LEARN, TEACH...

SUCCEED...

With **REA's FTCE General Knowledge**
test prep, you'll be in a class all your own.

FTCE GENERAL KNOWLEDGE

FLORIDA TEACHER CERTIFICATION EXAMINATIONS

Leasha M. Barry, Ph.D.
Associate Professor
University of West Florida

Laura Meiselman, M.S.
Former Teacher
Cold Springs, New York

Alicia Mendoza, Ed.D.
Associate Professor
Florida International University

And the Editors of
Research & Education Association

Research & Education Association

Planet Friendly Publishing
✔ Made in the United States
✔ Printed on Recycled Paper
Text: 10%   Cover: 10%
Learn more: www.greenedition.org

At REA we're committed to producing books in an Earth-friendly manner and to helping our customers make greener choices.

Manufacturing books in the United States ensures compliance with strict environmental laws and eliminates the need for international freight shipping, a major contributor to global air pollution.

And printing on recycled paper helps minimize our consumption of trees, water and fossil fuels. This book was printed on paper made with **10% post-consumer waste**. According to the Environmental Paper Network's Paper Calculator, by using this innovative paper instead of conventional papers, we achieved the following environmental benefits:

Trees Saved: 10 • Air Emissions Eliminated: 2223 pounds
Water Saved: 1991 gallons • Solid Waste Eliminated: 680 pounds

Courier Corporation, the manufacturer of this book, owns the Green Edition Trademark.
For more information on our environmental practices, please visit us online at **www.rea.com/green**

Research & Education Association
61 Ethel Road West
Piscataway, New Jersey 08854
E-mail: info@rea.com

Florida FTCE General Knowledge Test, 2ⁿᵈ Edition

Published 2014

Printed in the United States of America

Library of Congress Control Number 2011921171

ISBN-13: 978-0-7386-0947-8
ISBN-10: 0-7386-0947-1

The competencies presented in this book were created and implemented by the Florida Department of Education. For further information visit *www.fl.nesinc.com*.

Cover image: JGI/Blend Images/Getty Images

REA® and TestWare® are registered trademarks of Research & Education Association, Inc.

About Our Experts

Leasha M. Barry, Ph.D., received her graduate training in Special Education, disability, and at-risk populations at the University of California at Santa Barbara. She is an Associate Professor in the Division of Teacher Education within the College of Professional Studies at the University of West Florida. Her work focuses on early intervention with at-risk populations, including individuals with disabilities and those who experience traumatic stress at home and in educational and healthcare settings. Dr. Barry is interested in identifying and documenting developmentally appropriate supports and interventions that set the stage for independence and self-determination for individuals who are identified as at-risk.

Laura Meiselman, M.S. has taught math to both regular and special education students in public and independent schools in New York for over 15 years. She has two master's degrees from Bank Street College of Education, one in Special Education and one in Math Leadership. She is the author of two books: *Tic Tac Math: Grades 5–8* and *What's Your Angle? And 9 More Math Games*, published by Scholastic, Inc. and has contributed her expertise to several REA books. She lives in the Hudson Valley with her daughter. When she's not doing curriculum writing or test preparation work, Laura can be found doing yoga, taking cooking classes, or reading.

Alicia Mendoza, Ed.D., formerly chair of the Elementary Education Department at Florida International University, has held the position of Associate Professor at the same academic institution for more than 31 years. Before coming to FIU, she was an Associate Professor at Clarion State College in Clarion, Pennsylvania and served as a consultant to Head Start classes in Western Pennsylvania. She also taught in the public schools of New York City. She earned her Ed.D. and M.Ed. at the University of Miami, and her B.A. at Queens College in New York City. Dr. Mendoza has been the recipient of the Distinguished Member Award of the Association of Teacher Educators in 2005, a Teaching Incentive award, and an Excellence in Advising award during her time at Florida International University. She is the author of numerous published articles, book chapters, and curriculum materials. Dr. Mendoza also recently authored a book, titled *The Essentials of Elementary Education and Current Controversies.*

About Research & Education Association

Founded in 1959, Research & Education Association is dedicated to publishing the finest and most effective educational materials—including study guides and test preps—for students in middle school, high school, college, graduate school, and beyond.

Today, REA's wide-ranging catalog is a leading resource for teachers, students, and professionals. Visit *www.rea.com* to see a complete listing of all our titles.

Acknowledgments

We would like to thank Larry B. Kling, Vice President, Editorial, for supervising development; Pam Weston, Publisher, for setting the quality standards for production integrity and managing the publication to completion; Charlie Heinle, Senior Editor, for managing the project and coordinating revisions; Diane Goldschmidt, Managing Editor, and Alice Leonard, Senior Editor, for their editorial review; and Christine Saul, Senior Graphic Artist, for cover design.

We also gratefully acknowledge Kathy Caratozzolo of CaraGraphics for typesetting this edition.

CONTENTS

FTCE

Florida Teacher Certification Examinations
General Knowledge Test

Review

Passing the FTCE General Knowledge Test

About This Book

You are preparing to take the Florida Teacher Certification Exam General Knowledge Test (FTCE-GKT). Perhaps you are taking it for the first time. Perhaps you are retaking the exam. Whatever the case, this book will help you pass.

While working through this book, you will acquire a thorough and accurate understanding of what it takes to master the FTCE-GKT. The comprehensive review material in this book covers all subject areas known to appear on the FTCE-GKT, providing you with all the information you need to take this challenging certification exam.

Test-takers should note that every time the FTCE-GKT is administered, multiple versions of the exam are created and distributed to each testing center. These versions may contain a mix of different questions with different answers. This test versioning can add a greater level of uncertainty for the test-taker. Are you sure you are studying every topic enough? Are you adequately prepared for every test subject you may encounter on the FTCE-GKT? You can rest assured. One important purpose of this book is to prepare you for every possible version of the FTCE-GKT. We at REA believe you cannot prepare enough for this career-building exam.

About Our Practice Exams

You will be allotted three and one half hours to take the actual exam. This same amount of time is allotted to take each of our practice tests. REA's tests are carefully based on the current FTCE-GKT exams, and thus contain every type of question that you can expect to see on test day. Each practice test question is thoroughly explained in easy-to-follow detail. Sample responses are also provided for the essays to help you better understand and master the test material.

The FTCE is scored on a pass/fail basis. The following are the maximum percentages of questions in each subtest you need to answer correctly in order to pass:

- 65% Reading

- 73% English Language

- 60% Mathematics

In order to pass the Essay subtest, you need a score of at least 6 out of 12. Two raters will grade your exam independently and their grades will be combined to arrive at your final score.

About the Test

Who Takes the Test, and What Is It Used For?

The FTCE-GKT is used by the State of Florida to assess knowledge of teacher certification candidates. If you do not achieve a passing score on the FTCE-GKT, don't panic. You can take the test again, so you can work on improving your score in preparation for your next administration.

About Computer-Based Testing

The FTCE-GKT is offered only on computer at flexible times and locations throughout the year. Minimal computer and typing skills are required to complete the computer-based tests. You need to be comfortable with a Windows environment, using a mouse (including clicking, double-clicking, dragging, and scrolling), and typing at a rate that will allow you to complete the assignment in the allotted time (approximately 30 words per minute). In computer-based testing, examinees complete the tests by selecting answers on-screen to multiple-choice questions and typing or recording a response to a performance assessment component. The FTCE-GKT requires the examinee to type a response to the essay assignment.

When Should the FTCE-GKT Be Taken?

The FTCE-GKT is usually taken immediately before the completion of a teacher certification program at a college or university. This gives candidates enough time to retake the test if they are not pleased with their score. Our practice tests will familiarize you with the format of the exam so that you do not have to go through the anxiety of learning about the FTCE-GKT during the actual exam.

When and Where Is the Test Given?

The FTCE-GKT is administered five times a year at testing centers across Florida. Tests are usually administered on a Saturday; however, the test may be taken on an alternate day if a conflict, such as a religious obligation, exists.

The registration bulletin for the FTCE-GKT contains test dates and administration sites. You may obtain a registration bulletin by contacting:

> FTCE/FELE Program
> Evaluation Systems Group of Pearson
> PO Box 226
> Phone: (413) 256-2893
> Amherst, MA 01004
> Website: *www.fl.nesinc.com*

Is There a Registration Fee?

Yes, you must pay a fee to take the FTCE-GKT. Fee waivers are available for candidates who are unable to afford registration. You must be enrolled in a college undergraduate program and must prove that you are required by a registered score recipient to take the exam. Details regarding income eligibility levels are contained in the registration bulletin.

How to Use This Book

What should I Study First?

Read over our review material, and then take the first practice test. This will help you pinpoint your areas of weakness. Study those sections in which you had the most difficulty first, and then move on to those areas that presented less of a challenge to you.

When should I Start Studying?

It is never too early to begin studying for the FTCE-GKT. The earlier you begin, the more time you will have to sharpen your skills. Do not procrastinate! Cramming is not an effective way to study. Give yourself enough time to become familiar with the format of the test and the material it covers. The sooner you learn the format of the exam, the more comfortable and confident you will be on the day of the test.

Format of the FTCE-GKT

The FTCE-GKT is divided into four sections:

The Reading Test

The Reading Test measures your ability to understand and analyze written information. The test consists of several written passages and about 40 multiple-choice questions to test your understanding of those passages. You have 40 minutes to complete this section of the exam.

The Mathematics Test

The Mathematics Test measures competency in mathematical skills that an educated adult will require. It focuses on the ability to solve problems in a quantitative context. Several problems involve the integration of several skills into one problem-solving situation. The test consists of about 45 multiple-choice questions, which you have 100 minutes to complete.

The English Language Skills Test

The English Language Skills Test assesses your facility with the use of standard English, and you have 40 minutes to complete 40 multiple-choice questions.

The Essay Test

The Essay Test assesses the ability to communicate in written form using appropriate language and grammar. For your essay, you will choose between two topics. The 50 minutes allotted for this section of the exam includes time to prepare, write, and edit your essay.

About the Review Sections

The Reading Comprehension Review

The Reading Comprehension Review is designed to enhance the reading comprehension skills necessary to achieve a high score on the FTCE-GKT. Strategies for attacking reading comprehension questions are thoroughly explained, and a four-step approach to answering the test questions is completely outlined. In addition, a vocabulary enhancer is included to help you better understand the passages on the test.

The Basic Math Skills Review

The Mathematics Review will help you reinforce the arithmetic, algebraic, and geometric concepts that will be tested on the FTCE-GKT. Drill questions are included that will help you sharpen your mathematical skills. A valuable reference table offers quick access to important formulae and an index of mathematical symbols. Careful review of this section should give you all the information you need to pass this section of the FTCE-GKT.

The English Language Skills Review

The English Language Skills Review will help you prepare for the test by offering instruction and drills to enhance your conceptual and organizational skills; word choice skills; sentence structure skills; and grammar, spelling, capitalization, and punctuation skills.

The Writing Skills Review

The Writing Skills Review contains a wealth of information concerning the structure, content, and form of the FTCE-GKT essay. Regardless of the topic you are assigned on the exam, a concise, well-constructed essay is essential to achieve a passing score. Careful study of the Essay Writing Review will hone your essay writing abilities, so that you will be able to write your essay with confidence.

Studying for the FTCE-GKT

Everyone has a different learning environment that works best for them, and it is very important that you find the one that works best for you. Some students prefer to set aside a few hours every morning to study, while others prefer to study at night before going to sleep. Some students are capable of studying while waiting on line at the supermarket, or even while eating lunch. Other students require absolute silence in a well-lit room to study. Only you can determine what works best for you, but be consistent and use your time wisely. Develop a routine that works for you and stick to it.

When you are taking the practice tests, you should try to duplicate the testing conditions as closely as possible. Turn off the television and radio, and sit down in a quiet area as free from distraction as possible. Make sure to time yourself, and allow yourself no more time for the practice tests than you would have on the actual exam. Start off by setting a timer for the time that is allotted to each section of the exam, and be sure to reset it for the appropriate amount of time whenever you start a new section.

As you complete each practice test, score your exam and thoroughly review the detailed explanations to all the questions you answered incorrectly. Concentrate on one question at a time by reviewing the question and the explanation, and by studying the appropriate review material until you are confident that you completely understand the material.

Keep track of your scores on the individual practice tests. Doing this will enable you to gauge your progress and discover general weaknesses in particular sections. You should carefully study the review sections that cover your areas of difficulty to help reinforce your skills in those areas.

Test-Taking Tips

Even though you have probably taken standardized tests like the FTCE-GKT before, you may still be experiencing some anxiety about the exam. This is perfectly normal and there are several ways to help alleviate it listed below.

- **Become comfortable with the format of the FTCE-GKT.** When you are taking the practice tests, simulate the testing conditions as closely as possible. Stay calm and pace yourself. After simulating the test a few times, you will boost your chances of doing well. The test-taking experience will not be unfamiliar to you, and this will allow you to take the FTCE-GKT with much more confidence.

- **Read all of the possible answers.** Just because you think you have found the correct response, do not automatically assume that it is the best answer. Read all the answer choices so that you do not make a mistake by jumping to conclusions.

- **Use the process of elimination.** Go through all the answer choices and eliminate obviously incorrect answers immediately. If you are able to eliminate one or two answer choices, you will be able to make an educated guess.

- **Work quickly and steadily.** You have very specific time limits for each section, so pace yourself carefully. Do not spend too much time on any one question. By taking the practice tests included in this book, you will become better able to manage your time.

- **Learn the directions for each test section.** Familiarizing yourself with the directions for each section will not only save time, but also help you avoid anxiety and the mistakes that anxiety breeds.

- **Be sure that the answer oval you are marking corresponds to the number of the question in the test booklet.** Since the multiple-choice sections of the FTCE-GKT are graded by a machine, mismarking one response can throw off your entire score. Periodically check to be sure that you have not unintentionally left a space blank, or filled in two answer choices for a single question.

- **Guess, guess, guess.** You are not penalized for incorrect responses on the FTCE-GKT. Your score is based on the number of questions you have answered correctly. Therefore, even if you have absolutely no idea what the answer to a given question might be, you still have a 25 percent chance of being right. If you are able to eliminate even one or two of the answer choices, your chances of guessing correctly are greatly increased.

The Day of the Test

Before the Test

On the day of the test, you should wake up early after a good night's rest. You should have a good breakfast and dress in layers that can be removed or added as the conditions in the testing center require. Arrive at the testing center early. This will allow you to relax and collect your thoughts before the test, and will also spare you the anguish that comes with being late. As an added incentive to make sure that you arrive early, keep in mind that *no one will be admitted into the testing center after the test has begun.*

Before you leave for the testing site, make sure that you have your admission ticket and two unexpired forms of identification. The first form of identification must be government issued and must contain a recent photograph, your name, and a legible signature. This can be a driver's license, state-issued identification card, passport, or U.S. military identification. The second identification must have either a clear photograph or a signature. Examples of these could be a student ID or a Social Security card. If you do not have proper identification, you will not be admitted to the testing site. Be sure to check the FTCE website close to the date of your test just in case there are any changes to these requirements.

You must *bring several sharpened No. 2 pencils with erasers,* as well as *several blue or black ball point pens* for the essay, as none will be provided at the testing center!

There are also very strict rules about what you may not bring to the testing site. You may not bring cell phones or any other electronic communication devices. Scrap paper, written notes, books of any kind or any printed material is prohibited. You may not bring correction fluid or calculators. Smoking, eating, or drinking are not allowed, so do not bring any food or drinks, including water, to the site. Finally, weapons of any kind are banned, as are any visitors, including relatives.

During the Test

Once you enter the test center, follow all the rules and instructions given by your test supervisor. Failure to do so runs you the risk of being dismissed from the testing center. You may also have your scores canceled.

After all testing materials have been distributed, the test supervisor will give you directions for filling out your answer sheet. Fill out this sheet carefully since the information you enter will be printed on your score report. Remember to fill in your name exactly as it appears on the admission ticket to avoid confusion later on.

Scrap paper is not provided, but you are permitted to write in your test booklet. Mark your answers in the appropriate spaces on the answer sheet. Each numbered row will contain four ovals corresponding to each answer choice for that question. Fill in the oval that corresponds to your answer darkly, completely, and neatly. Should you change your answer, remember to erase the old answer entirely from the page. Only one answer should be marked for each question. This is very important, because answer sheets are machine scored, and stray marks can cause the machine to score your answers incorrectly.

After the Test

Once your test materials have been collected, you will be dismissed. Proceed to the exit.

Congratulations! You are well on your way to certification.

Talking to Your Fellow Test-Takers After the Test. Keep in mind that several versions of the FTCE-GKT are administered during each testing period. The test-takers around you were very likely working on tests with completely different questions and answers than yours. So, do not be alarmed when talking to friends and acquaintances about their FTCE-GKT test-taking experiences and you do not "remember" the questions they are discussing.

Reading Comprehension Review

Overview

This review was developed to prepare you for the Reading Section of the FTCE-GKT. You will be guided through a step-by-step approach to attacking reading passages and questions. Also included are tips to help you quickly and accurately answer the questions that will appear in this section. By studying our review, you will greatly increase your chances of achieving a passing score on the Reading Section of the FTCE-GKT.

Remember, the more you know about the skills tested, the better you will perform on the test. In this section, the skills you will be tested on are

1. Knowledge of literal comprehension
2. Knowledge of inferential comprehension

To help you master these skills, we present examples of the types of questions you will encounter and explanations of how to answer them. A drill section is also provided for further practice. Even if you are sure you will perform well on this section, make sure to complete the drills, as they will help sharpen your skills.

The Passages

The four reading passages in the Reading Section are specially designed to be on the level of the types of material that you will encounter in college textbooks. They will present you with very diverse subjects. The passages will be both expository and narrative. Although you will not be expected to have prior knowledge of the information presented in the passages, you will be expected to know the fundamental reading comprehension techniques presented in this chapter. Only your ability to read and comprehend material will be tested.

The Questions

Each passage will be followed by a number of questions, with the total number appearing in the section being 40 questions. The questions will ask you to make determinations based on what you have read. You will encounter 11 main types of questions in this test. These questions will ask you to

- recognize main ideas.
- identify supporting details.
- determine meaning of words or phrases in context.
- determine purpose.
- identify overall organizational pattern.
- distinguish between fact and opinion.
- recognize bias.
- recognize tone.
- determine relationships between sentences.
- analyze the validity of arguments.
- draw logical inferences and conclusions.

General Strategies

- Look over all the passages first and then attack the passages that seem easiest and most interesting.
- Identify and underline what sentences are the main ideas of each paragraph.
- When a question asks you to draw inferences, your answer should reflect what is implied in the passage, rather than what is directly stated.
- Use the context of the sentence to find the meaning of an unfamiliar word.
- Identify what sentences are example sentences and label them with an "E." Determine whether or not the writer is using facts or opinions.

- Circle key transitions and identify dominant patterns of organization.
- Make your final response and move on. Don't dawdle or get frustrated by the really troubling passages. If you haven't gotten answers after two attempts, answer as best you can and move on.
- If you have time at the end, go back to the passages that were difficult and review them again.

Strategies for Reading Passages

When reading the passage, this is your plan of attack:

Step 1: Read quickly while keeping in mind that questions will follow.

Step 2: Uncover the main idea or theme of the passage. Many times it is contained within the first few lines of the passage.

Step 3: Uncover the main idea of each paragraph. Usually it is contained in either the first or last sentence of the paragraph.

Step 4: Skim over the detailed points of the passage while circling key words or phrases. These are words or phrases such as *but, on the other hand, although, however, yet,* and *except.*

When you take the Reading Section of the FTCE-GKT, you will have two tasks:

1. to read the passage and
2. to answer the questions.

Of the two, carefully reading the passage is the most important; answering the questions is based on an understanding of the passage. Here is a four-step approach to reading:

Step 1: preview,

Step 2: read actively,

Step 3: review the passage, and

Step 4: answer the questions.

You should study the following exercises and use these four steps when you complete the Reading Section of the FTCE-GKT.

STEP 1: Preview

A preview of the reading passage will give you a purpose and a reason for reading; previewing is a good strategy to use in test-taking. Before beginning to read the passage (usually a four-minute activity if you preview and review), you should take about 30 seconds to look over the passage and questions. An effective way to preview the passage is to read quickly the first sentence of each paragraph, the concluding sentence of the passage, and the questions—not all the answers—following the passage. A passage is given below. Practice previewing the passage by reading the first sentence of each paragraph and the last line of the passage.

PASSAGE

1   That the area of obscenity and pornography is a difficult one for
the Supreme Court is well documented. The Court's numerous attempts
to define obscenity have proven unworkable and left the decision to
the subjective preferences of the justices. Perhaps Justice Stewart put it
5   best when, after refusing to define obscenity, he declared, "But I know it
when I see it." Does the Court literally have to see it to know it? Specifically, what role does the fact-pattern, including the materials' medium,
play in the Court's decision?

         Several recent studies employ fact-pattern analysis in modeling the
10   Court's decision making. These studies examine the fact-pattern or case
characteristics, often with ideological and attitudinal factors, as a determinant of the decision reached by the Court. In broad terms, these studies owe their theoretical underpinnings to attitude theory. As the name
suggests, attitude theory views the Court's attitudes as an explanation
15   of its decisions.

         These attitudes, however, do not operate in a vacuum. As Spaeth
explains, "the activation of an attitude involves both an object and the
situation in which that object is encountered." The objects to which the
court directs its attitudes are litigants. The situation—the subject matter
20   of the case—can be defined in broad or narrow terms. One may define
the situation as an entire area of the law (e.g., civil liberties issues). On
an even broader scale the situation may be defined as the decision to
grant certiorari or whether to defect from a minimum-winning coalition.

         Defining the situation with such broad strokes, however, does not
25   allow one to control for case content. In many specific issue areas,
the cases present strikingly similar patterns. In examining the Court's
search and seizure decisions, Segal found a relatively small number of
situational and case characteristic variables explain a high proportion of
the Court's decisions.

30   Despite Segal's success, efforts to verify the applicability of fact-
pattern analysis in other issue areas and using broad-based factors have
been slow in forthcoming. Renewed interest in obscenity and pornography by federal and state governments, the academic community,
and numerous antipornography interest groups indicates the Court's
35   decisions in this area deserve closer examination.

The Court's obscenity and pornography decisions also present an opportunity to study the Court's behavior in an area where the Court has granted significant decision-making authority to the states. In *Miller vs. California* (1973) the Court announced the importance of
40   local community standards in obscenity determinations. The Court's subsequent behavior may suggest how the Court will react in other areas where it has chosen to defer to the states (e.g., abortion).

QUESTIONS

1. The main idea of the passage is best stated in which of the following?

    (A)   The Supreme Court has difficulty convicting those who violate obscenity laws.

    (B)   The current definitions for obscenity and pornography provided by the Supreme Court are unworkable.

    (C)   Fact-pattern analysis is insufficient for determining the attitude of the Court toward the issues of obscenity and pornography.

    (D)   Despite the difficulties presented by fact-pattern analysis, Justice Segal found the solution in the patterns of search and seizure decisions.

2. The main purpose of the writer in this passage is to

    (A)   convince the reader that the Supreme Court is making decisions about obscenity based on their subjective views only.

    (B)   explain to the reader how fact-pattern analysis works with respect to cases of obscenity and pornography.

    (C)   define obscenity and pornography for the layperson.

    (D)   demonstrate the role fact-pattern analysis plays in determining the Supreme Court's attitude about cases in obscenity and pornography.

3. Of the following, which fact best supports the writer's contention that the Court's decisions in the areas of obscenity and pornography deserve closer scrutiny?

    (A)   The fact that a Supreme Court Justice said, "I know it when I see it."

    (B)   Recent studies that employ fact-pattern analysis in modeling the Court's decision-making process.

    (C)   The fact that attitudes do not operate in a vacuum.

    (D)   The fact that federal and state governments, interest groups, and the academic community show renewed interest in the obscenity and pornography decisions by the Supreme Court.

4.   Among the following statements, which states an opinion expressed by the writer rather than a fact?

   (A)   That the area of obscenity and pornography is a difficult one for the Supreme Court is well documented.

   (B)   The objects to which a court directs its attitudes are the litigants.

   (C)   In many specific issue areas, the cases present strikingly similar patterns.

   (D)   The Court's subsequent behavior may suggest how the Court will react in other legal areas.

5.   The list of topics below that best reflects the organization of the topics of the passage is

   (A)   I.   The difficulties of the Supreme Court

       II.   Several recent studies

       III. Spaeth's definition of "attitude"

       IV.   The similar patterns of cases

       V.   Other issue areas

       VI.   The case of *Miller vs. California*

   (B)   I.   The Supreme Court, obscenity, and fact-pattern analysis

       II.   Fact-pattern analyses and attitude theory

       III. The definition of "attitude" for the Court

       IV.   The definition of "situation"

       V.   The breakdown in fact-pattern analysis

       VI.   Studying Court behavior

   (C)   I.   Justice Stewart's view of pornography

       II.   Theoretical underpinnings

       III. A minimum-winning coalition

       IV.   Search and seizure decisions

       V.   Renewed interest in obscenity and pornography

       VI.   The importance of local community standards

   (D)   I.   The Court's numerous attempts to define obscenity

       II.   Case characteristics

       III. The subject matter of cases

       IV.   The Court's proportion of decisions

       V.   Broad-based factors

       VI.   Obscenity determination

6. Which paragraph below is the best summary of the passage?

(A) The Supreme Court's decision-making process with respect to obscenity and pornography has become too subjective. Fact-pattern analyses, used to determine the overall attitude of the Court, reveal only broad-based attitudes on the part of the Court toward the situations of obscenity cases. But these patterns cannot fully account for the Court's attitudes toward case content. Research is not conclusive that fact-pattern analyses work when applied to legal areas. Renewed public and local interest suggests continued study and close examination of how the Court makes decisions. Delegating authority to the states may reflect patterns for Court decisions in other socially sensitive areas.

(B) Though subjective, the Supreme Court decisions are well documented. Fact-pattern analyses reveal the attitude of the Supreme Court toward its decisions in cases. Spaeth explains that an attitude involves both an object and a situation. For the Court, the situation may be defined as the decision to grant certiorari. Cases present strikingly similar patterns, and a small number of variables explain a high proportion of the Court's decisions. Segal has made an effort to verify the applicability of fact-pattern analysis with some success. The Court's decisions on obscenity and pornography suggest weak Court behavior, such as in *Miller vs. California.*

(C) To determine what obscenity and pornography mean to the Supreme Court, we must use fact-pattern analysis. Fact-pattern analysis reveals the ideas that the Court uses to operate in a vacuum. The litigants and the subject matter of cases is defined in broad terms (such as an entire area of law) to reveal the Court's decision-making process. Search and seizure cases reveal strikingly similar patterns, leaving the Court open to grant certiorari effectively. Renewed public interest in the Court's decisions proves how the Court will react in the future.

(D) Supreme Court decisions about pornography and obscenity are under examination and are out of control. The Court has to see the case to know it. Fact-pattern analyses reveal that the Court can only define cases in narrow terms, thus revealing individual egotism on the part of the Justices. As a result of strikingly similar patterns in search and seizure cases, the Court should be studied further for its weakness in delegating authority to state courts, as in the case of *Miller vs. California.*

7. Based on the passage, the rationale for fact-pattern analyses arises out of what theoretical groundwork?

(A) Subjectivity theory

(B) The study of cultural norms

(C) Attitude theory

(D) Cybernetics

8. Based on data in the passage, what would most likely be the major cause for the difficulty in pinning down the Supreme Court's attitude toward cases of obscenity and pornography?

    (A) The personal opinions of the Court Justices

    (B) The broad nature of the situations of the cases

    (C) The ineffective logistics of certiorari

    (D) The inability of the Court to resolve the variables presented by individual case content

9. In the context of the passage, *subjective* might be most nearly defined as

    (A) personal.   (C) focused.

    (B) wrong.   (D) objective.

By previewing the passage, you should have learned the following:

- The fact that the area of obscenity and pornography is a difficult one for the Supreme Court is well documented.

- Several recent studies employ fact-pattern analysis in modeling the Court's decision making.

- These attitudes are not formed and expressed in a vacuum.

- Defining the situation with such broad strokes does not allow one to control for case content.

- Despite Segal's success, efforts to verify the applicability of fact-pattern analysis in other issue areas and using broad-based factors have been slow in coming.

- The Court's obscenity and pornography decisions also present an opportunity to study the Court's behavior in an area where the Court has granted significant decision-making authority to the states.

- The Court's subsequent behavior may suggest how the Court will react in other areas where it has chosen to defer to the states (e.g., abortion).

These few sentences tell you much about the entire passage.

As you begin to examine the passage, you should first determine the main idea of the passage and underline it, so that you can easily refer back to it if a question requires you to do so (see question 1). The main idea should be found in the first paragraph of the passage, and may even be the first sentence. From what you have read thus far, you now know that the main idea of this passage is that: the Supreme Court has difficulty in making obscenity and pornography decisions.

In addition, you also know that recent studies have used fact-pattern analysis in modeling the Court's decision. You have learned also that attitudes do not operate independently and that case content is important. The feasibility of using fact-pattern analysis in other areas and broad-based factors have not been quickly verified. To study the behavior of the Court in an area in which they have granted significant decision-making authority to the states, one has only to consider the obscenity and pornography decisions. In summary, the author suggests that the Court's subsequent behavior may suggest how the Court will react in those other areas in which decision-making authority has previously been granted to the states. As you can see, having this information will make the reading of the passage much easier.

You should have also looked at the stem of the question in your preview. You do not necessarily need to spend time reading the answers to each question in your preview. The stem alone can help to guide you as you read.

The stems in this case are:

1. The main idea of the passage is best stated in which of the following?

2. The main purpose of the writer in this passage is to

3. Of the following, which fact best supports the writer's contention that the Court's decisions in the areas of obscenity and pornography deserve closer scrutiny?

4. Among the following statements, which states an opinion expressed by the writer rather than a fact?

5. The list of topics below that best reflects the organization of the topics of the passage is

6. Which paragraph below is the best summary of the passage?

7. Based on the passage, the rationale for fact-pattern analyses arises out of what theoretical groundwork?

8. Based on data in the passage, what would most likely be the major cause for the difficulty in pinning down the Supreme Court's attitude toward cases of obscenity and pornography?

9. In the context of the passage, *subjective* might be most nearly defined as

STEP 2: Read Actively

After your preview, you are now ready to read actively. This means that as you read, you will be engaged in such things as underlining important words, topic sentences, main ideas, and words denoting the tone of the passage. If you think underlining can help you save time and help you remember the main ideas, when taking the test, feel free to use your pencil.

Read carefully the first sentence of each paragraph since this often contains the topic of the paragraph. You may wish to underline each topic sentence.

During this stage, you should also determine the writer's purpose in writing the passage (see question 2), as this will help you focus on the main points and the writer's key points in the organization of a passage. You can determine the author's purpose by asking yourself, Does *the relationship* between the writer's main idea plus evidence the writer uses answer one of four questions?

- What is the writer's overall primary goal or objective?

- Is the writer trying primarily to persuade you by proving or using facts to make a case for an idea? (P)

- Is the writer trying only primarily to inform and enlighten you about an idea, object, or event? (I)

- Is the writer attempting primarily to amuse you? To keep you fascinated? To keep you laughing? (A)

Read these examples and see if you can decide what the primary purpose of the following statements might be.

(A)   Jogging too late in life can cause more health problems than it solves. I will allow that the benefits of jogging are many: lowered blood pressure, increased vitality, better cardiovascular health, and better muscle tone. However, an older person may have a history of injury or chronic ailments that makes jogging counterproductive. For example, the elderly jogger may have hardening of the arteries, emphysema, or undiscovered aneurysms just waiting to burst and cause stroke or death. Chronic arthritis in the joints will only be aggravated by persistent irritation and use. Moreover, for those of us with injuries sustained in our youth—such as torn Achilles' tendons or torn knee cartilage—jogging might just make a painful life more painful, cancelling out the benefits the exercise is intended to produce.

(B)   Jogging is a sporting activity that exercises all the main muscle groups of the body. That the arms, legs, buttock, and torso voluntary muscles are engaged goes without question. Running down a path makes you move your upper body as well as your lower body muscles. People do not often take into account, however, how the involuntary muscle system is also put through its paces. The heart, diaphragm, even the eye and face muscles, take part as we hurl our bodies through space at speeds up to five miles per hour over distances as long as 26 miles.

(C)   It seems to me that jogging styles are as identifying as fingerprints! People seem to be as individual in the way they run as they are in personality. Here comes the Duck, waddling down the track, little wings going twice as fast as the feet in an effort to stay upright. At about the quarter mile mark, I see the Penguin, quite natty in the latest jogging suit, body stiff as a board from neck to ankles and the ankles flexing a mile a minute to cover the yards. And down there at the half-mile post—there comes the Giraffe—a tall fellow in a spotted electric yellow outfit, whose long strides cover about a dozen yards each, and whose neck waves around under some old army camouflage hat that probably served its time in a surplus store in the Bronx rather than in Desert Storm. Once you see the animals in the jogger woods once, you can identify them from miles away just by seeing their gait. And by the way, be careful whose hoof you're stepping on, it may be mine!

In (A) the writer makes a statement that a number of people would debate and which isn't clearly demonstrated in science or common knowledge. In fact, common wisdom usually maintains the opposite thesis. Many would say that jogging improves the health of the aging—even slows down the aging process. As soon as you see a writer point to or identify *an issue open to debate* and standing in need of proof, s/he is setting out to persuade you of one side or the other. You'll notice, too, that the writer in this case takes a stand here. It's almost as if s/he is saying, "I have concluded that . . ." But a thesis or arguable idea is only a *hypothesis* until evidence is summoned by the writer to prove it. Effective arguments are based on serious, factual, or demonstrable evidence, not opinion.

In (B) the writer is just stating a fact. This is not a matter for debate. From here, the writer's evidence is to *explain* and *describe* what is meant by the fact. S/he proceeds to *analyze* (break down into its elements) the way the different muscle groups come into play or do work when jogging, thus explaining the fact stated as a main point in the opening sentence. That jogging exercises all the muscle groups is not in question or a matter of debate. Besides taking the form of explaining how something works, what parts it is made of (for example, the basic parts of a bicycle are . . .), writers may show how the idea, object, or event functions. A writer may use this information to prove something. But if s/he doesn't argue to prove a debatable point, then the purpose must be either to inform (as here) or to entertain.

In (C) the writer is taking a stand, but s/he is not attempting to prove anything, merely pointing to a light-hearted observation. Moreover, all of the examples s/he uses to support the statement are either fanciful, funny, odd, or peculiar to the writer's particular vision. Joggers aren't really animals, after all.

Make sure to examine all of the facts that the author uses to support his/her main idea. This will allow you to decide whether or not the writer has made a case, and what sort of purpose s/he supports. Look for supporting details—facts, examples, illustrations, the testimony or research of experts, that are about the topic in question and *show* what the writer *says* is so. In fact, paragraphs and theses consist of *show* and *tell*. The writer *tells* you something is so or not so and then *shows* you facts, illustrations, expert testimony, or experience to back up what s/he says is or is not so. As you determine where the author's supporting details are, you may want to label them with an "S" so that you can refer back to them easily when answering questions (see question 3).

It is also important for you to be able to recognize the difference between the statements of fact presented and statements of the author's opinion. You will be tested on this skill in this section of the test (see question 4). Let's look at the following examples. In each case ask yourself if you are reading a fact or an opinion.

1. Some roses are red.
2. Roses are the most beautiful flower on earth.
3. After humans smell roses, they fall in love.
4. Roses are the worst plants to grow in your backyard.

Number 1 is a fact. All you have to do is go look at the evidence. Go to a florist. You will see that number 1 is true. A fact is anything that can be demonstrated to be true in reality or that has been demonstrated to be true in reality and is documented by others. For example, the moon is in orbit about 250,000 miles from the earth.

Number 2 is an opinion. The writer claims this as truth, but since it is an abstract quality (beauty), it remains to be seen. Others will hold different opinions. This is a matter of taste, not fact.

Number 3 is an opinion. There is probably some time-related coincidence between these two, but there is no verifiable or repeatable and observable evidence that this is always true—at least not the way it is true that if you throw a ball into the air, it will always come back down to earth if left on its own without interference. Opinions have a way of sounding absolute, are held by the writer with confidence, but are not backed up by factual evidence.

Number 4, though perhaps sometimes true, is a matter of opinion. Many variables contribute to the health of a plant in a garden: soil, temperature range, amount of moisture, number, and kinds of bugs. This is a debatable point that the writer would have to prove.

As you read, you should note the structure of the passage. There are several common structures for the passages. Some of these structures are described below.

Main Types of Paragraph Structures

1. The structure is a main idea plus supporting arguments.

2. The structure is a main idea plus examples.

3. The structure includes comparisons or contrasts.

4. There is a pro and a con structure.

5. The structure is chronological.

6. The structure has several different aspects of one idea. For example, a passage on education in the United States in the 1600s and 1700s might first define education, then describe colonial education, then give information about separation of church and state, and then outline the tax opposition and supportive arguments. Being able to recognize these structures will help you recognize how the author has organized the passage.

Examining the structure of the passage will help you answer questions that ask you to organize (see question 5) the information in the passage, or to summarize (see question 6) the information presented in that passage.

For example, if you see a writer using a transitional pattern that reflects a sequence moving forward in time, such as "In 1982 . . . Then, in the next five years . . . A decade later, in 1997, the xxxx will . . ." chances are the writer is telling a story, history, or the like. Writers often use transitions of classification to analyze an idea, object, or event. They may say something like, "The first part . . . Secondly . . . Thirdly . . . Finally." You may then ask yourself what is this analysis for? To explain or to persuade me of something? These transitional patterns may also help reveal the relationship of one part of a passage to another. For example, a writer may be writing "on the one hand, . . . on the other hand . . ." This should alert you to the fact that the writer is comparing two things or contrasting them. What for? Is one better than the other? Worse?

By understanding the *relationship* among the main point, transitions, and supporting information, you may more readily determine the pattern of organization as well as the writer's purpose in a given piece of writing.

As with the paragraph examples above showing the difference among possible purposes, you must look at the relationship between the facts or information presented (that's the show part) and what the writer is trying to point out to you (that's the tell part) with that data. For example, in the data given in number 6 above, the discussion presented about education in the 1600s might be used

- to prove that it was a failure (a form of argument),
- to show that it consisted of these elements (an analysis of the status of education during that time), or
- to show that education during that time was silly.

To understand the author's purpose, the main point and the evidence that supports it must be considered together to be understood. In number 6, no statement appears that controls these disparate areas of information. To be meaningful, a controlling main point is needed. You need to know that that main point is missing. You need to be able to distinguish between the writer showing data and the writer telling or making a point.

In the two paragraphs below, consider the different relationship between the same data above and the controlling statement, and how that controlling statement changes the discussion from explanation to argument:

(A) Colonial education was different than today's and consisted of several elements. Education in those days meant primarily studying the three "r's" (reading, writing, and arithmetic) and the Bible. The church and state were more closely aligned with one another—education was, after all, for the purpose of serving God better, not to make more money.

(B) Colonial "education" was really just a way to create a captive audience for the Church. Education in those days meant studying the three "r's" in order to learn God's word—the Bible—not commerce. The Church and state were closely aligned with one another, and what was good for the Church was good for the state—or else you were excommunicated, which kept you out of Heaven for sure.

The same information areas are brought up in both cases, but in (A) the writer treats it analytically (". . . consisted of several elements . . ."), not taking any real debatable stand on the issue. What is, is. However, the controlling statement in (B) puts forth a volatile hypothesis, and then uses the same information to support that hypothesis.

STEP 3: Review the Passage

After you finish reading actively, take 10 or 20 seconds to look over the main idea and the topic sentences that you have underlined, and the key words and phrases you have marked. Now you are ready to enter Step 4 and answer the questions.

STEP 4: Answer the Questions

In Step 2, Read Actively, you gathered enough information from the passage to answer questions dealing with the main idea, support, meaning, purpose, organization, fact vs. opinion, bias, tone, relationships between sentences, validity, and logic. Let's look again at these questions.

Strategies for Answering Questions

Competency 1: Knowledge of Literal Comprehension

When answering the questions, this is your plan of attack:

Step 1: Attack each question one at a time. Read it carefully.

Step 2: If the question is asking for a general answer, such as the main idea or the purpose of the passage, answer it immediately.

Step 3: If the question is asking for an answer that can only be found in a specific place in the passage, save it for last since this type of question requires you to go back to the passage and therefore takes more of your time.

Step 4: For the detail-oriented questions, try to eliminate or narrow down your choices before looking for the answer in the passage.

Step 5: Go back into the passage, utilizing the key words you circled, to find the answer.

Step 6: Any time you cannot find the answer, use the process of elimination to the greatest extent and then guess.

Skill 1: Recognize the Main Ideas

Looking back at the questions that follow the passage, you see that question 1 is a "main idea" question:

1.   The main idea of the passage is best stated in which of the following?

(A)   The Supreme Court has difficulty convicting those who violate obscenity laws.

(B)   The current definitions for obscenity and pornography provided by the Supreme Court are unworkable.

(C)   Fact-pattern analysis is insufficient for determining the attitude of the Court toward the issues of obscenity and pornography.

(D)   Despite the difficulties presented by fact-pattern analysis, Justice Segal found the solution in the patterns of search and seizure decisions.

In answering the question, you see that answer choice (C) is correct. The writer uses the second, third, fourth, and fifth paragraphs to show how fact-pattern analysis is an ineffective determinant of Court attitude toward obscenity and pornography.

Answer (A) is incorrect. Nothing is ever said directly about "convicting" persons accused of obscenity, only that the Court has difficulty defining it.

Choice (B) is also incorrect. Though it is stated as a fact by the writer, it is only used as an effect that leads the writer to examine how fact-pattern analysis does or does not work to reveal the "cause" or attitude of the Court toward obscenity and pornography.

Finally, answer choice (D) is incorrect. The statement is contrary to what Segal found when he examined search and seizure cases.

Skill 2: Identify Supporting Details

Question 3 requires you to analyze the author's supporting details:

3.   Of the following, which fact best supports the writer's contention that the Court's decisions in the areas of obscenity and pornography deserve closer scrutiny?

   (A)   The fact that a Supreme Court Justice said, "I know it when I see it."

   (B)   Recent studies that employ fact-pattern analysis in modeling the Court's decision-making process.

   (C)   The fact that attitudes do not operate in a vacuum.

   (D)   The fact that federal and state governments, interest groups, and the academic community show renewed interest in the obscenity and pornography decisions by the Supreme Court.

To answer this question, let's look at the answer choices. Choice (D) must be correct. In the fifth paragraph, the writer states that the "renewed interest"—a real and observable fact—from these groups "indicates the Court's decisions . . . deserve closer examination," another way of saying scrutiny.

Answer (A) is incorrect. The writer uses this remark to show how the Court cannot effectively define obscenity and pornography, relying on "subjective preferences" to resolve issues.

In addition, choice (B) is incorrect because the writer points to the data in (D), not fact-pattern analyses, to prove this.

(C), too, is incorrect. Although it is true, the writer makes this point to show how fact-pattern analysis doesn't help clear up the real-world "situation" in which the Court must make its decisions.

Skill 3: Determine the Meaning of Words or Phrases in Context

Returning to question 9, we can now determine an answer:

9.   In the context of the passage, *subjective* might be most nearly defined as

   (A)   personal.   (C)   focused.

   (B)   wrong.   (D)   objective.

Choice (A) is best. By taking note of the example of Justice Stewart provided by the writer, we can see that Justice Stewart's comment is not an example of right or wrong. (He doesn't talk about right or wrong. He uses the verb "know"—whose root points primarily to *know*ledge, understanding, and insight, *not* ethical considerations.) He probably doesn't mean "focused by" since the focus is provided by the appearance or instance of the case itself. By noting the same word ending and the appearance of the root "object"—meaning an observable thing existing outside of ourselves in time and space, and comparing it with the root of subjective, "subject"—often pointing to something personally studied, we can begin to rule out "objective" as the opposite of "subjective." Usually when we talk about people's "preferences," we are referring to matters of taste or quality; preferences don't usually result from scientific study or reasoning but instead arise out of a combination of personal taste and idiosyncratic intuitions. Thus, (A) becomes the most likely choice.

(C) is incorrect because the Court's focus is already in place—obscenity and pornography.

Answer (B) is incorrect. Nothing is implied or stated about the rightness or wrongness of the decisions themselves. Rather, it is the definition of obscenity that seems "unworkable."

(D) is also incorrect. "Objective" is the direct opposite of "subjective." To reason based on the object of study is the opposite of reasoning based upon the beliefs, opinions, or ideas of the one viewing the object, rather than consideration of the evidence presented by the object itself *independent* of the observer.

You may not have been familiar with the word "subjective," but from your understanding of the writer's intent, you should have been able to figure out what s/he was after. Surrounding words and phrases almost always provide clues in determining a word's meaning. In addition, any examples that appear in the text may also provide some hints.

Competency 2: Knowledge of Inferential Comprehension

Skill 1: Determine the Purpose

In examining question 2, you see that you must determine the author's purpose in writing the passage:

2.   The main purpose of the writer in this passage is to

   (A)   convince the reader that the Supreme Court is making decisions about obscenity based on their subjective views only.

   (B)   explain to the reader how fact-pattern analysis works with respect to cases of obscenity and pornography.

   (C)   define obscenity and pornography for the layperson.

   (D)   demonstrate the role fact-pattern analysis plays in determining the Supreme Court's attitude about cases in obscenity and pornography.

Looking at the answer choices, you see that choice (D) is correct. Though the writer never states it directly, s/he summons data consistently to show that fact-pattern analysis only gives us part of the picture, or "broad strokes" about the Court's attitude, but cannot account for the attitude toward individual cases.

Choice (A) is incorrect. The writer doesn't try to convince us of this fact, but merely states it as an opinion resulting from the evidence derived from the "well-documented" background to the problem.

(B) is also incorrect. The writer does more than just explain the role of fact-pattern analysis, but rather shows how it cannot fully apply.

The passage is about the Court's difficulty in defining these terms, not the man or woman in the street. Nowhere do definitions for these terms appear. Therefore, choice (C) is incorrect.

Skill 2: Identify Overall Organizational Pattern

Question 5 asks you to organize given topics to reflect the organization of the passage:

5.   The list of topics below that best reflects the organization of the topics of the passage is

    (A)   I.   The difficulties of the Supreme Court

            II.   Several recent studies

            III. Spaeth's definition of "attitude"

            IV. The similar patterns of cases

            V.   Other issue areas

            VI. The case of *Miller vs. California*

    (B)   I.   The Supreme Court, obscenity, and fact-pattern analysis

            II.   Fact-pattern analyses and attitude theory

            III. The definition of "attitude" for the Court

            IV. The definition of "situation"

            V.   The breakdown in fact-pattern analysis

            VI. Studying Court behavior

    (C)   I.   Justice Stewart's view of pornography

            II.   Theoretical underpinnings

            III. A minimum-winning coalition

            IV. Search and seizure decisions

     V.   Renewed interest in obscenity and pornography

    VI. The importance of local community standards

(D)   I.   The Court's numerous attempts to define obscenity

       II.   Case characteristics

      III. The subject matter of cases

      IV. The Court's proportion of decisions

       V.   Broad-based factors

      VI. Obscenity determination

After examining all of the choices, you will determine that choice (B) is the correct response. These topical areas lead directly to the implied thesis that the "role" of fact-pattern analysis is insufficient for determining the attitude of the Supreme Court in the areas of obscenity and pornography. (See question 1.)

Answer (A) is incorrect because the first topic stated in the list is not the topic of the first paragraph. It is too global. The first paragraph is about the difficulties the Court has with defining obscenity and how fact-pattern analysis might be used to determine the Court's attitude and clear up the problem.

(C) is incorrect because each of the items listed in this topic list are supporting evidence or data for the real topic of each paragraph. (See the list in (B) for correct topics.) For example, Justice Stewart's statement about pornography is only cited to indicate the nature of the problem with obscenity for the Court. It is not the focus of the paragraph itself.

Finally, (D) is incorrect. As with choice (C) these are all incidental pieces of information or data used to make broader points.

Skill 3: Distinguish Between Fact and Opinion

By examining question 4, you can see that you are required to know the difference between fact and opinion:

4.   Among the following statements, which states an opinion expressed by the writer rather than a fact?

(A)   That the area of obscenity and pornography is a difficult one for the Supreme Court is well documented.

(B)   The objects to which a court directs its attitudes are the litigants.

(C)   In many specific issue areas, the cases present strikingly similar patterns.

(D)   The Court's subsequent behavior may suggest how the Court will react in other legal areas.

Keeping in mind that an opinion is something that cannot be proven to hold true in all circumstances, you can determine that choice (D) is correct. It is the only statement among the four for which the evidence is yet to be gathered. It is the writer's opinion that this may be a way to predict the Court's attitudes.

(A), (B), and (C) are all taken from data or documentation in existence already in the world, and are, therefore, not the correct answers.

Skill 4: Recognize Bias

While reading, make a distinction between key ideas author bias, and the evidence for those ideas. *Evidence* is anything used to prove that an idea is true, real, correct, or probable. Bias is the author's personal feelings on the topic and what s/he believes which may not be based in fact.

Types of Evidence

Only a few forms of evidence are available to the writer. The kinds of evidence that a writer can summon to support his or her position or point are as follows: (1) facts and statistics, (2) the testimony of an authority, (3) personal anecdote, (4) hypothetical illustrations, and (5) analogy. Strictly speaking, the last two in this list are not true evidence but only offer commonsense probability to the support of an argument. In fact, there is a hierarchy for evidence similar to that of purpose. The most powerful evidence is fact, supported by statistics; the least powerful is analogy. The following table suggests the relationship:

Hierarchy of Validity of Evidence

Most Valid	Documented Facts and Statistics
(factual)	Expert Testimony
	Personal Experience and Anecdote
	Hypothetical Illustrations
Least Valid	Analogies
(may be influenced by bias)	

Documented facts and statistics are the most powerful evidence a writer can bring to bear on proving an idea or supporting a main thesis. Documented facts and statistics must be used fairly and come from reliable sources. For example, *Funk and Wagnall's Encyclopedia* is a reliable source but Joe the plumber's *Guide to Waterfowl in Hoboken* is not. This is true because, first of all, Joe is a plumber, not an ornithologist (a bird scientist), and second, no one has ever heard of Joe the plumber as an expert. Reliable sources for facts and statistics are the best information that can be offered.

Expert testimony is the reported positions, theses, or studies of people who are recognized experts in the field under discussion in the literature. A writer may use books, articles, essays, interviews, and so on by trained scientists and other professionals to support a thesis or position. Most often, this testimony takes the form of quotations from the expert or a paraphrasing of his or her important ideas or findings.

Personal experience and anecdote is the evidence of a writer's own personal experience, or a "little story" about an event, person, or idea that exemplifies the point he or she is trying to make. It holds weight if the reader trusts the writer, and it is valuable; it is not as powerful or as conclusive as documented facts or the testimony of experts (unless the writer is a recognized authority in the field about which he or she has written).

Hypothetical illustrations are examples that suggest probable circumstances in which something would be true. Strictly speaking, a hypothetical illustration is not "hard" evidence, but rather evidence of probability. For example, to demonstrate that "people will do whatever they can get away with," a writer might bring up the hypothetical illustration of someone at a ticket counter who gets back more change than he or she paid for the ticket. The chances are, the writer might point out, that the person would pocket the extra money rather than be honest and return it. In this case, the writer is not naming anybody in particular or citing statistics to make the point, but rather is pointing to *a situation that is likely but is not an actual documented case.* This situation has either the weight of common sense for the reader or none at all.

Analogies are the last and weakest form of evidence. It is not actually evidence at all. An analogy is simply a comparison between items that are different but that also have some striking similarities. Analogies often use the term "like" to show the relationship of ideas. For example, the writer might say, "Life is like a tree: we start out struggling in the dirt, grow into the full bloom of youth, and become deeply rooted in our ways, until, in the autumn of our years, we lose our hair like leaves, and succumb ultimately to the bare winter of death."

While reading, determine what sort of evidence the writer is using and how effective it is in proving his or her point.

Reasons for Evidence

To prove any thesis that the writer maintains is true, he or she may employ any one of the following seven strategies:

1. *show* that a process or a procedure does or should work step by step in time;

2. *compare or contrast* two or more things or ideas to show important differences or similarities;

3. *identify* a problem and then explain how to solve it;

4. *analyze* into its components, or *classify* by its types or categories, an idea or thing to show how it is put together, how it works, or how it is designed;

5. *explain* why something happens to produce a particular result or set of results;

6. *describe* the particular individual characteristics of a place, person, time, or idea;

7. *define* what a thing is or what an idea means.

Bias can be identified in passages in which the author is comparing and contrasting two arguments.

To analyze the relationship between ideas in opposition (pro and con), first identify the claim each side is making. (Of course, in many situations there are more than two sides.) Pay attention to the intricacies of the position; many arguments are not simply for or against something, but instead are qualified positions with exceptions. For example, the claim that Medicare should pay for standard prescriptions is different from the claim that Medicare should pay for prescriptions. The word 'standard' qualifies the argument; perhaps experimental drugs or preventative treatments are excluded from the proposal. In analyzing an argument, be sure to find the edges of the argument, where the arguer would not want to press the argument further and where there may be bias.

After analyzing the argument, locate and evaluate the reasons that the author uses to support the claim. Ask yourself, "Why is the author's claim important?" Then examine the reasons the author gives: are they good reasons and are they connected to the claim? Finally, examine the evidence the author uses to support the reasons. The evidence should come from reliable sources and be pertinent to the reasons and claim. In examining two or more opposing arguments, you will judge which best supports its claim. However, the best argument may fail to convince its reader, especially on politically volatile topics such as abortion rights.

Skill 5: Recognize Tone

The general tone of the passage can indicate something about the unfamiliar word. For instance, whether the word is positive or negative can often be deduced by tone clues.

> His speech <u>ostracized</u> his audience, who found his sarcastic, mordant, and rude comments disturbing. (*definition of ostracized:* to exclude willingly. The reader cannot miss the heavy negative tone of the words in the passage.)

Skill 6: Recognize Relationships Between Sentences

If the literature is a textbook, read the *introduction*, scan the *chapter titles*, and quickly review any *subheadings, charts, pictures, appendices,* and *indexes* that the book includes. If it is an article, read the first and last paragraphs. These are the most likely places to find the writer's *main point* or *thesis*.

Note that there is a significant difference between a thesis and a main point. Here is an example of a *main point*:

> The Rocky Mountains have three important geological features: abundant water, gold- and silver-bearing ore, and oil-bearing shale.

Notice that this statement is not a matter of the writer's opinion. It is a fact. Now, notice the following *thesis*:

> The Rocky Mountains are the most important source of geological wealth in the United States.

What is the difference? The second statement offers an arguable conclusion or informed opinion. It may be an informed opinion on the part of the writer, but it is still an opinion. A thesis, then, is a statement offered by a writer as true or correct, although it is actually a matter of opinion.

In the first statement, whether the author has an opinion about it or not, these features are an important part of the makeup of the Rocky Mountains. In the second statement, the author may have contrary evidence to offer about Alaska or the Everglades. The second statement bears proving; the first is self-evident. The writer would go on to show the existence of these features, not—as in the second case—the quality or value of those features. The writer of a main point paper is reporting to or informing his or her audience; the writer of a thesis is attempting to sway the audience to his or her point of view.

Key Sections to Recognize

In reading a particular passage, you want to identify what portions or sections of a whole essay you confront. Depending upon which section of an essay is offered, you may decide whether you are reading the writer's main point, thesis, purpose, or evidence.

Introduction: The introductory paragraph usually shows the writer's point of view, or thesis, and introduces that position with some lead-in or general data to support it. The thesis of an essay is the writer's stated or implied position on a particular issue or idea. Identify the writer's purpose and point of view.

Development: This part consists of three or more middle paragraphs that prove the writer's position from different angles, using evidence from real-life experience and knowledge. Evidence may take the form of facts, examples, statistics, illustrations, opinions, or analogies.

In addition, each paragraph within the development section will have a stated or implied main point used to support the thesis of the whole passage. For example, a thesis might be "Dogs are better than cats." Having said that, a whole paragraph might be written with supporting examples to show a main point in support of that idea. The main point of the paragraph that needs support, then, might be as follows:

First of all, dogs are more loyal than cats.

The evidence that is summoned to support that point which, in turn, supports the overall thesis would therefore have to be facts, statistics, expert testimony, or anecdotal knowledge that shows that dogs are indeed more loyal than cats. For example: "The A.S.P.C.A. reports that 99 out of 100 dogs cannot adjust to new owners after the death of their original masters, while only 2 out of 100 cats cannot adjust in the same situation."

Conclusion: The last paragraph usually (but not always) sums up the writer's position and may add some final reminder of what the issue is, some speculation, or some call to action that the writer suggests.

Skill 7: Analyze the Validity of Arguments

Induction, Deduction, and Fallacies

In formulating critical evaluations of a piece of writing, it is important to understand the problems, if any, with the logic of the piece that has been read. Does it make sense? If not, why doesn't it? It is up to the reader to find the errors in any piece of writing he or she reads. Of course, if the writer is effective, the reader won't find these fallacies. Be on the lookout for them because it is often a good way to refute, criticize, or counterargue if called upon to respond critically to any author's central idea, thesis, or main point. Make sure the evidence proves the writer's point and not something else.

Pay special attention to conclusions. The writer may not have proved the point. An essay is essentially a *syllogism* that proves something by *induction* or *deduction*. The *syllogism* is that *basic form of deductive reasoning* that is the cornerstone of most logic. It consists of a *major premise*, a *minor premise*, and a *conclusion*. Note how they are used in the discussion below. *Induction* is the sort of reasoning that arrives at a general conclusion based on the relationship among the contributing elements of an idea.

For example, a writer may observe under experimental conditions that whenever a spider begins to spin a web, it first rubs its back legs over its silk gland. The author may have observed 100,000 different species of spiders display this behavior. He or she may have also observed that they never rub their hind legs over the gland at any other time, only when they are about to put out silk to start a web. He or she may then *induce* from these observations that spiders must rub their hind legs over their silk glands in order to begin the production of silk to spin a web. Another individual may prove this theory wrong later because new evidence shows up to invalidate the induction. Until that happens, this will be the conclusion drawn from observations of the behavior of spiders.

Deduction, by way of contrast, reasons from the general to the particular. For example, an author may assert that all trees grow upward from the earth, not downward from the sky. Until someone finds a tree that grows from the sky to the earth, an individual will assume that every tree started growing out of the earth and base all other conclusions about the growth and flowering of trees upon this *deduction* as well.

Occasionally, however, the *premises* of a deductive argument are false or unprovable. The *premises* of an argument are those *definitions* or *assumptions* that are givens (concepts that do not stand in need of proof but are either self-evident, common knowledge, or agreed upon as terms between the writer and the reader). For example,

>   Major Premise: All goats have beards.
>
>   Minor Premise: Harry Jones has a beard.
>
>   Conclusion: Therefore, Harry is a goat.

The conclusion is incorrect. It could be true if only goats have beards, but this is not the case; male human beings may have beards as well. Therefore, the conclusion is insupportable. In this example, we lack sufficient information to draw a conclusion about who or what Harry is.

Typical Logical Fallacies

Below is a list of typical logical errors that weak writers commit. The list is not exhaustive. Know how they occur and practice finding them in others' arguments, either in conversation or in essays they may have written.

1. *Either/or:* The writer assumes only two opposing possibilities: "Either we abolish cars, or the environment is doomed." This argument is weak because other factors may contribute to the destruction of the environment as well.

2. *Oversimplification:* Here the author might first state, "Only motivated athletes become champions." Perhaps not; though unfortunate, unmotivated athletes who use enhancing steroids occasionally become champions, too.

3. *Begging the question:* The writer assumes he or she has proved something that has not been proven. "He is unintelligent because he is stupid." A lack of intelligence is almost synonymous with being stupid. It cannot be proven that he is stupid by saying he is unintelligent; that "he" is either or both of these is exactly what needs to be proved.

4. *Ignoring the issue:* An argument against the truth of a person's testimony in court shifts from what the witness observed to how the witness's testimony is inadmissible. "The witness is obviously unkempt and homeless." One has nothing to do with the other.

5. *Arguing against a person, not an idea:* The writer argues that somebody's idea has no merit because he or she is immoral or unintelligent: "John can't prove anything about dogs being faithful; he can't even understand basic mathematics."

6. *"It does not follow..."* or *non sequitur:* The writer leaps to a wrong conclusion: "John is tall; he must know a lot about mountains."

7. *Drawing the wrong conclusion from a sequence:* "He trained, read, then trained some more and, therefore, won the match." It is quite possible that other factors led to his winning the match.

Skill 8: Draw Logical Inferences and Conclusions

Returning to question 6 in the practice passage, you must be able to summarize the passage and draw logical inferences and conclusions.

6. Which paragraph below is the best summary of the passage?

(A) The Supreme Court's decision-making process with respect to obscenity and pornography has become too subjective. Fact-pattern analyses, used to determine the overall attitude of the Court, reveal only broad-based attitudes on the part of the Court toward the situations of obscenity cases. But these patterns cannot fully account for the Court's attitudes toward case content. Research is not conclusive that fact-pattern analyses work when applied to legal areas. Renewed public and local interest suggests continued study and close examination of how the Court makes decisions. Delegating authority to the states may reflect patterns for Court decisions in other socially sensitive areas.

(B)   Though subjective, the Supreme Court decisions are well documented. Fact-pattern analyses reveal the attitude of the Supreme Court toward its decisions in cases. Spaeth explains that an attitude involves both an object and a situation. For the Court, the situation may be defined as the decision to grant certiorari. Cases present strikingly similar patterns, and a small number of variables explain a high proportion of the Court's decisions. Segal has made an effort to verify the applicability of fact-pattern analysis with some success. The Court's decisions on obscenity and pornography suggest weak Court behavior, such as in *Miller vs. California.*

(C)   To determine what obscenity and pornography mean to the Supreme Court, we must use fact-pattern analysis. Fact-pattern analysis reveals the ideas that the Court uses to operate in a vacuum. The litigants and the subject matter of cases is defined in broad terms (such as an entire area of law) to reveal the Court's decision-making process. Search and seizure cases reveal strikingly similar patterns, leaving the Court open to grant certiorari effectively. Renewed public interest in the Court's decisions proves how the Court will react in the future.

(D)   Supreme Court decisions about pornography and obscenity are under examination and are out of control. The Court has to see the case to know it. Fact-pattern analyses reveal that the Court can only define cases in narrow terms, thus revealing individual egotism on the part of the Justices. As a result of strikingly similar patterns in search and seizure cases, the Court should be studied further for its weakness in delegating authority to state courts, as in the case of *Miller vs. California.*

The paragraph that best and most accurately reports what the writer demonstrated based on the implied thesis (see question 1) is answer choice (C) which is correct.

Choice (A) is incorrect. While it reflects some of the evidence presented in the passage, the passage does not imply that all Court decisions are subjective, just the ones about pornography and obscenity. Similarly, the writer does not suggest that delegating authority to the states as in *Miller vs. California* is a sign of some weakness, but merely that it is worthy of study as a tool for predicting or identifying the Court attitude.

Response (B) is also incorrect. The writer summons information over and over to show how fact-pattern analysis cannot pin down the Court's attitude toward case content.

(D) is incorrect. Nowhere does the writer say or suggest that the justice system is "out of control" or that the justices are "egotists," only that they are liable to be reduced to being "subjective" rather than based on an identifiable shared standard.

Drill 1: Vocabulary

➤ **Directions:** Determine a working meaning for the underlined word in each of the following passages.

1. Romeyn de Hooghe, the first limner to limit his work to narrative strips, used his talent to create pictorial criticism of the persecution of the Huguenots under Louis XIV.

2. The somber clouds and the dreary rain caused the child to mope about the house.

3. The veracity of the witness's testimony, revealed through his eye-to-eye contact with the jury and lack of stumbling over words, was not doubted.

4. Why isn't the evening sun described as moribund, not setting; after all, it is coming to the day's end?

5. As president, state warden, and security chief, the leader described in Gilbert and Sullivan's "The Mikado" is a poohbah.

6. Robin Hood's audacious actions included conducting dangerous rescues of Maid Marian and visiting enemy territory disguised as a local.

7. Among common household health products are St. John's Wort and Echinacea, herbs from the garden.

8. My father is a numismatist; he spends several hours each week studying his coins from other countries and time periods.

Drill 1: Answers

1. artist; line drawer

2. unhappily move about

3. truthfulness

4. dying or dead

5. leader who holds several offices

6. daring

7. herbs used for good health

8. coin collector

Drill 2: Inferential Comprehension

➤ **Directions:** Read the passages and answer the questions that follow.

Passage 1

The Mitsushita Electric Industrial Company of Japan has developed a computer program that can use photographs of faces to predict the aging process and, also, how an unborn child may look. The system can show how a couple may look after 40 years of marriage and how newlyweds' future children may look. The computer analyzes facial characteristics from a photograph, based on shading and coloring differences, and then creates a three-dimensional model in its memory. The system consists of a personal computer with a program and circuit board. It will be marketed soon by the Mitsushita Company.

1. This passage is written in the point of view called

    (A) first person.

    (B) second person.

    (C) third person.

    (D) a combination of first and third person.

2. The intended purpose of this passage is to

    (A) persuade a couple to send in their photographs to use to predict their children's appearance.

    (B) explain how the aging process of adults and the appearance of their children can be pre dicted by a computer.

    (C) express an opinion about the technology of the future in Japan.

    (D) describe one way a computer uses photographs.

Passage 2

As a farmer from Conrad, Montana, I might be the last person expected to invent and patent a motorcycle helmet. (No, I don't wear a helmet while I am driving my tractor.) The law in the United States requires that all cars sold must carry a third, high-mounted brake light on the rear of the vehicle. If cars need this light, I thought, how much safer life would be for motorcyclists if they, too, had such a light. The problem, however, was to install it "high-mounted." I have designed a helmet with a brake light in the rear. Thus, motorcyclists wearing a helmet like mine are much safer on the road.

3. The intended purpose of the passage is to

    (A) tell about a farmer in Montana.

    (B) explain a safety requirement for cars in the United States.

    (C) describe a man's motorcycle helmet invention that makes riding motorcycles safer.

    (D) show the versatility of some people.

4. The point of view of this passage is

    (A) first person.   (C) third person.

    (B) second person.   (D) first and third person.

Drill 2: Detailed Explanations of Answers

1. **(C)**

    Choice (C) is the correct answer because the passage employs the point of view of an outsider through the use of pronouns such as *he, she,* and *it.*

2. **(B)**

    The intended purpose is to explain. Although couples might be interested in sending in their photographs to see what their children may look like, choice (A), the passage is not encouraging this reaction from those who read it. Choice (C) is much too broad a response; also, the passage is not expressing an opinion. Choice (D) is too vague, although what it says is incomplete truth.

3. **(C)**

    The focus of the passage is the motorcycle helmet, and the intended purpose is to explain why and how the helmet was invented. Choice (A) is a fact about the inventor—he is a farmer. Choice (B) is a true statement as well, but it is what prompted the writer's idea for a helmet. (D) is a general statement that is unrelated to this passage.

4. **(A)**

    The personality of the speaker is revealed along with his ideas and actions. Notice also the use of the pronoun *I.* Choice (D) will attract some test-takers, but the first person point of view often uses third person pronouns along with first person pronouns.

Drill 3: Reading Comprehension

➤ **Directions:** Read the passage and answer the questions that follow.

WATER

1   The most important source of sediment is earth and rock material carried to the sea by rivers and streams; the same materials may also have been transported by glaciers and winds. Other sources are volcanic ash and lava, shells and skeletons of organisms, chemical precipitates

5   formed in seawater, and particles from outer space.

Water is a most unusual substance because it exists on the surface of the earth in its three physical states: ice, water, and water vapor. There are other substances that might exist in a solid and liquid or gaseous state at temperatures normally found at the earth's surface,

10   but there are fewer substances which occur in all three states.

Water is odorless, tasteless, and colorless. It is the only substance known to exist in a natural state as a solid, liquid, or gas on the surface of the earth. It is a universal solvent. Water does not corrode, rust, burn, or separate into its components easily. It is chemically in-

15   destructible. It can corrode almost any metal and erode the most solid rock. A unique property of water is that it expands and floats on water when frozen or in the solid state. Water has a freezing point of 0°C and a boiling point of 100°C. Water has the capacity for absorbing great quantities of heat with relatively little increase in temperature.

20   When *distilled*, water is a poor conductor of electricity but when salt is added, it is a good conductor of electricity.

Sunlight is the source of energy for temperature change, evaporation, and currents for water movement through the atmosphere. Sunlight controls the rate of photosynthesis for all marine plants,

25   which are directly or indirectly the source of food for all marine animals. Migration, breeding, and other behaviors of marine animals are affected by light.

Water, as the ocean or sea, is blue because of the molecular scattering of the sunlight. Blue light, being of short wavelength, is scat-

30   tered more effectively than light of longer wavelengths. Variations in color may be caused by particles suspended in the water, water depth, cloud cover, temperature, and other variable factors. Heavy concentrations of dissolved materials cause a yellowish hue, while algae will cause the water to look green. Heavy populations of plant and animal

35   materials will cause the water to look brown.

1. Which of the following lists of topics best organizes the information in the selection?

    (A) I.   Water as vapor

         II.   Water as ice

         III. Water as solid

    (B) I.   Properties of seawater

         II.   Freezing and boiling points of water

         III. Photosynthesis

         IV.   Oceans and seas

    (C) I.   Water as substance

         II.   Water's corrosion

         III. Water and plants

         IV.   Water and algae coloration

    (D) I.   Water's physical states

         II.   Properties of water

         III. Effects of the sun on water

         IV.   Reasons for color variation in water

2. According to the passage, what is the most unique property of water?

    (A) Water is odorless, tasteless, and colorless.

    (B) Water exists on the surface of the earth in three physical states.

    (C) Water is chemically indestructible.

    (D) Water is a poor conductor of electricity.

3. Which of the following best defines the word ***distilled*** as it is used in the last sentence of the third paragraph?

    (A) Free of salt content   (C) Dehydrated

    (B) Free of electrical energy   (D) Containing wine

4. The writer's main purpose in this selection is to

    (A) explain the colors of water.

    (B) examine the effects of the sun on water.

    (C) define the properties of water.

    (D) describe the three physical states of all liquids.

5. The writer of this selection would most likely agree with which of the following statements?

    (A)   The properties of water are found in most other liquids on this planet.

    (B)   Water should not be consumed in its most natural state.

    (C)   Water might be used to serve many different functions.

    (D)   Water is too unpredictable for most scientists.

➤ **Directions:** Read the passage and answer the questions that follow.

THE BEGINNINGS OF THE SUBMARINE

1   A submarine was first used as an offensive weapon during the American Revolutionary War. The Turtle, a one-man submersible designed by an American inventor named David Bushnell and hand-operated by a screw propeller, attempted to sink a British man-of-war

5   in New York Harbor. The plan was to attach a charge of gunpowder to the ship's bottom with screws and explode it with a time fuse. After repeated failures to force the screws through the copper sheathing of the hull of H.M.S. *Eagle*, the submarine gave up and withdrew, exploding its powder a short distance from the *Eagle*. Although the attack

10   was unsuccessful, it caused the British to move their blockading ships from the harbor to the outer bay.

    On 17 February 1864, a Confederate craft, a hand-propelled submersible, carrying a crew of eight men, sank a Federal corvette that was blockading Charleston Harbor. The hit was accomplished by a

15   torpedo suspended ahead of the Confederate *Hunley* as she rammed the Union frigate *Housatonic*, and is the first recorded instance of a submarine sinking a warship.

    The submarine first became a major component in naval warfare during World War I, when Germany demonstrated its full potential.

20   Wholesale sinking of Allied shipping by the German U-boats almost swung the war in favor of the Central Powers. Then, as now, the submarine's greatest advantage was that it could operate beneath the ocean surface where detection was difficult. Sinking a submarine was comparatively easy, once it was found—but finding it before it could

25   attack was another matter.

During the closing months of World War I, the Allied Submarine Devices Investigation Committee was formed to obtain from science and technology more effective underwater detection equipment. The committee developed a reasonably accurate device for locating a sub-
30 merged submarine. This device was a trainable hydrophone, which was attached to the bottom of the ASW ship, and used to detect screw noises and other sounds that came from a submarine. Although the committee disbanded after World War I, the British made improvements on the locating device during the interval between then and
35 World War II, and named it ASDIC after the committee.

American scientists further improved on the device, calling it SONAR, a name derived from the underlined initials of the words <u>so</u>und <u>n</u>avigation <u>a</u>nd <u>r</u>anging.

At the end of World War II, the United States improved the snor-
40 kel (a device for bringing air to the crew and engines when operating submerged on diesels) and developed the Guppy (short for greater underwater propulsion power), a conversion of the fleet-type submarine of World War II fame. The superstructure was changed by reducing the surface area, streamlining every protruding object, and
45 enclosing the periscope shears in a streamlined metal fairing. Performance increased greatly with improved electronic equipment, additional battery capacity, and the addition of the snorkel.

6. The passage implies that one of the most pressing modifications needed for the submarine was to

(A) streamline its shape.

(B) enlarge the submarine for accommodating more torpedoes and men.

(C) reduce the noise caused by the submarine.

(D) add a snorkel.

7. It is inferred that

(A) ASDIC was formed to obtain technology for underwater detection.

(B) ASDIC developed an accurate device for locating submarines.

(C) the hydrophone was attached to the bottom of the ship.

(D) ASDIC was formed to develop technology to defend U.S. shipping.

8. SONAR not only picked up the sound of submarines moving through the water but also

(A) indicated the speed at which the sub was moving.

(B) gave the location of the submarine.

(C) indicated the speed of the torpedo.

(D) placed the submarine within a specified range.

9.   According to the passage, the submarine's success was due in part to its ability to

    (A)   strike and escape undetected.

    (B)   move swifter than other vessels.

    (C)   submerge to great depths while being hunted.

    (D)   run silently.

10.   From the passage, one can infer

    (A)   David Bushnell was indirectly responsible for the sinking of the Federal corvette in Charlestown Harbor.

    (B)   David Bushnell invented the Turtle.

    (C)   the Turtle was a one-man submarine.

    (D)   the Turtle sank the *Eagle* on February 17, 1864.

Drill 3: Detailed Explanations of Answers

1.   **(D)**

The correct response is (D) because its precepts are summations of each of the composition's main paragraphs. (A) only mentions points made in the second paragraph. (B) and (C) only mention scattered points made throughout the passage, each of which does not represent a larger body of information within the passage.

2.   **(B)**

The second paragraph states that this is the reason that water is a most unusual substance. (A) and (C) list unusual properties of water, but are not developed in the same manner as the property stated in (B). (D) is not even correct under all circumstances.

3.   **(A)**

The sentence contrasts distilled water to that which contains salt, so (A) is correct. (B), (C), and (D) are not implied by the passage.

4.   **(C)**

The writer's didactic summary of water's properties is the only perspective found in the passage. (A) and (B) are the subjects of individual paragraphs within the passage, but hardly represent the entire passage itself. An in-depth discussion of the physical states of liquids (D) is not offered within the passage.

5. **(C)**

The correct choice is (C) because of the many properties of water ascribed to it in the passage, each of which might serve one practical purpose or another. (A) and (D) are contradicted within the passage, while (B) is not implied at all by the passage.

6. **(A)**

Answer (A) is correct because of the importance of streamlining mentioned in the final paragraph. (B) and (C) are not suggested in the paragraph, and (D) is secondary in importance to (A).

7. **(D)**

Since it may be inferred from the general purpose of underwater detection equipment, (D) is correct. While (A) and (B) are true statements, they are not inferences. (C) is not implied in the passage.

8. **(D)**

Answer (D) is correct because the "R" in SONAR stands for "Ranging." (A), (B), and (C) are neither mentioned nor implied by the passage.

9. **(A)**

As was mentioned in the third sentence of the third paragraph, (A) is correct. (B), (C), and (D) are not mentioned in the passage.

10. **(A)**

It may be inferred that Bushnell's invention led to the success of the later version of the submarine. (B) and (C) are true, but are not inferences because they are directly stated in the first paragraph. (D) is not a true statement; the Turtle had no direct link to the 1864 incident.

Mathematics Review

Are you ready to tackle the math section of the FTCE-GKT? Well, chances are you will be, but only after reviewing some basic concepts contained in this chapter. The more familiar you are with these fundamental concepts, the better you will do on the math section. Our math review represents the various mathematical topics that appear on the FTCE-GKT.

Competency 1: Knowledge of Number Sense, Concepts, and Operations

1.1: Compare the relative value of real numbers (e.g., integers, fractions, decimals, percents, irrational numbers, and numbers expressed in exponential or scientific notation).

Real Numbers

The numbers used in basic mathematics courses are called the **real numbers**. Real numbers are comprised of rational and irrational numbers. **Rational numbers** are numbers that can be written as a ratio of two integers. Rational numbers include integers, fractions, and decimals. **Integers** are the set of whole numbers and their opposites: {… –3, –2, –1, 0, 1, 2, 3…}. Whole numbers and counting numbers are subsets of integers. **Whole numbers** are all the positive integers and 0: {0, 1, 2, 3 …}. **Counting numbers** are the positive integers beginning with 1: {1, 2, 3, 4 …}. A **decimal number** is a number represented by the digits 0 to 9 and may include a decimal point. Examples of decimal numbers are 4.5, .003, and 367. **Fractions** are numbers used to express numbers that usually include parts of a whole. A fraction has a numerator and a denominator. The denominator is the number on the bottom, and it shows how many pieces the fraction is broken up into. The numerator shows how many parts of the fraction you have.

An **irrational number** is a number that cannot be expressed as the ratio of two integers. Decimals that never end (non-terminating) and do not repeat (repeating) are irrational. Square roots of numbers that are not perfect squares are irrational numbers. The ratio of a circle's circumference to its diameter is π, the most "well-known" irrational number.

Each number has a specific value and may be written in a number of different forms, such as a fraction, decimal, percent, or integer. All real numbers can be placed on a number line to show how they compare to each other. A number line is actually infinite, continuing in both directions forever. In order to make a physical representation of a number line, however, we are only able to draw a finite portion of it. Below is an example of a number line that shows the integers from −10 to +10. Although only the integers are marked, there are an infinite number of numbers that can be represented on the number line.

For example, between 0 and 1, you could place .3, .45, .8, $\frac{85}{100}$, and $\frac{9}{11}$ because they are numbers greater than 0 and less than 1.

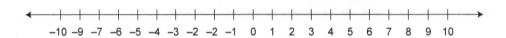

As you move to the right on a number line, numbers get larger. As you move to the left on a number line, numbers get smaller. You can choose to show as many or as few numbers as you wish on a number line. In addition, you can divide the number line into whatever divisions suit the situation. If you wanted to compare numbers between 0 and 1, for example, you could show just the portion of a number line between 0 and 1, divided up into tenths, if you wanted.

Fractions

Comparing fractions involves knowing which fraction is larger and which is smaller. If fractions are shown on a number line, the fraction to the right is the larger one. However, fractions are not always shown on a number line. Comparing fractions is simple when the fractions have the same denominator. Compare the numerators to see which fraction is larger. For example, which is larger, $\frac{9}{15}$ or $\frac{7}{15}$? Since 9 is larger than 7, you know that $\frac{9}{15}$ is larger than $\frac{7}{15}$.

If you want to compare two fractions that have different denominators, you have two options. You can convert each fraction into a decimal, or you can find a common denominator for the fractions and rewrite them with that common denominator.

Let's compare the two fractions $\frac{4}{7}$ and $\frac{5}{8}$ using both methods. To find the decimal equivalent of $\frac{4}{7}$, divide the numerator by the denominator. The resulting decimal is a repeating decimal; we can round it to the thousandths place. $\frac{4}{7} \approx .571$. The decimal equivalent of $\frac{5}{8}$ is .625. You can see that .625 is larger than .571. Therefore, $\frac{5}{8}$ is larger than $\frac{4}{7}$.

To compare the fractions using common denominators, we must rewrite the two fractions with a common denominator. To do that, find the least common multiple of the denominators, 7 and 8. The LCM is 56. Rewrite each fraction as an equivalent fraction with the denominator of 56. The fraction $\frac{4}{7}$ will be multiplied by $\frac{8}{8}$, and the fraction $\frac{5}{8}$ will be multiplied by $\frac{7}{7}$. Equivalent fractions have the same value; also, equivalent fractions both simplify to the same fraction when they are in lowest terms. See below:

$$\frac{4}{7} \times \frac{8}{8} = \frac{32}{56} \qquad\qquad \frac{5}{8} \times \frac{7}{7} = \frac{35}{56}$$

$$\frac{35}{56} > \frac{32}{56}. \text{ Therefore, } \frac{5}{8} > \frac{4}{7}.$$

PROBLEM

List the fractions shown from least to greatest: $\frac{3}{7}, \frac{8}{21}, \frac{7}{14}$

(A) $\frac{3}{7}, \frac{8}{21}, \frac{7}{14}$ (B) $\frac{8}{21}, \frac{7}{14}, \frac{3}{7}$

(C) $\frac{7}{14}, \frac{3}{7}, \frac{8}{21}$ (D) $\frac{8}{21}, \frac{3}{7}, \frac{7}{14}$

SOLUTION

Sometimes it is necessary to find a common denominator when ordering fractions. Other times, you can compare one fraction to another and determine which is larger without finding a common denominator. Notice that $\frac{7}{14}$ equals $\frac{1}{2}$. You can tell that $\frac{8}{21}$ and $\frac{3}{7}$ are less than $\frac{1}{2}$ because their numerators are less than half of their denominators. Half of 21 is 10.5; since 8 is less than 10.5, $\frac{8}{21}$ is less than $\frac{1}{2}$. Half of 7 is 3.5; since 3 is less than 3.5, $\frac{3}{7}$ is less than $\frac{1}{2}$. We know the largest fraction is $\frac{7}{14}$. All we have to do is compare $\frac{8}{21}$ and $\frac{3}{7}$. A common denominator for these two fractions is 21 since 7 is a factor of 21. $\frac{3}{7} \times \frac{3}{3} = \frac{9}{21}$, so $\frac{3}{7} = \frac{9}{21}$. $\frac{8}{21} < \frac{9}{21}$, which means that the fractions in order from least to greatest are $\frac{8}{21}, \frac{3}{7}, \frac{7}{14}$. The correct answer is (D).

Conversions

Quantities can be presented in a variety of ways: as decimals, percents, or fractions. Depending on the situation, it may be appropriate to use one form over another. Therefore, it is beneficial to know how to convert among the three forms.

Writing a fraction as a decimal is simple if the denominator of the fraction is a power of 10, such as 10, 100, or 1000. For example, $\frac{2}{10} = .2$, $\frac{17}{100} = .17$, and $\frac{45}{1000} = .045$. All you have to do is put the digits in their correct places. If the denominator is not a power of 10, then divide the numerator by the denominator. To write $\frac{4}{5}$ as a decimal, divide 4 by 5.

You need to add a decimal point and a 0 after the 4 to divide 4.0 by 5. Completing this division gives you .8; therefore, $\frac{4}{5}$ is equivalent to .8.

To write a decimal as a fraction, write the numbers of the decimal in the numerator of a fraction without the decimal point. Locate the digit that is farthest to the right in the number and write its place value as the denominator. If the fraction needs to be simplified, then rewrite it in lowest terms. To write .55 as a fraction, write 55 in the numerator and 100 in the denominator: $\frac{55}{100}$. Then simplify the fraction to $\frac{11}{20}$.

There are two steps to write a decimal as a percent. First move the decimal point two places to the right (this may result in the decimal point being at the end of the number; in that case, you can leave it off). The next step is to add the percent sign. Here's an example: Write .09 as a percent. Move the decimal point two places to the right and add the percent sign to get 9% (notice how the decimal point at the end of the number is not included because it is not necessary).

There are also two steps to write a percent as a decimal. First, move the decimal point in the number two places to the left. If there is no decimal point, it means that the number in front of the percent sign is a whole number. The decimal point in a whole number is actually at the end of the number. In the number 19, for example, the decimal point (not written) would be at the end of the number: 19. is the same as 19 without the decimal point. After moving the decimal point two places to the left, take away the percent sign.

PROBLEM

Find the decimal equivalent of 14%.

(A) 14   (B) .14   (C) .014   (D) 1.4

SOLUTION

When converting a percent to a decimal, remove the percent sign and divide the number by 100 (which is the same as moving the decimal point two places to the left). 14% as a decimal would be .14. (B) is the answer.

To write a percent as a fraction, write the number in front of the percent sign in the numerator of a fraction. Since we are working with percents, put 100 in the denominator. Remember to simplify the fraction, if necessary.

PROBLEM

How would you write 91% and 8% as fractions in *lowest terms*?

(A) $\dfrac{91}{100}$ and $\dfrac{2}{25}$ (B) $\dfrac{91}{100}$ and $\dfrac{8}{100}$

(C) $\dfrac{91}{10}$ and $\dfrac{2}{25}$ (D) $\dfrac{.91}{100}$ and $\dfrac{.08}{100}$

SOLUTION

To write a percent as a fraction, remove the percent sign. Put the number given as the numerator and 100 as the denominator. Simplify, if needed. 91% is equal to $\dfrac{91}{100}$. It is in lowest terms. 8% is equal to $\dfrac{8}{100}$. The greatest common factor of 8 and 100 is 4. Divide numerator and denominator by 4 to get $\dfrac{2}{25}$. (A) is the answer.

To write a fraction as a percent, follow the steps for writing a fraction as a decimal. Then follow the steps for writing a decimal as a percent. Example: Write $\dfrac{1}{8}$ as a percent. First $\dfrac{1}{8} = .125$. Then $.125 = 12.5\%$.

If you are asked to compare numbers to each other and they are presented in a variety of forms, it is helpful to put them all in the same form—whichever is easiest for you, or whichever form makes most sense in the problem. If you have to put the following numbers in order from least to greatest, .18, $\dfrac{1}{8}$, 15%, and 10%, you could rewrite $\dfrac{1}{8}$, 15%, and 10% as decimals. Then it would be easy to see how to order them. $\dfrac{1}{8} = .125$; 15% = .15; and 10% = .10. So, the numbers in order are 10%, $\dfrac{1}{8}$, 15%, and .18.

It is also helpful to know how to convert between mixed numbers and improper fractions. To explain how to rewrite a mixed number as an improper fraction, let's look at an example.

Write $5\frac{3}{8}$ as an improper fraction. Multiply the denominator of the fraction by the whole number, $8 \times 5 = 40$. Then, add that answer to the numerator of the fraction, $40 + 3 = 43$. That answer, 43, is the numerator of the equivalent improper fraction. The denominator remains the same; in this example, it is 8. Therefore, $5\frac{3}{8}$ is equivalent to $\frac{43}{8}$.

To write an improper fraction as a mixed number, you follow the opposite process of changing a mixed number into an improper fraction. Let's write $\frac{27}{4}$ as a mixed number. Divide the denominator into the numerator. See how many times it divides into the numerator without going over the numerator. In this case, 4 divides into 27 six times because $4 \times 6 = 24$. The number 6 becomes the whole number of the mixed number. As you can see, the numerator 27 is 3 more than 24. Therefore, 3 is the remainder, which will be the numerator of the fraction. The denominator remains 4. Therefore, $\frac{27}{4} = 6\frac{3}{4}$.

It is common to write all fractions in lowest terms. A fraction is in lowest terms if the largest factor that the numerator and denominator share is 1. For example, $\frac{8}{15}$, $\frac{14}{19}$, and $\frac{25}{54}$ are all in lowest terms because the only factor that the numerator and denominator of each fraction share is 1. If a fraction can be written in lowest terms, do so. When you rewrite a fraction to lowest terms, you are dividing the numerator and denominator by the same value; what you are doing, in fact, is dividing the fraction by a form of 1. Since 1 is the identity element for multiplication (and division), dividing by 1 will not change the value. To write a fraction in lowest terms, find the greatest factor that the numerator and denominator have in common. Then divide both numerator and denominator by that number.

Equivalent fractions are two fractions that are equal to each other, but have different denominators; equivalent fractions simplify to the same fraction written in lowest terms. Some examples of equivalent fractions are:

$$\frac{1}{8} \text{ and } \frac{2}{16}$$

$$\frac{4}{12} \text{ and } \frac{12}{36}$$

$$\frac{11}{22} \text{ and } \frac{1}{2}$$

PROBLEM

Simplify: $\dfrac{1}{10} + \dfrac{3}{5}$

SOLUTION

It is helpful to find an equivalent fraction with the following setup:

$$\frac{3}{5} \times \frac{?}{?} = \frac{?}{10}$$

You are looking for the number that multiplies by 5 to get 10. That number is 2. So, you also multiply the numerator, which is 3, by 2 to get 6. Since $\dfrac{2}{2} = 1$, you are multiplying $\dfrac{3}{5}$ by 1, which does not change the value of the fraction. $\dfrac{6}{10}$ is equivalent to $\dfrac{3}{5}$. Now that you have the same denominators, you can add $\dfrac{1}{10}$ and $\dfrac{6}{10}$, which gives $\dfrac{7}{10}$.

PROBLEM

Simplify: $\dfrac{11}{12} - \dfrac{3}{8}$

(A) $\dfrac{8}{4}$ 　　　(B) $\dfrac{11}{12}$ 　　　(C) $\dfrac{13}{24}$ 　　　(D) $\dfrac{1}{2}$

SOLUTION

To complete this problem, you need to find a common denominator for 12 and 8. The least common multiple of 12 and 8 is 24 because 24 is the smallest multiple that 12 and 8 share. The first four multiples of 12 are 12, 24, 36, 48. The first four multiples of 8 are 8, 16, 24, 32. As you can see, both numbers share the multiple 24, so that is the LCM.

$$\frac{11}{12} = \frac{22}{24} \quad \text{and} \quad \frac{3}{8} = \frac{9}{24}$$

Now that both fractions have a common denominator, we can subtract the numerators. $\dfrac{22}{24} - \dfrac{9}{24} = \dfrac{13}{24}$ The correct answer is (C).

Exponents and Exponential Notation

When a number is multiplied by itself a specific number of times, it is said to be **raised to a power**. This is written as $a^n = b$ where a is the number or **base**, n is the **exponent** or **power** that indicates the number of times the base is to be multiplied by itself, and b is the product of this multiplication. For example, in the expression 3^2, 3 is the base, and 2 is the exponent. This means that 3 is used as a factor two times (3×3); the product is 9. An exponent can be either positive or negative. A negative exponent implies a fraction such that if n is a negative integer, then b will be a fraction. For example, $3^{-2} = \dfrac{1}{3^2} = \dfrac{1}{9}$.

An exponent of 0 gives a result of 1, assuming that the base is not equal to 0. That is, $a^0 = 1$ for all values of a (except 0). When computing the value of an expression in exponential form, it is often a good idea to write the expression out in expanded form to make sure you arrive at the correct answer. If you have 2^5, a common error is to multiply 2 by 5 and get 10. 2^5 is the same as $2 \times 2 \times 2 \times 2 \times 2$, which is 32. Writing the expression out in expanded form ensures that you do not make a mistake when simplifying.

PROBLEM

Which of the statements below is true?

(A) $2^3 = 3^2$

(B) $4^0 \times 10^2 > 3^4$

(C) $5^3 + 5^2 = 5^5$

(D) $4^2 + 2^4 = 2^6$

SOLUTION

To select the correct answer, you must know how to evaluate and simplify exponential expressions. For (A), $2^3 = 2 \times 2 \times 2$, which is 8. $3^2 = 3 \times 3$, which is 9. These two expressions are not equal. In (B), 4^0 equals 1 because anything (except 0) to the 0 power is 1. $10^2 = 10 \times 10$, which is 100. $1 \times 100 = 100$. $3^4 = 3 \times 3 \times 3 \times 3$, which is 81. $100 > 81$, so this statement is true. Let's take a look at (C): $5^3 + 5^2$ is *not* the same as $5^3 \times 5^2$, which would be 5^5. The expression $5^3 + 5^2$ is $(5 \times 5 \times 5) + (5 \times 5)$. This simplifies to $125 + 25$, which equals 150. To simplify (D), $4^2 + 2^4$ equals $(4 \times 4) + (2 \times 2 \times 2 \times 2)$. This equals $16 + 16$, which is 32. When 32 is written as a power of 2, it is 2^5 (not 2^6). The correct answer is (B).

PROBLEM

Which of the statements below is *false*?

(A) $2^6 + 2^3 = 2^9$

(B) $5^3 \times 5^5 = 5^8$

(C) $\dfrac{10^9}{10^3} = 10^6$

(D) $\dfrac{8^5}{8^0} = 8^5$

SOLUTION

When multiplying exponents whose bases are the same, add the exponents and keep the base the same. When dividing exponents whose bases are the same, subtract the exponents and keep the base the same. If you know these two rules, you can see that answer choices (B), (C), and (D) are true. (A) is false because you do not add the exponents when *adding* exponential expressions. Each expression must be simplified separately, and then combined. That is, $2^6 + 2^3$ would be $64 + 8$, which equals 72. This is not the same as 2^9, which equals 512. The correct answer is (A) because it is the only false statement.

PROBLEM

Simplify the expression: $\dfrac{x^3 \times x^9}{x^2}$

   (A) x^6 (B) x^8 (C) x^{10} (D) x^{14}

SOLUTION

To solve this problem, you must know the rules of multiplying and dividing exponents with the same bases. First, simplify the numerator, and then simplify the rational expression by dividing the numerator by the denominator. Add the exponents in the numerator to get x^{12}. Then, divide x^{12} by x^2. Subtract the exponents because the bases are the same. The final answer is x^{10}, answer choice (C). Note: You do not divide exponents when you divide exponents with the same base. Answer choice (A), x^6, is not correct.

Square Numbers

Perfect square numbers are numbers that result from multiplying an integer by itself. The first 10 square numbers are 1, 4, 9, 16, 25, 36, 49, 64, 81, and 100.

There are an infinite number of square numbers; it is helpful to be able to recognize them. The reason they are called square numbers is because if you start with a positive integer, you can imagine that it is the side length of a square. When you multiply that number by itself, the answer you get can by represented by the area of a square. The diagrams below show the first six square numbers.

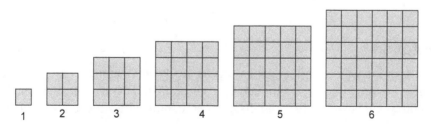

You can square any number by multiplying it by itself; however, if you do not square an integer, you will not get a perfect square number.

Square Roots

Just as you square a number, you can also find the **square root** of a number. The square root of a number is the number that if you multiply it by itself results in the number. Each number has two square roots, a positive one and a negative one. Thus, the square root of 81 is 9 since $9 \times 9 = 81$. However, –9 is also a root of 81 since $(-9)(-9) = 81$. Every positive number has two roots. The **principal root** is the positive one. Zero has only one square root, and negative numbers do not have real numbers as their square roots. Usually when asked for the square root of a number, you are looking for the principal square root. When you find the square root of a perfect square number, you will get an integer. If, however, you are finding the square root of a non-perfect square number, the square root will be an **irrational number**. That is, you can find the square root of numbers like 6, 15, and 30; however, they will be non-terminating, non-repeating decimal numbers, which are irrational numbers.

Radicals

A **radical** is a root sign. To multiply two or more radicals, we use the law that states: $\sqrt{a} \times \sqrt{b} = \sqrt{ab}$.

To divide two radicals, we use the law that states: $\dfrac{\sqrt{a}}{\sqrt{b}} = \sqrt{\dfrac{a}{b}}$.

To add or subtract radicals, the number underneath the radical must be the same. For example, $\sqrt{2} + 3\sqrt{2} = 4\sqrt{2}$. However, $3\sqrt{2} + \sqrt{5}$ cannot be simplified.

To find the square root of 100, you can write $\sqrt{100}$. Sometimes you will be asked to rewrite an expression with a radical in a different or simpler form. Therefore, it is important to know how to rewrite radicals in simplest form. If the number under a radical has a perfect square factor greater than 1, you should take that factor out. For example, $\sqrt{75}$ can be rewritten as $\sqrt{25} \bullet \sqrt{3}$. The square root of 25 is 5, so $\sqrt{75}$ in simplest form is $5\sqrt{3}$.

Scientific Notation

Scientific notation is a way of writing really large or really small numbers in a special format: There is a decimal number between 1 and 10 multiplied by a power of 10. For example, in scientific notation, the number 45,000,000 would be 4.5×10^7, and the number .00000347 would be 3.47×10^{-6}.

PROBLEM

Simplify the following and express the answer in scientific notation.

$$\frac{9.3 \times 10^6}{3.1 \times 10^2}$$

(A) 3.0×10^3

(B) 3.0×10^4

(C) 6.2×10^3

(D) 6.2×10^4

SOLUTION

It is not necessary to simplify the numerator and then the denominator. This problem can be done in parts. Divide 9.3 by 3.1. The answer is 3. Then divide 10^6 by 10^2. Subtract the exponents since the bases are the same. $10^6 \div 10^2 = 10^4$. The final answer is 3×10^4. The correct answer choice is (B).

PROBLEM

Calculate the expression shown below, and express the answer in scientific notation.

$$0.006 \times 1.34$$

(A) 0.804×10^{-2}

(B) 0.804×10^2

(C) 8.04×10^{-3}

(D) 8.04×10^3

SOLUTION

The first step is to multiply the decimal numbers together. The answer is .00804. The second step is to write that answer in scientific notation. The first number in scientific notation must be between 1 and 10. Where could you put the decimal point in .00804 to get a number between 1 and 10? The decimal point would go between the 8 and the 0: 8.04. Now you have to decide what power of 10 to multiply 8.04 by to get .00804. The decimal point needs to move three spaces to the left. This would be 10^{-3}. The final answer is 8.04×10^{-3}, which is answer choice (C).

1.2: Solve real-world problems involving addition, subtraction, multiplication, and division of rational numbers (e.g., whole numbers, integers, decimals, percents, and fractions including mixed numbers).

When you are trying to solve a problem, you must read the details in the problem carefully to figure out what information you need and what information you can ignore. It is recommended that you read word problems at least two times before attempting to solve them. Do not think that you must use every number that is given in a problem. Sometimes there is information included that is used to help clarify the situation, but the numbers are not needed to answer the question. If you find it helpful, you should underline key words such as "how many" or "at what time" to help you focus on what the question is asking.

Another important thing to remember when solving word problems is that they often do not tell you what operation to use or what process to follow. You have to figure out what to do based on the context of the problem. For example, the language, "all together" and "the total" indicate that you will use addition. The words, "how much more" or "how much taller" indicate subtraction. The chart below shows some vocabulary you may see that indicate each of the four operations.

Addition	Subtraction	Multiplication	Division
Add	Subtract	Multiply	Divide
And	Minus	Times	Quotient
Plus	Difference	Product	
More than	Less than		
Increased by	Decreased by		
Sum	Take away		
Total	Fewer		

PROBLEM

Mrs. Stanton is writing her will. She wishes to leave each of her five children an equal amount of her $800,000 estate. Which problem below will result in each child receiving the correct amount?

(A) 800,000 ÷ 5

(B) 5 × 800,000

(C) 5 ÷ 800,000

(D) 800,000 − 5

SOLUTION

To break up an amount into even groups, you must use division. To find how much money each child will receive, divide the total amount of money, $800,000 by the number of children, 5. 800,000 ÷ 5 is the correct expression. This is answer choice (A).

PROBLEM

Darnell put $2\frac{1}{4}$ cups of flour in a bowl along with $\frac{1}{2}$ cups of butter, and $\frac{2}{3}$ cups of sugar. How many cups of ingredients does Darnell have?

(A) $2\frac{4}{9}$ (B) $3\frac{5}{6}$ (C) $3\frac{5}{12}$ (D) $2\frac{7}{24}$

SOLUTION

To add these three fractions, find the common denominator for 2, 3, and 4. The least common multiple of 2, 3, and 4 is 12, so 12 is a common denominator you can use. The three fractions written as 12ths are $2\frac{3}{12}$, $\frac{6}{12}$, and $\frac{8}{12}$. When you add them together, you get $2\frac{17}{12}$. Notice the fractional part of the mixed number is an improper fraction. Rewrite $\frac{17}{12}$ as a mixed number. It is $1\frac{5}{12}$. Then add this mixed number to the whole number 2 from $2\frac{17}{12}$. $1\frac{5}{12}+2=3\frac{5}{12}$. The correct answer is (C).

Percents

There are several different types of problems that you may encounter involving percents. If you want to find the percent of a number, the easiest way is to rewrite the percent as its decimal equivalent and multiply. If you need to know what percent one number is of another as in the problem, you should set up and solve a proportion. One of the ratios will have 100 as a denominator. If you are asked to find the whole when given the part and the percent, you can also write a proportion.

PROBLEM

What percent of 80 is 5?

(A) 16   (B) 6.25   (C) .0625   (D) 40

SOLUTION

Write the proportion: $\frac{5}{80}=\frac{y}{100}$.

Cross-multiply. You get $80y = 500$. Then divide both sides by 80 to get 6.25. Therefore 5 is 6.25% of 80. (B) is the correct answer.

PROBLEM

15% of what number is 30?

(A) 4.5   (B) 20   (C) 15   (D) 200

SOLUTION

The biggest challenge with this problem is not interpreting it correctly. You are not asked to find 15% of 30. You need to find what number, when you find 15% of it, gives 30. Write the following proportion to find the number: $\frac{15}{100} = \frac{30}{z}$. Cross multiply, which gives you $15z = 3000$. Then divide both sides by 30 to get $z = 200$. That means that 15% of 200 is 30. (D) is the correct answer.

PROBLEM

Tom bought a piece of land selling for $65,000. If he had to pay 12% of the price as a down payment, how much was his down payment?

(A) $5,416   (B) $7,800   (C) $6,500   (D) $5,000

SOLUTION

The most efficient way to find 12% of $65,000 is to multiply the decimal equivalent of 12% by 65,000. .12 $\times$ 65,000 = 7800. Therefore, $7,800 is the down payment Tom must pay. (B) is the correct answer.

PROBLEM

A diamond necklace sells for $7,300. If you purchase it on black Friday, the price is reduced by 18%. What is the sale price of the necklace?

(A) $1,314   (B) $405   (C) $2908   (D) $5,986

SOLUTION

The price of the necklace is being reduced 18%. That means the price you pay for the necklace will be 100% − 18%, which is 82% of the original price. To find the sale price of the necklace, you can find 82% of $7,300 or find 18% of $7,300 and subtract it from $7,300. The first way is more efficient because it requires only one step. To find 82% of $7,300, rewrite 82% as a decimal (.82) and multiply it by 7,300. .82 × 7300 = 5,986. The correct answer is (D). Answer choice (A) is the amount of discount (not the sale price).

1.3: Apply basic number theory concepts including the use of primes, composites, factors, and multiples in solving problems.

Factors

Factors are the numbers that you multiply to get another number. For example, 8 and 2 are factors of 16 because 8 × 2 = 16. Factors must divide evenly into a number with no remainder. That is, 5 is not a factor of 12 because even though 5 divides into 12 two times, there is a remainder of 2. To find the **greatest common factor** of two numbers, the **GCF**, you must find the largest factor that both numbers have in common. If you wanted to find the GCF of 8 and 12, list the factors of each number, and then select the largest factor that both numbers have in common. Factors of 8 are 1, 2, 4, 8. Factors of 12 are 1, 2, 3, 4, 6, 12. The common factors are 1, 2, and 4. The greatest common factor is 4. Finding the GCF of two numbers is useful when you want to simplify fractions. To simplify $\frac{25}{30}$, divide the numerator and denominator by the GCF of 5. Therefore, $\frac{25}{30} = \frac{5}{6}$ when simplified.

Divisibility

There are times you will want to know what numbers are factors of other numbers. In this case, you are looking for numbers that divide evenly into another number. Familiarity with divisibility rules will help you recognize factors quickly.

How can you tell if a number is evenly divisible by another?

- Divisible by 1: All whole numbers are divisible by 1.
- Divisible by 2 (also called even): If a number ends in 0, 2, 4, 6, or 8, it is an even number.
- Divisible by 3: Add up the digits of the number; if that sum is divisible by 3, then the number is divisible by 3.
- Divisible by 5: A number is divisible by 5 if it ends in 5 or 0.
- Divisible by 9: A number is divisible by 9 if the sum of its digits is divisible by 9.
- Divisible by 10: If a number ends in 0 it is divisible by 10.

Every whole number is divisible by 1 and itself. If a number is only divisible by 1 and itself and has no other factors (therefore having only 2 factors), it is a **prime number**. The prime numbers less than 20 are 2, 3, 7, 11, 13, 17, and 19. There are an infinite number of prime numbers. If a number has more than two factors, it is a **composite number**. The number 1 has only one factor; therefore, it is neither prime nor composite.

PROBLEM

Which answer choice shows a number that is *not* a factor of 384?

(A) 1   (B) 9   (C) 2   (D) 3

SOLUTION

To identify the factors of a number is easy if you know the divisibility rules. 1 is a factor of every number, so 1 is a factor of 384. 384 is an even number because it ends with a 4; therefore, 2 is a factor of 384. The sum of the digits of 384 is 15 because $3 + 8 + 4 = 15$. If the sum of the digits is a multiple of 3, then 3 is a factor. If the sum of the digits is a multiple of 9, then 9 is a factor. 15 is not a multiple of 9; therefore, 9 is not a factor. The answer choice that shows a number that is not a factor of 384 is answer choice (B).

The **Fundamental Theorem of Arithmetic** points out that there is one unique set of prime factors for each composite number. For example, the prime factorization of 100 is $2^2 \times 5^2$. There is no other way to factor 100 into its primes. That is, you can change the order of the prime factors, but there is only *one set* of prime factors possible.

PROBLEM

Which is the correct prime factorization of 150?

(A) (10)(5)(5)   (B) (2)(3)(5^2)

(C) (2^2)(5)(3)   (D) (2)(5)(5)(5)(5)

SOLUTION

The prime factorization of a number must only contain prime numbers. The order of the factors is not important. Answer choice (A) cannot be correct because 10 is not a prime number. An efficient way to find the prime factors of a number is to start with any two factors of the number and then break those factors down into primes (this may remind you of "factor trees"). $150 = 15 \times 10$. Then you can break 15 into 5×3, and you can break 10 into 2×5. Put all the factors together, and you see there are two factors of 5, one factor or 3, and one factor of 2. These factors are shown in answer choice (B), so this is the correct answer.

Multiples

To find the multiples of a number, multiply that number by any integer. Every number has an infinite number of multiples. Some multiples of 4 are: –8, 0, 12, and 20 because 4 × –2 = 8, 4 × 0 = 0, 4 × 3 = 12, and 4 × 5 = 20. The **least common multiple**, or **LCM**, of two numbers is the smallest number that is a multiple of both numbers. To find the LCM of 6 and 9, you will need to list the non-zero multiples of each until you find a common one. The first five non-zero multiples of 6 are: 6, 12, 18, 24, and 30, and the first five non-zero multiples of 9 are: 9, 18, 27, 36, and 45. The LCM is 18.

PROBLEM

Note cards come in packages of 6, and pens come in packages of 8. If Mr. Morton ordered the same number of note cards and pens, what is the fewest number of packages of each item he could have ordered?

    (A) 6 packages of note cards and 8 packages of pens

    (B) 4 packages of note cards and 3 packages of pens

    (C) 3 packages of note cards and 4 packages of pens

    (D) 2 packages of note cards and 3 packages of pens

SOLUTION

This problem is asking you to find the least common multiple of 6 and 8. That number is 24. 24 is the LCM, but it is not the answer to the problem. You have to find the number of boxes of note cards and pens that have 24 items in them. Since there are 6 note cards to a package, you will need 4 packages to have 24 note cards. There are 8 pens to a package, so you will need 3 packages to have 24 pens. The correct answer is (B).

Mathematical Properties

The **Commutative Property** works for addition and multiplication only. The Commutative Property of Addition states that if you add two terms (they may be numbers or variables), the order does not affect the sum. That is, 4 + 3 = 3 + 4. In this example, you can see that the answers on both sides of the equal sign are the same even though the order of the two numbers is different. This property works with variables as well. 12 + y = y + 12. Even though we do not know the value of y, we can be certain that both sides of the equation are equal because the same two terms are being added on each side. The Commutative Property also works for multiplication. 9 × 5 = 5 × 9 illustrates the Commutative Property of multiplication. Both sides of the equation equal 45. If there are variables involved, such as in the example, $ab = ba$, we know both sides are equal because we are multiplying the same two numbers, just in a different order.

The **Associative Property** is a grouping property that works for both addition and multiplication. The Order of Operations tells us that the first thing we must do when simplifying expressions is to simplify operations within grouping symbols. Therefore, if given the following expression, $(4 + 6) + 2$, you would add 4 and 6 together before adding 2. However, let's compare the following expressions: $(4 + 6) + 2$ and $4 + (6 + 2)$. Notice that both expressions contain only addition, the same three numbers, and a set of parentheses. The difference is that the first expression groups 4 and 6 together while the second expression groups 6 and 2 together. How do the answers compare?

$(4 + 6) + 2 =$	$4 + (6 + 2) =$
$10 + 2 =$	$4 + 8 =$
12	12

Notice that both expressions yield the same answer. The Associative Property changes the numbers that are grouped together, but it does not change the answer.

To see how the Associative Property of multiplication works, we can compare the following two expressions that contain only multiplication, the same three numbers, and one set of grouping symbols. The only difference is which numbers are grouped together.

$(5 \times 8) \times 6 =$	$5 \times (8 \times 6) =$
$40 \times 6 =$	$5 \times 48 =$
240	240

As you can see, both answers are the same even though in one expression, we multiplied 5 and 8 before multiplying by 6, and in the other expression, we multiplied 8 by 6 before multiplying by 5.

The **Distributive Property** of multiplication over addition shows that $a(b + c)$ is equal to $ab + ac$. You can prove this property is true by substituting in some numbers.

EXAMPLE   Does $4(30 + 6) = (4 \times 30) + (4 \times 6)$?

Original Problem	$4(30 + 6)$	$(4 \times 30) + (4 \times 6)$
Step #1	$4(36)$	$(120) + (24)$
Step #2	144	144

As you can see, the two expressions are equal. When dealing with numbers only, it does not make sense to use the Distributive Property; that is, it is not more efficient. However, when working with variables, using the Distributive Property is necessary to simplify an expression to remove parentheses. For example, $5(x + 3)$ can be rewritten as $5x + 15$. There is no other way to simplify the expression except to use the Distributive Property.

PROBLEM

Which of the expressions below is equivalent to $35y + 60$?

(A) $95y$ (D) $5 + (7y + 12)$

(B) $(35 + y + 60)$ (E) $(35)(y)(60)$

(C) $5(7y + 12)$

SOLUTION

This problem requires being able to work with the Distributive Property. The two terms in the given expression have a GCF of 5. Therefore, you can divide both terms by 5 and take out 5 as a factor. Write the 5 on the outside of a set of parentheses. Inside the parentheses write $7y$ and 12 because those are the two terms that result when you divide $35y$ and 60 by 5. (C) is the correct answer. To check that it is correct, use the Distributive Property. Multiply 5 by both $7y$ and 12. You will get $35y + 60$; this checks your answer.

1.4: Apply the order of operations with or without grouping symbols.

Mathematics follows rules and procedures. If you encounter a problem with different operations, or one that also has parentheses and exponents in it, you must know in what order to simplify the problem. Without being given any instruction on this topic, you might think that you would simplify from left to right; however, this is not always correct. To make sure that everyone who completes the same problem gets the same answer, there is an order of operations to follow. The order of operations is as follows:

1 Simplify everything inside grouping symbols.

2 Simplify exponents.

3 Do multiplication and division from left to right.

4. Do addition and subtraction from left to right

People often use the mnemonic, "Please Excuse My Dear Aunt Sally" to remember the order of operations, PEMDAS.

Let's start by looking at problems that contain only the four operations of addition, subtraction, multiplication, and division. By following the rules of the order of operations, do multiplication and division from left to right before addition and subtraction, which you also do from left to right. Therefore, in the following problem: $4 + 7 \times 2$, multiply 7 by 2 first, then add that answer to 4. The answer is 18.

Let's look at this problem: $12 \div 3 \times 5$. This problem has both multiplication and division. Neither multiplication nor division comes *before* the other; they are to be done as they occur from left to right. In this problem, do 12 divided by 3 and then multiply that answer by 5. You get 4×5, which is 20.

If, in addition to any of the four operations, a problem has parentheses or exponents, you must do what's inside the parentheses before exponents.

Let's look at a problem that has parentheses, exponents, and several operations. $6 \times (8 + 2) \div 5 - 3^2$

Follow the order of operations to complete the problem in the following order:

$6 \times (8 + 2) \div 5 - 3^2$	The original problem
$6 \times 10 \div 5 - 3^2$	Simplify inside parentheses.
$6 \times 10 \div 5 - 9$	Simplify exponents.
$60 \div 5 - 9$	Do multiplication and division from left to right.
$12 - 9$	Do multiplication and division from left to right.
3	Do addition and subtraction from left to right.

PROBLEM

Simplify by following the order of operations: $18 - 12 \div (3 - 1)^2 \times 5 + 8$

(A) 15.5   (B) 8.3   (C) 4   (D) 11

SOLUTION

Following the order of operations, the problem is simplified as follows:

$18 - 12 \div 4 \times (3 - 1)^2 \times 5 + 8$	The original problem
$18 - 12 \div (2)^2 \times 5 + 8$	Simplify inside parentheses.
$18 - 12 \div 4 \times 5 + 8$	Simplify exponents.
$18 - 3 \times 5 + 8$	Do multiplication and division from left to right.
$18 - 15 + 8$	Do multiplication and division from left to right.
$3 + 8$	Do addition and subtraction from left to right.
11	Do addition and subtraction from left to right.

The correct answer is choice (D).

Absolute Value

The absolute value of a number is its distance from 0 on the number line and is written as $|a|$. The absolute value of a number is always positive because distance is always positive. For example, $|+4| = 4$, and $|-4| = 4$ because both numbers are four units from 0 on the number line. When simplifying expressions involving absolute value, pay attention to positive and negative signs and be sure to follow the correct order of operations. For example, the expression $-3|-5| - 1$ simplifies to -16.

PROBLEM

Simplify the following: $|3 - 12| + 6 \div 2 \times 3^2 - 5$

    (A) 13   (B) 62.5   (C) 8.5   (D) 31

SOLUTION

In addition to following the order of operations, for this problem you have to know how to simplify expressions that have absolute value bars. The expression in the bars, $|3 - 12|$, simplifies to -9. Then take the absolute value of -9 to get 9. The steps below show how to get the simplified answer to this expression.

$|3 - 12| + 6 \div 2 \times 3^2 - 5$	The original problem
$9 + 6 \div 2 \times 3^2 - 5$	Simplify absolute value expression.
$9 + 6 \div 2 \times 9 - 5$	Simplify exponents.
$9 + 3 \times 9 - 5$	Do multiplication and division from left to right.
$9 + 27 - 5$	Do multiplication and division from left to right.
$36 - 5$	Do addition and subtraction from left to right.
31	Do addition and subtraction from left to right.

Competency 2: Knowledge of Measurement (Using Customary or Metric Units)

2.1: Solve real-world problems involving length, weight, mass, perimeter, area, capacity, and volume.

There are a variety of measurements that you may encounter when solving problems: length, weight, mass, perimeter, area, capacity, and volume, to name some. It is important that you know what each measure is used for as well as familiarize yourself with the various units within each system. Length and perimeter are measures of distance. Area is a two-dimensional measurement. Volume and capacity are three-dimensional measurements. For solids, volume can be measured in terms of cubic units. For liquids, volume can be measured in ounces, cups, pints, quarts, and gallons. Weight measures the force from gravity on an object and can be measured in grams, ounces, pounds, and tons. Mass measures the amount of matter an object has.

Measuring can be done using either the metric system or customary units. It is important to be comfortable with both systems. Some people find working with the metric system easier than working with customary measurements because it uses base 10, so it is easier to convert from one unit to another. In addition, the metric system allows you to use decimal numbers, rather than fractions, which many find more accessible. The standard unit of measurement in the United States is the foot, which has 12 inches in it. Three feet make up a yard, and there are 5,280 feet in a mile. Customary units are based on inches, feet, and yards. There are 12 inches in a foot and 3 feet to a yard. Inches are broken up into fractional parts such as halves, fourths, eighths, and sixteenths. These fractions do not lend themselves to conversion to decimal numbers. Some people find working with fractions more challenging. The metric system is an international system of measurement, which is simpler to work with than standard measurements because all its measures are in base 10. Metric units of length include millimeters, centimeters, meters, and kilometers. A meter (m) has 100 centimeters (cm) and 1000 mm (mm). A centimeter has 10 millimeters (mm).

The ruler below shows the relationship between centimeters and millimeters. Notice that the markings between centimeters show millimeters, which are $\frac{1}{10}$ of a centimeter.

Metric units of weight include grams and kilograms. The gram is the basic metric unit of mass (which for many purposes is the same as *weight*). A large paper clip weighs about 1 gram. It takes about 28 grams to make 1 ounce. Metric units of capacity include milliliters and liters. The liter is the basic metric unit of volume (or capacity). A liter is slightly larger than a quart, so it takes fewer than four liters to make a gallon.

An important step in solving problems involving measurement is figuring out its category. Generally, such problems will fall under one of these categories: length, area, angles, volume, mass, time, money, and temperature. Solving measurement problems will likely have you calling on your knowledge in several other areas of mathematics, especially algebra.

The following is an example measurement problem that requires knowledge of several math topics:

> Sophie's Carpet Store charges $19.40 per square yard for the type of carpeting you'd like (padding and labor included). How much will you pay to carpet your 9 foot by 12 foot room?

One way to find the solution is to convert the room dimensions to yards (3 yards by 4 yards), then multiply to get 12 square yards. Finally, multiply 12 by the price of $19.40 per square yard, for a total price of $232.80.

Remember to read word problems thoroughly to determine what information you need. For example, if you are given the length and width of a room, and you need to buy carpeting for the room, what measurement do you need to find? Perimeter? Area? Volume? You need to find the area of the room. Here's another example: A rectangular shaped backyard has a length of 25 feet and an area of 550 ft². If you need to know how much fence to buy to surround the yard, what measurement do you need to find? Perimeter? Area? Volume? You need to find the perimeter because the fence will surround the yard. You are given the length, which is 25 feet, but not the width. However, you are given the area, so you can find the width by dividing the area by the length. 550 ÷ 25 = 22. Therefore, the width is 22 feet. The perimeter of the yard is found by adding both lengths and both widths. 25 + 25 + 22 + 22 = 94. The perimeter of the yard requires 94 feet of fencing.

A ruler with customary units is often broken up into sixteenths. The marks on the ruler below show sixteenths.

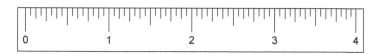

The large line in the middle of each inch indicates a half-inch. The slightly smaller line between each inch and half-inch indicates fourths of an inch. The marks that are slightly smaller than the quarter-inch marks represent eighths of an inch. The marks that are the smallest represent sixteenths of an inch. Depending on the level of accuracy that is needed, measurements may be to the closest half-inch, quarter-inch, eighth-inch, or sixteenth-inch.

PROBLEM

To the nearest millimeter, what is the length of the black line below?

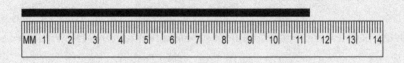

(A) 11.4 cm   (B) 11.4 mm   (C) 114 cm   (D) 1140 mm

SOLUTION

Each number represents a centimeter, and each small mark represents a millimeter. The red line is 4 millimeters past the 11-centimeter mark, so the measure is 11.4 cm (which could also be written as 114 mm.) The correct answer is (A).

PROBLEM

To the nearest sixteenth of an inch, what is the measurement of the black line below?

(A) $4\frac{1}{16}$ (B) $4\frac{2}{16}$ (C) $4\frac{4}{16}$ (D) $4\frac{6}{16}$

SOLUTION

The red line is between 4 and 5 inches. Each of the smallest markets represents $\frac{1}{16}$ of an inch. This line is $4\frac{4}{16}$ inches long. The correct answer is (C).

PROBLEM

It took Carla $1\frac{1}{2}$ minutes to run 160 meters. At that same rate, how many meters would she run in an hour?

   (A) 9600   (B) 6400   (C) 240   (D) 430

SOLUTION

To solve the problem, you can write a proportion. $\dfrac{1.5}{160} = \dfrac{60}{x}$

Cross-multiply and then divide. $x = 6400$. Carla will run 6400 meters in 1 hour (60 minutes). The correct answer is (B).

Rate

A rate is a value describing one quantity in terms of another, such as miles per hour (mph) or meters per second (mps). An important formula used when working with rate is Distance = Rate × Time. This formula is a familiar one. For example, if you are driving 40 mph for 2 hours, how many miles will you cover? When you multiply 40 by 2 and get 80 (miles), you are using the formula, Distance = Rate × Time.

Another rate that is useful to know is the cost per unit. For example, if you want to compare two different size containers of laundry detergent to figure out which is the better deal, you would want to know how to find the cost per ounce. If a 50-ounce container of Detergent A costs $5.99, and a 32-ounce container of Detergent B costs $4.15, which detergent costs less (per ounce)? Divide the cost by the number of ounces to find the cost per ounce. Detergent A is approximately $0.12 per ounce and Detergent B is approximately $0.13 per ounce. Detergent A is cheaper.

PROBLEM

Which unit price shows the best buy?

   (A) 15 sodas for $8.10   (B) 12 sodas for $6.96

   (C) 5 sodas for $2.80   (D) 13 sodas for $7.41

SOLUTION

To find the unit price, divide the total price by the number of sodas. The unit price for (A) is 0.54 cents. The unit price for (B) is 0.58 cents. The unit price for (C) is 0.56 cents, and the unit price for (D) is 0.57 cents. The best buy is 15 sodas for $8.10, answer choice (A).

2.3: Solve real-world problems involving scaled drawings (e.g., maps, blueprints, and models).

Scale Drawings

A scale drawing is a drawing of an object that is proportional in size to the actual object. Scale drawings are based on a certain conversion scale. If you know this scale, you can determine the measurements of the actual objects. For example, the scale drawing of a volleyball court shown below is drawn using the scale 1-centimeter equals 2 meters.

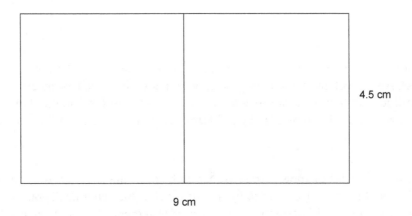

4.5 cm

9 cm

Calculate the area of this volleyball court in square meters. In the scale drawing, length is equal to 9 centimeters and width is equal to 4.5 centimeters. The scale is 1 centimeter equals 2 meters. So, the length of the court is 18 meters, and the width is 9 meters. To find the area, multiply length times width: $18 \times 9 = 162$. The volleyball court is 162 square meters.

Scale is often used for maps and models of real-life objects. For example, an architect wanted to draw a lighthouse that was 144.5 feet tall. She was using the scale of 1 inch = 34 feet. How many inches high would the lighthouse be in the drawing? You could set up a proportion: $\dfrac{1}{34} = \dfrac{x}{144.5}$. Notice that the numerators represent the heights in the drawing and the denominators represent the heights in real life. Solving the proportion gives $x = 4.25$. The height of the lighthouse on the drawing would be 4.25 inches.

2.4: Solve real-world problems involving the change of units of measures of length, weight, mass, capacity, and time.

If you need to convert inches to feet, you need to divide by 12 since there are 12 inches in each foot. For example, if you have 42 inches, how many feet do you have? When you divide 42 by 12, you get 3 with a remainder of 6. Since your divisor is 12, $\frac{6}{12} = \frac{1}{2}$; therefore, you have $3\frac{1}{2}$ feet. Here's another example: If you have 16 inches, how many feet do you have? When you divide 16 by 12, you get 1 with a remainder of 4. Since your divisor is 12, $\frac{4}{12} = \frac{1}{3}$; therefore, you have $1\frac{1}{3}$ feet. If you want to find out how many feet you have in a given number of yards, multiply by 3 because every yard has 3 feet. Let's look at this example: If you have 8 yards, how many feet do you have? Since $8 \times 3 = 24$, you have 24 feet. If you wanted to know how many inches that was, multiply 24 by 12 since 1 foot has 12 inches. $12 \times 24 = 288$. There are 288 inches in 24 feet and 8 yards.

Converting within the metric system is straightforward, involving multiplying or dividing by a power of 10. If something is 4 m long, it is 400 cm long because 1 m $\times$ 100 cm = 400 cm. If an object is 8.4 m long, then it would be 840 cm because 8.4 m $\times$ 100 cm = 840 cm. How many meters are in 735 cm? Since there are 100 cm in one meter, you must divide 735 by 100, which gives you 7.35. Therefore 735 cm = 7.35 m. If you wanted to know how many mm there are in a number of meters, multiply by 1000 because there are 1000 mm in one meter. How many mm are in 5.8 meters? $5.8 \times 1000 = 5800$. So, there are 5800 mm in 5.8 meters.

PROBLEM

The distance between two posts is 8.4 meters. How many centimeters is this distance?

(A) 84   (B) 840   (C) 8,400   (D) 84,000

SOLUTION

To solve this problem, you must know that there are 100 centimeters in 1 meter. Therefore, if you multiply 8.4 by 100, you will find the number of centimeters in 8.4 meters. There are 840 centimeters in 8.4 meters. The correct answer is (B).

PROBLEM

> A marathon is 26.2 miles long. How many kilometers are in a marathon if there are approximately 1.61 kilometers in 1 mile? Round your answer to the nearest tenth of a kilometer.
>
>   (A) 42.2   (B) 16.3   (C) 33.6   (D) 24.6

SOLUTION

To solve this problem, you can set up and solve a proportion. $\frac{1}{1.61} = \frac{26.2}{x}$. Cross-multiply to find that there are approximately 42.2 kilometers in 26.2 miles. The correct answer is (A).

2.5: Solve real-world problems involving estimates of measures including length, weight, mass, temperature, time, money, perimeter, area, and volume.

Sometimes it is helpful to estimate before performing the actual calculation to be sure your answer is reasonable. You may also estimate an answer if you do not need an exact answer. If you want to know how long it will take you to complete some errands before meeting a friend, you probably will not need an exact answer. There are times when an estimate is good enough. Estimating the result of a calculation sometimes involves rounding. If you bought a package of 8 cookies for $1.99 and wanted to know what the price per cookie is, you would divide 1.99 by 8. When you do so, you get .24875. That is the exact answer. However, when talking about price, we usually go to the nearest cent. So, in this example, each cookie costs approximately 25 cents.

If you needed to estimate the area of a field that was 190 meters by 217 meters, you could round 190 meters up to 200 meters, and you could round 217 meters down to 200 meters. Therefore, the approximate or estimated area would be about 200 × 200, which is 40,000 meters. Estimating can sometimes save time when you have to compare fractions to one another. If, for example, you are asked to list a group of fractions with different denominators in order from least to greatest, you may be able to do so without going through the laborious work of finding a common denominator. Let's look at an example. Put the following fractions in order from least to greatest: $\frac{2}{5}, \frac{7}{8}, \frac{3}{4}, \frac{6}{17}, \frac{13}{14}$. At first glance, this looks like a very time-consuming problem because all of the fractions have different denominators. However, when you look closely, you should notice that you can use your estimation skills to put the fractions in order. Ask yourself if any of the fractions are less than $\frac{1}{2}$? Notice that $\frac{2}{5}$ and $\frac{6}{17}$ are the only fractions that are less than $\frac{1}{2}$. You can tell because their numerators are less than half of their denominators. Therefore, you know that either $\frac{2}{5}$ or $\frac{6}{17}$ will be the smallest fraction. Can you use your estimating skills again to figure out which of the two fractions is smallest? Notice that $\frac{2}{5}$ is very close to $\frac{1}{2}$. $\frac{2.5}{5}$ would be exactly $\frac{1}{2}$. What about $\frac{6}{17}$? Notice that $\frac{6}{18}$ would be exactly $\frac{1}{3}$ and $\frac{6}{17}$ is very close to that. $\frac{1}{3}$ is smaller than $\frac{1}{2}$. Therefore, $\frac{6}{17}$ is smaller than $\frac{2}{5}$. Now, you have two of the five fractions in order $\frac{6}{17}$ and $\frac{2}{5}$. Now examine the other three fractions: $\frac{7}{8}$, $\frac{3}{4}$, and $\frac{13}{14}$. Notice that $\frac{3}{4}$ can be easily rewritten as $\frac{6}{8}$. Which is smaller, $\frac{6}{8}$ or $\frac{7}{8}$? $\frac{6}{8}$ is smaller, so you know that $\frac{3}{4}$ comes before $\frac{7}{8}$. The final fraction, $\frac{13}{14}$, is very close to one whole, which would be $\frac{14}{14}$. Therefore, you can order all five fractions from least to greatest as follows: $\frac{6}{17}, \frac{2}{5}, \frac{3}{4}, \frac{7}{8}, \frac{13}{14}$. Be sure to see if you can use estimation rather than exact computation. If you can, it will often be more efficient than performing tedious calculations

2.6: Choose the correct reading, to a specified degree of accuracy, using instruments (e.g., scales, rulers, thermometers, measuring cups, protractors, and gauges).

When you measure an object, you want to be as precise as you can be. In addition, you want to use the most appropriate unit of measure. If you are measuring the length of a pencil, you would not use meters (because that is too large a unit of measure). You may use centimeters or millimeters. If you want to measure the volume of a swimming pool, you would not use milliliters (because that is too small a unit of measure). Choosing the most appropriate unit of measure is important. It is also important to know how to label your units of measure. Length, width, height, diameter, radius, and circumference are all one dimension, so those units will be to the first power. Area involves two dimensions, so those units will be to the second power. Volume has three dimensions, so those units will be to the third power.

How precise your measurement needs to be depends on the task. For example, when using a ruler, you may be asked to measure to the nearest inch, half-inch, or quarter-inch. When using a thermometer, you may need to find the temperature to the nearest degree or tenth of a degree. When using a protractor, it is customary to measure to the nearest degree.

Competency 3: Knowledge of Geometry and Spatial Sense

3.1: Identify and/or classify simple two- and three-dimensional figures according to their properties.

Intersecting Lines and Angles

An **angle** is a collection of points that is the union of two rays having the same endpoint. An angle such as the one illustrated below can be referred to in any of the following ways:

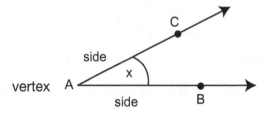

A)   by a capital letter which names its **vertex** (common endpoint), i.e., $\angle A$;

B)   by a lowercase letter or number placed inside the angle, i.e., $\angle x$;

C)   by three capital letters, where the middle letter is the vertex and the other two letters are not on the same ray, i.e., $\angle CAB$ or $\angle BAC$, both of which represent the angle illustrated in the figure.

Types of Angles

A)   **Vertical angles** are formed when two lines intersect. These angles are equal.

B)   **Adjacent angles** are two angles with a common vertex and a common side, but no common interior points. In the following figure, $\angle DAC$ and $\angle BAC$ are adjacent angles. $\angle DAB$ and $\angle BAC$ are not.

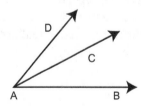

C)   A **right angle** is an angle whose measure is 90°.

D)   An **acute angle** is an angle whose measure is larger than 0° but less than 90°.

E)   An **obtuse angle** is an angle whose measure is larger than 90° but less than 180°.

F) A **straight angle** is an angle whose measure is 180°. Such an angle is, in fact, a straight line.

G) A **reflex angle** is an angle whose measure is greater than 180° but less than 360°.

H) **Complementary angles** are two angles, the sum of the measures of which equals 90°.

I) **Supplementary angles** are two angles, the sum of the measures of which equals 180°.

J) **Congruent angles** are angles of equal measure.

PROBLEM

In the diagram below, ∠2 is equal to 128°. What is the measure of ∠3?

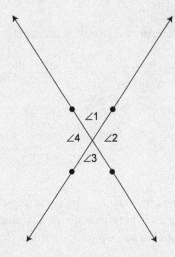

(A) 52 degrees

(B) 48 degrees

(C) It cannot be determined from the diagram.

(D) 128 degrees

SOLUTION

Two intersecting lines create two pairs of **vertical angles**. Vertical angles are congruent (they have the same measure). The angles that are not congruent are supplementary (they add up to 180 degrees). Therefore, if you know the measure of one of the four angles, you can find the other three. In this problem, you are told that ∠2 is 128 degrees and asked to find ∠3. You can see that ∠3 is supplementary to ∠2. Therefore, 180 degrees – 128 degrees will give you the measure of ∠3, which is 52 degrees.

PROBLEM

Find the measure of ∠B in right triangle ABC.

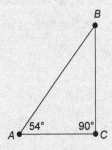

(A)   It cannot be determined from the diagram.

(B)   36°

(C)   90°

(D)   44°

SOLUTION

In a right triangle, the two angles that are not the right angle are complementary (they add up to 90 degrees). The sum of the three angles in any triangle is 180 degrees. Therefore, if one of the angles is 90 degrees, then the other two must also add up to 90 degrees (to have a total of 180 degrees in all three angles).

Solve the equation: $90 - 54 = x$ to find the measure of ∠B. ∠B = 36°.

Working with two-dimensional geometric shapes involves measures of one-dimension (length, width, height, perimeter, circumference, radius, and diameter) and two-dimensions (area) measurements. Being able to recognize and name two-dimensional shapes is important.

Number of sides in polygon	Name of polygon
3	Triangle
4	Quadrilateral
5	Pentagon
6	Hexagon
7	Septagon
8	Octagon
9	Nonagon
10	Decagon

Triangles

A closed three-sided geometric figure is called a **triangle**. The points of the intersection of the sides of a triangle are called the **vertices** of the triangle.

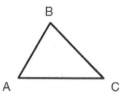

The **perimeter** of a triangle is the sum of the measures of the sides of the triangle.

A triangle with no equal sides is called a **scalene** triangle.

A triangle having at least two equal sides is called an **isosceles** triangle. The third side is called the **base** of the triangle.

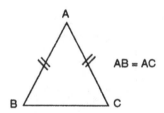

A side of a triangle is a line segment whose endpoints are the vertices of two angles of the triangle.

An interior angle of a triangle is an angle formed by two sides and includes the third side within its collection of points.

An equilateral triangle is a triangle having three equal sides. $AB = AC = BC$

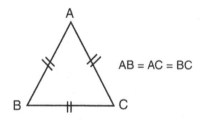

A triangle with an obtuse angle (greater than 90°) is called an **obtuse triangle**.

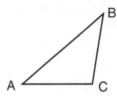

An **acute triangle** is a triangle with three acute angles (less than 90°).

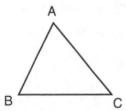

A triangle with a right angle is called a **right triangle**. The side opposite the right angle in a right triangle is called the hypotenuse of the right triangle. The other two sides are called arms or legs of the right triangle.

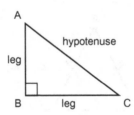

The area of a triangle is given by the formula $A = \frac{1}{2} bh$, where b is the length of a base, which can be any side of the triangle and h is the corresponding height of the triangle, which is the perpendicular line segment from the vertex opposite the base to the base itself.

$$A = \frac{1}{2} bh$$
$$A = \frac{1}{2} (10)(3)$$
$$A = 15$$

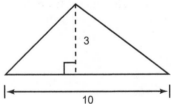

The area of a right triangle is found by taking $\frac{1}{2}$ the product of the lengths of its two arms.

$$A = \frac{1}{2} (5)(12)$$
$$A = 30$$

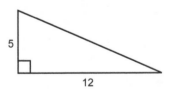

Similar Triangles

The measures of the angles of a pair of similar triangles are equal in a one-to-one fashion. Therefore, a triangle whose angles are 30º, 60º, and 90º is similar to every other triangle with those angle measurements, even though the sides of the two triangles may be different. The sides, however, are proportional, meaning they correspond to one another. The following figure shows two similar triangles, but one is three times the size of the other, so the corresponding sides are three times as long (even though the angles remain the same).

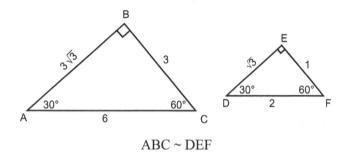

ABC ~ DEF

The sign for similar is ~ and the corresponding angles are listed in the same order: ∠A = ∠D, ∠B = ∠E, and ∠C = ∠F.

There are many "special" quadrilaterals. Knowing their specific properties helps define them accurately.

Special Quadrilateral	Properties
Trapezoid	• Exactly one pair of parallel sides
Parallelogram	• Two pairs of parallel sides • Opposite sides congruent
Rhombus	• All four sides congruent
Rectangle	• Two pairs of parallel sides • Opposite sides congruent • Four right angles
Square	• Two pairs of parallel sides • All four sides congruent • Four right angles
Kite	• Two pairs of adjacent sides are congruent • One pair of opposite angles congruent • Diagonals are perpendicular to each other • Longer diagonal bisects the shorter diagonol

Area Review

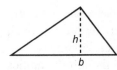

Triangle $A = \dfrac{1}{2}bh$

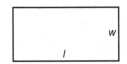

Rectangle $A = lw$

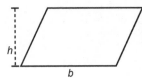

Parallelogram $A = bh$

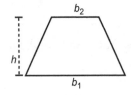

Trapezoid $A = \dfrac{1}{2}h(b_1 + b_2)$

PROBLEM

Find the area of the trapezoid in the diagram in square units.

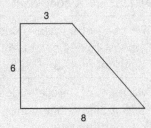

(A) 66   (B) 33   (C) 48   (D) 57

SOLUTION

Use the formula for the area of a trapezoid: $A = \frac{1}{2}h(b_1 + b_2)$.

The height of this trapezoid is 6. The two bases are 3 and 8. Substitute the numbers into the formula to find the area of the trapezoid.

$$A = \frac{1}{2}(6)(3+8)$$

$$A = (3)(11)$$

$$A = 33$$

The area is 33 square units. The correct answer is (B).

Circles

A circle is a special two-dimensional geometric figure whose circumference is found my multiplying its diameter by the irrational number π. A circle's diameter is twice its radius. The area of a circle is found by the formula $A = \pi r^2$, and the circumference can be found by the formula $C = 2\pi r$ or $C = \pi d$. The diagram below shows the parts of a circle. The circumference of a circle is the distance around the circle. The radius is a segment from the center of a circle to a point on its circumference. The diameter is a segment from one point on the circumference to another point on the circumference passing through the center of the circle.

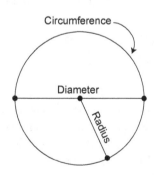

PROBLEM

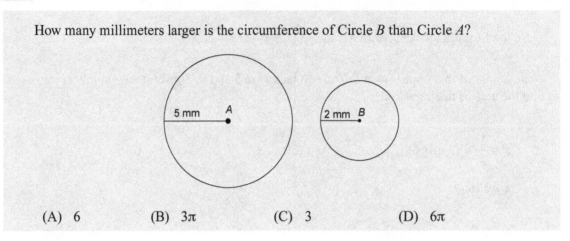

How many millimeters larger is the circumference of Circle *B* than Circle *A*?

(A) 6　　　　(B) 3π　　　　(C) 3　　　　(D) 6π

SOLUTION

The formula for the circumference of a circle is $C = 2\pi r$. The question asks you to compare the circumferences of Circles A and B. Find the circumference of each circle.

Circle A	Circle B
$C = 2\pi r$	$C = 2\pi r$
$C = 2\pi 5$	$C = 2\pi 2$
$C = 10\pi$	$C = 4\pi$

Circle A's circumference is $10\pi - 4\pi = 6\pi$ mm larger than Circle B's circumference. The correct answer is (D).

Three-Dimensional Figures

There are many different three-dimensional geometric shapes: prisms, pyramids, cylinders, cones, and spheres. A prism is a solid whose opposite lateral faces are congruent. A pyramid has a polygon as its base and triangular shaped lateral faces. The lateral faces meet at a point at the top of the figure called the apex. A "pyramid" with a circular base is called cone. A cylinder is a solid whose bases are congruent circles. Its lateral face is in the shape of a rectangle that is rolled up (think of a can of soup). A sphere is shaped like a ball.

Prisms

A solid with lateral faces and bases that are congruent polygons is called a **prism**. If the congruent polygons and lateral faces are all rectangles, it is called a **rectangular solid**.

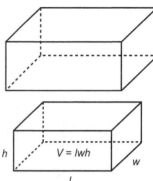

The surface area of a prism is the sum of the areas of all the faces. The area of each face is referred to as a lateral area.

The volume of a prism equals the area of the base (B) times the height (h).

$$V = Bh$$

The volume of a rectangular solid is equal to the product of its length, width, and height.

$$V = lwh$$

Pyramid

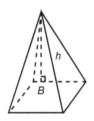

The figure formed when the vertices of a plane polygon (called the base) are joined by line segments to a point not in the same plane is called a **pyramid**.

The surface area of a pyramid equals the sum of areas of all faces.

The volume of a pyramid or cone equals $\frac{1}{3}$ times the <u>Area of the Base</u> (B) times the height (h).

$$V = \frac{1}{3} Bh$$

Cone

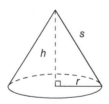

A "pyramid" with a circular base is called a **cone**. The distance from any point on the circular base to the point of the cone is called the slant height.

The surface area of a cone is given by

$$A = \pi r s + \pi r^2$$

The volume of a cone is given by

$$V = \frac{1}{3} \pi r^2 h$$

Cylinder

A solid with bases that are congruent circles is called a **cylinder**.

The surface area of a cylinder equals the sum of the areas of the bases and the rectangular "wrap".

$$A = 2(\pi r^2) + 2(\pi r)h$$

The volume of a cylinder equals the Area of the Base (B) times the height (h).

$$V = Bh$$

PROBLEM

A particular three-dimensional figure has two congruent triangular shaped faces and three rectangular shaped faces. What is the best name for this figure?

(A) Triangular pyramid   (B) Rectangular pyramid

(C) Triangular prism   (D) Rectangular prism

SOLUTION

To solve this problem correctly, you must know the difference between a pyramid and a prism. A pyramid is named by the shape of its base. No matter what the shape of the base of a pyramid, its lateral faces will always be triangular. A prism is named by the shape of its base, and it has two congruent bases. With the given information, you know that the shape described is a triangular prism, answer choice (C).

The net of a triangular prism is shown below:

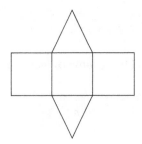

PROBLEM

What is the best name for a three-dimensional figure with the following characteristics?

- 6 vertices
- 1 pentagonal base
- 4 triangular lateral faces

(A) pentagonal prism   (B) pentagonal pyramid

(C) triangular prism   (D) triangular pyramid

SOLUTION

A three-dimensional figure with triangular lateral faces will be a pyramid. The shape of the base tells you the name of the pyramid. The figure described above is a pentagonal pyramid. Answer choice (B) is the correct answer.

3.2: Solve real-world and mathematical problems involving ratio, proportion, similarity, congruence, and the Pythagorean relationship.

A **ratio** is a comparison of two quantities. There was once a commercial, which stated 4 out of 5 dentists prefer Trident; that is a ratio. Ratios can be written three different ways:

- With the word "to": 4 to 5

- With a colon: 4:5

- As a fraction: $\frac{4}{5}$

Ratios are used frequently in daily life. A teacher might say, "Eight of the twenty-five students are sick." A bakery owner could say, "We sold 56 of the 200 croissants."

When two ratios are equal to each other, that is called a **proportion**. An example of a proportion is $\frac{12}{36} = \frac{9}{27}$. An easy way to see if two ratios are equivalent is to simplify both ratios into their lowest terms. A fraction is in lowest terms if the only factor the numerator and denominator have in common is 1. If both ratios simplify to the same fraction, then the ratios are equivalent and it is a proportion. Often times, we use the principle of a proportion to solve for an unknown quantity.

Here's an example: There are 150 calories in an 8-ounce serving of whole milk. How many calories are in a 12-ounce serving?

You can set up the following proportion to answer the question: $\dfrac{8}{150} = \dfrac{12}{C}$

The first ratio has an 8 in the numerator; this represents the number of ounces given in the problem. In the denominator of the first ratio is 150. This represents the number of calories in 8 ounces of milk. This information is given in the problem. The other ratio has a 12 in the numerator because 12 represents the number of ounces of milk you are asked about in the problem. Notice how both numbers that represent the number of ounces are in the numerator. Numbers representing the same quantity must be in the same places in the ratios. The second ratio has a C in the denominator. This C represents the unknown number of calories we are trying to find in 12 ounces of milk.

When given three of the four numbers in a proportion, you can solve for the unknown number by following a procedure. The first step is cross-multiplying. That means multiplying the numerator of one ratio by the denominator in the other ratio. Then, set those products equal to each other. The final step is to divide both sides by the number that is multiplied by the variable.

- $\dfrac{8}{150} = \dfrac{12}{C}$
- $8C = 1800$
- $C = 225$

Therefore, there are 225 calories in 12-ounces of whole milk.

PROBLEM

An automobile dealer has to sell 3.5 cars for every 1 truck to achieve the optimum profit. This year, it is estimated that 3,500 cars will be sold. How many trucks must he sell to achieve the optimum profit?

(A) 1,000   (B) 500   (C) 350   (D) 2,000

SOLUTION

Step 1 is to determine the ratio of cars to trucks.

$$3.5 \text{ cars}:1 \text{ truck} = 3.5:1$$

Make both sides of the ratio an integer. To do this, multiply both sides of the ratio by 2.

$$2(3.5):2(1) = 7:2$$

Step 2 is to write the problem as a proportion.

$$\frac{7}{2} = \frac{3,500}{?}$$

Step 3 is to put the proportion in the following format:

$$7(?) = 2(3,500)$$

Step 4 is to solve the right side of the proportion.

$$2(3,500) = 7,000$$

Step 5 is to rewrite the proportion.

$$7(?) = 7,000$$

Step 6 is to find the missing integer that solves the proportion. To do this, divide both sides by the known extreme, 7.

$$\frac{7(?)}{7} = ? \qquad \frac{7,000}{7} = 1,000$$

Step 7 is to rewrite the proportion.

$$? = 1,000$$

The solution is 1,000 trucks.

The correct answer is (A).

PROBLEM

A baker is making a new recipe for cookies. For every 6 cups of flour, he is using 1 cup of sugar. He puts 30 cups of flour and 2 cups of sugar into the batter. How many more cups of sugar does he need to add to maintain the ratio?

    (A) 2   (B) 5   (C) 3   (D) 7

SOLUTION

To solve this problem, first find the ratio of flour to sugar that the baker is using. It is 6:1. Then write a proportion using the amount of flour he is going to use: $\dfrac{6}{1} = \dfrac{30}{S}$ where S represents the number of cups of sugar. Solve the proportion by cross-multiplying and then dividing. S = 5. The baker needs to use 5 cups of sugar for 30 cups of flour. However, the answer to the problem is not 5 (cups) because the baker has already put 2 cups of sugar in the batter. Therefore, he needs 5 – 2 = 3 (cups of sugar). Answer (C) is the correct answer.

Similar Figures

In mathematics, similar figures are two-dimensional figures that have the same shape. Usually similar figures have different sizes; however, two identical figures (which are congruent) are considered similar because they fit the definition of similar figures. Corresponding sides of similar figures have the same ratio to each other, called the scale factor. The ratio of any pair of corresponding sides of similar figures is the same. The corresponding angles of similar figures are congruent.

The two triangles below are similar.

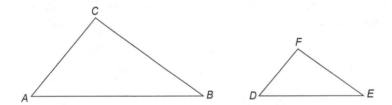

Side *AC* corresponds to side *DF*. Side *CB* corresponds to side *FE*. Side *ED* corresponds to side *BA*. The ratios of corresponding sides have the same ratio. If side *AC* is 12 cm and side *DF* is 4 cm, then the ratio of each pair of corresponding sides is 3 to 1. Therefore, we can find a missing side length of either of the triangles if we know that the triangles are similar and know the ratio of the sides. In this example, if side *ED* is 8 cm, we can find the length of side *BA* because we know that it will be three times larger than *ED*. Side BA would be 24 cm. The corresponding angles of similar figures are congruent. So, in this example, $\angle A \cong \angle D$; $\angle C \cong \angle F$; and $\angle B \cong \angle E$.

The areas of similar figures are also proportional; however, they do not have the same ratio as the side lengths do. One right triangle has a base of 6 cm and a height of 10 cm. What would be the base and height of a similar triangle with a scale factor of 2? The base would be 12 cm and the height would be 20 cm. Let's examine the area of both triangles. The formula for finding the area of a triangle is $A = \dfrac{1}{2}bh$, where b is the base and h is the height. So the area of the original triangle is (1/2)(6)(10) = 30 cm². The area of the larger triangle is $\left(\dfrac{1}{2}\right)(12)(20) = 120$ cm². The area of the larger triangle is not double the area of the original triangle, as one would have expected. The area of the larger triangle is four times greater. So, what is the ratio of the areas of similar figures? The area will be the scale factor *squared*. So, if the scale factor is 3, then the area will be 3^2 or 9 times larger.

When two figures are similar, they have 6 pairs of corresponding parts—the sides and the angles. Corresponding parts are in the same place in each similar figure.

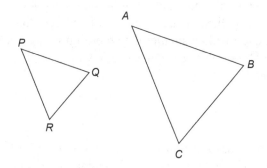

The six corresponding parts for these two similar triangles shown are:

1. *PQ* and *AB*

2. *QR* and *BC*

3. *RP* and *CA*

4. $\angle P$ and $\angle A$

5. $\angle Q$ and $\angle B$

6. $\angle R$ and $\angle C$

PROBLEM

Jerome has a photograph that is 6 inches by 9 inches. He wants to enlarge it by a scale factor of 2. What would be the area in square inches of Jerome's enlarged photograph?

(A) 108   (B) 216

(C) 60   (D) 120

SOLUTION

To solve this problem correctly, you must know that the length and width of the enlarged photograph will be twice the length and width of the original photograph. The enlarged photograph will be 12 inches by 18 inches. To find the area, multiply the length times the width. This answer is 216 square inches. The correct answer is (B).

Congruent Figures

When two figures are **congruent**, they are the same size and shape. Corresponding parts of congruent figures are congruent. That means corresponding sides and corresponding angles are congruent. If you have two congruent regular pentagons, for example, and you know the length of one side of one of the pentagons, you can find the length of the sides of the other pentagon. Congruent figures are also considered similar. Similar figures are figures whose side lengths are proportional. The angles of similar figures are the same. If a figure is scaled up, then the new figure will be larger than the original figure. If a figure is scaled down, then the new figure will be smaller than the original figure. For example, a right triangle with sides 3, 4, and 5 cm would be similar to a right triangle with sides 18, 24, and 30 cm because 18, 24, and 30 are six times larger than 3, 4, and 5.

Pythagorean Theorem

The **Pythagorean theorem** is used to find the missing side length of a right triangle. If you know two of the three sides, you can find the third using the Pythagorean theorem. The Pythagorean theorem is $a^2 + b^2 = c^2$, where a and b are the legs and c is the hypotenuse of the right triangle. The legs are the two sides that make up the right angle (it does not matter which leg is a and which leg is b. The hypotenuse is the longest side of the right triangle and is opposite the right angle.

There are many situations in real life where you can apply the Pythagorean theorem. Often times, these problems do not explicitly state that you need to use the Pythagorean theorem. By reading the problem, you have to recognize that the information you are looking for is a side length of a right triangle. If you are given the length of a ladder and how far its base is from a building, you may be asked how high up the building the top of the ladder falls. In the diagram below, if you knew the length of the ladder and the distance of the base of the ladder from the building, you could find how high up the building the top of the ladder is. In this example, the ladder is the hypotenuse and the other two measures are the legs of a right triangle.

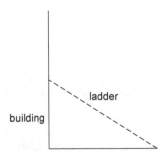

If the ladder is 23 feet, and the base of the ladder is 12 feet from the building, how high up the building is the top of the ladder to the nearest tenth of a foot? Use the Pythagorean theorem and substitute the numbers given in their correct places. The ladder is the hypotenuse, and the distance from the building is one of the legs of the triangle.

$a^2 + b^2 = c^2$

$12^2 + b^2 = 23^2$

$144 + b^2 = 529$

$b^2 = 529 - 144$

$b^2 = 385$

$b = \sqrt{385}$

$b \approx 19.6$

PROBLEM

A group of neighbors were creating a community garden in the shape of a right triangle. Two of the three dimensions are shown below. To the nearest foot, what would be the length of the missing side below?

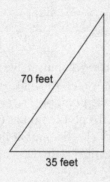

70 feet

35 feet

(A) 61   (B) 78   (C) 94   (D) 105

SOLUTION

To solve this problem correctly, you must recognize that the missing side is a leg of the right triangle (not the hypotenuse). Substitute the numbers given into the Pythagorean theorem to find the missing length.

$a^2 + b^2 = c^2$

$35^2 + b^2 = 70^2$

$1225 + b^2 = 4900$

$b^2 = 4900 - 1225$

$b^2 = 3675$

$b = \sqrt{3675}$

$b \approx 61$

3.3: Identify the location of ordered pairs of integers in all four quadrants of a coordinate system (graph) and use the coordinate system to apply the concepts of slope and distance to solve problems.

The **coordinate plane** is made up of two perpendicular axes. The **x-axis** is horizontal, and the **y-axis** is vertical. Where the two axes intersect is called the **origin**; this point has the coordinates (0, 0). The intersection of the two axes creates four separate areas called quadrants. **Quadrant I** is in the upper right hand corner. **Quadrants II, III, and IV** are located counterclockwise to Quadrant I.

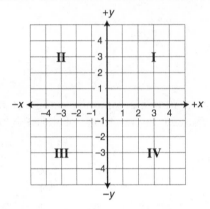

To plot a point on the coordinate plane, you must have both an **x-coordinate** and a **y-coordinate**. The x-coordinate tells how many spaces to move left or right, and the y-coordinate tells you how many spaces to move up or down. If you want to plot the point (4, 3), for example, start at the origin. Move four spaces to the right, then move three spaces up. To plot the point (–2, 5), start at the origin. Move two spaces to the left, then move five spaces up. To plot (1, –8), start at the origin. Move one space to the right and then eight spaces down. To plot (0, –3), start at the origin. Do not move any spaces left or right, then move three spaces down. See the three points plotted below.

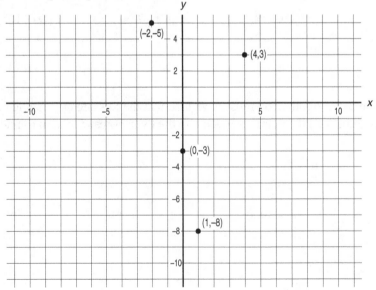

To figure out the coordinates of points that are plotted, start at the origin. Move left or right on the *x*-axis until you are directly above or below the point. Count the spaces you moved. Moving right is positive and moving left is negative. Then move up or down until you get to the point. Moving up is positive and moving down is negative.

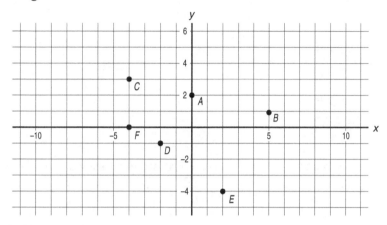

The coordinates for the points above are as follows: *A* (0, 2), *B* (5, 1), *C* (–4, 3), *D* (–2, –1), *E* (2, –4), and *F* (–4, 0).

Distance Betweeen Two Points

The distance between two points on a graph can be found using the principles of the Pythagorean theorem. Consider segment *AB* below.

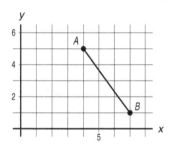

To find the distance between the two points, construct a right triangle with a hypotenuse as the given segment.

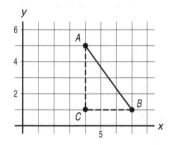

Notice that AC and BC are both legs of the right triangle with hypotenuse AB. AC is 4 units, and BC is 3 units. Substitute those numbers into the Pythagorean theorem to find the length of AB.

$$a^2 + b^2 = c^2$$

$$4^2 + 3^2 = c^2$$

$$16 + 9 = c^2$$

$$25 = c^2$$

$$\sqrt{25} = c$$

$$5 = c$$

To find the distance between two points, you can also use the distance formula, which is just a form of the Pythagorean theorem: Distance $= \sqrt{(x_2 - x_1)^2 + (y_2 - y_1)^2}$.

For example, if you wanted to find the distance between the points (3, 5) and (4, 9) using the distance formula, substitute the points in the formula. It does not matter which point you label point 1 and which you label point 2. Let's call (3, 5) point 1 and (4, 9) point 2.

$$\text{Distance} = \sqrt{(x_2 - x_1)^2 + (y_2 - y_1)^2}$$

$$\text{Distance} = \sqrt{(4 - 3)^2 + (9 - 5)^2}$$

$$\text{Distance} = \sqrt{(1)^2 + (4)^2}$$

$$\text{Distance} = \sqrt{1 + 16}$$

$$\text{Distance} = \sqrt{17}\text{, which is approximately 4.1 units.}$$

Slope

If you know two points on a line, you can find the **slope** of the line. The slope of a line is the steepness of the line, and it can be found by dividing the vertical change between two points by the horizontal change of the two points. We can use any two points on a line to find its slope because the slope of a line is constant. The diagram below shows line AC which has an infinite number of points. Three of the points are labeled: A, B, and C.

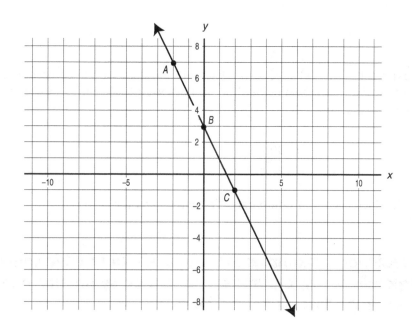

Let's use Points B and C to find the slope of the line. The coordinates of point B are $(0, 3)$, and the coordinates of point C are $(2, -1)$. We can consider point B as point 1 and point C as point 2.

$$\frac{y_2 - y_1}{x_2 - x_1} = \frac{-1 - 3}{2 - 0} = \frac{-4}{2} = -2$$

Therefore, the slope passing through $(0, 3)$ and $(2, -1)$ is -2.

PROBLEM

Laura gets an hourly rate for helping out at her mom's office. The graph below shows Laura's earnings. What is the slope of the graph, and what does it represent?

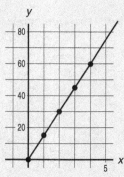

(A) The slope is $15, and it is Laura's hourly rate.

(B) The slope is 5, and it is the number of hours Laura worked.

(C) The slope is $75, and it is the total amount of money Laura earned.

(D) The slope is 0, and it is the number of hours Laura worked for 0 dollars.

SOLUTION

The slope of a line is its rate of change. In this example, the slope would represent Laura's hourly rate. To find the slope of the line, select two points from it. Let's use (2, 30) and (4, 60). Substitute them into the slope formula to find the slope.

$$\frac{y_2 - y_1}{x_2 - x_1} = \frac{60-30}{4-2} = 15$$

The slope is 15, which is Laura's hourly rate. The correct answer is (A).

3.4: Identify real-world examples that represent geometric concepts including perpendicularity, parallelism, tangency, symmetry, and transformations (e.g., flips, slides, and turns).

Tangency

A line that has only one point of intersection with a circle is said to be **tangent** to the circle. In the diagram below, line *BD* is tangent to circle *A* at point *C*. If you draw a radius from the point of tangency to the center of the circle, you will always create two right angles at the point of tangency.

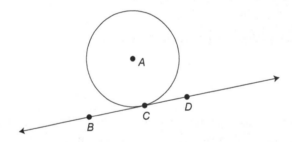

In the diagram below, radius *AC* creates two right angles: ∠*BCA* and ∠*DCA*.

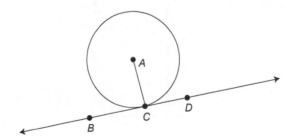

Symmetry

An object has symmetry if it is the same on both sides. A "line of symmetry" separates the object into two identical halves. The arrow below is symmetric. If you folded the arrow on the dotted line, you would see that both sides are exactly the same.

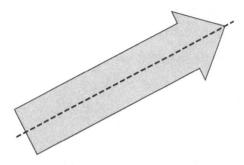

PROBLEM

Ms. Martin had a square piece of land. She wanted to cut her land in half so that each half was a mirror image of the other half. How many different cuts are possible?

    (A) 1   (B) 2   (C) 3   (D) 4

SOLUTION

A square has four different lines of symmetry. One is a cut through the square horizontally. One is a cut through the square vertically. There are also two cuts through the diagonals. The sketch below shows all four possible lines of symmetry. The correct answer is (D).

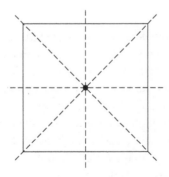

Parallel

Two lines are parallel if they lie in the same plane and do not intersect. The symbol for parallel is ‖. In the diagram below, line *XY* is parallel to line *VW*.

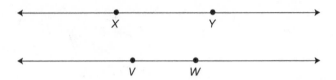

Perpendicular

Two lines or line segments are perpendicular if they intersect and form right angles. The symbol for perpendicular is ⊥. In the diagram below, segment *AB* ⊥ segment *CD*.

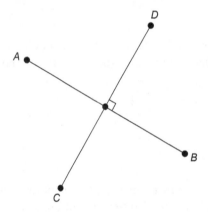

Transformations

There are four different types of transformations: **translations**, **reflections**, **rotations**, and **dilations**. No matter which transformation you apply, the transformed shape is called the image. Translations are sometimes called slides and result from moving a figure up, down, left, or right. In a translation, the original shape and its translation are the same size and shape and have the same orientation on the page. A reflection, sometimes called a flip, results from reflecting a shape over a line of reflection. Often this line of reflection is the *x* or *y*-axis, although other lines of reflection can be used as well. In a reflection, the original shape and its image are the same size and shape, although the orientation is not the same. A rotation results from rotating the original shape about a point of rotation. Rotations of specific number of degrees are common, such as 90 degrees, 180 degrees, and 270 degrees. In a rotation, the original shape and its image are the same size and shape; however, the orientation is not the same. The last transformation is a dilation. A dilation is a shrinking or stretching of the original shape. As a result of a dilation, the image remains the same shape as the original figure, but the size is different. The orientation remains the same, however.

PROBLEM

A triangle has the following coordinates: A (5, 1), B (10, 2), and C (7, –4). What are the coordinates of $A'B'C'$ after a reflection over the x-axis?

(A) A' (5, –1), B' (10, –2), C' (7, 4)

(B) A' (–5, 1), B' (–10, 2), C' (–7, –4)

(C) A' (–5, –1), B' (–10, –2), C' (–7, 4)

(D) A' (5, 1), B' (10, 2), C' (7, –4)

SOLUTION

When a shape is reflected over the x-axis, the x-coordinates stay the same, and the y-coordinates switch to their opposite sign. The correct answer is (A). The graph below shows the original triangle ABC and its reflection $A'B'C'$.

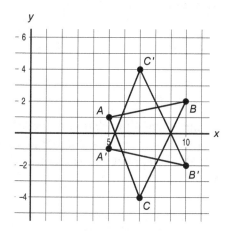

PROBLEM

What are the coordinates of triangle *XYZ*, shown below, translated 5 units to the left and 2 units down?

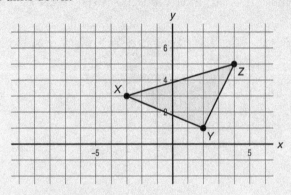

(A) X' (–3, 3), Y' (2, 1), Z' (4, 5)

(B) X' (2, 5), Y' (7, 3), Z' (9, 7)

(C) X' (–8, 1), Y' (–3, –1), Z' (–1, 3)

(D) X' (2, 5), Y' (7, 3), Z' (9, 7)

SOLUTION

   To solve this problem, you must know that a translation to the left 5 units will decrease the *x*-coordinates by 5. A translation down 2 units will decrease the *y*-coordinates by 2. The coordinates of triangle *XYZ* are X (–3, 3), Y (2, 1), and Z (4, 5). The correct answer choice is (C). The original triangle and the translated triangle are shown below.

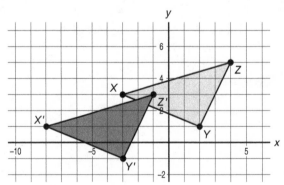

Competency 4: Knowledge of Algebraic Thinking

4.1: Analyze and generalize patterns including arithmetic and geometric sequences.

A **sequence** of numbers is an ordered set of numbers. Sometimes a sequence is **arithmetic**, which means that in order to find the next number in the sequence, you have to add (or subtract) the same number. For example, the sequence (2, 5, 8, 11...) starts with the number 2, and each subsequent number is found by adding 3 to the previous number. That is, 2 + 3 = 5; 5 + 3 = 8, and so on. If you want to find the next number in an **arithmetic sequence**, then you need to find the **difference** between any two consecutive numbers of the sequence. Once you have discovered this **difference**, you can continue the sequence infinitely. If you wanted to continue the arithmetic sequence 2, 5, 8, 11, keep adding 3 to the previous value, like so: (2, 5, 8, 11, 14, 17, 20...)

Here's another example of an arithmetic sequence: (45, 40, 35, 30...) Starting with 45, each subsequent number is found by subtracting 5. You can see that 45 − 5 = 40; 40 − 5 = 35, etc. The next number in the **sequence** after 30 is 25 because 30 − 5 = 25.

Sequences of numbers can also be **geometric**, which means that you multiply (or divide) by the same number to find the next number. An example of a **geometric sequence** is (1, 2, 4, 8...). Examine the numbers to see what you need to multiply (or divide) each number by to get the next number. In this case, it is times 2 because 1 × 2 = 2, 2 × 2 = 4, and 4 × 2 = 8. The next number in the sequence is found by multiplying 8 by 2, which gives 16. It may not always be easily apparent whether a sequence is arithmetic or geometric, and sometimes it is neither. To check if it is an arithmetic sequence, see if there is a common difference between each number and the one that follows it. If there is, then you know it is an arithmetic sequence. If not, then you can see if it is geometric by dividing each term by the one before it. If you get the same **quotient** each time, then it is **geometric**. Once you have determined the kind of **sequence** you have, it is easy to find the next number. Number patterns may be neither arithmetic nor geometric. The sequence (1, 2, 4, 5, 7, 8, 10...) shows a pattern. The pattern is +1, +2, +1, +2, etc. Because the amount being added is not the same each time, it is not an arithmetic sequence. However, it is a recognizable pattern, and you could continue the pattern by repeating +1, +2, etc.

PROBLEM

Which number pattern below shows a geometric sequence?

    (A) (2, 7, 12, 17, 22...)   (B) (4, 5, 10, 11, 22...)

    (C) (4, 8, 12, 16, 20...)   (D) (2, 6, 18, 54, 162...)

SOLUTION

A geometric sequence is found by multiplying or dividing each number in the sequence by the same number. Answer choice (A) shows an arithmetic sequence (add 5 to each number). Answer choice (B) is neither arithmetic nor geometric (add 1, multiply by 2, repeat). Answer choice (C) is an arithmetic sequence (add 4). Answer choice (D) is a geometric sequence (multiply by 3), and it is the correct answer.

PROBLEM

Which number sequence below is neither arithmetic nor geometric?

(A) 1, 10, 100, 1000…   (B) 95, 90, 85, 80…

(C) 2, 5, 8, 11…   (D) 2, 3, 5, 8…

SOLUTION

Answer choice (A) is a geometric sequence because the pattern is multiply by 10. Answer choice (B) is an arithmetic sequence because the pattern is subtract 5. Answer choice (C) is an arithmetic sequence because the pattern is add 3. The correct answer is (D) because the pattern is add 1, add 2, add 3. The amount that is added every time is not the same; therefore, it cannot be considered an arithmetic sequence.

4.2: Interpret algebraic expressions using words, symbols, variables, tables, and graphs.

An algebraic expression is a collection of numbers and variables or just variables that may include any of the four operations. Some examples of algebraic expressions are $3x$, $8x^2 - 3y$, y^3, $\dfrac{2x}{-5}$. It is important to be able to interpret algebraic expressions as well as to evaluate them. Being able to translate algebraic expressions into word phrases and word phrases into algebraic expressions is a useful skill. The chart below shows some different ways to translate a variety of algebraic expressions.

Algebraic Expressions	Word Phrases
$y + 3$	• y increased by 3 • y plus 3 • 3 more than y • y and 3
$7x$	• 7 times x • the product of x and 7 • x multiplied by 7
$\dfrac{p}{3}$	• p divided by 3 • the quotient of p and 3
$m - 1$	• m decreased by 1 • 1 less than m • m minus 1 • 1 subtracted from m

Sometimes you have to translate words into algebraic expressions. For example, you could be told that Sophia is 4 years older than Gabriella and asked to write an algebraic expression for Sophia's age. Let's say Gabriella is G years old; then Sophia would be $G + 4$ years old because she is 4 years older than Gabriella.

PROBLEM

Which expression does *not* show multiplication?

    (A) $4(z)$ (B) 2×6 (C) 49   (D) $3y$

SOLUTION

To correctly answer this question, you must be familiar with the different ways to write multiplication. In addition to the $\times$ sign as shown in (B), there are other ways to show multiplication. A common way is using parentheses as shown in answer choice (A). If you are multiplying a number and a variable, two variables or more, or a number and two or more variables, you can put the symbols next to each other without any multiplication sign at all. For example, yz, $4p$, and $2xy$ all indicate multiplication. You cannot, however, put two numbers together to indicate multiplication. 34 means $30 + 4$; it never means 3 times 4. Another common way to indicate multiplication is using a raised dot: $5 \cdot 7$ means 5 times 7. Therefore, answer choice (C) is the only expression that does not show multiplication and is the correct answer to this problem.

PROBLEM

> Harriet is *H* years old. Her cousin Martha is 2 years less than three times Harriet's age. Which expression below shows the sum of Harriet's and Martha's ages?
>
> (A) $3H - 2$ (B) $3H - 2 + H$
>
> (C) $2H - 3$ (D) $2H - 3 + H$

SOLUTION

To find the correct expression, you could make a "key", which clarifies what each algebraic expression means.

$$H = \text{Harriet's age}$$

$$3H - 2 = \text{Martha's age}$$

After you have written the key, you can use it to write the algebraic expression that means the sum of Harriet's and Martha's ages. Remember that "sum" indicates addition.

Either of the expressions below would be correct because addition is Commutative.

$$H + 3H - 2 \quad \text{or} \quad 3H - 2 + H$$

Answer choice (B) is the right answer.

PROBLEM

> Which word phrase could be the translation of the following expression?
>
> $$\frac{y}{3} - 5$$
>
> (A) The quotient of *y* and three less than five
>
> (B) The quotient of *y* and three, decreased by five
>
> (C) Three less than *y*, minus five
>
> (D) The difference between five and y divided by three

SOLUTION

To select the correct translation of this algebraic expression, you must be familiar with the different ways to indicate subtraction and division. In addition, you need to translate the expression in the correct order. Answer choice (A) would be $5 - \dfrac{y}{3}$, so that is not correct. Answer choice (C) would be $(y - 3) - 5$, which is not accurate. The algebraic expression for (D) would be $\dfrac{5 - y}{3}$, which is not correct. The correct answer choice is (B).

Interpreting a geometric diagram algebraically is a necessary skill. The diagram below shows 1 x^2 tile, 3 x tiles, and 2 ones tiles. This rectangular model can be used to represent the product of two algebraic factors. To find the two factors, determine the length of the horizontal side of the rectangle as well as the length of the vertical side of the rectangle. The horizontal length is $x + 1$. The vertical length is $x + 2$.

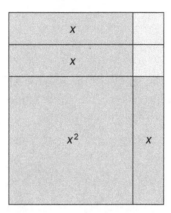

This model is saying $(x + 1)(x + 2) = x^2 + 3x + 2$. Below, you can see the two factors of the rectangle on the left side and along the bottom of the rectangle.

PROBLEM

Which expression shows the area in the diagram below?

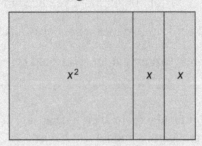

(A) $x(x + 1)$ (B) $x(x + 2)$ (C) $(x)(x)$ (D) $x(x + x)$

SOLUTION

To find the two factors, determine the length of the horizontal side of the rectangle, and then find the length of the vertical side of the rectangle. The horizontal length is $x + 2$, and the vertical length is x. The correct answer is (B). The two factors are shown below.

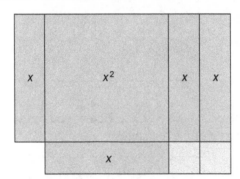

Evaluating algebraic expressions

To "evaluate" an algebraic expression means to substitute in the values given for the variables to find the value of the expression. For example, the expression $x + 3y$ cannot be evaluated *until* you are given the values for both x and y. Let's say $x = -5$ and $y = 7$. We can substitute those values into the expression:

$x + 3y$	The given algebraic expression
$-5 + 3(7)$	Substitute in the values given.
$-5 + 21$	Evaluate following the order of operations (multiply).
16	Evaluate following the order of operations (add).

The value of the expression $x + 3y$ is 16 when $x = -5$ and $y = 7$.

You must remember to follow the order of operations when evaluating algebraic expressions. The four steps to the order of operations are:

1. Simplify inside parentheses.

2. Simplify expressions with exponents.

3. Do multiplication and division from left to right.

4. Do addition and subtraction from left to right.

A typical mistake when simplifying and evaluating algebraic expressions is to work from left to right without regard to the correct order of operations. Be sure to pay attention to the order of operations when evaluating algebraic expressions.

The same expression can have different values depending on what value(s) you substitute in for the variable(s). Take a look at the same expression evaluated with different values for y.

Evaluate the expression $y + 12$ for $y = 3$

$$y + 12$$
$$3 + 12$$
$$15$$

Evaluate the expression $y + 12$ for $y = -18$

$$y + 12$$
$$-18 + 12$$
$$-6$$

PROBLEM

Evaluate the expression for the given values.

$$(x + z)^2 - 3z \div x \quad x = 3 \quad \text{and} \quad z = 5$$

(A) 11 (B) 59 (C) $16\dfrac{1}{3}$ (D) $\dfrac{1}{3}$

SOLUTION

Substitute the values for x and z in the algebraic expression and evaluate the expression, following the order of operations.

$(x + z)^2 - 3z \div x$	The given expression
$(3 + 5)^2 - 3(5) \div 3$	Substitute in the given values.
$(8)^2 - 3(5) \div 3$	Evaluate following the order operations (parentheses).
$64 - 3(5) \div 3$	Evaluate following the order operations (exponents).
$64 - 15 \div 3$	Evaluate following the order operations (multiply).
$64 - 5$	Evaluate following the order operations (divide).
59	Evaluate following the order operations (add).

PROBLEM

Evaluate the expression below for $x = 2$ and $y = -3$

$$-5y + x^3$$

(A) 23   (B) –7   (C) 21   (D) –9

SOLUTION

$-5y + x^3$	The problem
$-5(-3) + (2)^3$	Substitute in the values given.
$-5(-3) + 8$	Evaluate following order of operations (exponents).
$15 + 8$	Evaluate following order of operations (multiply).
23	Evaluate following order of operations (add).

Like Terms

Algebraic expressions can have one or more terms. Some terms can be combined, and other terms cannot. If an expression has two or more terms are *like terms*, then they can be combined. You recognize like terms because they have the same variable to the same power ($4x^4$ and $2x^4$ are like terms). Numbers with no variables, of course, are like terms (3 and –5 are like terms). The table below shows some examples of like terms and unlike terms.

	Like Terms	Unlike Terms
1.	$8 + 2 - 1$	$4c + 3c^2$
2.	$5x + 2x - 9x$	$2y - 5x$
3.	$2xy + 5xy$	$x^3 - 3x^2$
4.	$-5y^2 - 3y^2$	$3xy + 8x^2y$

Since like terms can be combined, the expressions in the first column of the table can be simplified. The simplified expressions are shown below:

1. 9 　　　　2. $-2x$ 　　　　3. $7xy$ 　　　　4. $-8y^2$

Graphs

Graphs can represent situations visually. The graph below shows the distance and time it took for a woman to walk from her home to her office. Her office is 160 meters from her home. Even if you are not told specifically about her trip, you can create a legitimate story of her trip by following the graph. For example, during the first 50 seconds after the woman left her home, she walked at a steady rate toward work. Notice that as the time increases steadily, the distance increases steadily. From 50 seconds to 70 seconds, the woman walked at a steady pace back toward her home. Notice that although the time is increasing, the distance from home is decreasing. Perhaps she thought she forgot something and headed back toward home. Then she found what she was looking for in her pocket and did not need to continue home. From 70 seconds to 100 seconds, she walked toward her office at a steady pace. Notice that as the time increases, the distance also increases. At 100 seconds, she gets to her office (it is 160 meters from her home). Notice that from 100 seconds until 120 seconds, the distance does not change. Perhaps she ran into a friend in front of her office and talked with her for 20 seconds. Other "stories" for the graph below are possible, as long as they make sense with the given information in the graph.

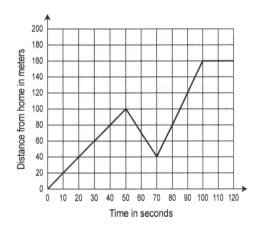

PROBLEM

Which statement below correctly describes the air temperature on Wednesday shown in the line graph?

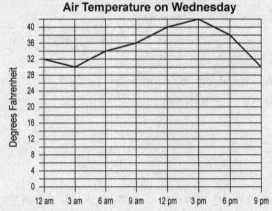

Air Temperature on Wednesday

(A) The temperature rises steadily from 12 am until 6 am, then decreases until 6 pm, and then increases until 9 pm.

(B) The temperature decreases after 9 am, increases until 12 pm, decreases until 6 pm, and then holds steady until 9 pm.

(C) The temperature decreases slightly after 12 am, then increases until 3 pm, and then decreases until 9 pm.

(D) The temperature increases until 12 pm, then decreases until 9 pm.

SOLUTION

Reading a line graph requires paying close attention to the labels on the axes. This line graph shows the time on the *x*-axis and the temperature on the *y*-axis. Before reading the answer choices, take a look at the line graph and see what you notice. You can see that the temperature goes down, then up, and then down again. Now, read the answer choices to find the one that matches up with the information on the line graph. Answer choice (C) is the only correct answer.

Interpreting Tables

Tables can show relationships between two variables. Recognizing the pattern allows you to generate more values in the table. For example, look at the table below. What is the pattern between the *x*-values and the *y*-values? Notice that the *y*-values are all twice the *x*-values. Knowing that, what would be the missing *y*-value in the table?

x-values	y-values
7	14
9	18
−3	−6
−1	

The missing y-value will be twice the x-value, which is −1. $2(-1) = -2$. The missing y-value is −2.

x-values	y-values
7	14
9	18
−3	−6
−1	−2

PROBLEM

Which equation shows the relationship between the x- and y-values in the table?

x-values	y-values
18	12
10	4
4	−2

(A) $y = x - 6$

(B) $y = 2x$

(C) $x = y - 6$

(D) $x = 2y$

SOLUTION

To find the relationship in the table, look at the relationship between the x-values and y-values. Each y-value is found by taking the corresponding x-value and subtracting 6 from it. The correct answer is $y = x - 6$, which is answer choice (A).

PROBLEM

Which equation shows the relationship between x and y in the table of values?

x	y
10	6
12	7
14	8
16	9

(A) $y = x - 1$

(B) $y = x - 4$

(C) $y = \dfrac{x}{2} - 1$

(D) $y = \dfrac{x}{2} + 1$

SOLUTION

When looking for the relationship in a table of values, it is important to remember that the relationship has to be the same for each input and output value. Answer choice (B) could be correct for the first (x, y) pair, but it does not hold true for all other pairs in the table. The relationship in the table of values is divide the input value by 2, and then add 1. This holds true for all (x, y) pairs in the table. The correct answer is (D).

4.3: Solve equations and inequalities graphically or algebraically.

Solving Algebraic Equations

A linear equation is an algebraic equation whose independent variable is to the first power. To solve an equation involving one operation, you must apply the inverse operation to solve it. The inverse operation means the opposite operation. The opposite of addition is subtraction and vice versa. The opposite of multiplication is division and vice versa. You must always do the same thing to both sides of an equation to keep it balanced. When you are presented with an equation, the expression on the left is equal to the expression on the right. Therefore, if you manipulate the equation in any way, you must be sure to do the same thing to both expressions. For example, if you subtract 5 from one side of an equation, you must subtract 5 from the other side, as shown below.

$$y + 5 = 12$$
$$-5 + y + 5 = 12 - 5$$
$$y = 7$$

PROBLEM

A box of pens costs $1.89. Which equation shows how to find the total cost, *C*, of *B* boxes of pens?

(A) $B = 1.89C$ (B) $C = 1.89B$

(C) $C = \dfrac{1.89}{B}$ (D) $B = \dfrac{1.89}{C}$

SOLUTION

If you want, you can create a table for this problem. The relationship in the problem shows that for each box of pens, the cost is $1.89. Therefore, 2 boxes would be 2($1.89). Three boxes would be 3($1.89), etc. So, to find the total cost of *B* boxes of pens, multiply the price for 1 box ($1.89) by *B*. The correct answer is (B), $C = 1.89B$.

Solving Two-step equations

A two-step equation is an equation that requires performing two inverse operations to find the solution. A two-step equation has multiplication or division and addition or subtraction. You must do addition or subtraction before you do multiplication or division

See the examples below:

$$6y - 3 = 27$$
$$ +3 \; +3$$
$$6y = 30$$

$$\div 6 \; \div 6$$
$$y = 5$$

$$\frac{m}{4} + 7 = 10$$
$$\phantom{\frac{m}{4}} -7 \; -7$$
$$\frac{m}{4} = 3$$

$$(4)\frac{m}{4} = 3(4)$$
$$m = 12$$

Some word problems lend themselves to being solved by writing and solving two-step equations. Let's take a look at one: Jon is 5 years older than Zachary. Ben is twice Jon's age. The sum of all three of their ages is 39. Find Ben's age. You can solve this algebraically. First start by making a key. A key indicates what each algebraic expression represents.

$z =$ Zachary's age

$z + 5 =$ Jon's age

$2(z + 5) =$ Ben's age

Write an equation based on the information given in the problem.

$$z + z + 5 + 2(z + 5) = 39 \qquad \text{Zachary's age + Jon's age + Ben's age} = 39$$
$$z + z + 5 + 2z + 10 = 39 \qquad \text{Do the Distributive Property}$$
$$4z + 15 = 39 \qquad \text{Collect like terms}$$
$$4z = 24 \qquad \text{Subtract 15 from both sides.}$$
$$z = 6 \qquad \text{Divide both sides by 4.}$$

Since you know that $z = 6$, use your key to determine that Zachary is 6. Jon is 11 and Ben is 22. Check to see that all three ages add up to 39, which they do, so you know you are correct.

PROBLEM

The sum of three consecutive integers is 165. Find the largest of the three integers.

(A) 54   (B) 55   (C) 56   (D) 57

SOLUTION

In order to solve this problem, you can write an algebraic equation. First start with writing a key. Integers that are consecutive "follow" one another, like 1, 2, and 3.

$$x = \text{first integer}$$
$$x + 1 = \text{second integer}$$
$$x + 2 = \text{third integer}$$

Write an equation showing that the sum of these three integers is 165.

$$x + x + 1 + x + 2 = 165 \qquad \text{Write the equation.}$$
$$3x + 3 = 165 \qquad \text{Combine like terms.}$$
$$3x = 162 \qquad \text{Subtract 3 from both sides.}$$
$$x = 54 \qquad \text{Divide both sides by 3}$$

Since $x = 54$, the smallest of the three integers is 54. The question asks for the *largest* of the three consecutive integers, which is 56, because $x + 2 = 56$. The correct answer is (C).

Solving Linear Inequalities

Inequalities are statements that show the relationship between two quantities.

There are four inequality symbols:

$>$	Greater than
$\geq$	Greater than or equal to
$<$	Less than
$\leq$	Less than or equal to

Inequalities are solved in a similar manner to solving equations. Just as in an equation, an inequality requires you use the inverse operation of the operation that is in the problem to solve it. Also, you must do the same thing to both sides of an equation and both sides of an inequality to keep the relationship true. The main difference between solving equations and inequalities occurs when you multiply or divide an inequality by a negative number. When you do, you must *reverse* the inequality symbol to keep the inequality true. Examine the solution to the inequality below.

$-8x + 2 < 26$	Original inequality
$-8x < 24$	Subtract 2 from both sides.
$-8x < 24$	Divide both sides by -8 and *flip* the inequality symbol.
$x > -3$	The solution set.

Another difference between equations and inequalities is that for most equations, there is only one solution, while an inequality has a *range* of solutions. For example, if the solution to an inequality is $x > 5$, then any number greater than 5 is a solution. There are an infinite number of numbers that are greater than 5. In addition to whole numbers, there are also fractions and decimals.

Graphing Linear Inequalities

Because there are often an infinite number of solutions to an inequality, they are sometimes shown on a number line.

$>$ means "greater than" is indicated with an open circle and an arrow pointing to the right.

$\geq$ means "greater than or equal to" is indicated by a solid circle and an arrow pointing to the right.

<   means "less than" is indicated by an open circle and an arrow pointing to the left.

≤   means "less than or equal to" is indicated by a solid circle and an arrow pointing to the left.

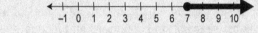

PROBLEM

Which number line shows the solutions to the inequality: $-2x - 9 \leq 5$

(A) Show $x \geq 7$

(B) Show $x \geq -7$

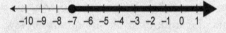

(C) Show $x \leq 7$

(D) Show $x \leq -7$

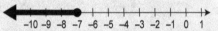

SOLUTION

To solve the following two-step inequality, first add 9 to both sides and then divide both sides by –2. Remember to flip the inequality symbol.

$$-2x - 9 \leq 5$$
$$+9 \quad +9$$
$$-2x \leq 14$$
$$x \geq -7$$

The correct answer is (B).

PROBLEM

Solve the inequality: $-2(x - 8) \leq 3x + 1$

   (A) $x \geq 3$ (B) $x \leq 3$ (C) $x \geq -3$ (D) $x \leq -3$

SOLUTION

$-2(x - 8) \leq 3x + 1$	The original inequality
$-2x + 16 \leq 3x + 1$	Do the distributive property.
$\underline{-16 \quad\quad -16}$	Subtract 16 from both sides.
$-2x \leq 3x - 15$	
$\underline{-3x \quad -3x}$	Subtract $3x$ from both sides.
$\dfrac{-5x}{-5} \leq \dfrac{-15}{-5}$	Divide both sides by -5.
$x \geq 3$	Flip the inequality symbol.

The correct answer is (A).

4.4: Determine whether a number or ordered pair is among the solutions of given equations or inequalities.

If a number is a solution to an equation, it will make the equation true. If a number is not a solution to an equation, it will make the equation false. For example, given the equation, $-19 + x = 3$, which value in the set $(22, -22, -16, 16)$ is a solution to the equation? Substitute each of the values of the set into the equation, and look for the one that makes the equation true. The only value that works is 22.

$-19 + x = 3$	The equation given.
$-19 + 22 = 3$	Substitute in 22 for the variable.
$3 = 3$	The statement is true; therefore, 22 is the solution.

In contrast, if we substitute in any of the other values given, we will get a false statement. Let's try -22.

$-19 + x = 3$	The equation given
$-19 + (-22) = 3$	Substitute in -22 for the variable.
$-41 \neq 3$	The statement is false; therefore, -22 is not a solution.

Linear equations have two variables, a dependent variable and an independent variable. An equation in two variables to the first power represents a line, and a line has an infinite number of points on it. Therefore, there are an infinite number of ordered pairs that lie on the line. If an ordered pair is a solution to an equation, it will make the equation true. If an ordered pair is *not* a solution to an equation, it will make the equation false.

For example, given the equation, $y = 3x - 7$, which value(s) in the set of ordered pairs [(2,–1), (5, 22), (–3, 0), (–4, –19)]) is a solution to the equation? You must substitute in each of the points because more than one of the ordered pairs may lie on the line. The first value in the ordered pair is the x-coordinate, and the second value is the y-coordinate.

$y = 3x - 7$	The equation
$-1 = 3(2) - 7$	Substitute in (2, –1).
$-1 = 6 - 7$	Simplify.
$-1 = -1$	The statement is *true*. (2, –1) is a solution.
$y = 3x - 7$	The equation
$22 = 3(5) - 7$	Substitute in (5, 22).
$22 = 15 - 7$	Simplify.
$22 \neq 8$	The statement is *false*. (5, 22) is *not* a solution.
$y = 3x - 7$	The equation
$0 = 3(-3) - 7$	Substitute in (–3, 0).
$0 = -9 - 7$	Simplify.
$0 \neq -16$	The statement is *false*. (–3, 0) is *not* a solution.
$y = 3x - 7$	The equation
$-19 = 3(-4) - 7$	Substitute in (–4, –19).
$-19 = -12 - 7$	Simplify.
$-19 = -19$	The statement is *true*. (–4, –19) is a solution.

PROBLEM

Which ordered pairs in the set are solutions to the linear equation?
$$-2x + y = 3$$
$$[(-3, -3), (-1, -5), (4, 11), (1, 3)]$$

(A) $(-3, -3)$ only

(B) $(-1, -5)$ only

(C) $(-3, -3)$ and $(4, 11)$

(D) $(-1, -5)$ and $(4, 11)$

SOLUTION

Insert each ordered pair into the equation to see if you get a true statement. If you do, you know the ordered pair lies on the line.3

$-2x + y = 3$	The equation
$-2(-3) + (-3) = 3$	Substitute in $(-3, -3)$.
$6 + (-3) = 3$	Simplify.
$3 = 3$	This is a true statement $(-3, -3)$ is a solution.
$-2x + y = 3$	The equation
$-2(-1) + (-5) = 3$	Substitute in $(-1, -5)$.
$2 + (-5) = 3$	Simplify.
$-3 \neq 3$	This is a false statement. $(-1, -5)$ is *not* a solution.
$-2x + y = 3$	The equation
$-2(4) + (11) = 3$	Substitute in $(4, 11)$.
$-8 + (11) = 3$	Simplify.
$3 = 3$	This is a true statement. $(4, 11)$ is a solution.
$-2x + y = 3$	The equation
$-2(1) + (3) = 3$	Substitute in $(1, 3)$.
$-2 + (3) = 3$	Simplify.
$1 \neq 3$	This is a false statement. $(1, 3)$ is *not* a solution.

Since both $(-3, -3)$ and $(4, 11)$ make the equations true, then both are solutions. The correct answer is (C).

PROBLEM

Which ordered pair satisfies the given equation?

$$y = \frac{10}{x}$$

(A) (10, 100)   (B) (2, .5)   (C) (.1, 100)   (D) (20, .05)

SOLUTION

The equation shows an inverse relationship, which means that as the *x*-value increases, the *y*-value decreases. The product of each *xy* pair is 10. Try the ordered pairs given in the answer choice to find the one that is correct. The only pair that is correct is (.1, 100), answer choice (C).

Solutions To Quadratic Equations

A second-degree equation is called a **quadratic equation**. Quadratic equations form parabolas, which are U-shaped curves, when they are graphed. Below is the quadratic equation $y = x^2 - 4$. Notice that the points on the graph lie along a curve.

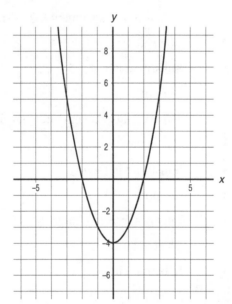

To determine whether a specific point lies on the curve, you can substitute the ordered pair into the equation. We can test to see which of the ordered pairs in the following set satisfy the equation $y = x^2 - 4$. [(0, –4), (3, 5), (1, –2)]

$$y = x^2 - 4 \qquad \text{The equation.}$$
$$-4 = (0)^2 - 4 \qquad \text{Substitute } (0, -4) \text{ in equation.}$$
$$-4 = 0 - 4 \qquad \text{Simplify.}$$
$$-4 = -4 \qquad \text{The equation is true. } (0, -4) \text{ satisfies the equation.}$$

$$y = x^2 - 4 \qquad \text{The equation.}$$
$$5 = (3)^2 - 4 \qquad \text{Substitute } (3, 5) \text{ in equation.}$$
$$5 = 9 - 4 \qquad \text{Simplify.}$$
$$5 = 5 \qquad \text{The equation is true. } (3, 5) \text{ satisfies the equation.}$$

$$y = x^2 - 4 \qquad \text{The equation.}$$
$$-2 = (1)^2 - 4 \qquad \text{Substitute } (1, -2) \text{ in equation.}$$
$$-2 = 1 - 4 \qquad \text{Simplify.}$$
$$-2 \neq -3 \qquad \text{The equation is false. } (1, -2) \text{ does not satisfy the equation.}$$

PROBLEM

Which ordered pair satisfies the equation $y = x^2 - 3x + 6$?

   (A) (5, 5)   (B) (2, 4)   (C) (0, –3)   (D) (–3, 2)

SOLUTION

Substitute in each of the ordered pairs until you find the one that makes a true statement. The only point that satisfies the equation $y = x^2 - 3x + 6$ is $(2, 4)$.

$$y = x^2 - 3x + 6$$
$$4 = 2^2 - 3(2) + 6$$
$$4 = 4 - 6 + 6$$
$$4 = 4 \qquad \text{This is a true statement. } (2, 4) \text{ satisfies the equation.}$$

Solutions To Inequalities

If a number is a solution to an inequality, it makes the inequality true. There are an infinite number of solutions to most inequalities. For example, the solution set to $x \leq 2$ includes every number less than or equal to 2. In the set that follows, which are solutions to $x \leq 2$? (–3, –1, 0, 2, 3, 9, 100) The solutions are (–3, –1, 0, and 2) from the set given.

If an ordered pair is a solution to a linear inequality, the point lies in the solution set.

Consider the linear inequality $y \geq 2x - 4$ shown in the graph below.

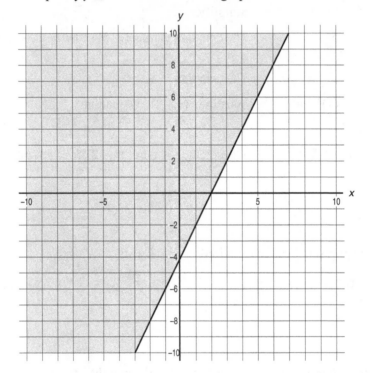

Every point that lies in the shaded area (including the line itself) is a solution to the inequality. As you can see, there are an infinite number of points that will satisfy the inequality.

The graph shows that the origin, (0, 0) is a solution. When you substitute the point into the inequality, you will get a true statement.

$y \geq 2x - 4$	The inequality.
$(0) \geq 2(0) - 4$	Substitute (0, 0).
$(0) \geq 0 - 4$	Simplify.
$0 \geq -4$	This statement is true. This proves (0, 0) is a solution.

The point (4, 0) is not in the shaded area of the linear inequality. Therefore, it is not a solution. When you substitute the point into the inequality, you will get a false statement.

$$y \geq 2x - 4 \qquad \text{The inequality.}$$

$$(0) \geq 2(4) - 4 \qquad \text{Substitute (4, 0).}$$

$$(0) \geq 8 - 4 \qquad \text{Simplify.}$$

$$0 \geq 4 \qquad \text{This statement is false. This proves (4, 0) is not a solution.}$$

PROBLEM

Which one of the ordered pairs is a solution to the inequality $y \leq -3x - 1$?

     (A)   (2, 3)   (B)   (–5, 15)   (C)   (1, –2)   (D)   (0, –1)

SOLUTION

Although there are an infinite number of solutions to a second-degree inequality, not all ordered pairs will be solutions. To find which of the answer choices is a solution, substitute in each ordered pair until you find a true statement.

$$y \leq -3x - 1$$

$$3 \leq -3(2) - 1 \qquad \text{Substitute in (2, 3).}$$

$$3 \leq -6 - 1$$

$$3 \leq -7 \qquad \text{This is a false statement. (2, 3) is not a solution to the inequality.}$$

$$y \leq -3x - 1$$

$$15 \leq -3(-5) - 1 \qquad \text{Substitute in (–5, 15).}$$

$$15 \leq 15 - 1$$

$$15 \leq 14 \qquad \text{This is a false statement. (–5, 15) is not a solution to the inequality.}$$

$$(1, -2)$$

$$-2 \leq -3(1) - 1$$

$$-2 \leq -3 - 1$$

$$-2 \leq -4 \qquad \text{This is a false statement. (1, –2) is not a solution to the inequality.}$$

(0, −1)

$-1 \leq -3(0) - 1$

$-1 \leq 0 - 1$

$-1 \leq -1$ This is a true statement. (0, −1) is a solution to the inequality.

The correct answer is choice (D).

Competency 5: Knowledge of Data Analysis and Probability

5.1: Analyze data and solve problems using data presented in histograms, bar graphs, circle graphs, pictographs, tables, and charts.

Information, or data, can be displayed in charts, tables, or a variety of graphs. The main reason that data is collected is so that it can be analyzed. Some data is better suited for being displayed in one form rather than another. For example, data that shows change over time is well suited for a line graph. Scatter plots are useful for examining trends. Venn diagrams help to see where two or more sets of data intersect. When you are given data in a chart, table, or graph, the best thing you can do is take your time reading the information. Some questions you might ask yourself: What is the title? What information is on the *x*-axis and the *y*-axis? What is the scale being used? What is the time period being covered? If you are examining a pictograph, don't assume that each picture represents one unit; often the picture represents larger numbers, such as 10, 100, or 1000.

Circle Graphs

Circle graphs, also known as pie graphs or pie charts, are good for showing how the parts to a whole relate to one another. The circle graph below shows the percentages consumers spent on different areas in 1992. Notice that the portions of the pie chart are given in percents. It is possible, however, to find the amount of money spent on each category by using the average total expenditure of $29,846 that is given. To find how much money was spent on housing, you could find 32% of $29,846 by completing the following computation: .32 × 29846 = 9550.72. $9,550.72 is spent on housing. So, even though the dollar amounts are not given in the pie graph, they can be found.

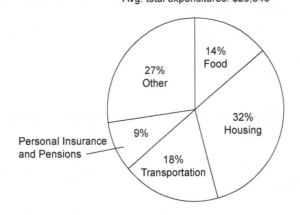

Consumer Expenditures in 1992

Avg. total expenditures: $29,846

After data is collected and then organized, it can be put into a graphic representation allowing you to make observations, comparisons, predictions, or extrapolations. It is important to remember that data is collected and organized so that we can make observations from it.

Frequency Tables and Histograms

A **frequency table** is a way to organize data to see how frequently each value occurs. A common way to organize a frequency table is to make three columns. The first column contains the data values. The second column is for tally marks, and the third column shows the number of times each data value occurs. Below is a sample of a frequency table showing how often the numbers 1 – 6 were tossed when a die was thrown.

Number	Tally	Frequency
1	IIII	4
2	⤫HIL	5
3	III	3
4	III	3
5	II	2
6	III	3

A **histogram** is a type of bar graph that is similar to a frequency table in that it shows the frequency that data occurs. It is different from a frequency table because it shows the data in bar graph form (with no spaces between the bars) rather than in a table. Often histograms group data into intervals. For example, when looking at the weights of a group of individuals, the weights might be grouped in the following ways: 90–109, 100–109, 110–119, etc. When there is a lot of data, it makes more sense to group the data items in intervals rather than graph each piece of data individually.

Below is an example of a histogram that shows the breakdown of students' grades on an exam. Notice that each bar represents a range of scores rather than a specific score. Looking at the histogram, it is easily apparent that more students scored in the 60–80 range than in any other range.

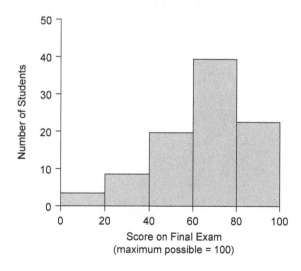

PROBLEM

The histogram shows the number of books a group of students read last school year. Which statement about the histogram is *not* true?

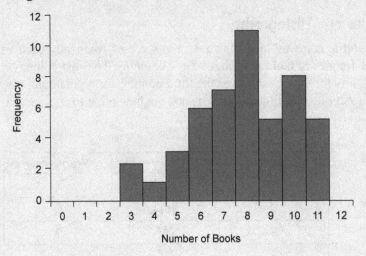

(A) The number of students who read 7 books is less than the number of students who read 8 books.

(B) The number of students who read 11 books is more than the sum of the number of students who read 3 books and 4 books.

(C) More students read 10 books than read 9 books.

(D) Four students read one book.

SOLUTION

   Answer choices (A), (B), and (C) are all true. The only statement that is not true is (D). The statement for (D) could be confusing because it says, "Four students read one book," which is false. What is true, however, is "One student read four books." When interpreting any graph, be sure that you are reading it correctly.

Bar Graphs

Look at the following bar graph showing students' scores on a math test. There are many observations that can be made from the data.

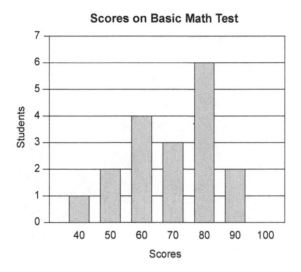

Some possible observations:

- More students scored 80 than any other score (the **mode**)

- 18 students took the test

- The **range** on the test was 50

- Almost half of the students scored less than 70 on the test

- No one achieved a perfect score

- The **median** score was 70

PROBLEM

A group of seventh grade students was asked what was their favorite subject in school. Their results are depicted in the bar graph. Which statement about the results is *not* true?

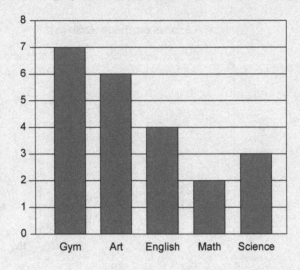

(A)   Fewer students chose Math than any other subject.

(B)   Four more students chose Gym than chose Math.

(C)   Twice as many students chose Art than chose Science.

(D)   Four students chose English as their favorite subject.

SOLUTION

To answer this question correctly, you have to identify the statement that is not true from the answer choices. Answer choice (A) is true because only 2 students chose Math; this was the least popular subject. Answer choice (C) is true because 3 students chose Science and 6 students chose Art. Twice as many chose Art as Science. Answer choice (D) is true because the bar for English shows that 4 students chose that subject. The only answer choice that is not true is (B); 7 students chose Gym and 2 students chose Math. The difference between those two numbers is 5, not 4. Therefore, answer choice (B) is the only false statement and is the correct answer.

Line Graphs

Line graphs are useful for looking at the change of some value over time. What predictions or extrapolations can you make from the line graph of the temperature of water that is being heated over time, shown in the line graph below?

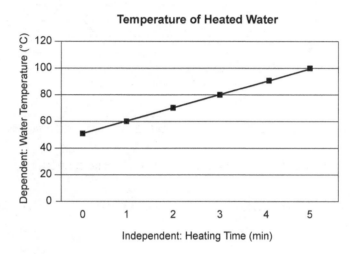

As you can see, the line graph shows a constant increase of about 10 degrees every minute. So even though the graph does not show the temperature of the water after 6 or more minutes, we can extrapolate what the temperature will be based on the information that we are given. What temperature would you expect the water to be after 8 minutes? At 5 minutes, the temperature is 100 degrees; the graph shows that the water increases 10 degrees every minute. You would expect the water to be at 130 degrees after 8 minutes. Although this temperature would follow the pattern of the graph (and it would be a logical extrapolation), it does not make sense in the real world as water boils at 100 degrees. Therefore, it cannot get any hotter than that! Therefore, you must pay attention to the patterns that you see in graphs, but you must also pay attention to what you know to be true in the real world. Using this "real world" knowledge, you can predict that after reaching its highest temperature at 5 minutes, the temperature of the water will remain the same, 100 degrees, as time goes on. So, at 8 minutes the temperature would still be 100 degrees.

PROBLEM

The line graph shows the amount of money the Patterson's have saved over the years. The *x*-axis shows the years, and the *y*-axis shows the total amount of money in dollars in the account.

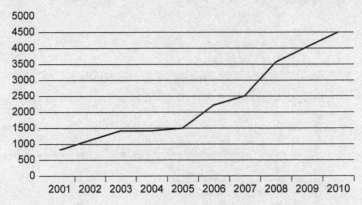

How much money did the Patterson's save from 2001 until 2010?

(A) $4,500   (B) $4,000   (C) $3,750   (D) $3,500

SOLUTION

The question is asking you how much money the Patterson's saved over 9 years. It is *not* asking you how much money they have in their account in 2010. Therefore, you must find the difference between the amount of money in their account in 2010 and the amount of money in their account in 2001. $4,500 – $750 = $3,750. The correct answer is (C).

Pictographs

A **pictograph** is a visual presentation of data using pictures or symbols instead of bars, lines or points. The pictures in a pictograph represent a particular number. Sometimes each picture represents one; however, other times each picture represents a larger number such as 10, 100, or 1000. Based on the size of the data, the person who is making the pictograph chooses what number each picture will represent.

Here is a sample pictograph of the different sports played by a group of elementary school students. Notice that the key indicates each soccer ball is equivalent to 10 students.

baseball	⚽ ⚽ ⚽ ⚽ ⚽
football	⚽ ⚽ ⚽
soccer	⚽ ⚽ ⚽ ⚽ ⚽ ⚽
hockey	⚽ ⚽
basketball	⚽ ⚽ ⚽ ⚽

Key: ⚽ = 10 students

Therefore, you must be able to "read" a pictograph accurately. The number of students who play baseball is 50 (not 5).

5.2: Identify how the presentation of data can lead to different or inappropriate interpretations.

Data that is presented in a graph gives the impression of being "correct". However, it is important to know that data can be presented in a variety of ways that can lead to a variety of conclusions. Depending on the scale used in the graphs, the number of years included, or the number of people included in a survey, the data can communicate different things. People who put together data are often trying to influence their audiences to see things a certain way that benefits them. Therefore, you must be cautious when reading "results," recognizing that you may not be seeing the whole picture. Do not assume that the graph you are seeing is depicting the data in an unbiased way.

PROBLEM

Shaniqua wants to find the average weight of a student in her high school. Which sample would give Shaniqua the most representative results?

(A) All of the boys in 11th grade

(B) The 24 members of the boys' wrestling team

(C) The 21 students in her 9th grade science class

(D) 18 students from each of the grades 9 through 12

SOLUTION

Results from a sample are only as good as the sample chosen. So, in this case, you are looking for the best sample to show the average weight of a high school student. High school consists of grades 9–12 and includes both boys and girls. Therefore, choose a sample that represents all four grades and both genders. Answer choices (A), (B), and (C) all are too narrow of a sample group. Answer choice (D) includes a varied sample, which will yield the best results. Answer choice (D) is the correct answer.

5.3: Calculate range, mean, median, and mode(s) from sets of data and interpret the meaning of the measures of central tendency (i.e., mean, median, and mode) and dispersion (i.e., range and standard deviation).

Familiarity with the central tendencies of mean, median, and mode are important. You must know how to find them. The **mean** is found by adding up all the data items and dividing by the number of data items there are: The mean of 4, 5, and 12 is found by adding $4 + 5 + 12$, which equals 21, and then dividing by 3; the mean is 7. The **median** is found by putting the data in order from least to greatest and then finding the middle data item. When there is an odd number of items, this is fairly straightforward. To find the median of 10, 6, 4, 8, and 12, put the data in order from least to greatest: 4, 6, 8, 10, 12; the middle number, the median, is 8. If there is an even number of data items, the median is found by finding the average of the two middle numbers. To find the median of 3, 8, 4, and 11, put the data in order: 3, 4, 8, 11. The two middle numbers are 4 and 8. Find the average of 4 and 8 by adding them together and dividing by 2. $4 + 8 = 12$. $12 \div 2 = 6$; the median is 6. The data item which occurs more often than any other data item is the **mode**. In the data set (4, 5, 5, 7, 7, 7, 9, 9), the mode is 7 because the number 7 occurs more than any other number.

PROBLEM

Which data set has a mean of 10?

    (A) (4, 5, 10, 13, 17)   (B) (3, 5, 5, 8, 13)

    (C) (2, 10, 10, 10, 11)   (D) (7, 8, 8, 12, 15)

SOLUTION

To find the correct set of data, the sum of all five data items must be 50 because $5 \times 10 = 50$. Therefore, whichever set has a sum of 50 is the correct answer. The sum of the data items in (B) is 34. The sum of the data items in answer choice (C) is 43. The sum of the data items in answer choice (A) is 49. The sum of the data items in answer choice (D) is 50, so that is the correct answer.

PROBLEM

Which group of numbers does *not* have a mean of 30?

(A) (20, 30, 30, 40)   (B) (22, 24, 15, 19, 40, 60)

(C) (10, 10, 70)   (D) (15, 49)

SOLUTION

To find the mean of a set of numbers, find the sum of all of the numbers and then divide by the number of numbers there are.

The mean for answer choice (A) is $(20 + 30 + 30 + 40) \div 4 = 30$

The mean for answer choice (B) is $(22 + 24 + 15 + 19 + 40 + 60) \div 6 = 30$

The mean for answer choice (C) is $(10 + 10 + 70) \div 3 = 30$

The mean for answer choice (D) is $(15 + 49) \div 2 = 32$

The only answer choice, which does not have a mean of 30 is answer choice (D), which is the correct answer.

There are two values that give you information about how varied the data is. Knowing the **range** of data is important as it shows you how spread out the data is. To find the range, subtract the smallest data item from the largest data item. A small range lets you know that the data is grouped together closely. A large range tells you that the data is spread apart. The **standard deviation** is a statistic that shows how close the set of data is to the mean. When the data is close together around the mean, the standard deviation is small. However, when the data is spread farther apart, the standard deviation is larger. Both the range and the standard deviation give information about the data set that may be helpful when analyzing data.

PROBLEM

Mr. Potts gave a math test to his students and found that the mean was 82. He also found that the standard deviation for the test scores was 27. Based on the information given, what observation could be made from the test scores of Mr. Potts' students?

(A) Some of the students scored 27 on the test.

(B) There were 27 students who took the test.

(C) The highest score earned was 82.

(D) On average, each student's test score was 27 points from the mean.

SOLUTION

The mean is found by adding all of the test scores and dividing by the number of tests. We are told that the mean of the scores was 82. We do not know how many students took the test, so answer choice (B) cannot be correct. We also do not know any of the individual test scores, so answer choices (A) and (C) cannot be correct. The standard deviation tells, on average, how far each test score is from the mean. In this case, the standard deviation is 27, which means that the scores were not grouped tightly around the mean of 82. Answer choice (D) is the correct answer.

PROBLEM

The weekly salaries of 12 employees in a company are listed below:

(500, 500, 500, 500, 500, 550, 550, 550, 600, 800, 825, 950)

Which measure of central tendency will be the highest: the mean, median, or the mode?

(A) The mode and mean will be the highest.

(B) The mean and the median will be the highest.

(C) The mean will be the highest.

(D) The median will be the highest.

SOLUTION

Even though the mean, median, and mode are all measures of central tendency, they may not be the same value, depending on the values of the data. Solving this problem is not as difficult as you may think. It is easy to find the mode; it is 500. It is easy to find the median; it is 550. The mean, however, is harder to find, but it is not necessary to find its exact value to answer this question correctly. Notice that there are some larger values in the data. These values will pull the mean up above 500 and 550. Therefore, you know that answer choice (C) is the correct answer. (The actual mean is approximately 610.) If you state the average weekly salary is $610, that is accurate, but you are referring to the mean. If you state the average weekly salary is $500, that is also accurate, but that is the mode. That is, you can describe the "average" using three different numbers, and all will communicate something slightly different.

5.4: Identify how the measures of central tendency (i.e., mean, median, or mode) can lead to different interpretations.

Sometimes one measure of central tendency is a better representation of the data than another. The mode is useful when data is qualitative rather than quantitative. That is, if a group of people is asked their favorite movie, their answers will be movie titles and not numbers. The best way to indicate the movie that most people named as their favorite is to use the mode. In a group of data, if there is a number or numbers that is much larger or much smaller than most of the data, it is called an **outlier**. When looking at data that has no outliers and is evenly spread out, any of the three measures of central tendency may be good. However, if a data set has an outlier or two, the mean will be skewed by these very high or very low values; as a result, it would not be the best representation of the data.

PROBLEM

A company has 90 employees. Eighty-nine employees make $50,000 a year, and one employee makes $2,000,000 a year. Which measure of central tendency would be the least representative of the data?

(A) the mean

(B) the median

(C) the mode

(D) All measures of central tendency would be equally representative.

SOLUTION

Notice that in this problem, all but one piece of the data are the same value. There is only one value that is much higher than all of the others. As a result, the mean will pull the "average" up, while the mode and the median will be $50,000. Therefore, the mean would be least representative of the data. Answer choice (A) is the correct answer.

5.5: Calculate the probability of a specified outcome.

Probability is a measure of how likely it is for an event to occur. To find the probability of an event occurring, you need to write a ratio. The numerator of the ratio is the number of times the favorable event will occur, and the denominator is the total number of events possible. For example, if you toss a penny, the probability that the penny will land tails up is $\frac{1}{2}$ because there is one tails and two possible outcomes (heads or tails). Another example is if you want to find the probability of choosing a caramel-filled chocolate out of a box of chocolates, you need to know how many chocolates are caramel-filled and how many chocolates there are total. So, if there are 8 caramel-filled chocolates and there are 24 chocolates in the box, then the probability of choosing a caramel-filled chocolate from the box at random is $\frac{8}{24}$. It is customary to write a probability ratio in lowest terms, so the probability of choosing a caramel-filled chocolate from the box can also be written as $\frac{1}{3}$.

PROBLEM

> A bag contains 12 blue tiles, 6 red tiles, and 2 green tiles. What is the probability that you will select a green tile if you pick a tile from the bag at random?
>
> (A) $\dfrac{2}{18}$ (B) $\dfrac{2}{20}$ (C) $\dfrac{1}{20}$ (D) $\dfrac{1}{18}$

SOLUTION

To find the probability of selecting a green tile at random, you must know how many green tiles there are and how many tiles there are total (including the green tiles). There are 2 green tiles and a total of 20 tiles. So the probability of choosing a green tile is $\dfrac{2}{20}$. Answer choice (B) is correct.

5.6: Solve and interpret real-world problems involving probability using counting procedures, tables, tree diagrams, and the concepts of permutations and combinations.

There are a multitude of problems that can be solved using probability. The important thing is to recognize what type of problem you are presented with so that you will know how to solve it correctly. The **Fundamental Counting Principle** is a method used to calculate all of the possible combinations of a given number of events. If an event has m possible outcomes and another independent event has n possible outcomes, then there are $m \times n$ possible outcomes for the two events to occur together. Let's look at specific example. If you are choosing an outfit to wear from 2 pairs of pants and 3 shirts (assuming all outfits will match), there are 6 possible outfits for you to wear because $2 \times 3 = 6$.

PROBLEM

> Laura has a 4-digit combination lock on her briefcase, and she has forgotten the combination. If she remembers that the first digit is a 5, and the second digit is prime, how many numbers must Laura try before the lock is sure to open?
>
> (A) 40   (B) 400   (C) 100   (D) 1000

SOLUTION

This problem can be solved using the fundamental counting principle. There are four digits in the combination lock. The first digit is a 5, which means there is only one possibility for that digit. The second number is prime, which means there are four possible numbers for that digit (the prime numbers between

0 and 9 are 2, 3, 5, and 7). The problem does not give any information about the third and the fourth digits, which means that there are 10 possible numbers for each of the third and fourth digits. To find the final answer, solve the following: $1 \times 4 \times 10 \times 10$, which equals 400. The correct answer is (B).

Tree diagrams

In probability, the **sample space** is the set of all possible outcomes of an event. For example, the sample space for throwing a six-sided number cube is (1, 2, 3, 4, 5, 6). When more than one event is occurring at the same time, it is sometimes helpful to illustrate the sample space with a tree diagram. In such a way, you can see all the possible outcomes. A tree diagram shows all the possible outcomes of an event in a diagram that looks like branches of a tree. Below is a tree diagram showing all possible outcomes when tossing two coins. The last column shows in words what the tree diagram shows in branches. That is, the four ways two coins could land are (Head, Head), (Head, Tail), (Tail, Head), and (Tail, Tail).

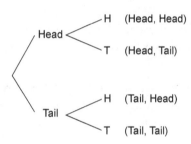

PROBLEM

Caroline tossed three coins. Use the tree diagram below to find the probability that only one of the three coins will land on heads.

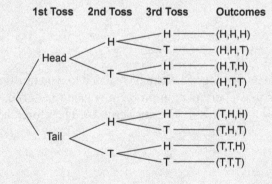

(A) $\dfrac{3}{8}$ (B) $\dfrac{1}{2}$ (C) $\dfrac{1}{4}$ (D) $\dfrac{5}{8}$

SOLUTION

The last column of the tree diagram shows the various ways three coins can land. Count the ways that show one head only (and two tails) to find that the answer is $\frac{3}{8}$, which is answer choice (A).

Permutations

A permutation is a list of all possible arrangements of a collection of items. Order is important. An example of a problem that is a permutation problem follows. Let's say you have 3 pictures to put up on the wall in a row. How many different arrangements are possible? To illustrate this problem before showing the mathematical way to solve it, let's call each of the pictures A, B, and C. Below lists the different ways the pictures can be hung.

ABC   ACB   BAC   BCA   CAB   CBA

As you can see, there are six different ways. The answer to this problem can be solved by solving 3! which means $3 \times 2 \times 1$. 3! is translated as 3 factorial.

If you wanted to find the number of ways you could put 4 pictures on a wall in a row, you could list all the permutations, but that would take a long time and might be confusing. To find the answer, find 4! which is $4 \times 3 \times 2 \times 1$. There are 24 ways to arrange four pictures in a row on a wall.

PROBLEM

Danny bought 4 new CDs. In how many different orders can he listen to his 4 CDs?

    (A) 16   (B) 24   (C) 12   (D) 4

SOLUTION

To find the different orders that four CDs can be listened to, you must recognize that this is a permutation problem. The way to solve a permutation problem is using factorial. Since there are four items, the answer is 4! which means $4 \times 3 \times 2 \times 1$. The answer is 24. Therefore, the correct answer choice is (B).

Combinations

A combination is a way of selecting several things out of a larger group where order does not matter. For example, if you are choosing three books from your bookshelf (which has 25 books) to take on vacation with you, the order that you choose the books does not matter. That is, they are the same three books no matter what order you choose them. The formula for combinations of *n* objects taken *r* at a time is written $_nC_r = \dfrac{n!}{r!(n-r)!}$.

To solve the problem described above using the combinations formula, substitute the numbers given into the formula.

$$\frac{25!}{3!(25-3)!} = \frac{25!}{3!(22!)} = 2300$$

There are 2300 ways you can select 3 books from 25.

PROBLEM

There are 10 students in the chess club. If the teacher wants to choose 3 students to represent the chess club during the next school assembly, how many different groups of 3 students can he choose?

(A) 30 (B) 120 (C) 600 (D) 300

SOLUTION

In order to solve this problem correctly, you must identify it as a combinations problem. Notice that the order the three students are picked is not important. The students John, Carol, and Tanisha are the same three students as Tanisha, John, and Carol, for example. Substituting the values of 10 and 3 in the combinations formula, you will find that there are 120 ways to select 3 students from 10. $\dfrac{10!}{3!(10-3)!} = \dfrac{10!}{3!(7!)} = 120$.

Drill Section for Competency 1

Drill: Integers and Real Numbers

Addition

1. Simplify $4 + (-7) + 2 + (-5)$.

   (A) -6 (B) -4 (C) 0 (D) 6 (E) 18

2. Simplify $144 + (-317) + 213$.

   (A) -357 (B) -40 (C) 40 (D) 257 (E) 674

3. What integer makes the equation $-13 + 12 + 7 + ? = 10$ a true statement?

   (A) -22 (B) -10 (C) 4 (D) 6 (E) 10

4. Simplify $4 + 17 + (-29) + 13 + (-22) + (-3)$.

   (A) -44 (B) -20 (C) 23 (D) 34 (E) 78

Subtraction

5. Simplify $319 - 428$.

   (A) -111 (B) -109 (C) -99 (D) 109 (E) 747

6. Simplify $91{,}203 - 37{,}904 + 1{,}073$.

   (A) $54{,}372$ (B) $64{,}701$ (C) $128{,}034$ (D) $129{,}107$ (E) $130{,}180$

7. Simplify $|43 - 62| - |-17 - 3|$.

   (A) -39 (B) -19 (C) -1 (D) 1 (E) 39

8. Simplify $-(-4 - 7) + (-2)$.

   (A) -22 (B) -13 (C) -9 (D) 7 (E) 9

9. In the St. Elias Mountains, Mt. Logan rises from 1,292 meters above sea level to 7,243 meters above sea level. How tall is Mt. Logan?

   (A) $4{,}009$ m   (B) $5{,}951$ m   (C) $5{,}699$ m   (D) $6{,}464$ m   (E) $7{,}885$ m

Multiplication

10. Simplify $(-3) \times (-18) \times (-1)$.

    (A) -108 (B) -54 (C) -48 (D) 48 (E) 54

11. Simplify $|-42| \times |7|$.

    (A) -294 (B) -49 (C) -35 (D) 284 (E) 294

12. Simplify $(-6) \times 5 \times (-10) \times (-4) \times 0 \times 2$.

    (A) $-2,400$ (B) -240 (C) 0 (D) 280 (E) $2,700$

13. Simplify $-|-6 \times 8|$.

    (A) -48 (B) -42 (C) 2 (D) 42 (E) 48

14. A city in Georgia had a record low temperature of $-3°F$ one winter. During the same year, a city in Michigan experienced a record low that was nine times the record low set in Georgia. What was the record low in Michigan that year?

    (A) $-31°F$ (B) $-27°F$ (C) $-21°F$ (D) $-12°F$ (E) $-6°F$

Division

15. Simplify $(-24) \div 8$.

    (A) -4 (B) -3 (C) -2 (D) 3 (E) 4

16. Simplify $(-180) \div (-12)$.

    (A) -30 (B) -15 (C) 1.5 (D) 15 (E) 216

17. Simplify $|-76| \div |-4|$.

    (A) -21 (B) -19 (C) 13 (D) 19 (E) 21.5

18. Simplify $|216 \div (-6)|$

    (A) -36 (B) -12 (C) 36 (D) 38 (E) 43

19. At the end of the year, a small firm has $2,996 in its account for bonuses. If the entire amount is equally divided among the 14 employees, how much does each one receive?

    (A) $107   (B) $114   (C) $170   (D) $210   (E) $214

Order of Operations

20. Simplify $\dfrac{4+8\times 2}{5-1}$.

    (A) 4   (B) 5   (C) 6   (D) 8   (E) 12

21. $96 \div 3 \div 4 \div 2 =$
    (A) 65   (B) 64   (C) 16   (D) 8   (E) 4

22. $3 + 4 \times 2 - 6 \div 3 =$

    (A) -1 (B) $\dfrac{5}{3}$ (C) $\dfrac{8}{3}$ (D) 9   (E) 12

23. $[(4+8) \times 3] \div 9 =$
    (A) 4   (B) 8   (C) 12   (D) 24   (E) 36

24. $18 + 3 \times 4 \div 3 =$
    (A) 3   (B) 5   (C) 10   (D) 22   (E) 28

25. $(29 - 17 + 4) \div 4 + |-2| =$

    (A) $2\dfrac{2}{3}$ (B) 4   (C) $4\dfrac{2}{3}$ (D) 6   (E) 15

26. $(-3) \times 5 - 20 \div 4 =$

    (A) -75 (B) -20 (C) -10 (D) $-8\dfrac{3}{4}$ (E) 20

27. $\dfrac{11 \times 2 + 2}{16 - 2 \times 2} =$

    (A) $\dfrac{11}{16}$ (B) 1   (C) 2   (D) $3\dfrac{2}{3}$ (E) 4

28. $|-8 - 4| \div 3 \times 6 + (-4) =$
    (A) 20   (B) 26   (C) 32   (D) 62   (E) 212

29. $32 \div 2 + 4 - 15 \div 3 =$
    (A) 0   (B) 7   (C) 15   (D) 23   (E) 63

30. Simplify $|4 + (-3)| + |-2|$.
    (A) -2 (B) -1 (C) 1   (D) 3   (E) 9

Drill: Fractions

Changing an Improper Fraction to a Mixed Number

➤ **Directions:** Write each improper fraction as a mixed number in simplest form.

1. $\dfrac{50}{4}$

    (A) $10\dfrac{1}{4}$　　(B) $11\dfrac{1}{2}$　　(C) $12\dfrac{1}{4}$　　(D) $12\dfrac{1}{2}$　　(E) 25

2. $\dfrac{17}{5}$

    (A) $3\dfrac{2}{5}$　　(B) $3\dfrac{3}{5}$　　(C) $3\dfrac{4}{5}$　　(D) $4\dfrac{1}{5}$　　(E) $4\dfrac{2}{5}$

3. $\dfrac{42}{3}$

    (A) $10\dfrac{2}{3}$　　(B) 12　　(C) $13\dfrac{1}{3}$　　(D) 14　　(E) $21\dfrac{1}{3}$

Changing a Mixed Number to an Improper Fraction

➤ **Directions:** Change each mixed number to an improper fraction in simplest form.

4. $2\dfrac{3}{5}$

    (A) $\dfrac{4}{5}$　　(B) $\dfrac{6}{5}$　　(C) $\dfrac{11}{5}$　　(D) $\dfrac{13}{5}$　　(E) $\dfrac{17}{5}$

5. $4\dfrac{3}{4}$

    (A) $\dfrac{7}{4}$　　(B) $\dfrac{13}{4}$　　(C) $\dfrac{16}{3}$　　(D) $\dfrac{19}{4}$　　(E) $\dfrac{21}{4}$

6. $6\dfrac{7}{6}$

    (A) $\dfrac{13}{6}$　　(B) $\dfrac{43}{6}$　　(C) $\dfrac{19}{36}$　　(D) $\dfrac{42}{36}$　　(E) $\dfrac{48}{6}$

Adding Fractions with the Same Denominator

➤ **Directions:** Add and write the answer in simplest form or as a mixed number.

7. $\dfrac{5}{12} + \dfrac{3}{12} =$

   (A) $\dfrac{5}{24}$ (B) $\dfrac{1}{3}$ (C) $\dfrac{8}{12}$ (D) $\dfrac{2}{3}$ (E) $1\dfrac{1}{3}$

8. $\dfrac{5}{8} + \dfrac{7}{8} + \dfrac{3}{8} =$

   (A) $\dfrac{15}{24}$ (B) $\dfrac{3}{4}$ (C) $\dfrac{5}{6}$ (D) $\dfrac{7}{8}$ (E) $1\dfrac{7}{8}$

9. $131\dfrac{2}{15} + 28\dfrac{3}{15} =$

   (A) $159\dfrac{1}{6}$ (B) $159\dfrac{1}{5}$ (C) $159\dfrac{1}{3}$ (D) $159\dfrac{1}{2}$ (E) $159\dfrac{3}{5}$

Subtracting Fractions with the Same Denominator

➤ **Directions:** Subtract and write the answer in simplest form or as a mixed number.

10. $4\dfrac{7}{8} - 3\dfrac{1}{8} =$

   (A) $1\dfrac{1}{4}$ (B) $1\dfrac{3}{4}$ (C) $1\dfrac{12}{16}$ (D) $1\dfrac{7}{8}$ (E) 2

11. $132\dfrac{5}{12} - 37\dfrac{3}{12} =$

   (A) $94\dfrac{1}{6}$ (B) $95\dfrac{1}{12}$ (C) $95\dfrac{1}{6}$ (D) $105\dfrac{1}{6}$ (E) $169\dfrac{2}{3}$

12. $19\dfrac{1}{3} - 2\dfrac{2}{3} =$

   (A) $16\dfrac{2}{3}$ (B) $16\dfrac{5}{6}$ (C) $17\dfrac{1}{3}$ (D) $17\dfrac{2}{3}$ (E) $17\dfrac{5}{6}$

Finding the LCD

➤ **Directions:** Find the lowest common denominator of each group of fractions.

13. $\frac{2}{3}, \frac{5}{9},$ and $\frac{1}{6}$

(A) 9   (B) 18   (C) 27   (D) 54   (E) 162

14. $\frac{7}{16}, \frac{5}{6},$ and $\frac{2}{3}$

(A) 3   (B) 6   (C) 12   (D) 24   (E) 48

15. $\frac{2}{3}, \frac{1}{5},$ and $\frac{5}{6}$

(A) 15   (B) 30   (C) 48   (D) 90   (E) 120

16. $\frac{4}{9}, \frac{2}{5},$ and $\frac{1}{3}$

(A) 15   (B) 17   (C) 27   (D) 45   (E) 135

17. $\frac{3}{7}, \frac{5}{21},$ and $\frac{2}{3}$

(A) 21   (B) 42   (C) 31   (D) 63   (E) 441

Adding Fractions with Different Denominators

➤ **Directions:** Add and write the answer in simplest form.

18. $\frac{1}{3} + \frac{5}{12} =$

(A) $\frac{2}{5}$ (B) $\frac{1}{2}$ (C) $\frac{9}{12}$ (D) $\frac{3}{4}$ (E) $1\frac{1}{3}$

19. $12\frac{9}{16} + 17\frac{3}{4} + 8\frac{1}{8} =$

(A) $37\frac{7}{16}$ (B) $38\frac{7}{16}$ (C) $38\frac{1}{2}$ (D) $38\frac{2}{3}$ (E) $39\frac{3}{16}$

20. $28\dfrac{4}{5}+11\dfrac{16}{25}=$

    (A) $39\dfrac{2}{3}$ (B) $39\dfrac{4}{5}$ (C) $40\dfrac{9}{25}$ (D) $40\dfrac{2}{5}$ (E) $40\dfrac{11}{25}$

Subtracting Fractions with Different Denominators

➤ **Directions:** Subtract and write the answer in simplest form.

21. $8\dfrac{9}{12}-2\dfrac{2}{3}=$

    (A) $6\dfrac{1}{12}$ (B) $6\dfrac{1}{6}$ (C) $6\dfrac{1}{3}$ (D) $6\dfrac{7}{12}$ (E) $6\dfrac{2}{3}$

22. $185\dfrac{11}{15}-107\dfrac{2}{5}=$

    (A) $77\dfrac{2}{15}$ (B) $78\dfrac{1}{5}$ (C) $78\dfrac{3}{10}$ (D) $78\dfrac{1}{3}$ (E) $78\dfrac{9}{15}$

23. $34\dfrac{2}{3}-16\dfrac{5}{6}=$

    (A) 16 (B) $16\dfrac{1}{3}$ (C) 17 (D) 17 (E) $17\dfrac{5}{6}$

Multiplying Fractions

➤ **Directions:** Multiply and reduce the answer.

24. $\dfrac{2}{3}\times\dfrac{4}{5}=$

    (A) $\dfrac{6}{8}$ (B) $\dfrac{3}{4}$ (C) $\dfrac{8}{15}$ (D) $\dfrac{10}{12}$ (E) $\dfrac{6}{5}$

25. $5\dfrac{1}{3}\times\dfrac{3}{8}=$

    (A) $\dfrac{4}{11}$ (B) 2 (C) $\dfrac{8}{5}$ (D) $5\dfrac{1}{8}$ (E) $5\dfrac{17}{24}$

26. $6\frac{1}{2} \times 3 =$

   (A) $9\frac{1}{2}$ (B) $18\frac{1}{2}$ (C) $19\frac{1}{2}$ (D) 20   (E) $12\frac{1}{2}$

Dividing Fractions

➤ **Directions:** Divide and reduce the answer.

27. $\frac{3}{16} \div \frac{3}{4} =$

   (A) $\frac{9}{64}$ (B) $\frac{1}{4}$ (C) $\frac{6}{16}$ (D) $\frac{9}{16}$ (E) $\frac{3}{4}$

28. $\frac{4}{9} \div \frac{2}{3} =$

   (A) $\frac{1}{3}$ (B) $\frac{1}{2}$ (C) $\frac{2}{3}$ (D) $\frac{7}{11}$ (E) $\frac{8}{9}$

29. $5\frac{1}{4} \div \frac{7}{10} =$

   (A) $2\frac{4}{7}$ (B) $3\frac{27}{40}$ (C) $5\frac{19}{20}$ (D) $7\frac{1}{2}$ (E) $8\frac{1}{4}$

Drill: Decimals

Addition

➤ **Directions:** Perform the following additions.

1. $1.032 + 0.987 + 3.07 =$
   (A) 4.089   (B) 5.089   (C) 5.189   (D) 6.189   (E) 13.972

2. $7.1 + 0.62 + 4.03827 + 5.183 =$
   (A) 0.2315127   (B) 16.45433   (C) 16.94127   (D) 18.561   (E) 40.4543

3.   8 + 17.43 + 9.2 =

(A) 34.63   (B) 34.86   (C) 35.63   (D) 176.63   (E) 189.43

Subtraction

➤ **Directions:** Perform the following subtractions.

4.   16.047 − 13.06 =

(A) 2.887   (B) 2.987   (C) 3.041   (D) 3.141   (E) 4.741

5.   87.4 − 56.27 =

(A) 30.27   (B) 30.67   (C) 31.1   (D) 31.13   (E) 31.27

6.   1,046.8 − 639.14 =

(A) 303.84   (B) 313.74   (C) 407.66   (D) 489.74   (E) 535.54

Multiplication

➤ **Directions:** Perform the following multiplications.

7.   1.03 × 2.6 =

(A) 2.18   (B) 2.678   (C) 2.78   (D) 3.38   (E) 3.63

8.   93 × 4.2 =

(A) 39.06   (B) 97.2   (C) 223.2   (D) 390.6   (E) 3,906

9.   0.04 × 0.23 =

(A) 0.0092   (B) 0.092   (C) 0.27   (D) 0.87   (E) 0.920

Division

➤ **Directions:** Perform the following divisions.

10.   123.39 ÷ 3 =

(A) 31.12   (B) 41.13   (C) 401.13   (D) 411.3   (E) 4,113

11.   1,428.6 ÷ 6

(A) 0.2381   (B) 2.381   (C) 23.81   (D) 238.1   (E) 2,381

12. $25.2 \div 0.3 =$

    (A) 0.84   (B) 8.04   (C) 8.4   (D) 84   (E) 840

Comparing

➤ **Directions:** Answer the following questions.

13. In which set below are the numbers arranged correctly from smallest to largest?

    (A) {0.98, 0.9, 0.993}   (B) {0.113, 0.3, 0.31}

    (C) {7.04, 7.26, 7.2}   (D) {0.006, 0.061, 0.06}

    (E) {12.84, 12.801, 12.6}

14. In which set below are the numbers arranged correctly from largest to smallest?

    (A) {1.018, 1.63, 1.368}   (B) {4.219, 4.29, 4.9}

    (C) {0.62, 0.6043, 0.643}   (D) {16.34, 16.304, 16.3}

    (E) {12.98, 12.601, 12.86}

15. Which is the **largest** number in this set—{0.87, 0.89, 0.889, 0.8, 0.987}?

    (A) 0.87   (B) 0.89   (C) 0.889   (D) 0.8   (E) 0.987

Drill: Percent

Finding Percents

➤ **Directions:** Solve to find the correct percentages.

1. Find 3% of 80.

    (A) 0.24   (B) 2.4   (C) 24   (D) 240   (E) 2,400

2. Find 125% of 400.

    (A) 425   (B) 500   (C) 525   (D) 600   (E) 825

3. Find 300% of 4.

    (A) 12   (B) 120   (C) 1,200   (D) 12,000   (E) 120,000

4. Forty-eight percent of the 1,200 students at Central High are males. How many male students are there at Central High?

    (A) 57   (B) 576   (C) 580   (D) 600   (E) 648

5. Of every 1,000 people who take a certain medicine, 0.2% develop severe side effects. How many people out of every 1,000 who take the medicine develop the side effects?

    (A) 0.2   (B) 2   (C) 20   (D) 22   (E) 200

6. Of 220 applicants for a job, 75% were offered an initial interview. How many people were offered an initial interview?

    (A) 75   (B) 110   (C) 120   (D) 155   (E) 165

Changing Percents to Fractions

➤ **Directions:** Solve to find the correct fractions.

7. What is 25% written as a fraction?

    (A) $\dfrac{1}{25}$ (B) $\dfrac{1}{5}$ (C) $\dfrac{1}{4}$ (D) $\dfrac{1}{3}$ (E) $\dfrac{1}{2}$

8. What is 200% written as a fraction?

    (A) $\dfrac{1}{2}$ (B) $\dfrac{2}{1}$ (C) $\dfrac{20}{1}$ (D) $\dfrac{200}{1}$ (E) $\dfrac{2,000}{1}$

9. What is 2% written as a fraction?

    (A) $\dfrac{1}{50}$ (B) $\dfrac{1}{25}$ (C) $\dfrac{1}{10}$ (D) $\dfrac{1}{4}$ (E) $\dfrac{1}{2}$

Changing Fractions to Percents

➤ **Directions:** Solve to find the following percentages.

10. What is $\dfrac{3}{5}$ written as a percent?

    (A) 30%   (B) 35%   (C) 53%   (D) 60%   (E) 65%

11. What is $\dfrac{17}{20}$ written as a percent?

    (A) 17%   (B) 70%   (C) 75%   (D) 80%   (E) 85%

12. What is $1\dfrac{1}{4}$ written as a percent?

    (A) 114%   (B) 120%   (C) 125%   (D) 127%   (E) 133%

Changing Percents to Decimals

➤ **Directions:** Convert the percentages to decimals.

13. What is 42% written as a decimal?

(A) 0.42   (B) 4.2   (C) 42   (D) 420   (E) 422

14. What is 8% written as a decimal?

(A) 0.0008   (B) 0.008   (C) 0.08   (D) 0.80   (E) 8

15. What is 34% written as a decimal?

(A) 0.00034   (B) 0.0034   (C) 0.034   (D) 0.34   (E) 3.4

Changing Decimals to Percents

➤ **Directions:** Convert the following decimals to percents.

16. What is 1 written as a percent?

(A) 1%   (B) 10%   (C) 100%   (D) 111%   (E) 150%

17. What is 0.08 written as a percent?

(A) 0.08%   (B) 8%   (C) 8.8%   (D) 80%   (E) 800%

18. What is 0.645 written as a percent?

(A) 64.5%   (B) 65%   (C) 69%   (D) 70%   (E) 645%

Drill: Radicals

Multiplication

➤ **Directions:** Multiply and simplify each answer.

1. $\sqrt{6} \times \sqrt{5} =$

(A) $\sqrt{11}$ (B) $\sqrt{30}$ (C) $2\sqrt{5}$ (D) $3\sqrt{10}$ (E) $2\sqrt{3}$

2. $\sqrt{3} \times \sqrt{12} =$

(A) 3   (B) $\sqrt{15}$ (C) $\sqrt{36}$ (D) 6   (E) 8

Division

➤ **Directions:** Divide and simplify the answer.

3. $\sqrt{10} \div \sqrt{2} =$

   (A) $\sqrt{8}$ (B) $2\sqrt{2}$ (C) $\sqrt{5}$ (D) $2\sqrt{5}$ (E) $2\sqrt{3}$

4. $\sqrt{30} \div \sqrt{15} =$

   (A) $\sqrt{2}$ (B) $\sqrt{45}$ (C) $3\sqrt{5}$ (D) $\sqrt{15}$ (E) $5\sqrt{3}$

Addition

➤ **Directions:** Simplify each radical and add.

5. $\sqrt{7} + 3\sqrt{7} =$

   (A) $3\sqrt{7}$ (B) $4\sqrt{7}$ (C) $3\sqrt{14}$ (D) $4\sqrt{14}$ (E) $3\sqrt{21}$

6. $\sqrt{5} + 6\sqrt{5} + 3\sqrt{5} =$

   (A) $9\sqrt{5}$ (B) $9\sqrt{15}$ (C) $5\sqrt{10}$ (D) $10\sqrt{5}$ (E) $18\sqrt{15}$

Subtraction

➤ **Directions:** Simplify each radical and subtract.

7. $8\sqrt{5} - 6\sqrt{5} =$

   (A) $2\sqrt{5}$ (B) $3\sqrt{5}$ (C) $4\sqrt{5}$ (D) $14\sqrt{5}$ (E) $48\sqrt{5}$

8. $16\sqrt{33} - 5\sqrt{33} =$

   (A) $3\sqrt{33}$ (B) $33\sqrt{11}$ (C) $11\sqrt{33}$ (D) $11\sqrt{0}$ (E) $\sqrt{33}$

Drill: Exponents

Multiplication

➤ **Directions:** Simplify.

1. $4^6 \times 4^2 =$

   (A) 4^4 (B) 4^8 (C) 4^{12} (D) 16^8 (E) 16^{12}

2. $2^2 \times 2^5 \times 2^3 =$

   (A) 2^{10} (B) 4^{10} (C) 8^{10} (D) 2^{30} (E) 8^{30}

3. $m^8 n^3 \times m^2 n \times m^4 n^2 =$

   (A) $3m^{16}n^6$ (B) $m^{14}n^6$ (C) $3m^{14}n^5$ (D) $3m^{14}n^5$ (E) m^2

Division

➤ **Directions:** Simplify.

4. $6^5 \div 6^3 =$

   (A) 0 (B) 1 (C) 6 (D) 12 (E) 36

5. $x^{10}y^8 \div x^7 y^3 =$

   (A) $x^2 y^5$ (B) $x^3 y^4$ (C) $x^3 y^5$ (D) $x^2 y^4$ (E) $x^5 y^3$

Power to a Power

➤ **Directions:** Simplify.

6. $(3^6)^2 =$

   (A) 3^4 (B) 3^8 (C) 3^{12} (D) 9^{12} (E) 9^8

7. $(a^4 b^3)^2 =$

   (A) $(ab)^9$ (B) $a^8 b^6$ (C) $(ab)^{24}$ (D) $a^6 b^5$ (E) $2a^4 b^3$

8. $(m^6 n^5 q^3)^2 =$

   (A) $2m^6 n^5 q^3$ (B) $m^4 n^3 q$ (C) $m^8 n^7 q^5$ (D) $m^{12} n^{10} q^6$ (E) $2m^{12} n^{10} q^6$

Competency 1: Arithmetic Drills Answer Key

Drill: Integers and Real Numbers

1. (A)	7. (C)	13. (A)	19. (E)	25. (D)
2. (C)	8. (E)	14. (B)	20. (B)	26. (B)
3. (C)	9. (B)	15. (B)	21. (E)	27. (C)
4. (B)	10. (B)	16. (D)	22. (D)	28. (A)
5. (B)	11. (E)	17. (D)	23. (A)	29. (C)
6. (A)	12. (C)	18. (C)	24. (D)	30. (D)

Drill: Fractions

1. (D)	7. (D)	13. (B)	19. (B)	25. (B)
2. (A)	8. (E)	14. (E)	20. (E)	26. (C)
3. (D)	9. (C)	15. (B)	21. (A)	27. (B)
4. (D)	10. (B)	16. (D)	22. (D)	28. (C)
5. (D)	11. (C)	17. (A)	23. (E)	29. (D)
6. (B)	12. (A)	18. (D)	24. (C)	

Drill: Decimals

1. (B)	4. (B)	7. (B)	10. (B)	13. (B)
2. (C)	5. (D)	8. (D)	11. (D)	14. (D)
3. (A)	6. (C)	9. (A)	12. (D)	15. (E)

Drill: Percent

1. (B)	5. (B)	8. (A)	13. (A)	17. (B)
2. (B)	6. (E)	10. (D)	14. (C)	18. (A)
3. (A)	7. (C)	11. (E)	15. (D)	
4. (B)	7. (B)	12. (C)	16. (C)	

Drill: Radicals

1. (B)	5. (B)
2. (D)	6. (D)
3. (C)	7. (A)
4. (A)	8. (C)

Drill: Exponents

1. (B)	5. (C)
2. (A)	6. (C)
3. (B)	7. (B)
4. (E)	8. (D)

Drill Section for Competency 2

Drill: Measurement

1. A brick walkway measuring 3 feet by 11 feet is to be built. The bricks measure 4 inches by 6 inches. How many bricks will it take to complete the walkway?

    (A) 132　　　(B) 198　　　(C) 330　　　(D) 1927　　　(E) 4752

2. A wall to be papered is three times as long as it is wide. The total area to be covered is 192 ft². Wall-paper comes in rolls that are 2 feet wide by 8 feet long. How many rolls will it take to cover the wall?

    (A) 8　　　(B) 12　　　(C) 16　　　(D) 24　　　(E) 32

3. A bottle of medicine containing 2 kg is to be poured into smaller containers that hold 8 grams each. How many of these smaller containers can be filled from the 2 kg bottle?

    (A) 0.5　　　(B) 1　　　(C) 5　　　(D) 50　　　(E) 250

Drill: Metric Conversions

1. How many centimeters are in 4.8 meters?

    (A) .48　　　(B) 48　　　(C) 480　　　(D) 4,800　　　(E) 48,000

2. How many meters are in 330 millimeters?

    (A) .33　　　(B) 3.3　　　(C) 3,300　　　(D) 33,000　　　(E) 330,000

3. How many kilometers is 475 meters?

    (A) 4750　　　(B) 47.5　　　(C) 4.75　　　(D) .475　　　(E) .0475

4. How many millimeters in 7.3 centimeters?

    (A) .73　　　(B) 73　　　(C) 730　　　(D) 7,300　　　(E) 73,000

5. How many centimeters in 3560 millimeters?

    (A) 35.6　　　(B) 356　　　(C) 3,560　　　(D) 35,600　　　(E) 356,000

Drill: Customary Conversions

1. How many inches in 45 feet?

    (A) 3.75   (B) 540   (C) 1620   (D) 135   (E) 450

2. How many feet in 114 inches?

    (A) 9.5   (B) 1368   (C) 38   (D) 12.5   (E) 1140

3. How many miles in 14520 feet?

    (A) 1210   (B) $403\frac{1}{3}$ (C) 2.75   (D) 8.25   (E) 14.52

4. How many yards in 96 inches?

    (A) 8   (B) 288   (C) $2\frac{2}{3}$ (D) $10\frac{2}{3}$ (E) 467

Drill: Unit Price

1. Find the unit price: 18 pieces of gum for 90 cents

    (A) 0.04   (B) 0.05   (C) 0.06   (D) 16.20   (E) 1.62

2. Find the unit price: 8 balloons for $1.00

    (A) 0.125   (B) 1.25   (C) 8.00   (D) 0.80   (E) 0.08

Competency 2: Knowledge of Measurement Drill Answer Key

Drill: Measurement

1. (B)
2. (B)
3. (E)

Drill: Metric Conversions

1. (C) 4. (B)
2. (A) 5. (B)
3. (D)

Drill: Customary Conversions

1. (B) 3. (C)
2. (A) 4. (C)

Drill: Unit Price

1. (B)
2. (A)

Drill Section for Competency 3

Drill: Lines and Angles

Intersection Lines

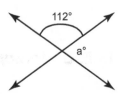

1. Find *a*.

    (A) 38°   (B) 68°   (C) 78°

    (D) 90°   (E) 112°

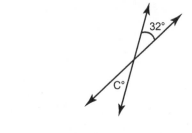

2. Find *c*.

    (A) 32°   (B) 48°   (C) 58°

    (D) 82°   (E) 148°

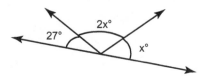

3. Determine *x*.

    (A) 21°   (B) 23°   (C) 51°

    (D) 102°   (E) 153°

Perpendicular Lines

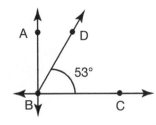

4. $\overline{BA} \perp \overline{BC}$ and $m \angle DBC = 53$. Find $m \angle ABD$.

    (A) 27°   (B) 33°   (C) 37°

    (D) 53°   (E) 90°

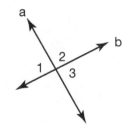

5. $m \angle 1 = 90°$. Find $m \angle 2$.

    (A) 80°   (B) 90°   (C) 100°

    (D) 135°   (E) 180°

6. If $n \perp p$, which of the following statements is true?

    (A) $\angle 1 \cong \angle 2$

    (B) $\angle 4 \cong \angle 5$

    (C) $m \angle 4 + m \angle 5 > m \angle 1 + m \angle 2$

    (D) $m \angle 3 > m \angle 2$

    (E) $m \angle 4 = 90°$

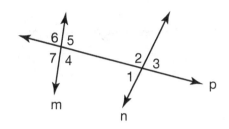

Drill: Triangles

Angle Measures

1. In $\triangle PQR$, $\angle Q$ is a right angle. Find $m \angle R$.

    (A) 27°   (B) 33°   (C) 54°

    (D) 67°   (E) 157°

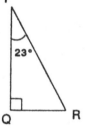

2. $\triangle MNO$ is isosceles. If the vertex angle, $\angle N$, has a measure of 96°, find the measure of $\angle M$.

    (A) 21°   (B) 42°   (C) 64°

    (D) 84°   (E) 96°

3. Find x.

    (A) 15°   (B) 25°   (C) 30°

    (D) 45°   (E) 90°

Similar Triangles

4. The two triangles shown are similar. Find b.

    (A) 2 2/3   (B) 3   (C) 4

    (D) 16   (E) 24

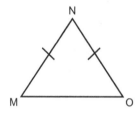

5. The two triangles shown are similar. Find $m \angle 1$.

    (A) 48   (B) 53   (C) 74

    (D) 127   (E) 180

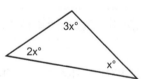

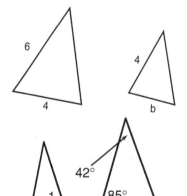

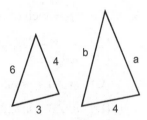

6. The two triangles shown are similar. Find *a* and *b*.

    (A) 5 and 10   (B) 4 and 8   (C) 4 2/3 and 7 1/3
    (D) 5 and 8   (E) 5 1/3 and 8

Area

7. Find the area of Δ *MNO*.

    (A) 22   (B) 49   (C) 56
    (D) 84   (E) 112

8. Find the area of Δ *STU*.

    (A) $4\sqrt{2}$ (B) $8\sqrt{2}$ (C) $12\sqrt{2}$
    (D) $16\sqrt{2}$ (E) $32\sqrt{2}$

9. Find the area of Δ *ABC*.

    (A) 54 cm²   (B) 81 cm²   (C) 108 cm²
    (D) 135 cm²   (E) 180 cm²

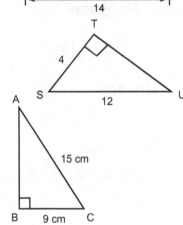

Drill: Quadrilaterals

Parallelograms, Rectangles, Rhombi, Squares, Trapezoids

1. Find the area of parallelogram *STUV*.

    (A) 56   (B) 90   (C) 108
    (D) 162   (E) 180

2. Find the perimeter of rectangle *PQRS*, if the area is 84 in².

    (A) 31 in   (B) 38 in   (C) 40 in
    (D) 44 in   (E) 121 in

3. In rectangle *ABCD*, *AD* = 6 cm and *DC* = 8 cm.
    Find the length of the diagonal *AC*.

    (A)   10 cm   (B)   12 cm   (C)   20 cm
    (D)   28 cm   (E)   48 cm

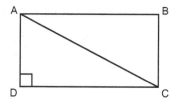

4. Find the area of rectangle *UVXY*.

    (A)   17 cm²   (B)   34 cm²   (C)   35 cm²
    (D)   70 cm²   (E)   140 cm²

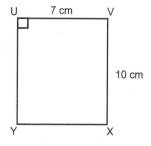

5. In rhombus *DEFG*, *DE* = 7 cm. Find the perimeter of the rhombus.

    (A)   14 cm   (B)   28 cm   (C)   42 cm
    (D)   49 cm   (E)   56 cm

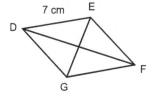

6. Quadrilateral *ATUV* is a square. If the perimeter of the square is 44 cm, find the length of $\overline{AT}$.

    (A)   4 cm   (B)   11 cm   (C)   22 cm   (D)   30 cm   (E)   40 cm

7. The area of square *XYZW* is 196 cm².
    Find the perimeter of the square.

    (A)   28 cm   (B)   42 cm   (C)   56 cm
    (D)   98 cm   (E)   196 cm.

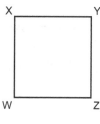

8. In square *MNOP*, *MN* is 6 cm. Find the length of diagonal $\overline{MO}$.

    (A)   6 cm   (B) $6\sqrt{2}$ cm   (C) $6\sqrt{3}$ cm
    (D) $6\sqrt{6}$ cm   (E)   12 cm

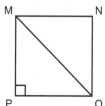

9.   In square *ABCD*, *AB* = 3 cm. Find the area of the square.

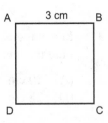

(A)   9 cm²   (B)   12 cm²   (C)   15 cm²
(D)   18 cm²   (E)   21 cm²

10.   *ABCD* is an isosceles trapezoid. Find the perimeter.

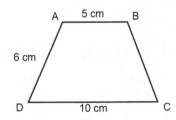

(A)   21 cm   (B)   27 cm   (C)   30 cm
(D)   50 cm   (E)   54 cm

11.   Trapezoid *XYZW* is isosceles. If $m \angle W = 58°$
and $m \angle Z = 4x - 6°$, find *x*.

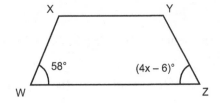

(A)   8   (B)   12   (C)   13
(D)   16   (E)   58

Drill: Circles

Circumference, Area, Concentric Circles

1.   Find the circumference of circle *A* if its radius is 3 mm.

(A) 3π mm   (B) 6π mm   (C) 9π mm   (D) 12π mm   (E) 15π mm

2.   The circumference of circle *H* is 20π cm. Find the length of the radius.

(A)   10 cm   (B)   20 cm   (C) 10π cm   (D) 15π cm   (E) 20π cm

3.   If the diameter of circle *X* is 9 cm and if $\pi = 3.14$, find the circumference of the circle to the nearest tenth.

(A)   9 cm   (B)   14.1 cm   (C)   21.1 cm   (D)   24.6 cm   (E)   28.3 cm

4.   Find the area of circle *I*.

(A)   22 mm²   (B)   121 mm²   (C)   121π mm²
(D)   132 mm²   (E)   132π mm²

5.   The diameter of circle *Z* is 27 mm. Find the area of the circle.

(A)   91.125 mm²   (B)   182.25 mm²   (C)   191.5π mm²
(D)   182.25π mm² (E)   729 mm²

6.   The area of circle *B* is 225π cm². Find the length of the diameter of the circle.

(A)   15 cm   (B)   20 cm   (C)   30 cm   (D)   20π cm   (E)   25π cm

Drill: Solids

1.   Find the surface area of the rectangular prism shown.

(A)   138 cm²   (B)   336 cm²   (C)   381 cm²
(D)   426 cm²   (E)   540 cm²

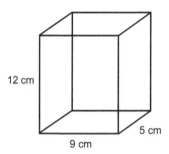

2.   Find the volume of the rectangular storage tank shown.

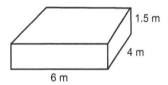

(A)   24 m³   (B)   36 m³   (C)   38 m³   (D)   42 m³   (E)   45 m³

Drill: Coordinate Geometry

1. Which point shown has the coordinates (–3, 2)?

   (A) A   (B) B   (C) C
   (D) D   (E) E

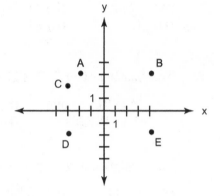

2. Name the coordinates of point A.

   (A) (4, 3)   (B) (3, –4)   (C) (3, 4)
   (D) (–4, 3)   (E) (4, –3)

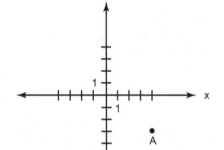

3. Which point shown has the coordinates (2.5, –1)?

   (A) M   (B) N   (C) P
   (D) Q   (E) R

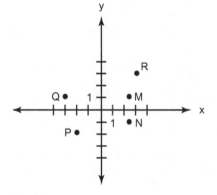

4. The correct *x*-coordinate for point *H* is what number?

    (A) 3   (B) 4   (C) –3

    (D) –4   (E) –5

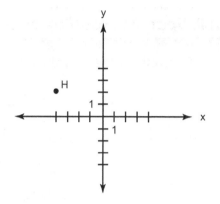

5. The correct *y*-coordinate for point *R* is what number?

    (A) –7   (B) 2   (C) –2

    (D) 7   (E) 8

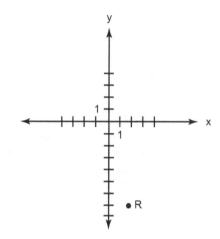

6. Find the distance between (4, –7) and (–2, –7).

    (A) 4   (B) 6   (C) 7   (D) 14   (E) 15

7. Find the distance between the point (–4, 2) and (3, –5).

    (A) 3   (B) $3\sqrt{3}$ (C) 7   (D) $7\sqrt{2}$ (E) $7\sqrt{3}$

Drill: Spatial Sense/Relationships

1. The triangle in Fig. 9 is reflected across the *y*-axis. Which one of the configurations, A to E, is the result?

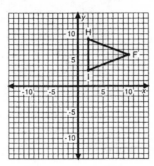

Fig. 9

(A)

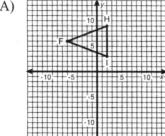

(D)

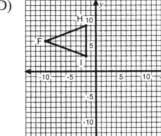

(B)

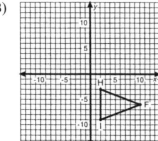

(E)

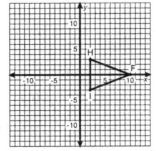

(C)

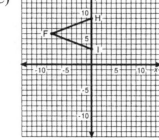

2.   In Fig. 10, which transformation will map $\triangle ABC$ onto $\triangle DEF$?

   (A)   Reflect $\triangle ABC$ over the y-axis and shift up 6 spaces.

   (B)   Reflect $\triangle ABC$ over the x-axis and shift up 6 spaces.

   (C)   Reflect $\triangle ABC$ over the y-axis and shift down 6 spaces.

   (D)   Reflect $\triangle ABC$ over the y-axis, reflect over the x-axis, and shift down 4 spaces.

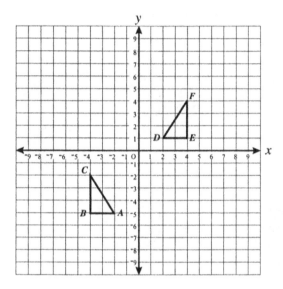

Fig. 10

Competency 3: Geometry and Spatial Sense Drills Answer Key

Drill: Lines and Angles

1. (B)	3. (C)	5. (B)
2. (A)	4. (C)	6. (A)

Drill: Triangles

1. (D)	4. (A)	7. (C)
2. (B)	5. (B)	8. (D)
3. (C)	6. (E)	9. (A)

Drill: Quadrilaterals

1. (D)	5. (B)	9. (A)
2. (C)	6. (B)	10. (B)
3. (A)	7. (C)	11. (D)
4. (D)	8. (B)	

Drill: Circles

1. (B)	4. (C)
2. (A)	5. (D)
3. (E)	6. (C)

Drill: Solids

1. (D)
2. (B)

Drill: Coordinate Geometry

1. (C)	5. (A)
2. (E)	6. (B)
3. (B)	7. (D)
4. (D)	

Drill: Spatial Sense/Relationships

1. (D)
2. (A)

Drill Section for Competency 4

Drill: Operations with Polynomials

Addition

➤ **Directions:** Add the following polynomials.

1. $14m^2n^3 + 6m^2n^3 + 3m^2n^3 =$

    (A) $20m^2n^3$ (B) $23m^6n^9$ (C) $23m^2n^3$

    (D) $32m^6n^9$ (E) $23m^8n^{27}$

2. $3x + 2y + 16x + 3z + 6y =$

    (A) $19x + 8y$ (B) $19x + 11yz$ (C) $19x + 8y + 3z$

    (D) $11xy + 19xz$ (E) $30xyz$

3. $(4d^2 + 7e^3 + 12f) + (3d^2 + 6e^3 + 2f) =$

    (A) $23d^2e^3f$ (B) $33d^2e^2f$ (C) $33d^4e^6f^2$

    (D) $7d^2 + 13e^3 + 14f$ (E) $23d^2 + 11e^3f$

Subtraction

➤ **Directions:** Subtract the following polynomials.

4. $14m^2n - 6m^2n =$

    (A) $20m^2n$ (B) $8m^2n$ (C) $8m$

    (D) 8 (E) $8m^4n^2$

5. $7b^3 - 4c^2 - 6b^3 + 3c^2 =$

    (A) $b^3 - c^2$ (B) $-11b^2 - 3c^2$ (C) $13b^3 - c$

    (D) $7b - c$ (E) 0

Multiplication

➤ **Directions:** Multiply the following polynomials.

6. $5p^2t \times 3p^2t =$

    (A) $15p^2t$ (B) $15p^4t$ (C) $15p^4t^2$

    (D) $8p^2t$ (E) $8p^4t^2$

7. $(2r + s)\, 14r =$

    (A) $28rs$ (B) $28r^2 + 14sr$ (C) $16r^2 + 14rs$

    (D) $28r + 14sr$ (E) $17r^2s$

8. $(6t^2 + 2t + 1)\, 3t =$

    (A) $9t^2 + 5t + 3$ (B) $18t^2 + 6t + 3$ (C) $9t^3 + 6t^2 + 3t$

    (D) $18t^3 + 6t^2 + 3t$ (E) $12t^3 + 6t^2 + 3t$

Division

➤ **Directions:** Divide the following polynomials.

9. $24b^4c^3 \div 6b^2c =$

    (A) $3b^2c^2$ (B) $4b^4c^3$ (C) $4b^3c^2$

    (D) $4b^2c^2$ (E) $3b^4c^3$

Drill: Linear Equations

➤ **Directions:** Solve for x.

1. $4x - 2 = 10$

    (A) -1 (B)   2   (C)   3   (D)   4   (E)   6

2. $7z + 1 - z = 2z - 7$

    (A) -2 (B)   0   (C)   1   (D)   2   (E)   3

3. $\dfrac{1}{3}b + 3 = \dfrac{1}{2}b$

     (A) $\dfrac{1}{2}$ (B)   2   (C) $3\dfrac{3}{5}$ (D)   6   (E)   18

4. $0.4p + 1 = 0.7p - 2$

     (A)   0.1   (B)   2   (C)   5   (D)   10   (E)   12

5. $4(3x + 2) - 11 = 3(3x - 2)$

     (A)   –3   (B)   –1   (C)   2   (D)   3   (E)   7

Drill: Inequalities

➤ **Directions:** Find the solution set for each inequality.

1. $3m + 2 < 7$

     (A) $m \geq \dfrac{5}{3}$ (B) $m \leq 2$ (C) $m < 2$

     (D) $m > 2$ (E) $m < \dfrac{5}{3}$

2. $\dfrac{1}{2}x - 3 \leq 1$

     (A) $-4 \leq x \leq 8$ (B) $x \geq -8$ (C) $x \leq 8$

     (D) $2 \leq x \leq 8$ (E) $x \geq 8$

3. $-3p + 1 \geq 16$

     (A) $p \geq -5$ (B) $p \geq \dfrac{-17}{3}$ (C) $p \leq \dfrac{-17}{3}$

     (D) $p \leq -5$ (E) $p \geq 5$

Drill: Algebraic Word Problems

➤ **Directions:** Solve the following word problems algebraically.

1. The sum of two numbers is 41. One number is one less than twice the other. Find the larger of the two numbers.

    (A) 13   (B) 14   (C) 21   (D) 27   (E) 41

2. The sum of two consecutive integers is 111. Find the value of the smaller integer.

    (A) 55   (B) 56   (C) 58   (D) 111   (E) 112

3. The difference between two integers is 12. The sum of the two integers is 2. Find both integers.

    (A) 7 and 5   (B) 7 and –5   (C) –7 and 5   (D) 2 and 12   (E) –2 and 12

Competency 4: Algebraic Thinking Drills Answer Key

Drill: Operations with Polynomials

1. (C)	4. (B)	7. (B)
2. (C)	5. (A)	8. (D)
3. (D)	6. (C)	9. (D)

Drill: Linear Equations

1. (C)	4. (D)
2. (A)	5. (B)
3. (E)	

Drill: Inequalities

1. (E)
2. (C)
3. (D)

Drill: Algebraic Word Problems

1. (D)
2. (A)
3. (B)

Drill Section for Competency 5

Drill: Data Interpretation

➤ **Directions:** Determine the correct response from the information provided.

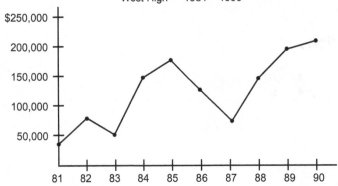

Amount of Scholarship Money Awarded to Graduating Seniors
West High — 1981 – 1990

1. What was the approximate amount of scholarship money awarded in 1985?

   (A) $150,000 (B) $155,000 (C) $165,000 (D) $175,000 (E) $190,000

2. By how much did the scholarship money increase between 1987 and 1988?

   (A) $25,000 (B) $30,000 (C) $50,000 (D) $55,000 (E) $75,000

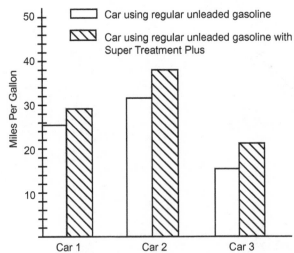

Changes in Average Mileage

☐ Car using regular unleaded gasoline

▨ Car using regular unleaded gasoline with Super Treatment Plus

3. By how much did the mileage increase for Car 2 when the new product was used?

    (A) 5 mpg   (B) 6 mpg   (C) 7 mpg

    (D) 10 mpg   (E) 12 mpg

4. Which car's mileage increased the most in this test?

    (A) Car 1   (B) Car 2   (C) Car 3

    (D) Cars 1 and 2   (E) Cars 2 and 3

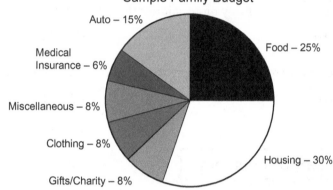

Sample Family Budget

Auto – 15%

Food – 25%

Medical Insurance – 6%

Miscellaneous – 8%

Clothing – 8%

Housing – 30%

Gifts/Charity – 8%

5. Using the budget shown, a family with an income of $4,500 a month would plan to spend what amount on housing?

    (A) $900   (B) $1125   (C) $1350   (D) $1470   (E) $1560

6. In this sample family budget, how does the amount spent on an automobile compare to the amount spent on housing?

    (A) $\dfrac{1}{3}$ (B) $\dfrac{1}{2}$ (C) $\dfrac{2}{3}$ (D) $1\dfrac{1}{2}$ (E) 2

7. A family with a monthly income of $3,720 spends $375 a month on clothing. By what amount do they exceed the sample budget?

    (A) $3.00   (B) $15.60   (C) $30.00   (D) $77.40   (E) $95.25

CALORIE CHART — BREADS

Bread	Amount	Calories
French Bread	2 oz	140
Bran Bread	1 oz	95
Whole Wheat Bread	1 oz	115
Oatmeal Bread	0.5 oz	55
Raisin Bread	1 oz	125

8. One dieter eats two ounces of French bread. A second dieter eats two ounces of bran bread. The second dieter has consumed how many more calories than the first dieter?

    (A) 40   (B) 45   (C) 50   (D) 55   (E) 65

9. One ounce of whole wheat bread has how many more calories than an ounce of oatmeal bread?

    (A) 5   (B) 15   (C) 60   (D) 75   (E) 125

Drill: Measures of Central Tendency

Mean

➤ **Directions:** Find the mean of each set of numbers.

1. 18, 25, and 32

    (A) 3   (B) 25   (C) 50   (D) 75   (E) 150

2. 97, 102, 116, and 137

    (A) 40   (B) 102   (C) 109   (D) 113   (E) 116

3. 12, 15, 18, 24, and 31

    (A) 18   (B) 19.3   (C) 20   (D) 25   (E) 100

4. 7, 4, 6, 3, 11, and 14

    (A) 5   (B) 6.5   (C) 7   (D) 7.5   (E) 8

Median

➤ **Directions:** Find the median value of each set of numbers.

5.   3, 8, and 6

   (A)   3   (B)   6   (C)   8   (D)   17   (E)   20

6.   19, 15, 21, 27, and 12

   (A)   19   (B)   15   (C)   21   (D)   27   (E)   94

7.   29, 18, 21, and 35

   (A)   29   (B)   18   (C)   21   (D)   35   (E)   25

8.   8, 15, 7, 12, 31, 3, and 28

   (A)   7   (B)   11.6   (C)   12   (D)   14.9   (E)   104

Mode

➤ **Directions:** Find the mode(s) of each set of numbers.

9.   1, 3, 7, 4, 3, and 8

   (A)   1   (B)   3   (C)   7   (D)   4   (E)   None

10.   12, 19, 25, and 42

   (A)   12   (B)   19   (C)   25   (D)   42   (E)   None

11.   16, 14, 12, 16, 30, and 28

   (A)   6   (B)   14   (C)   16   (D) $19.\overline{3}$ (E)   None

12.   4, 3, 9, 2, 4, 5, and 2

   (A)   3 and 9   (B)   5 and 9   (C)   4 and 5   (D)   2 and 4   (E)   None

Competency 5: Data Analysis Drills Answer Key

Drill: Data Interpretation

1. (D)	4. (E)	7. (D)	
2. (E)	5. (C)	8. (C)	
3. (B)	6. (B)	9. (A)	

Drill: Measures of Central Tendency

1. (B)	4. (D)	7. (E)	10. (E)
2. (D)	5. (B)	8. (C)	11. (C)
3. (C)	6. (A)	9. (B)	12. (D)

English Language Skills

Overview

This review offers comprehensive coverage of Florida's required competencies and provides 21 drills that will help build your English language skills. On the FTCE-GKT, you will have 40 minutes to complete the 40-question section, which covers the following:

- conceptual and organizational skills

- word choice skills

- sentence structure skills

- grammar, spelling, capitalization, and punctuation skills

Competency 1: Conceptual and Organizational Skills

Skill 1: Identify Logical Order in a Written Passage

The unit of work for revising is the paragraph. After you have read a passage, spend some time reviewing the passage by looking to see whether the author needed to indent for paragraphs anywhere. If so, make a proofreader's mark to indicate to the reader that you think a paragraph should start-here. Check to see whether the author should add anything that would make the point of view more convincing. Be sure to check for useful transitions to keep up the flow and maintain the focus of ideas. If the paragraphs are out of order, add that paragraph and indicate with a number or some other mark where you want it to go.

Skill 2: Identify Irrelevant Sentences

Identify content that does not contribute to the purpose of a passage or provides irrelevent or illogical information.

- Either/Or—The writer assumes that only two opposing possibilities may be attained: "Either _____, or this _____."

- Oversimplification—The writer simplifies the subject: "The rich only want one thing."

- Begging the question—The writer assumes she has proven something (often counterintuitive) that may need to be proven to the reader: "The death penalty actually increases, rather than deters, violent crime."

- Ignoring the issue—The writer argues against the truth of an issue due to its conclusion: "John is a good boy and, therefore, did not rob the store."

- Arguing against a person, not an idea—The writer argues that somebody's idea has no merit because he is immoral or personally stupid: "Eric will fail out of school because he is not doing well in gym class."

- Non sequitur—The writer leaps to the wrong conclusion: "Jake is from Canada; he must play hockey."

- Drawing the wrong conclusion from a sequence—The author attributes the outcome to the wrong reasons: "Betty married at a young age to an older man and now has three children and is therefore a housewife."

Competency 2: Word Choice Skills

Skill 1: Choose Appropriate Word or Expression in Context

Consider this sentence: The high school *principal* resigned for two *principal* reasons. If you think that the second *principal* is the wrong word (that it should be *principle*), think again. This usage is correct. You may be asked about words that are commonly confused and misused, as well as the use of words based on their grammatical appropriateness in a sentence, such as the distinction between *principal* and *principle*, *fewer* and *less*, and *lie* and *lay*. Here are some commonly confused pairs:

principal—as an adjective, most important; as a noun, the chief authority.

principle—always a noun: a fundamental law. "We hold these principles to be self-evident."

affect—usually a verb, meaning to *influence*; sometimes a noun, with a specific meaning in psychology. "Her performance was adversely affected by the heat."

effect—usually a noun, meaning something that results from something else; occasionally a verb, meaning *to cause to come into being*. "The heat had no effect on his performance." "Her persistence helped to effect the new zoning ordinance."

Skill 2: Recognize Commonly Confused or Misused Words or Phrases

It is important to understand the meanings of all words—not just the ones you are asked to define. A good vocabulary is a strength that can help you perform well on all sections of this test. The following information will build your skills in determining the meanings of words.

Similar Forms and Sounds

The complex nature of language sometimes makes reading difficult. Words often become confusing when they have similar forms and sounds. Indeed the author may have a correct meaning in mind, but an incorrect word choice can alter the meaning of the sentence or even make it totally illogical.

NO: Martha was always part of that *cliché.*

YES: Martha was always part of that *clique.*

(A *cliché* is a trite or hackneyed expression; a *clique* is an exclusive group of people.)

NO: The minister spoke of the soul's *immorality.*

YES: The minister spoke of the soul's *immortality.*

(*Immorality* means wickedness; *immortality* means imperishable or unending life.)

NO: Where is the nearest *stationary* store?

YES: Where is the nearest *stationery* store?

(*Stationary* means immovable; *stationery* is paper used for writing.)

Below are groups of words that are often confused because of their similar forms and sounds.

1. accent – *v.* – to stress or emphasize (You must *accent* the last syllable.)

    ascent – *n.* – a climb or rise (John's *ascent* of the mountain was dangerous.)

    assent – *n.* – consent; compliance (We need your *assent* before we can go ahead with the plans.)

2. accept – *v.* – to take something offered (She *accepted* the gift.)

    except – *prep.* – other than; but (Everyone was included in the plans *except* him.)

3. advice – *n.* – opinion given as to what to do or how to handle a situation (Her sister gave her *advice* on what to say at the interview.)

    advise – *v.* – to counsel (John's guidance counselor *advised* him on which colleges to apply to.)

4. affect – *v.* – to influence (Mary's suggestion did not *affect* me.)

   effect – 1. *v.* – to cause to happen (The plan was *effected* with great success.); 2. *n.* – result (The *effect* of the medicine is excellent.)

5. allusion – *n.* – indirect reference (In the poem, there are many biblical *allusions.*)

   illusion – *n.* – false idea or conception; belief or opinion not in accord with the facts (Greg was under the *illusion* that he could win the race after missing three weeks of practice.)

6. already – *adv.* – previously (I had *already* read that novel.)

   all ready – *adv.* + *adj.* – prepared (The family was *all ready* to leave on vacation.)

7. altar – *n.* – table or stand used in religious rites (The priest stood at the *altar.*)

   alter – *v.* – to change (Their plans were *altered* during the strike.)

8. capital – 1. *n.* – a city where the government meets (The senators had a meeting in Albany, the *capital* of New York.); 2. money used in business (They had enough *capital* to develop the industry.)

   capitol – *n.* – building in which the legislature meets (Senator Brown gave a speech at the *capitol* in Washington.)

9. choose – *v.* – to select (Which camera did you *choose*?)

   chose – (past tense, *choose*) (Susan *chose* to stay home.)

10. cite – *v.* – to quote (The student *cited* evidence from the text.)

    site – *n.* – location (They chose the *site* where the house would be built.)

11. clothes – *n.* – garments (Because she got caught in the rain, her *clothes* were wet.)

    cloths – *n.* – pieces of material (The *cloths* were used to wash the windows.)

12. coarse – *adj.* – rough; unrefined (Sandpaper is *coarse.*)

    course – 1. *n.* – path of action (She did not know what *course* would solve the problem.); 2. passage (We took the long *course* to the lake.); 3. series of studies (We both enrolled in the physics *course.*); 4. part of a meal (She served a five *course* meal.)

13. consul – *n.* – a person appointed by the government to live in a foreign city and represent the citizenry and business interests of his native country there (The *consul* was appointed to Naples, Italy.)

    council – *n.* – a group used for discussion, advisement (The *council* decided to accept his letter of resignation.)

    counsel – *v.* – to advise (Tom *counsels* Jerry on tax matters.)

14. decent – *adj.* – proper; respectable (He was very *decent* about the entire matter.)

    descent – 1. *n.* – moving down (In Dante's *Inferno,* the *descent* into Hell was depicted graphically.); 2. ancestry (He is of Irish *descent.*)

15. device – 1. *n.* – plan; scheme (The *device* helped her win the race.); 2. invention (We bought a *device* that opens the garage door automatically.)

    devise – *v.* – to contrive (He *devised* a plan so John could not win.)

16. emigrate – *v.* – to go away from a country (Many Japanese *emigrated* from Japan in the late 1800s.)

    immigrate – *v.* – to come into a country (Her relatives *immigrated* to the United States after World War I.)

17. eminent – *n.* – prominent (He is an *eminent* member of the community.)

    imminent – *adj.* – impending (The decision is *imminent.*)

    immanent – *adj.* – existing within (Maggie believed that religious spirit is *immanent* in human beings.)

18. fair – 1. *adj.* – beautiful (She was *a fair* maiden.); 2. just (She tried to be *fair.*); 3. *n* – festival (There were many games at the *fair.*)

    fare – *n.* – amount of money paid for transportation (The city proposed that the subway *fare* be raised.)

19. forth – *adv.* – onward (The soldiers moved *forth* in the blinding snow.)

    fourth – *n., adj.* – 4th (She was the *fourth* runner-up in the beauty contest.)

20. its – possessive form of *it* (Our town must improve *its* roads.)

    it's – contraction of "it is" (*It's* time to leave the party.)

21. later – *adj., adv.* – at a subsequent date (We will take a vacation *later* this year.)

    latter – *n.* – second of the two (Susan can visit Monday or Tuesday. The *latter,* however, is preferable.)

22. lead – 1. *n.* – (led) a metal (The handgun was made of *lead.*); 2. *v.t.* – (leed) to show the way (The camp counselor *leads* the way to the picnic grounds.)

    led – past tense of *lead* (#2 above) (The dog *led* the way.)

23. loose – *adj.* – free; unrestricted (The dog was let *loose* by accident.)

    lose – *v.* – to suffer the loss of (He was afraid he would *lose* the race.)

24. moral – 1. *adj.* – virtuous (She is a *moral* woman with high ethical standards.); 2. *n.* – lesson taught by a story, incident, etc. (Most fables end with a *moral*.)

    morale – *n.* – mental condition (After the team lost the game, their *morale* was low.)

25. of – *prep.* – from (She is *of* French descent.)

    off – *adj.* – away; at a distance (The television fell *off* the table.)

26. passed – *v.* – having satisfied some requirement (He *passed* the test.)

    past – 1. *adj.* – gone by or elapsed in time (His *past* deeds got him in trouble.); 2. *n.* – a period of time gone by (His *past* was shady.); 3. *prep.* – beyond (She ran *past* the house.)

27. personal – *adj.* – private (Jack was unwilling to discuss his childhood; it was too *personal*.)

    personnel – *n.* – staff (The *personnel* at the department store was made up of young adults.)

28. principal – *n.* – head of a school (The *principal* addressed the graduating class.)   -adj.- most important

    principle – *n.* – the ultimate source, origin, or cause of something; a law, truth (The *principles* of physics were reviewed in class today.)

29. prophecy – *n.* – prediction of the future (His *prophecy* that he would become a doctor came true.)

    prophesy – *v.* – to declare or predict (He *prophesied* that we would win the lottery.)

30. quiet – *adj.* – still; calm (At night all is *quiet*.)

    quite – *adv.* – really; truly (She is *quite* a good singer.)

    quit – *v.* – to free oneself (Peter had little time to spare so he *quit* the chorus.)

31. respectfully – *adv.* – with respect, honor, esteem (He declined the offer *respectfully*.)

    respectively – *adv.* – in the order mentioned (Jack, Susan and Jim, who are members of the club, were elected president, vice president, and secretary *respectively*.)

32. stationary – *adj.* – immovable (The park bench is *stationary*.)

    stationery – *n.* – paper used for writing (The invitations were printed on yellow *stationery*.)

33. straight – *adj.* – not curved (The road was *straight*.)

    strait – 1. *adj.* – restricted; narrow; confined (The patient was put in a *strait* jacket.); 2. *n.* – narrow waterway (He sailed through the *Straits* of Magellan.)

34. than – *conj.* – used most commonly in comparisons (Maggie is older *than* I.)

    then – *adv.* – soon afterward (We lived in Boston, *then* we moved to New York.)

35. their – possessive form of *they* (That is *their* house on Tenafly Drive.)

    they're – contraction of "they are" (*They're* leaving for California next week.)

    there – *adv.* – at that place (Who is standing *there* under the tree?)

36. to – *prep.* – in the direction of; toward; as (She made a turn *to* the right on Norman Street.)

    too – 1. *adv.* – more than enough (She served *too* much for dinner.); 2. also (He is going to Maine *too*.)

    two – *n.* – 2; one and one (We have *two* pet rabbits.)

37. weather – *n.* – the general condition of the atmosphere (The *weather* is expected to be clear on Sunday.)

    whether – *conj.* – if it be a case or fact (We don't know *whether* the trains are late.)

38. who's – contraction of "who is" or "who has" (*Who's* willing to volunteer for the night shift?)

    whose – possessive form of *who* (*Whose* book is this?)

39. your – possessive form of *you* (Is this *your* seat?)

    you're – contraction of you and are (I know *you're* going to do well on the test.)

Multiple Meanings

In addition to words that sound alike, you must be careful when dealing with words that have multiple meanings. For example:

> The boy was thrilled that his mother gave him a piece of chewing *gum*.

> Dentists advise people to floss their teeth to help prevent *gum* disease.

As you can see, one word can have different meanings depending on the context in which it is used.

Connotation and Denotation

Language can become even more complicated. Not only can a single word have numerous definitions and subtle meanings, it may also take on added meanings through implication. The **connotation** is the idea suggested by its place near or association with other words or phrases. The **denotation** of a word is the direct explicit meaning.

Connotation

Sometimes, you will be asked to tell the meaning of a word in the context of the paragraph. You may not have seen the word before, but from your understanding of the writer's intent, you should be able to figure out what it is s/he's after. For example, read the following paragraph:

> Paris is a beautiful city, perhaps the most beautiful on earth. Long, broad avenues are lined with seventeenth- and eighteenth-century apartments, office buildings, and cafes. Flowers give the city a rich and varied look. The bridges and the river lend an air of lightness and grace to the whole urban landscape.

1. In this paragraph, "rich" most nearly means

   (A) wealthy.

   (B) polluted.

   (C) colorful.

   (D) dull.

If you chose "colorful" you would be right. Although "rich" literally means "wealthy" (that is its *denotation*, its literal meaning), here the writer means more than the word's literal meaning, and seems to be highlighting the variety and color that the flowers add to the avenues, that is, richness in a figurative sense.

The writer is using a non-literal meaning, or *connotation* that we associate with the word "rich" to show what s/he means. When we think of something "rich," we usually also think of abundance, variety, color, and not merely numbers.

Denotation

Determining the denotation of a word is different from determining a word's connotation. Read this paragraph:

> Many soporifics are on the market to help people sleep. Take a glass of water and two *Sleepeze* and you get the "zzzzz" you need. *Sominall* supposedly helps you get the sleep you need so you can go on working. With *Morpho*, your head hits the pillow and you're asleep before the light goes out.

1. From this paragraph, a "soporific" is probably

   (A) a drug that stimulates you to stay awake.

   (B) a kind of sleeping bag.

   (C) a kind of bed.

   (D) a drug that helps you sleep.

What is a soporific? You can figure out what it means by looking at what is said around it. People take these "soporifics" to go to sleep, not to wake up. So it can't be (A). You can't take two beds and a glass of water to go to sleep, either. So, it can't be (C). Anyway, you might be able to identify what a soporific is because you recognize the brand names used as examples. So, it must be some sort of pill that you take to sleep. Well, pills are usually drugs of some kind. Therefore, the answer is (D).

Figures of Speech

Figurative language helps to create imaginative and detailed writing. A figure of speech is used in the imaginative rather than the literal sense. It helps the reader to make connections between the writer's thoughts and the external world. Knowing the different types of figures of speech can help you determine the context in which a word is being used and, thereby, help you determine the meaning of that word. The following are some commonly used figures of speech.

Simile

A simile is an explicit comparison between two things. The comparison is made by using *like* or *as*.

> Her hair was *like* straw.
>
> The blanket was *as* white as snow.

Metaphor

Like the simile, the metaphor likens two things. However, *like* or *as* are not used in the comparison.

> "All the world's a stage." Shakespeare
>
> Grass is nature's blanket.

A common error is the mixed metaphor. This occurs when a writer uses two inconsistent metaphors in a single expression.

> The blanket of snow clutched the earth with icy fingers.

Hyperbole

A hyperbole is a deliberate overstatement or exaggeration used to express an idea.

> I have told you a thousand times not to play with matches.

Personification

Personification is the attribution of human qualities to an object, animal, or idea.

> The wind laughed at their attempts to catch the flying papers.

Skill 3: Recognize Diction and Tone Appropriate to a Given Audience

The denotative meaning of a word is its *literal,* dictionary definition: what the word denotes or "means." The connotative meaning of a word is what the word connotes or "suggests"; it is a meaning apart from what the word literally means. A writer should choose a word based on the tone and context of the sentence; this ensures that a word bears the appropriate connotation while still conveying some exactness in denotation. For example, a gift might be described as "cheap," but the directness of this word has a negative connotation—something cheap is something of little or no value. The word "inexpensive" has a more positive connotation, though "cheap" is a synonym for "inexpensive." Questions of this type require you to make a decision regarding the appropriateness of words and phrases for the context of a sentence.

Wordiness and Conciseness

Effective writing is concise. Wordiness, on the other hand, decreases the clarity of expression by cluttering sentences with unnecessary words.

Wordiness questions test your ability to detect redundancies (unnecessary repetitions), circumlocution (failure to get to the point), and padding with loose synonyms. Wordiness questions require you to choose sentences that use as few words as possible to convey a message clearly, economically, and effectively.

Notice the difference in impact between the first and second sentences in the following pairs:

INCORRECT:	The medical exam that he gave me was entirely complete.
CORRECT:	The medical exam he gave me was complete.

INCORRECT:	Larry asked his friend John, who was a good, old friend, if he would join him and go along with him to see the foreign film made in Japan.
CORRECT:	Larry asked his good, old friend John if he would join him in seeing the Japanese film.

INCORRECT:	I was absolutely, totally happy with the present that my parents gave to me at 7 a.m. on the morning of my birthday.
CORRECT:	I was happy with the present my parents gave me on the morning of my birthday.

Competency 3: Sentence Structure Skills

Skill 1: Recognize Correct Placement of Modifiers

A misplaced modifier is one that is in the wrong place in the sentence. Misplaced modifiers come in all forms—words, phrases, and clauses. Sentences containing misplaced modifiers are often very comical: *Mom made me eat the spinach instead of my brother.* Misplaced modifiers, like the one in this sentence, are usually too far away from the word or words they modify. This sentence should read: *Mom made me, instead of my brother, eat the spinach.*

Modifiers like *only, nearly,* and *almost* should be placed next to the word they modify and not in front of some other word, especially a verb, that they are not intended to modify.

A modifier is misplaced if it appears to modify the wrong part of the sentence or if we cannot be certain what part of the sentence the writer intended it to modify. To correct a misplaced modifier, move the modifier next to the word it describes.

> INCORRECT: She served hamburgers to the men on paper plates.
>
> CORRECT: She served hamburgers on paper plates to the men.

Split infinitives also result in misplaced modifiers. Infinitives consist of the marker *to* plus the plain form of the verb. The two parts of the infinitive make up a grammatical unit that should not be split. Splitting an infinitive is placing an adverb between the *to* and the verb.

> INCORRECT: The weather service expects temperatures to not rise.
>
> CORRECT: The weather service expects temperatures not to rise.

Sometimes a split infinitive may be natural and preferable, though it may still bother some readers.

> EXAMPLE: Several U.S. industries expect *to* more than *triple* their use of
> robots within the next decade.

A squinting modifier is one that may refer to either a preceding or a following word, leaving the reader uncertain about what it is intended to modify. Correct a squinting modifier by moving it next to the word it is intended to modify.

> INCORRECT: Snipers who fired on the soldiers often escaped capture.
>
> CORRECT: Snipers who often fired on the soldiers escaped capture. OR
>
> Snipers who fired on the soldiers escaped capture often.

A dangling modifier is a modifier or verb in search of a subject: the modifying phrase (usually an *-ing* word group, an *-ed* or *-en* word group, or a *to + a verb* word group—participle phrase or infinitive phrase respectively) either appears to modify the wrong word or has nothing to modify. It is literally dangling at the beginning or the end of a sentence. The sentences often look and sound correct: *To be a student government officer, your grades must be above average.* (However, the verbal modifier has nothing to describe. Who is *to be a student government officer*? Your grades?) Questions of this type require you to determine whether a modifier has a headword or whether it is dangling at the beginning or the end of the sentence.

To correct a dangling modifier, reword the sentence by either: 1) changing the modifying phrase to a clause with a subject, or 2) changing the subject of the sentence to the word that should be modified. The following are examples of a dangling gerund, a dangling infinitive, and a dangling participle:

INCORRECT:	Shortly after leaving home, the accident occurred.
	Who is <u>leaving home</u>, the accident?
CORRECT:	Shortly after we left home, the accident occurred.
INCORRECT:	To get up on time, a great effort was needed.
	<u>To get up</u> needs a subject.
CORRECT:	To get up on time, I made a great effort.

Skill 2: Recognize Parallelism

This skill requires recognition of parallel expressions for parallel ideas. Parallel structure is used to express matching ideas. It refers to the grammatical balance of a series of any of the following:

Phrases:

The squirrel ran *along the fence, up the tree,* and *into his burrow* with a mouthful of acorns.

Adjectives:

The job market is flooded with *very talented, highly motivated,* and *well-educated* young people.

Nouns:

You will need a *notebook, pencil,* and *dictionary* for the test.

Clauses:

The children were told to decide *which toy they would keep* and *which toy they would give away.*

Verbs:

The farmer *plowed, planted,* and *harvested* his corn in record time.

Verbals:

Reading, writing, and *calculating* are fundamental skills that all of us should possess.

Correlative conjunctions:

Either you will do your homework *or* you will fail.

Repetition of structural signals:

(such as articles, auxiliaries, prepositions, and conjunctions)

> INCORRECT: I have quit my job, enrolled in school, and am looking for a reliable babysitter.

> CORRECT: I *have quit* my job, *have enrolled* in school, and *am looking* for a reliable babysitter.

Note: Repetition of prepositions is considered formal and is not necessary.

> You can travel *by car, by plane, or by train*; it's all up to you.

OR

> You can travel *by car, plane, or train*; it's all up to you.

When a sentence contains items in a series, check for both punctuation and sentence balance. When you check for punctuation, make sure the commas are used correctly. When you check for parallelism, make sure that the conjunctions connect similar grammatical constructions, such as all adjectives or all clauses.

Skill 3: Recognize Fragments, Comma Splices, and Run-on Sentences

A fragment is an incomplete construction that may or may not have a subject and a verb. Specifically, a fragment is a group of words pretending to be a sentence. Not all fragments appear as separate sentences, however. Often, fragments are separated by semicolons.

> INCORRECT: Traffic was stalled for ten miles on the freeway. Because repairs were being made on potholes.

> CORRECT: Traffic was stalled for ten miles on the freeway because repairs were being made on potholes.

INCORRECT:	It was a funny story; one that I had never heard before.
CORRECT:	It was a funny story, one that I had never heard before.

Comma Splices

A comma splice is the unjustifiable use of only a comma to combine what really is two separate sentences.

INCORRECT:	One common error in writing is incorrect spelling, the other is the occasional use of faulty diction.
CORRECT:	One common error in writing is incorrect spelling; the other is the occasional use of faulty diction.

Both run-on sentences and comma splices may be corrected in one of the following ways:

RUN-ON:	Neal won the award he had the highest score.
COMMA SPLICE:	Neal won the award, he had the highest score.

Separate the sentences with a period:

Neal won the award. He had the highest score.

Separate the sentences with a comma and a coordinating conjunction (*and, but, or, nor, for, yet, so*):

Neal won the award for he had the highest score.

Separate the sentences with a semicolon:

Neal won the award; he had the highest score.

Separate the sentences with a subordinating conjunction such as *although, because, since, if*:

Neal won the award because he had the highest score.

Run-on/Fused Sentences

A run-on/fused sentence is not necessarily a long sentence or a sentence that the reader considers too long; in fact, a run-on may be two short sentences: *Dry ice does not melt it evaporates.* A run-on results when the writer fuses or runs together two separate sentences without any correct mark of punctuation separating them.

INCORRECT:	Knowing how to use a dictionary is no problem each dictionary has a section in the front of the book telling how to use it.

CORRECT: Knowing how to use a dictionary is no problem. Each dictionary has a section in the front of the book telling how to use it.

Even if one or both of the fused sentences contains internal punctuation, the sentence is still a run-on.

INCORRECT: Bob bought dress shoes, a suit, and a nice shirt he needed them for his sister's wedding.

CORRECT: Bob bought dress shoes, a suit, and a nice shirt. He needed them for his sister's wedding.

Subordination, Coordination, and Predication

Suppose, for the sake of clarity, you wanted to combine the information in these two sentences to create one statement:

I studied a foreign language. I found English quite easy.

How you decide to combine this information should be determined by the relationship you'd like to show between the two facts. *I studied a foreign language, and I found English quite easy* seems rather illogical. The **coordination** of the two ideas (connecting them with the coordinating conjunction *and*) is ineffective. Using **subordination** instead (connecting the sentences with a subordinating conjunction) clearly shows the degree of relative importance between the expressed ideas:

After I studied a foreign language, I found English quite easy.

When using a conjunction, be sure that the sentence parts you are joining are in agreement.

INCORRECT: She loved him dearly but not his dog.

CORRECT: She loved him dearly but she did not love his dog.

A common mistake that is made is to forget that each member of the pair must be followed by the same kind of construction.

INCORRECT: They complimented them for their bravery and they thanked them for their being kind.

CORRECT: They complimented them for their bravery and thanked them for their kindness.

While refers to time and should not be used as a substitute for *although*, *and*, or *but*.

INCORRECT: While I'm usually interested in Fellini movies, I'd rather not go tonight.

CORRECT: Although I'm usually interested in Fellini movies, I'd rather not go tonight.

Where refers to place and should not be used as a substitute for *that*.

> INCORRECT: We read in the paper where they are making great strides in DNA research.
>
> CORRECT: We read in the paper that they are making great strides in DNA research.

After words like "reason" and "explanation", use *that*, not *because*.

> INCORRECT: His explanation for his tardiness was because his alarm did not go off.
>
> CORRECT: His explanation for his tardiness was that his alarm did not go off.

Competency 4: Grammar, Spelling, Capitalization, and Punctuation Skills

Skill 1: Identify Standard Verb Forms

Verb Forms

This section covers the principal parts of some irregular verbs including troublesome verbs like *lie* and *lay*. The use of regular verbs like *look* and *receive* poses no real problem to most writers since the past and past participle forms end in *-ed*; it is the irregular forms that pose the most serious problems—for example, *seen, written,* and *begun.*

Skill 2: Identify Inappropriate Shifts in Verb Tense

Tense sequence indicates a logical time sequence.

Use present tense

in statements of universal truth:

> I learned that the sun *is* 90 million miles from the earth.

in statements about the contents of literature and other published works:

> In this book, Sandy *becomes* a nun and *writes* a book on psychology.

Use past tense

in statements concerning writing or publication of a book:

> He *wrote* his first book in 1949, and it *was published* in 1952.

Use present perfect tense

for an action that began in the past but continues into the future:

> I *have lived* here all my life.

Use past perfect tense

for an earlier action that is mentioned in a later action:

> Cindy ate the apple that she *had picked.*

(First she picked it, then she ate it.)

Use future perfect tense

for an action that will have been completed at a specific future time:

> By May, I *shall have graduated.*

Use a present participle

for action that occurs at the same time as the verb:

> *Speeding* down the interstate, I saw a cop's flashing lights.

Use a perfect participle

for action that occurred before the main verb:

> *Having read* the directions, I started the test.

Use the subjunctive mood

to express a wish or state a condition contrary to fact:

> *If it were not raining,* we could have a picnic.

in *that* clauses after verbs like *request, recommend, suggest, ask, require,* and *insist*; and after such expressions as *it is important* and *it is necessary*:

> It is necessary that all papers *be* submitted on time.

Skill 3: Identify Agreement Between Subject and Verb

Agreement is the grammatical correspondence between the subject and the verb of a sentence: *I do; we do; they do; he, she, it does.*

Every English verb has five forms, two of which are the bare form (plural) and the *-s* form (singular). Simply put, singular verb forms end in *-s*; plural forms do not.

Study these rules governing subject-verb agreement:

A verb must agree with its subject, not with any additive phrase in the sentence such as a prepositional or verbal phrase. Ignore such phrases.

> Your *copy* of the rules *is* on the desk.
>
> Ms. Craig's *record* of community service and outstanding teaching *qualifies* her for a promotion.

In an inverted sentence beginning with a prepositional phrase, the verb still agrees with its subject.

> At the end of the summer *come* the best *sales.*
>
> Under the house *are* some old Mason *jars.*

Prepositional phrases beginning with compound prepositions such as *along with, together with, in addition to,* and *as well as* should be ignored, for they do not affect subject-verb agreement.

> *Gladys Knight*, as well as the Pips, *is* riding the midnight train to Georgia.

A verb must agree with its subject, not its subject complement.

> *Taxes are* a problem.
>
> A *problem is* taxes.

When a sentence begins with an expletive such as *there, here,* or *it,* the verb agrees with the subject, not the expletive.

> Surely, there *are* several *alumni* who would be interested in forming a group.
>
> There *are* 50 *students* in my English class.
>
> There *is* a horrifying *study* on child abuse in *Psychology Today.*

Indefinite pronouns such as *each, either, one, everyone, everybody,* and *everything* are singular.

> *Somebody* in Detroit *loves* me.
>
> *Does either* [one] of you have a pencil?
>
> *Neither* of my brothers *has* a car.

Indefinite pronouns such as *several, few, both,* and *many* are plural.

> *Both* of my sorority sisters *have* decided to live off campus.
>
> *Few seek* the enlightenment of transcendental meditation.

Indefinite pronouns such as *all, some, most,* and *none* may be singular or plural depending on their referents.

> *Some* of the food *is* cold.
>
> *Some* of the vegetables *are* cold.
>
> I can think of some retorts, but *none seem* appropriate.
>
> *None* of the children *is* as sweet as Sally.

Fractions such as *one-half* and *one-third* may be singular or plural depending on the referent.

> *Half* of the mail *has* been delivered.
>
> *Half* of the letters *have* been read.

Subjects joined by *and* take a plural verb unless the subjects are thought to be one item or unit.

> *Jim* and *Tammy were* televangelists.
>
> *Earth, Wind, and Fire is* my favorite group.

In cases when the subjects are joined by *or, nor, either . . . or,* or *neither . . . nor,* the verb must agree with the subject closer to it.

> Either the teacher or the *students are* responsible.
>
> Neither the students nor the *teacher is* responsible.

Relative pronouns, such as *who, which,* or *that,* which refer to plural antecedents require plural verbs. However, when the relative pronoun refers to a singular subject, the pronoun takes a singular verb.

> She is one of the girls *who cheer* on Friday nights.

> She is the only cheerleader *who has* a broken leg.

Subjects preceded by *every, each,* and *many a* are singular.

> *Every* man, woman, and child *was* given a life preserver.

> *Each* undergraduate *is* required to pass a proficiency exam.

> *Many a* tear *has* to fall before one matures.

A collective noun, such as *audience, faculty, jury,* etc., requires a singular verb when the group is regarded as a whole, and a plural verb when the members of the group are regarded as individuals.

> The *jury has* made its decision.

> The *faculty are* preparing their grade rosters.

Subjects preceded by *the number of* or *the percentage of* are singular, while subjects preceded by *a number of* or *a percentage of* are plural.

> *The number of* vacationers in Florida *increases* every year.

> *A number of* vacationers *are* young couples.

Titles of books, companies, name brands, and groups are singular or plural depending on their meaning.

> *Great Expectations is* my favorite novel.

> The *Rolling Stones are* performing in the Super Dome.

Certain nouns of Latin and Greek origin have unusual singular and plural forms.

Singular	Plural
criterion	criteria
alumnus	alumni
datum	data
medium	media

The *data are* available for inspection.

The only *criterion* for membership *is* a high GPA.

Some nouns such as *deer, shrimp,* and *sheep* have the same spellings for both their singular and plural forms. In these cases, the meaning of the sentence will determine whether they are singular or plural.

> *Deer are* beautiful animals.
>
> The spotted *deer is* licking the sugar cube.

Some nouns like *scissors, jeans,* and *wages* have plural forms but no singular counterparts. These nouns almost always take plural verbs.

> The *scissors are* on the table.
>
> My new *jeans fit* me like a glove.

Words used as examples, not as grammatical parts of the sentence, require singular verbs.

> *Can't is* the contraction for "cannot."
>
> *Cats is* the plural form of "cat."

Mathematical expressions of subtraction and division require singular verbs, while expressions of addition and multiplication take either singular or plural verbs.

> Ten *divided* by two *equals* five.
>
> Five *times* two *equals* ten. OR
>
> Five *times* two *equal* ten.

Nouns expressing time, distance, weight, and measurement are singular when they refer to a unit and plural when they refer to separate items.

> *Fifty yards is* a short distance.
>
> *Ten years have* passed since I finished college.

Expressions of quantity are usually plural.

> *Nine out of ten* dentists *recommend* that their patients floss.

Some nouns ending in *-ics,* such as *economics* and *ethics,* take singular verbs when they refer to principles or a field of study; however, when they refer to individual practices, they usually take plural verbs.

> *Ethics is* being taught in the spring.
>
> His unusual business *ethics are* what got him into trouble.

Some nouns like *measles, news,* and *calculus* appear to be plural but are actually singular in number. These nouns require singular verbs.

> *Measles is* a very contagious disease.
>
> *Calculus requires* great skill in algebra.

A verbal noun (infinitive or gerund) serving as a subject is treated as singular, even if the object of the verbal phrase is plural.

> *Hiding* your mistakes *does* not make them go away.
>
> *To run* five miles *is* my goal.

A noun phrase or clause acting as the subject of a sentence requires a singular verb.

> *What I need is* to be loved.
>
> *Whether there is any connection between them is* unknown.

Clauses beginning with *what* may be singular or plural depending on the meaning, that is, whether *what* means "the thing" or "the things."

> *What I want for Christmas is* a new motorcycle.
>
> *What matters are* Smith's ideas.

A plural subject followed by a singular appositive requires a plural verb; similarly, a singular subject followed by a plural appositive requires a singular verb.

> When the girls throw a party, *they* each bring a *gift*.
>
> The *board,* all ten members, *is* meeting today.

Skill 4: Identify Agreement Between Pronoun and Antecedent

These kinds of questions test your knowledge of using an appropriate pronoun to agree with its antecedent in number (singular or plural form) and gender (masculine, feminine, or neuter). An antecedent is a noun or pronoun to which another noun or pronoun refers.

Here are the two basic rules for pronoun reference-antecedent agreement:

1. Every pronoun must have a conspicuous antecedent.

2. Every pronoun must agree with its antecedent in number, gender, and person.

When an antecedent is one of dual gender like *student, singer, artist, person, citizen,* etc., use *his* or *her.* Some careful writers change the antecedent to a plural noun to avoid using the sexist, singular masculine pronoun *his*:

> INCORRECT: Everyone hopes that he will win the lottery.
>
> CORRECT: Most people hope that they will win the lottery.

Ordinarily, the relative pronoun *who* is used to refer to people, *which* to refer to things and places, *where* to refer to places, and *that* to refer to places or things. The distinction between *that* and *which* is a grammatical distinction (see the section on Word Choice Skills).

Many writers prefer to use *that* to refer to collective nouns.

> EXAMPLE: A family *that* traces its lineage is usually proud of its roots

Skill 5: Identify Inappropriate Pronoun Shifts

Many writers, especially students, are not sure when to use the reflexive case pronoun and when to use the possessive case pronoun. The rules governing the usage of the reflexive case and the possessive case are quite simple.

Use the possessive case

before a noun in a sentence:

> *Our* friend moved during the semester break.
>
> *My* dog has fleas, but *her* dog doesn't.

before a gerund in a sentence:

> *Her* running helps to relieve stress.
>
> *His* driving terrified her.

as a noun in a sentence:

> *Mine* was the last test graded that day.

to indicate possession:

> Karen never allows anyone else to drive *her* car.
>
> Brad thought the book was *his,* but it was someone else's.

Use the reflexive case

as a direct object to rename the subject:

I kicked *myself.*

as an indirect object to rename the subject:

Henry bought *himself* a tie.

as an object of a prepositional phrase:

Tom and Lillie baked the pie for *themselves.*

as a predicate pronoun:

She hasn't been *herself* lately.

Do not use the reflexive in place of the nominative pronoun:

INCORRECT: Both Randy and *myself* plan to go.

CORRECT: Both Randy and *I* plan to go.

INCORRECT: *Yourself* will take on the challenges of college.

CORRECT: *You* will take on the challenges of college.

INCORRECT: Either James or *yourself* will paint the mural.

CORRECT: Either James or *you* will paint the mural.

Watch out for careless use of the pronoun form:

INCORRECT: George *hisself* told me it was true.

CORRECT: George *himself* told me it was true.

INCORRECT: They washed the car *theirselves.*

CORRECT: They washed the car *themselves.*

Notice that reflexive pronouns are not set off by commas:

INCORRECT: Mary, *herself,* gave him the diploma.

CORRECT: Mary *herself* gave him the diploma.

| INCORRECT: | I will do it, *myself.* |
| CORRECT: | I will do it *myself.* |

Skill 6: Identify Clear Pronoun References

Pronoun reference questions require you to determine whether the antecedent is conspicuously written in the sentence or whether it is remote, implied, ambiguous, or vague, none of which results in clear writing. Make sure that every italicized pronoun has a conspicuous antecedent and that one pronoun substitutes only for another noun or pronoun, not for an idea or a sentence.

Pronoun reference problems occur

when a pronoun refers to either of two antecedents:

| INCORRECT: | Joanna told Tim that *she* was getting fat. |
| CORRECT: | Joanna told Tim, "*I'm* getting fat." |

when a pronoun refers to a remote antecedent:

| INCORRECT: | A strange car followed us closely, and *he* kept blinking his lights at us. |
| CORRECT: | A strange car followed us closely, and *its driver* kept blinking his lights at us. |

when *this, that,* and *which* refer to the general idea of the preceding clause or sentence rather than the preceding word:

INCORRECT:	The students could not understand the pronoun reference handout, *which* annoyed them very much.
CORRECT:	The students could not understand the pronoun reference handout, a *fact which* annoyed them very much.
OR	The students were annoyed *because* they could not understand the pronoun reference handout.

when a pronoun refers to an unexpressed but implied noun:

| INCORRECT: | My husband wants me to knit a blanket, but I'm not interested in *it*. |
| CORRECT: | My husband wants me to knit a blanket, but I'm not interested in *knitting*. |

when *it* is used as something other than an expletive to postpone a subject:

INCORRECT: *It* says in today's paper that the newest shipment of cars from Detroit, Michigan, seems to include outright imitations of European models.

CORRECT: *Today's paper* says that the newest shipment of cars from Detroit, Michigan, seems to include outright imitations of European models.

INCORRECT: The football game was canceled because *it* was bad weather.

CORRECT: The football game was canceled because *the weather* was bad.

when *they* or *it* is used to refer to something or someone indefinitely, and there is no definite antecedent:

INCORRECT: At the job placement office, *they* told me to stop wearing ripped jeans to my interviews.

CORRECT: At the job placement office, *I was told* to stop wearing ripped jeans to my interviews.

when the pronoun does not agree with its antecedent in number, gender, or person:

INCORRECT: Any graduate student, if *they* are interested, may attend the lecture.

CORRECT: Any graduate student, if *he or she* is interested, may attend the lecture.

OR   *All* graduate students, if *they* are interested, may attend the lecture.

INCORRECT: Many Americans are concerned that the overuse of slang and colloquialisms is corrupting *the* language.

CORRECT: Many Americans are concerned that the overuse of slang and colloquialisms is corrupting *their* language.

INCORRECT: The Board of Regents will not make a decision about tuition increase until *their* March meeting.

CORRECT: The Board of Regents will not make a decision about tuition increase until *its* March meeting.

when a noun or pronoun has no expressed antecedent:

INCORRECT:	In the *President's* address to the union, *he* promised no more taxes.
CORRECT:	In *his* address to the union, *the President* promised no more taxes.

Skill 7: Identify Proper Case Forms

Pronoun case questions test your knowledge of the use of nominative and objective case pronouns:

Nominative Case	Objective Case
I	me
he	him
she	her
we	us
they	them
who	whom

This review section answers the most frequently asked grammar questions: when to use *I* and when to use *me*; when to use *who* and when to use *whom*. Some writers avoid *whom* altogether, and instead of distinguishing between *I* and *me*, many writers incorrectly use *myself.*

Use the nominative case (subject pronouns)

for the subject of a sentence:

> *We* students studied until early morning for the final.
>
> Alan and *I* "burned the midnight oil," too.

for pronouns in apposition to the subject:

> Only two students, Alex and *I,* were asked to report on the meeting.

for the predicate nominative/subject complement:

> The actors nominated for the award were *she* and *I.*

for the subject of an elliptical clause:

> Molly is more experienced than *he.*

for the subject of a subordinate clause:

> Robert is the driver *who* reported the accident.

for the complement of an infinitive with no expressed subject:

> I would not want to be *he.*

Use the objective case (object pronouns)

for the direct object of a sentence:

> Mary invited *us* to her party.

for the object of a preposition:

> The books that were torn belonged to *her.*
> Just between you and *me,* I'm bored.

for the indirect object of a sentence:

> Walter gave a dozen red roses to *her.*

for the appositive of a direct object:

> The committee elected two delegates, Barbara and *me.*

for the object of an infinitive:

> The young boy wanted to help *us* paint the fence.

for the object of a gerund:

> Enlisting *him* was surprisingly easy.

for the object of a past participle:

> Having called the other students and *us,* the secretary went home for the day.

for a pronoun that precedes an infinitive (the subject of an infinitive):

> The supervisor told *him* to work late.

for the complement of an infinitive with an expressed subject:

> The fans thought the best player to be *him.*

for the object of an elliptical clause:

> Bill tackled Joe harder than *me.*

for the object of a verb in apposition:

> Charles invited two extra people, Carmen and *me,* to the party.

When a conjunction connects two pronouns or a pronoun and a noun, remove the "and" and the other pronoun or noun to determine what the correct pronoun form should be:

> Mom gave ~~Tom and~~ myself a piece of cake.
>
> Mom gave ~~Tom and~~ I a piece of cake.
>
> Mom gave ~~Tom and~~ me a piece of cake.

Removal of these words reveals what the correct pronoun should be:

> Mom gave *me* a piece of cake.

The only pronouns that are acceptable after *between* and other prepositions are: *me, her, him, them,* and *whom.* When deciding between *who* and *whom,* try substituting *he* for *who* and *him* for *whom*; then follow these easy transformation steps:

1. Isolate the *who* clause or the *whom* clause:

   > whom we can trust

2. Invert the word order, if necessary. Place the words in the clause in the natural order of an English sentence, subject followed by the verb:

   > we can trust whom

3. Read the final form with the *he* or *him* inserted:

   > We can trust ~~whom~~ him.

When a pronoun follows a comparative conjunction like *than* or *as,* complete the elliptical construction to help you determine which pronoun is correct.

> EXAMPLE: She has more credit hours than me [do].
> She has more credit hours than I [do].

Skill 8: Identify Correct Use of Adjectives and Adverbs

Correct Usage

Adjectives are words that modify nouns or pronouns by defining, describing, limiting, or qualifying those nouns or pronouns.

Adverbs are words that modify verbs, adjectives, or other adverbs and that express such ideas as time, place, manner, cause, and degree. Use adjectives as subject complements with linking verbs; use adverbs with action verbs.

EXAMPLE:	The old man's speech was *eloquent.*	ADJECTIVE
	Mr. Brown speaks *eloquently.*	ADVERB
	Please be *careful.*	ADJECTIVE
	Please drive *carefully.*	ADVERB

Good or well

Good is an adjective; its use as an adverb is colloquial and nonstandard.

INCORRECT:	He plays *good.*
CORRECT:	He looks *good* to be an octogenarian.
	The quiche tastes very *good.*

Well may be either an adverb or an adjective. As an adjective, *well* means "in good health."

CORRECT:	He plays *well.*	ADVERB
	My mother is not *well.*	ADJECTIVE

Bad or badly

Bad is an adjective used after sense verbs such as *look, smell, taste, feel,* or *sound,* or after linking verbs (*is, am, are, was, were*).

INCORRECT:	I feel *badly* about the delay.
CORRECT:	I feel *bad* about the delay.

Badly is an adverb used after all other verbs.

INCORRECT:	It doesn't hurt very *bad.*
CORRECT:	It doesn't hurt very *badly.*

Real or really

Real is an adjective; its use as an adverb is colloquial and nonstandard. It means "genuine."

INCORRECT:	He writes *real* well.
CORRECT:	This is *real* leather.

Really is an adverb meaning "very."

INCORRECT:	This is *really* diamond.	
CORRECT:	Have a *really* nice day.	
EXAMPLE:	This is *real* amethyst.	ADJECTIVE
	This is *really* difficult.	ADVERB
	This is a *real* crisis.	ADJECTIVE
	This is *really* important.	ADVERB

Sort of and kind of

Sort of and *kind of* are often misused in written English by writers who actually mean *rather* or *somewhat*.

INCORRECT:	Jan was *kind of* saddened by the results of the test.
CORRECT:	Jan was *somewhat* saddened by the results of the test.

Skill 9: Comparisons and Superlatives

Skill 9 requires identification of appropriate comparative and superlative degree forms.

Sentences containing a faulty comparison often sound correct because their problem is not one of grammar but of logic. Read these sentences closely to make sure that like things are being compared, that the comparisons are complete, and that the comparisons are logical.

When comparing two persons or things, use the comparative, not the superlative form, of an adjective or an adverb. Use the superlative form for comparison of more than two persons or things. Use *any, other,* or *else* when comparing one thing or person with a group of which it/he or she is a part.

Most one- and two-syllable words form their comparative and superlative degrees with *-er* and *-est* suffixes. Adjectives and adverbs of more than two syllables form their comparative and superlative degrees with the addition of *more* and *most*.

Positive	Comparative	Superlative
good	better	best
old	older	oldest
friendly	friendlier	friendliest
lonely	lonelier	loneliest
talented	more talented	most talented
beautiful	more beautiful	most beautiful

A double comparison occurs when the degree of the modifier is changed incorrectly by adding both *-er* and *more* or *-est* and *most* to the adjective or adverb.

INCORRECT: He is the *most nicest* brother.

CORRECT: He is the *nicest* brother.

INCORRECT: She is the *more meaner* of the sisters.

CORRECT: She is the *meaner* sister.

Illogical comparisons occur when there is an implied comparison between two things that are not actually being compared or that cannot be logically compared.

INCORRECT: The interest at a loan company is higher *than* a bank.

CORRECT: The interest at a loan company is higher *than* that *at* a bank.

OR   The interest at a loan company is higher *than at a* bank.

Ambiguous comparisons occur when elliptical words (those omitted) create for the reader more than one interpretation of the sentence.

INCORRECT: I like Mary better than you. (than you *what*?)

CORRECT: I like Mary better than I like you.

OR   I like Mary better than you do.

Incomplete comparisons occur when the basis of the comparison (the two categories being compared) is not explicitly stated.

INCORRECT: Skywriting is *more* spectacular.

CORRECT: Skywriting is *more* spectacular *than* billboard advertising.

Do not omit the words *other, any,* or *else* when comparing one thing or person with a group of which it/he or she is a part.

> INCORRECT: Joan writes better *than any* student in her class.
>
> CORRECT: Joan writes better *than any other* student in her class.

Do not omit the second *as* of *as . . . as* when making a point of equal or superior comparison.

> INCORRECT: The University of West Florida is *as large* or larger than the University of North Florida.
>
> CORRECT: The University of West Florida is *as large as* or larger than the University of Northern Florida.

Do not omit the first category of the comparison, even if the two categories are the same.

> INCORRECT: This is one of the best, if not the best, college in the country.
>
> CORRECT: This is one of the best colleges in the country, if not the best.

The problem with the incorrect sentence is that *one of the best* requires the plural word *colleges,* not *college.*

Skill 10: Identify Standard Spelling

Spelling questions test your ability to recognize misspelled words. This section reviews spelling tips and rules to help you spot incorrect spellings. Problems such as the distinction between *to* and *too* and *lead* and *led* are covered under the Word Choice Skills section of this review.

- Remember, *i* before *e* except after *c,* or when sounded as "a" as in *neighbor* and *weigh.*

- There are only three words in the English language that end in *-ceed*:

    proceed, succeed, exceed

- There are several words that end in *-cede*:

    secede, recede, concede, precede

- There is only one word in the English language that ends in *-sede*:

    supersede

Many people learn to read English phonetically; that is, by sounding out the letters of the words. However, many English words are not pronounced the way they are spelled, and those who try to spell English words phonetically often make spelling *errors*. It is better to memorize the correct spelling of English words rather than relying on phonetics to spell correctly.

Skill 11: Identify Standard Punctuation

Commas

Commas should be placed according to standard rules of punctuation for purpose, clarity, and effect. The proper use of commas is explained in the following rules and examples:

In a series:

When more than one adjective describes a noun, use a comma to separate and emphasize each adjective. The comma takes the place of the word *and* in the series.

> the long, dark passageway
>
> another confusing, sleepless night
>
> an elaborate, complex, brilliant plan
>
> the old, grey, crumpled hat

Some adjective-noun combinations are thought of as one word. In these cases, the adjective in front of the adjective-noun combination needs no comma. If you inserted *and* between the adjective-noun combination, it would not make sense.

> a stately oak tree
>
> an exceptional wine glass
>
> my worst report card
>
> a china dinner plate

The comma is also used to separate words, phrases, and whole ideas (clauses); it still takes the place of *and* when used this way.

> an apple, a pear, a fig, and a banana
>
> a lovely lady, an elegant dress, and many admirers
>
> She lowered the shade, closed the curtain, turned off the light, and went to bed.

The only question that exists about the use of commas in a series is whether or not one should be used before the final item. It is standard usage to do so, although many newspapers and magazines have stopped using the final comma. Occasionally, the omission of the comma can be confusing.

> INCORRECT: He got on his horse, tracked a rabbit and a deer and rode on to Canton.
>
> CORRECT: We planned the trip with Mary and Harold, Susan, Dick and Joan, Gregory and Jean and Charles.

With a long introductory phrase:

Usually if a phrase of more than five or six words or a dependent clause precedes the subject at the beginning of a sentence, a comma is used to set it off.

> After last night's fiasco at the disco, she couldn't bear the thought of looking at him again.
>
> Whenever I try to talk about politics, my wife leaves the room.
>
> Provided you have said nothing, they will never guess who you are.

It is not necessary to use a comma with a short sentence.

> In January she will go to Switzerland.
>
> After I rest I'll feel better.
>
> During the day no one is home.

If an introductory phrase includes a verb form that is being used as another part of speech (a *verbal*), it must be followed by a comma.

> INCORRECT: When eating Mary never looked up from her plate.
>
> CORRECT: When eating, Mary never looked up from her plate.

> INCORRECT: Because of her desire to follow her faith in James wavered.
>
> CORRECT: Because of her desire to follow, her faith in James wavered.

> INCORRECT: Having decided to leave Mary James wrote her a letter.
>
> CORRECT: Having decided to leave Mary, James wrote her a letter.

To separate sentences with two main ideas:

To understand this use of the comma, you need to be able to recognize compound sentences. When a sentence contains more than two subjects and verbs (clauses), and the two clauses are joined by a conjunction (*and, but, or, nor, for, yet*), use a comma before the conjunction to show that another clause is coming.

> I thought I knew the poem by heart, but he showed me three lines I had forgotten.
>
> Are we really interested in helping the children, or are we more concerned with protecting our good names?
>
> He is supposed to leave tomorrow, but he is not ready to go.
>
> Jim knows you are disappointed, and he has known it for a long time.

If the two parts of the sentence are short and closely related, it is not necessary to use a comma.

He threw the ball and the dog ran after it.

Jane played the piano and Michael danced.

Be careful not to confuse a sentence that has a compound verb and a single subject with a compound sentence. If the subject is the same for both verbs, there is no need for a comma.

INCORRECT:	Charles sent some flowers, and wrote a long letter explaining why he had not been able to attend.
CORRECT:	Charles sent some flowers and wrote a long letter explaining why he had not been able to attend.
INCORRECT:	Last Thursday we went to the concert with Julia, and afterwards dined at an old Italian restaurant.
CORRECT:	Last Thursday we went to the concert with Julia and afterwards dined at an old Italian restaurant.
INCORRECT:	For the third time, the teacher explained that the literacy level for high school students was much lower than it had been in previous years, and, this time, wrote the statistics on the board for everyone to see.
CORRECT:	For the third time, the teacher explained that the literacy level for high school students was much lower than it had been in previous years and this time wrote the statistics on the board for everyone to see.

In general, words and phrases that stop the flow of the sentence or are unnecessary for the main idea are set off by commas.

Abbreviations after names:

Did you invite John Paul, Jr., and his sister?

Martha Harris, Ph.D., will be the speaker tonight.

Interjections (an exclamation without added grammatical connection):

Oh, I'm so glad to see you.

I tried so hard, alas, to do it.

Hey, let me out of here.

Direct address:

Roy, won't you open the door for the dog?

I can't understand, Mother, what you are trying to say.

May I ask, Mr. President, why you called us together?

Hey, lady, watch out for that car!

Tag questions:

You're really hungry, aren't you?

Jerry looks like his father, doesn't he?

Geographical names and addresses:

The concert will be held in Chicago, Illinois, on August 12.

The letter was addressed to Mrs. Marion Heartwell, 1881 Pine Lane, Palo Alto, CA 95824.

(Note: No comma is needed before the zip code, because it is already clearly set off from the state name.)

Transitional words and phrases:

On the other hand, I hope he gets better.

In addition, the phone rang constantly this afternoon.

I'm, nevertheless, going to the beach on Sunday.

You'll find, therefore, that no one is more loyal than I am.

Parenthetical words and phrases:

You will become, I believe, a great statesman.

We know, of course, that this is the only thing to do.

In fact, I planted corn last summer.

The Mannes affair was, to put it mildly, a surprise.

Unusual word order:

The dress, new and crisp, hung in the closet.

Intently, she stared out the window.

With nonrestrictive elements:

Parts of a sentence that modify other parts are sometimes essential to the meaning of the sentence and sometimes not. When a modifying word or group of words is not vital to the meaning of the sentence, it is set off by commas. Since it does not restrict the meaning of the words it modifies, it is called "nonrestrictive." Modifiers that are essential to the meaning of the sentence are called "restrictive" and are not set off by commas.

ESSENTIAL:	The girl *who wrote the story* is my sister.
NONESSENTIAL:	My sister, *the girl who wrote the story,* has always loved to write.
ESSENTIAL:	John Milton's famous poem *Paradise Lost* tells a remarkable story.
NONESSENTIAL:	Dante's greatest work, *The Divine Comedy,* marked the beginning of the Renaissance.
ESSENTIAL:	The cup *that is on the piano* is the one I want.
NONESSENTIAL:	The cup, *which my brother gave me last year,* is on the piano.
ESSENTIAL:	The people *who arrived late* were not seated.
NONESSENTIAL:	George, *who arrived late,* was not seated.

To set off direct quotations:

Most direct quotes or quoted materials are set off from the rest of the sentence by commas.

"Please read your part more loudly," the director insisted.

"I won't know what to do," said Michael, "if you leave me."

The teacher said sternly, "I will not dismiss this class until I have silence."

Who was it who said "Do not ask for whom the bell tolls; it tolls for thee"?

Note: Commas always go inside the closing quotation mark, even if the comma is not part of the material being quoted.

Be careful not to set off indirect quotes or quotes that are used as subjects or complements.

"To be or not to be" is the famous beginning of a soliloquy in Shakespeare's *Hamlet.* (subject)

She said she would never come back. (indirect quote)

Back then my favorite poem was "Evangeline." (complement)

To set off contrasting elements:

Her intelligence, not her beauty, got her the job.

Your plan will take you a little further from, rather than closer to, your destination.

It was a reasonable, though not appealing, idea.

He wanted glory, but found happiness instead.

In dates:

Both forms of the date are acceptable.

She will arrive on April 6, 1998.

He left on 5 December 1980.

In January 1967, he handed in his resignation.

On October 22, 1992, Frank and Julie were married.

Usually, when a subordinate clause is at the end of a sentence, no comma is necessary preceding the clause. However, when a subordinate clause introduces a sentence, a comma should be used after the clause.

Some common subordinating conjunctions are:

after	so that
although	though
as	till
as if	unless
because	until
before	when
even though	whenever
if	while
inasmuch as	since

Semicolons

Questions testing semicolon usage require you to be able to distinguish between the semicolon and the comma, and the semicolon and the colon. This review section covers the basic uses of the semicolon: to separate independent clauses not joined by a coordinating conjunction, to separate independent clauses separated by a conjunctive adverb, and to separate items in a series with internal commas. It is important to be consistent; if you use a semicolon between *any* of the items in the series, you must use semicolons to separate *all* of the items in the series.

Usually, a comma follows the conjunctive adverb. Note also that a period can be used to separate two sentences joined by a conjunctive adverb. Some common conjunctive adverbs are:

accordingly	nevertheless
besides	next
consequently	nonetheless
finally	now
furthermore	on the other hand
however	otherwise
indeed	perhaps
in fact	still
moreover	therefore

Then is also used as a conjunctive adverb, but it is not usually followed by a comma.

Use the semicolon

to separate independent clauses that are not joined by a coordinating conjunction:

I understand how to use commas; the semicolon I have not yet mastered.

to separate two independent clauses connected by a conjunctive adverb:

He took great care with his work; *therefore,* he was very successful.

to combine two independent clauses connected by a coordinating conjunction if either or both of the clauses contain other internal punctuation:

Success in college, some maintain, requires intelligence, industry, and perseverance; *but* others, fewer in number, assert that only personality is important.

to separate items in a series when each item has internal punctuation:

I bought an old, dilapidated chair; an antique table, which was in beautiful condition; and a new, ugly, blue and white rug.

Call our customer service line for assistance: Arizona, 1-800-555-6020; New Mexico, 1-800-555-5050; California, 1-800-555-3140; or Nevada, 1-800-555-3214.

Do not use the semicolon

to separate a dependent and an independent clause:

> INCORRECT: You should not make such statements; even though they are correct.

> CORRECT: You should not make such statements even though they are correct.

to separate an appositive phrase or clause from a sentence:

> INCORRECT: His immediate aim in life is centered around two things; becoming an engineer and learning to fly an airplane.

> CORRECT: His immediate aim in life is centered around two things: becoming an engineer and learning to fly an airplane.

to precede an explanation or summary of the first clause:

Note: Although the sentence below is punctuated correctly, the use of the semicolon provides a miscue, suggesting that the second clause is merely an extension, not an explanation, of the first clause. The colon provides a better clue.

> WEAK: The first week of camping was wonderful; we lived in cabins instead of tents.

> BETTER: The first week of camping was wonderful: we lived in cabins instead of tents.

to substitute for a comma:

> INCORRECT: My roommate also likes sports; particularly football, basketball, and baseball.

> CORRECT: My roommate also likes sports, particularly football, basketball, and baseball.

to set off other types of phrases or clauses from a sentence:

> INCORRECT: Being of a cynical mind; I should ask for a recount of the ballots.

> CORRECT: Being of a cynical mind, I should ask for a recount of the ballots.

INCORRECT: The next meeting of the club has been postponed two weeks; inasmuch as both the president and vice president are out of town.

CORRECT: The next meeting of the club has been postponed two weeks, inasmuch as both the president and vice president are out of town.

Note: The semicolon is not a terminal mark of punctuation; therefore, it should not be followed by a capital letter unless the first word in the second clause ordinarily requires capitalization.

Colons

While it is true that a colon is used to precede a list, one must also make sure that a complete sentence precedes the colon. The colon signals the reader that a list, explanation, or restatement of the preceding will follow. It is like an arrow, indicating that something is to follow. The difference between the colon and the semicolon and between the colon and the period is that the colon is an introductory mark, not a terminal mark. Look at the following examples:

The Constitution provides for a separation of powers among the three branches of government.

government.   The period signals a new sentence.

government;   The semicolon signals an interrelated sentence.

government,   The comma signals a coordinating conjunction followed by another independent clause.

government: The colon signals a list.

The Constitution provides for a separation of powers among the three branches of *government:* executive, legislative, and judicial.

Ensuring that a complete sentence precedes a colon means following these rules:

Use the colon to introduce a list (one item may constitute a list):

I hate this one course: English.

Three plays by William Shakespeare will be presented in repertory this summer at the University of Michigan: *Hamlet, Macbeth,* and *Othello.*

To introduce a list preceded by *as follows* or *the following*:

The reasons he cited for his success are as follows: integrity, honesty, industry, and a pleasant disposition.

To separate two independent clauses, when the second clause is a restatement or explanation of the first:

> All of my high school teachers said one thing in particular: college is going to
> be difficult.

To introduce a word or word group that is a restatement, explanation, or summary of the first sentence:

> These two things he loved: an honest man and a beautiful woman.

To introduce a formal appositive:

> I am positive there is one appeal that you can't overlook: money.

To separate the introductory words from a quotation that follows, if the quotation is formal, long, or paragraphed separately:

> The actor then stated: "I would rather be able to adequately play the part of
> Hamlet than to perform a miraculous operation, deliver a great lecture, or build
> a magnificent skyscraper."

The colon should only be used after statements that are grammatically complete.

Do *not* use a colon after a verb:

INCORRECT:	My favorite holidays are: Christmas, New Year's Eve, and Halloween.
CORRECT:	My favorite holidays are Christmas, New Year's Eve, and Halloween.

Do *not* use a colon after a preposition:

INCORRECT:	I enjoy different ethnic foods such as: Greek, Chinese, and Italian.
CORRECT:	I enjoy different ethnic foods such as Greek, Chinese, and Italian.

Do *not* use a colon interchangeably with the dash:

INCORRECT:	Mathematics, German, English: these gave me the greatest difficulty of all my studies.
CORRECT:	Mathematics, German, English—these gave me the greatest difficulty of all my studies.

Information preceding the colon should be a complete sentence regardless of the explanatory information following the clause.

Do *not* use the colon before the words *for example, namely, that is,* or *for instance* even though these words may be introducing a list.

INCORRECT: We agreed to it: namely, to give him a surprise party.

CORRECT: There are a number of well-known American women writers: for example, Nikki Giovanni, Phillis Wheatley, Emily Dickinson, and Maya Angelou.

Colon usage questions test your knowledge of the colon preceding a list, restatement, or explanation. These questions also require you to be able to distinguish between the colon and the period, the colon and the comma, and the colon and the semicolon.

Apostrophes

Apostrophe questions require you to know when an apostrophe has been used appropriately to make a noun possessive, not plural. Remember the following rules when considering how to show possession.

Add *'s* to singular nouns and indefinite pronouns:

    Tiffany's flowers

    a dog's bark

    everybody's computer

    at the owner's expense

    today's paper

Add *'s* to singular nouns ending in *s,* unless this distorts the pronunciation:

    Delores's paper

    the boss's pen

    Dr. Yots' class

    for righteousness' sake

    Dr. Evans's office OR Dr. Evans' office

Add *an apostrophe* to plural nouns ending in *s* or *es*:

    two cents' worth

    ladies' night

    thirteen years' experience

    two weeks' pay

Add '*s* to plural nouns not ending in *s:*

> men's room
>
> children's toys

Add '*s* to the last word in compound words or groups:

> brother-in-law's car
>
> someone else's paper

Add '*s* to the last name when indicating joint ownership:

> Joe and Edna's home
>
> Julie and Kathy's party
>
> women and children's clinic

Add '*s* to both names if you intend to show ownership by each person:

> Joe's and Edna's trucks
>
> Julie's and Kathy's pies
>
> Ted's and Jane's marriage vows

Possessive pronouns change their forms *without* the addition of an apostrophe:

> her, his, hers
>
> your, yours
>
> their, theirs
>
> it, its

Use the possessive form of a noun preceding a gerund:

> His driving annoys me.
>
> My bowling a strike irritated him.
>
> Do you mind our stopping by?
>
> We appreciate your coming.

Add '*s* to words and initials to show that they are plural:

> no if's, and's, or but's
>
> the do's and don't's of dating
>
> three A's
>
> IRA's are available at the bank.

Add *s* to numbers, symbols, and letters to show that they are plural:

> TVs
>
> VCRs
>
> the 1800s
>
> the returning POWs

Quotation Marks and Italics

These kinds of questions test your knowledge of the proper use of quotation marks with other marks of punctuation, with titles, and with dialogue. These kinds of questions also test your knowledge of the correct use of italics and underlining with titles and words used as sample words (for example, *the word is is a common verb*).

The most common use of double quotation marks (") is to set off quoted words, phrases, and sentences.

> "If everybody minded their own business," said the Duchess in a hoarse growl, "the world would go round a great deal faster than it does."
>
> "Then you would say what you mean," the March Hare went on.
>
> "I do," Alice hastily replied: "at least—at least I mean what I say—that's the same thing, you know."
>
> > —from Lewis Carroll's *Alice in Wonderland*

Single quotation marks are used to set off quoted material within a quote.

> "Shall I bring 'Rime of the Ancient Mariner' along with us?" she asked her brother.
>
> Mrs. Green said, "The doctor told me, 'Go immediately to bed when you get home!'"
>
> "If she said that to me," Katherine insisted, "I would tell her, 'I never intend to speak to you again! Goodbye, Susan!'"

When writing dialogue, begin a new paragraph each time the speaker changes.

> "Do you know what time it is?" asked Jane.
>
> "Can't you see I'm busy?" snapped Mary.
>
> "It's easy to see that you're in a bad mood today!" replied Jane.

Use quotation marks to enclose words used as words (sometimes italics are used for this purpose).

"Judgment" has always been a difficult word for me to spell.

Do you know what "abstruse" means?

"Horse and buggy" and "bread and butter" can be used either as adjectives or as nouns.

If slang is used within more formal writing, the slang words or phrases should be set off with quotation marks.

Harrison's decision to leave the conference and to "stick his neck out" by flying to Jamaica was applauded by the rest of the conference attendees.

When words are meant to have an unusual or specific significance to the reader, for instance irony or humor, they are sometimes placed in quotation marks.

For years, women were not allowed to buy real estate in order to "protect" them from unscrupulous dealers.

The "conversation" resulted in one black eye and a broken nose.

To set off titles of TV shows, poems, stories, and book chapters, use quotation marks. (Book, motion picture, newspaper, and magazine titles are underlined when handwritten and italicized when printed.)

The article "Moving South in the Southern Rain," by Jergen Smith in the *Southern News,* attracted the attention of our editor.

The assignment is "Childhood Development," Chapter 18 of *Human Behavior.*

My favorite essay by Montaigne is "On Silence."

"Happy Days" led the TV ratings for years, didn't it?

You will find Keats' "Ode to a Grecian Urn" in Chapter 3, "The Romantic Era," in Lastly's *Selections from Great English Poets.*

Errors to avoid:

Be sure to remember that quotation marks always come in pairs. Do not make the mistake of using only one set.

INCORRECT: "You'll never convince me to move to the city, said Thurman. I consider it an insane asylum."

CORRECT: "You'll never convince me to move to the city," said Thurman. "I consider it an insane asylum."

INCORRECT:	"Idleness and pride tax with a heavier hand than kings and parliaments," Benjamin Franklin is supposed to have said. If we can get rid of the former, we may easily bear the latter."
CORRECT:	"Idleness and pride tax with a heavier hand than kings and parliaments," Benjamin Franklin is supposed to have said. "If we can get rid of the former, we may easily bear the latter."

When a quote consists of several sentences, do not put the quotation marks at the beginning and end of each sentence; put them at the beginning and end of the entire quotation.

INCORRECT:	"It was during his student days in Bonn that Beethoven fastened upon Schiller's poem." "The heady sense of liberation in the verses must have appealed to him." "They appealed to every German."—John Burke
CORRECT:	"It was during his student days in Bonn that Beethoven fastened upon Schiller's poem. The heady sense of liberation in the verses must have appealed to him. They appealed to every German."—John Burke

Instead of setting off a long quote with quotation marks, if it is longer than five or six lines you may want to indent and single space it. If you do indent, do not use quotation marks.

In his *First Inaugural Address,* Abraham Lincoln appeals to the war-torn American people:

> We are not enemies, but friends. We must not be enemies. Though passion may have strained, it must not break, our bonds of affection. The mystic chords of memory, stretching from every battlefield and patriot grave to every living heart and hearthstone all over this broad land, will yet swell the chorus of the Union when again touched, as surely they will be, by the better angels of our nature.

Be careful not to use quotation marks with indirect quotations.

INCORRECT:	Mary wondered "if she would get over it."
CORRECT:	Mary wondered if she would get over it.

INCORRECT:	The nurse asked "how long it had been since we had visited the doctor's office."
CORRECT:	The nurse asked how long it had been since we had visited the doctor's office.

When you quote several paragraphs, it is not sufficient to place quotation marks at the beginning and end of the entire quote. Place quotation marks at the *beginning of each paragraph,* but only at the *end of the last paragraph.* Here is an abbreviated quotation for an example:

> "Here begins an odyssey through the world of classical mythology, starting with the creation of the world . . .
>
> "It is true that themes similar to the classical may be found in any corpus of mythology . . . Even technology is not immune to the influence of Greece and Rome . . .
>
> "We need hardly mention the extent to which painters and sculptors . . . have used and adapted classical mythology to illustrate the past, to reveal the human body, to express romantic or antiromantic ideals, or to symbolize any particular point of view."

Remember that commas and periods are *always* placed inside the quotation marks even if they are not actually part of the quote.

INCORRECT:	"Life always gets colder near the summit", Nietzsche is purported to have said, "—the cold increases, responsibility grows".
CORRECT:	"Life always gets colder near the summit," Nietzsche is purported to have said, "—the cold increases, responsibility grows."
INCORRECT:	"Get down here right away", John cried. "You'll miss the sunset if you don't."
CORRECT:	"Get down here right away," John cried. "You'll miss the sunset if you don't."
INCORRECT:	"If my dog could talk", Mary mused, "I'll bet he would say, 'Take me for a walk right this minute'."
CORRECT:	"If my dog could talk," Mary mused, "I'll bet he would say, 'Take me for a walk right this minute'."

Other marks of punctuation, such as question marks, exclamation points, colons, and semicolons, go inside the quotation marks if they are part of the quoted material. If they are not part of the quotation, however, they go outside the quotation marks. Be careful to distinguish between the guidelines for the comma and period, which always go inside the quotation marks, and those for other marks of punctuation.

INCORRECT:	"I'll always love you"! he exclaimed happily.
CORRECT:	"I'll always love you!" he exclaimed happily.

INCORRECT:	Did you hear her say, "He'll be there early?"
CORRECT:	Did you hear her say, "He'll be there early"?

INCORRECT:	She called down the stairs, "When are you going"?
CORRECT:	She called down the stairs, "When are you going?"

INCORRECT:	"Let me out"! he cried. "Don't you have any pity"?
CORRECT:	"Let me out!" he cried. "Don't you have any pity?"

Remember to use only one mark of punctuation at the end of a sentence ending with a quotation mark.

INCORRECT:	She thought out loud, "Will I ever finish this paper in time for that class?".
CORRECT:	She thought out loud, "Will I ever finish this paper in time for that class?"

INCORRECT:	"Not the same thing a bit!", said the Hatter. "Why, you might just as well say that 'I see what I eat' is the same thing as 'I eat what I see'!".
CORRECT:	"Not the same thing a bit!" said the Hatter. "Why, you might just as well say that 'I see what I eat' is the same thing as 'I eat what I see'!"

Skill 12: Identify Standard Capitalization

When a word is capitalized, it calls attention to itself. This attention should be for a good reason. There are standard uses for capital letters. In general, capitalize (1) all proper nouns, (2) the first word of a sentence, and (3) the first word of a direct quotation.

You should also capitalize

Names of ships, aircraft, spacecraft, and trains:

Apollo 13	*Mariner IV*
DC-10	S.S. *United States*
Sputnik II	Boeing 707

Names of deities:

God	Jupiter
Allah	Holy Ghost
Buddha	Venus
Jehovah	Shiva

Geological periods:

Neolithic age	Cenozoic era
late Pleistocene times	Ice Age

Names of astronomical bodies:

Mercury	Big Dipper
the Milky Way	Halley's comet
Ursa Major	North Star

Personifications:

Reliable Nature brought her promised Spring.

Bring on Melancholy in his sad might.

She believed that Love was the answer to all her problems.

Historical periods:

the Middle Ages	World War I
Reign of Terror	Great Depression
Christian Era	Roaring Twenties
Age of Louis XIV	Renaissance

Organizations, associations, and institutions:

Girl Scouts	North Atlantic Treaty Organization
Kiwanis Club	League of Women Voters
Florida Marlins	Unitarian Church
Smithsonian Institution	Common Market
Library of Congress	Franklin Glen High School
New York Philharmonic	Harvard University

Government and judicial groups:

United States Court of Appeals	Senate
Committee on Foreign Affairs	Parliament
New Jersey City Council	Peace Corps
Arkansas Supreme Court	Census Bureau
House of Representatives	Department of State

A general term that accompanies a specific name is capitalized only if it follows the specific name. If it stands alone or comes before the specific name, it is put in lowercase:

Washington State	the state of Washington
Senator Martinez	the senator from Florida
Central Park	the park
Golden Gate Bridge	the bridge
President Bush	the president of the United States
Pope Benedict	the pope
Queen Elizabeth I	the queen of England
Tropic of Capricorn	the tropics
Monroe Doctrine	the doctrine of expansion
the Mississippi River	the river
Easter Day	the day
Treaty of Versailles	the treaty
Webster's Dictionary	the dictionary
Equatorial Current	the equator

Use a capital to start a sentence:

Our car would not start.

When will you leave? I need to know right away.

Never!

Let me in! Please!

When a sentence appears within a sentence, start it with a capital letter:

We had only one concern: When would we eat?

My sister said, "I'll find the Monopoly game."

He answered, "We can only stay a few minutes."

The most important words of titles are capitalized. Those words not capitalized are conjunctions (*and, or, but*) and short prepositions (*of, on, by, for*). The first and last word of a title must always be capitalized:

A Man for All Seasons	*Crime and Punishment*
Of Mice and Men	*Rise of the West*
Strange Life of Ivan Osokin	"Sonata in G Minor"
"Let Me In"	"Ode to Billy Joe"
"Rubaiyat of Omar Khayyam"	"All in the Family"

Capitalize newspaper and magazine titles:

U.S. News & World Report

National Geographic

the *New York Times*

the *Washington Post*

Capitalize radio and TV station call letters:

ABC	NBC
WNEW	WBOP
CNN	HBO

Do not capitalize compass directions or seasons:

west	north
east	south
spring	winter
autumn	summer

Capitalize regions:

the South	the Northeast
the West	Eastern Europe
BUT:	the south of France
	the east part of town

Capitalize specific military units:

> the U.S. Army
>
> the 7th Fleet
>
> the German Navy
>
> the 1st Infantry Division

Capitalize political groups and philosophies:

Democrat	Communist
Marxist	Nazism
Whig	Federalist
Existentialism	Transcendentalism

BUT do not capitalize systems of government or individual adherents to a philosophy:

democracy	communism
fascist	agnostic

Vocabulary Builder

Although the context in which a word appears can help you determine the meaning of the word, one sure-fire way to know a definition is to learn it. By studying the following lists of words and memorizing their definition(s), you will be better equipped to answer Reading Section questions that deal with word meanings.

To benefit most from this vocabulary list, study the words and their definitions, then answer all of the drill questions that appear at the end of the review. Make sure to check your answers with the answer key.

Group 1

> abstract – *adj.* – not easy to understand; theoretical
>
> acclaim – *n.* – loud approval; applause
>
> acquiesce – *v.* – agree or consent to an opinion
>
> adamant – *adj.* – not yielding; firm
>
> adversary – *n.* – an enemy; foe
>
> advocate – 1. *v.* – to plead in favor of; 2. *n.* – supporter; defender

aesthetic – *adj.* – showing good taste; artistic

alleviate – *v.* – to lessen or make easier

aloof – *adj.* – distant in interest; reserved; cool

altercation – *n.* – controversy; dispute

altruistic – *adj.* – unselfish

amass – *v.* – to collect together; accumulate

ambiguous – *adj.* – not clear; uncertain; vague

ambivalent – *adj.* – undecided

ameliorate – *v.* – to make better; to improve

amiable – *adj.* – friendly

amorphous – *adj.* – having no determinate form

anarchist – *n.* – one who believes that a formal government is unnecessary

antagonism – *n.* – hostility; opposition

apathy – *n.* – lack of emotion or interest

appease – *v.* – to make quiet; to calm

apprehensive – *adj.* – fearful; aware; conscious

arbitrary – *adj.* – based on one's preference or whim

arrogant – *adj.* – acting superior to others; conceited

articulate – 1. *v.* – to speak distinctly; 2. *adj.* – eloquent; fluent; 3. *adj.* – capable of speech; 4. *v.* – to hinge; to connect; 5. *v.* – to convey; to express effectively

Drill 1

➤ **Directions:** Match each word in the left column with the word in the right column that is most *opposite* in meaning.

Word				Match		
1. ___ articulate	6. ___ abstract	A.	hostile	F.	disperse
2. ___ apathy	7. ___ acquiesce	B.	concrete	G.	enthusiasm
3. ___ amiable	8. ___ arbitrary	C.	selfish	H.	certain
4. ___ altruistic	9. ___ amass	D.	reasoned	I.	resist
5. ___ ambivalent	10. ___ adversary	E.	ally	J.	incoherent

➤ **Directions:** Match each word in the left column with the word in the right column that is most *similar* in meaning.

Word		**Match**	

11. ___ adamant   14. ___ antagonism   A. afraid   D. insistent

12. ___ aesthetic   15. ___ altercation   B. disagreement   E. hostility

13. ___ apprehensive   C. tasteful

Group 2

assess – *v.* – to estimate the value of

astute – *adj.* – cunning; sly; crafty

atrophy – *v.* – to waste away through lack of nutrition

audacious – *adj.* – fearless; bold

augment – *v.* – to increase or add to; to make larger

austere – *adj.* – harsh; severe; strict

authentic – *adj.* – real; genuine; trustworthy

authoritarian – *adj.* – acting as a dictator; demanding obedience

banal – *adj.* – common; petty; ordinary

belittle – *v.* – to make small; to think lightly of

benefactor – *n.* – one who helps others; a donor

benevolent – *adj.* – kind; generous

benign – *adj.* – mild; harmless

biased – *adj.* – prejudiced; influenced; not neutral

blasphemous – *adj.* – irreligious; away from acceptable standards

blithe – *adj.* – happy; cheery; merry

brevity – *n.* – briefness; shortness

candid – *adj.* – honest; truthful; sincere

capricious – *adj.* – changeable; fickle

caustic – *adj.* – burning; sarcastic; harsh

censor – *v.* – to examine and delete objectionable material

censure – *v.* – to criticize or disapprove of

charlatan – *n.* – an imposter; fake

coalesce – *v.* – to combine; come together

collaborate – *v.* – to work together; cooperate

Drill 2

➤ **Directions:** Match each word in the left column with the word in the right column that is most *opposite* in meaning.

	Word				Match		
1.	___ augment	6.	___ authentic	A.	permit	F.	malicious
2.	___ biased	7.	___ candid	B.	religious	G.	neutral
3.	___ banal	8.	___ belittle	C.	praise	H.	mournful
4.	___ benevolent	9.	___ blasphemous	D.	diminish	I.	unusual
5.	___ censor	10.	___ blithe	E.	dishonest	J.	ersatz

➤ **Directions:** Match each word in the left column with the word in the right column that is most *similar* in meaning.

	Word				Match		
11.	___ collaborate	14.	___ censure	A.	harmless	D.	cooperate
12.	___ benign	15.	___ capricious	B.	cunning	E.	criticize
13.	___ astute			C.	changeable		

Group 3

compatible – *adj.* – in agreement; harmonious

complacent – *adj.* – content; self-satisfied; smug

compliant – *adj.* – yielding; obedient

comprehensive – *adj.* – all-inclusive; complete; thorough

compromise – *v.* – to settle by mutual adjustment

concede – 1. *v.* – to acknowledge; admit; 2. to surrender; to abandon one's position

concise – *adj.* – in few words; brief; condensed

condescend – *v.* – to come down from one's position or dignity

condone – *v.* – to overlook; to forgive

conspicuous – *adj.* – easy to see; noticeable

consternation – *n.* – amazement or terror that causes confusion

consummation – *n.* – the completion; finish

contemporary – *adj.* – living or happening at the same time; modern contempt – *n.* – scorn; disrespect

contrite – *adj.* – regretful; sorrowful

conventional – *adj.* – traditional; common; routine

cower – *v.* – crouch down in fear or shame

defamation – *n.* – any harm to a name or reputation; slander

deference – *n.* – a yielding to the opinion of another

deliberate – 1. *v.* – to consider carefully; weigh in the mind; 2. *adj.* – intentional

denounce – *v.* – to speak out against; condemn

depict – *v.* – to portray in words; present a visual image

deplete – *v.* – to reduce; to empty

depravity – *n.* – moral corruption; badness

deride – *v.* – to ridicule; laugh at with scorn

Drill 3

➤ **Directions:** Match each word in the left column with the word in the right column that is most *opposite* in meaning.

	Word			Match		
1.	___ deplete	6.	___ condone	A. unintentional	F.	support
2.	___ contemporary	7.	___ conspicuous	B. disapprove	G.	beginning
3.	___ concise	8.	___ consummation	C. invisible	H.	ancient
4.	___ deliberate	9.	___ denounce	D. respect	I.	virtue
5.	___ depravity	10.	___ contempt	E. fill	J.	verbose

➤ **Directions:** Match each word in the left column with the word in the right column that is most *similar* in meaning.

	Word			Match		
11.	___ compatible	14.	___ comprehensive	A. portray	D.	thorough
12.	___ depict	15.	___ complacent	B. content	E.	common
13.	___ conventional			C. harmonious		

Group 4

desecrate – *v.* – to violate a holy place or sanctuary

detached – *adj.* – separated; not interested; standing alone

deter – *v.* – to prevent; to discourage; hinder

didactic – 1. *adj.* – instructive; 2. dogmatic; preachy

digress – *v.* – stray from the subject; wander from topic

diligence – *n.* – hard work

discerning – *adj.* – distinguishing one thing from another

discord – *n.* – disagreement; lack of harmony

discriminating – 1. *v.* – distinguishing one thing from another; 2. *v.* – demonstrating bias; 3. *adj.* – able to distinguish

disdain – 1. *n.* – intense dislike; 2. *v.* – look down upon; scorn

disparage – *v.* – to belittle; undervalue

disparity – *n.* – difference in form, character, or degree

dispassionate – *adj.* – lack of feeling; impartial

disperse – *v.* – to scatter; separate

disseminate – *v.* – to circulate; scatter

dissent – *v.* – to disagree; differ in opinion

dissonance – *n.* – harsh contradiction

diverse – *adj.* – different; dissimilar

document – 1. *n.* – official paper containing information; 2. *v.* – to support; substantiate; verify

dogmatic – *adj.* – stubborn; biased; opinionated

dubious – *adj.* – doubtful; uncertain; skeptical; suspicious

eccentric – *adj.* – odd; peculiar; strange

efface – *v.* – wipe out; erase

effervescence – 1. *n.* – liveliness; spirit; enthusiasm; 2. bubbliness

egocentric – *adj.* – self-centered

Drill 4

➤ **Directions:** Match each word in the left column with the word in the right column that is most *opposite* in meaning.

Word				Match			
1. ___ detached	6. ___ dubious	A.	agree	F.	respect
2. ___ deter	7. ___ diligence	B.	certain	G.	compliment
3. ___ dissent	8. ___ disdain	C.	lethargy	H.	sanctify
4. ___ discord	9. ___ desecrate	D.	connected	I.	harmony
5. ___ efface	10. ___ disparage	E.	assist	J.	restore

➤ **Directions:** Match each word in the left column with the word in the right column that is most *similar* in meaning.

Word				Match		
11. ___ effervescence	14. ___ document	A.	stubborn	D.	liveliness
12. ___ dogmatic	15. ___ eccentric	B.	distribute	E.	odd
13. ___ disseminate		C.	substantiate		

Group 5

elaboration – *n.* – the act of clarifying or adding details

eloquence – *n.* – the ability to speak well

elusive – *adj.* – hard to catch; difficult to understand

emulate – *v.* – to imitate; copy; mimic

endorse – *v.* – support; to approve of; recommend

engender – *v.* – to create; bring about

enhance – *v.* – to improve; compliment; make more attractive

enigma – *n.* – mystery; secret; perplexity

ephemeral – *adj.* – temporary; brief; short-lived

equivocal – *adj.* – doubtful; uncertain

erratic – *adj.* – unpredictable; strange

erroneous – *adj.* – untrue; inaccurate; not correct

esoteric – *adj.* – incomprehensible; obscure

euphony – *n.* – pleasant sound

execute –1. *v.* – put to death; kill; 2. to carry out; fulfill

exemplary – *adj.* – serving as an example; outstanding

exhaustive – *adj.* – thorough; complete

expedient – *adj.* – helpful; practical; worthwhile

expedite – *v.* – speed up

explicit – *adj.* – specific; definite

extol – *v.* – praise; commend

extraneous – *adj.* – irrelevant; not related; not essential

facilitate – *v.* – make easier; simplify

fallacious – *adj.* – misleading

fanatic – *n.* – enthusiast; extremist

Drill 5

➤ **Directions:** Match each word in the left column with the word in the right column that is most *opposite* in meaning.

	Word				Match		
1.	___ extraneous	6.	___ erratic	A.	incomplete	F.	eternal
2.	___ ephemeral	7.	___ explicit	B.	delay	G.	condemn
3.	___ exhaustive	8.	___ euphony	C.	dependable	H.	relevant
4.	___ expedite	9.	___ elusive	D.	comprehensible	I.	indefinite
5.	___ erroneous	10.	___ extol	E.	dissonance	J.	accurate

➤ **Directions:** Match each word in the left column with the word in the right column that is most *similar* in meaning.

	Word				Match		
11.	___ endorse	14.	___ fallacious	A.	enable	D.	worthwhile
12.	___ expedient	15.	___ engender	B.	recommend	E.	deceptive
13.	___ facilitate			C.	create		

Group 6

fastidious – *adj.* – fussy; hard to please

fervent – *n.* – passionate; intense

fickle – *adj.* – changeable; unpredictable

fortuitous – *adj.* – accidental; happening by chance; lucky

frivolity – *n.* – giddiness; lack of seriousness

fundamental – *adj.* – basic; necessary

furtive – *adj.* – secretive; sly

futile – *adj.* – worthless; unprofitable

glutton – *n.* – overeater

grandiose – *adj.* – extravagant; flamboyant

gravity – *n.* – seriousness

guile – *n.* – slyness; deceit

gullible – *adj.* – easily fooled

hackneyed – *adj.* – commonplace; trite

hamper – *v.* – interfere with; hinder

haphazard – *adj.* – disorganized; random

hedonistic – *adj.* – pleasure seeking

heed – *v.* – obey; yield to

heresy – *n.* – opinion contrary to popular belief

hindrance – *n.* – blockage; obstacle

humility – *n.* – lack of pride; modesty

hypocritical – *adj.* – two-faced; deceptive

hypothetical – *adj.* – assumed; uncertain

illuminate – *v.* – make understandable

illusory – *adj.* – unreal; false; deceptive

Drill 6

➤ **Directions:** Match each word in the left column with the word in the right column that is most *opposite* in meaning.

	Word				Match		
1. ___ heresy		6. ___ fervent		A. predictable		F. beneficial	
2. ___ fickle		7. ___ fundamental		B. dispassionate		G. orthodoxy	
3. ___ illusory		8. ___ furtive		C. simple		H. organized	
4. ___ frivolity		9. ___ futile		D. extraneous		I. candid	
5. ___ grandiose		10. ___ haphazard		E. real		J. seriousness	

➤ **Directions:** Match each word in the left column with the word in the right column that is most *similar* in meaning.

	Word				Match		
11. ___ glutton		14. ___ hackneyed		A. hinder		D. overeater	
12. ___ heed		15. ___ hindrance		B. obstacle		E. obey	
13. ___ hamper				C. trite			

Group 7

immune – *adj.* – protected; unthreatened by

immutable – *adj.* – unchangeable; permanent

impartial – *adj.* – unbiased; fair

impetuous – 1. *adj.* – rash; impulsive; 2. forcible; violent

implication – *n.* – suggestion; inference

inadvertent – *adj.* – not on purpose; unintentional

incessant – *adj.* – constant; continual

incidental – *adj.* – extraneous; unexpected

inclined – 1. *adj.* – apt to; likely to; 2. angled

incoherent – *adj.* – illogical; rambling

incompatible – *adj.* – disagreeing; disharmonious

incredulous – *adj.* – unwilling to believe; skeptical

indifferent – *adj.* – unconcerned

indolent – *adj.* – lazy; inactive

indulgent – *adj.* – lenient; extravagant

inevitable – *adj.* – sure to happen; unavoidable

infamous – *adj.* – having a bad reputation; notorious

infer – *v.* – form an opinion; conclude

initiate – 1. *v.* – begin; admit into a group; 2. *n.* – a person who is in the process of being admitted into a group

innate – *adj.* – natural; inborn

innocuous – *adj.* – harmless; innocent

innovate – *v.* – introduce a change; depart from the old

insipid – *adj.* – uninteresting; bland

instigate – *v.* – start; provoke

intangible – *adj.* – incapable of being touched; immaterial

Drill 7

➤ **Directions:** Match each word in the left column with the word in the right column that is most *opposite* in meaning.

Word		Match	
1. ___ immutable	6. ___ innate	A. intentional	F. changeable
2. ___ impartial	7. ___ incredulous	B. articulate	G. avoidable
3. ___ inadvertent	8. ___ inevitable	C. gullible	H. harmonious
4. ___ incoherent	9. ___ intangible	D. material	I. learned
5. ___ incompatible	10. ___ indolent	E. biased	J. energetic

➤ **Directions:** Match each word in the left column with the word in the right column that is most *similar* in meaning.

Word		Match	
11. ___ impetuous	14. ___ instigate	A. lenient	D. conclude
12. ___ incidental	15. ___ indulgent	B. impulsive	E. extraneous
13. ___ infer		C. provoke	

Group 8

ironic – *adj.* – contradictory; inconsistent; sarcastic

irrational – *adj.* – not logical

jeopardy – *n.* – danger

kindle – *v.* – ignite; arouse

languid – *adj.* – weak; fatigued

laud – *v.* – to praise

lax – *adj.* – careless; irresponsible

lethargic – *adj.* – lazy; passive

levity – *n.* – silliness; lack of seriousness

lucid – 1. *adj.* – shining; 2. easily understood

magnanimous – *adj.* – forgiving; unselfish

malicious – *adj.* – spiteful; vindictive

marred – *adj.* – damaged

meander – *v.* – wind on a course; go aimlessly

melancholy – *n.* – depression; gloom

meticulous – *adj.* – exacting; precise

minute – *adj.* – extremely small; tiny

miser – *n.* – penny pincher; stingy person

mitigate – *v.* – alleviate; lessen; soothe

morose – *adj.* – moody; despondent

negligence – *n.* – carelessness

neutral – *adj.* – impartial; unbiased

nostalgic – *adj.* – longing for the past; filled with bittersweet memories

novel – *adj.* – new

Drill 8

➤ **Directions:** Match each word in the left column with the word in the right column that is most *opposite* in meaning.

	Word			Match		
1.	___ irrational	6.	___ magnanimous	A. extinguish	F.	ridicule
2.	___ kindle	7.	___ levity	B. jovial	G.	kindly
3.	___ meticulous	8.	___ minute	C. selfish	H.	sloppy
4.	___ malicious	9.	___ laud	D. logical	I.	huge
5.	___ morose	10.	___ novel	E. seriousness	J.	stale

➤ **Directions:** Match each word in the left column with the word in the right column that is most *similar* in meaning.

	Word			Match		
11.	___ ironic	14.	___ jeopardy	A. lessen	D.	carelessness
12.	___ marred	15.	___ negligence	B. damaged	E.	danger
13.	___ mitigate			C. sarcastic		

Group 9

nullify – *v.* – cancel; invalidate

objective – 1. *adj.* – open-minded; impartial; 2. *n.* – goal

obscure – *adj.* – not easily understood; dark

obsolete – *adj.* – out of date; passe

ominous – *adj.* – threatening

optimism – *n.* – hope for the best; seeing the good side

orthodox – *adj.* – traditional; accepted

pagan – 1. *n.* – polytheist; 2. *adj.* – polytheistic

partisan – 1. *n.* – supporter; follower; 2. *adj.* – biased; one sided

perceptive – *adj.* – full of insight; aware

peripheral – *adj.* – marginal; outer

pernicious – *adj.* – dangerous; harmful

pessimism – *n.* – seeing only the gloomy side; hopelessness phenomenon – 1. *n.* – miracle; 2. occurrence

philanthropy – *n.* – charity; unselfishness

pious – *adj.* – religious; devout; dedicated

placate – *v.* – pacify

plausible – *adj.* – probable; feasible

pragmatic – *adj.* – matter-of-fact; practical

preclude – *v.* – inhibit; make impossible

predecessor – *n.* – one who has occupied an office before another

prodigal – *adj.* – wasteful; lavish

prodigious – *adj.* – exceptional; tremendous

profound – *adj.* – deep; knowledgeable; thorough

profusion – *n.* – great amount; abundance

Drill 9

➤ **Directions:** Match each word in the left column with the word in the right column that is most *opposite* in meaning.

Word		Match	
1. ___ objective	6. ___ plausible	A. scantiness	F. minute
2. ___ obsolete	7. ___ preclude	B. assist	G. anger
3. ___ placate	8. ___ prodigious	C. mundane	H. pessimism
4. ___ profusion	9. ___ profound	D. biased	I. modern
5. ___ peripheral	10. ___ optimism	E. improbable	J. central

➤ **Directions:** Match each word in the left column with the word in the right column that is most *similar* in meaning.

Word		Match	
11. ___ nullify	14. ___ pernicious	A. invalidate	D. threatening
12. ___ ominous	15. ___ prodigal	B. follower	E. harmful
13. ___ partisan		C. lavish	

Group 10

prosaic – *adj.* – tiresome; ordinary

provincial – *adj.* – regional; unsophisticated

provocative – 1. *adj.* – tempting; 2. irritating

prudent – *adj.* – wise; careful; prepared

qualified – *adj.* – experienced; indefinite

rectify – *v.* – correct

redundant – *adj.* – repetitious; unnecessary

refute – *v.* – challenge; disprove

relegate – *v.* – banish; put to a lower position

relevant – *adj.* – of concern; significant

remorse – *n.* – guilt; sorrow

reprehensible – *adj.* – wicked; disgraceful

repudiate – *v.* – reject; cancel

rescind – *v.* – retract; discard

resignation – 1. *n.* – quitting; 2. submission

resolution – *n.* – proposal; promise; determination

respite – *n.* – recess; rest period

reticent – *adj.* – silent; reserved; shy

reverent – *adj.* – respectful

rhetorical – *adj.* – having to do with verbal communication

rigor – *n.* – severity

sagacious – *adj.* – wise; cunning

sanguine – 1. *adj.* – optimistic; cheerful; 2. red

saturate – *v.* – soak thoroughly; drench

scanty – *adj.* – inadequate; sparse

Drill 10

➤ **Directions:** Match each word in the left column with the word in the right column that is most *opposite* in meaning.

Word			Match	
1. ___ provincial	6. ___ remorse	A. inexperienced	F. affirm
2. ___ reticent	7. ___ repudiate	B. joy	G. extraordinary
3. ___ prudent	8. ___ sanguine	C. pessimistic	H. sophisticated
4. ___ qualified	9. ___ relevant	D. unrelated	I. forward
5. ___ relegate	10. ___ prosaic	E. careless	J. promote

➤ **Directions:** Match each word in the left column with the word in the right column that is most *similar* in meaning.

Word			Match	
11. ___ provocative	14. ___ rescind	A. drench	D. severity
12. ___ rigor	15. ___ reprehensible	B. tempting	E. blameworthy
13. ___ saturate		C. retract	

Group 11

scrupulous – *adj.* – honorable; exact

scrutinize – *v.* – examine closely; study

servile – *adj.* – slavish; groveling

skeptic – *n.* – doubter

slander – *v.* – defame; maliciously misrepresent

solemnity – *n.* – seriousness

solicit – *v.* – ask; seek

stagnant – *adj.* – motionless; uncirculating

stanza – *n.* – group of lines in a poem having a definite pattern

static – *adj.* – inactive; changeless

stoic – *adj.* – detached; unruffled; calm

subtle – *adj.* – understated

superficial – *adj.* – on the surface; narrow-minded; lacking depth superfluous – *adj.* – unnecessary; extra

surpass – *v.* – go beyond; outdo

sycophant – *n.* – flatterer

symmetry – *n.* – correspondence of parts; harmony

taciturn – *adj.* – reserved; quiet; secretive

tedious – *adj.* – time-consuming; burdensome; uninteresting

temper – *v.* – soften; pacify; compose

tentative – *adj.* – not confirmed; indefinite

thrifty – *adj.* – economical; pennywise

tranquility – *n.* – peace; stillness; harmony

trepidation – *n.* – apprehension; uneasiness

trivial – *adj.* – unimportant; small; worthless

Drill 11

➤ **Directions:** Match each word in the left column with the word in the right column that is most *opposite* in meaning.

Word				Match			
1. ___ scrutinize	6. ___ tentative	A.	frivolity	F.	skim
2. ___ skeptic	7. ___ thrifty	B.	enjoyable	G.	turbulent
3. ___ solemnity	8. ___ tranquility	C.	prodigal	H.	active
4. ___ static	9. ___ solicit	D.	chaos	I.	believer
5. ___ tedious	10. ___ stagnant	E.	give	J.	confirmed

➤ **Directions:** Match each word in the left column with the word in the right column that is most *similar* in meaning.

Word			Match	
11. ___ symmetry	14. ___ subtle	A.	understated	D.	fear
12. ___ superfluous	15. ___ trepidation	B.	unnecessary	E.	flatterer
13. ___ sycophant		C.	balance		

Group 12

tumid – *adj.* – swollen; inflated

undermine – *v.* – weaken; ruin

uniform – *adj.* – consistent; unvaried; unchanging

universal – *adj.* – concerning everyone; existing everywhere

unobtrusive – *adj.* – inconspicuous; reserved

unprecedented – *adj.* – unheard of; exceptional

unpretentious – *adj.* – simple; plain; modest

vacillation – *n.* – fluctuation

valid – *adj.* – acceptable; legal

vehement – *adj.* – intense; excited; enthusiastic

venerate – *v.* – revere

verbose – *adj.* – wordy; talkative

viable – 1. *adj.* – capable of maintaining life; 2. possible; attainable

vigorous – *adj.* – energetic; forceful

vilify – *v.* – slander

virtuoso – *n.* – highly skilled artist

virulent – *adj.* – deadly; harmful; malicious

vital – *adj.* – important; spirited

volatile – *adj.* – changeable; undependable

vulnerable – *adj.* – open to attack; unprotected

wane – *v.* – grow gradually smaller

whimsical – *adj.* – fanciful; amusing

wither – *v.* – wilt; shrivel; humiliate; cut down

zealot – *n.* – believer; enthusiast; fan

zenith – *n.* – point directly overhead in the sky

Drill 12

➤ **Directions:** Match each word in the left column with the word in the right column that is most *opposite* in meaning.

Word				Match			
1. ___ uniform	6. ___ vigorous	A.	amateur	F.	support
2. ___ virtuoso	7. ___ volatile	B.	trivial	G.	constancy
3. ___ vital	8. ___ vacillation	C.	visible	H.	lethargic
4. ___ wane	9. ___ undermine	D.	placid	I.	wax
5. ___ unobtrusive	10. ___ valid	E.	unacceptable	J.	varied

➤ **Directions:** Match each word in the left column with the word in the right column that is most *similar* in meaning.

Word				Match			
11. ___ wither	14. ___ vehement	A.	intense	D.	possible
12. ___ whimsical	15. ___ virulent	B.	deadly	E.	shrivel
13. ___ viable		C.	amusing		

Drill 13

➤ **Directions:** Each of the following questions provides a given word in capitalized letters followed by five word choices. Choose the word that is *opposite* in meaning to the given word.

1. AUTHENTIC:

(A) cheap   (B) competitive   (C) false

(D) biased   (E) irrational

2. MISERLY:

(A) unhappy   (B) generous   (C) optimistic

(D) reticent   (E) golden

3. DILIGENT:

    (A) lethargic   (B)   morose   (C) silly

    (D) nostalgic   (E)   poor

4. PRECLUDE:

    (A) commence   (B)   include   (C) produce

    (D) perpetuate   (E)   enable

5. EXTOL:

    (A) criticize   (B)   expedite   (C) pay

    (D) deport   (E)   defer

6. DIVERSE:

    (A) solo   (B)   furtive   (C) jovial

    (D) wrinkled   (E)   similar

7. DISPERSE:

    (A) despair   (B)   belittle   (C) renew

    (D) renege   (E)   amass

8. ENDURING:

    (A) fallacious   (B)   temporal   (C) dismal

    (D) minute   (E)   disseminating

9. BREVITY:

    (A) gravity   (B)   gluttony   (C) cowardice

    (D) authenticity   (E)   verbosity

10. DEMUR:

    (A) assemble   (B)   bereave   (C) approve

    (D) add   (E)   ascribe

11. UNWONTED:

    (A) perceptive   (B)   ordinary   (C) tepid

    (D) desirable   (E)   qualified

12. CHASTISE:

    (A) repudiate   (B) immortalize   (C) endorse

    (D) virility   (E) congratulate

13. INFAMOUS:

    (A) revered   (B) resolute   (C) obscure

    (D) contiguous   (E) unknown

14. DISPASSIONATE:

    (A) resigned   (B) profound   (C) fanatical

    (D) torrid   (E) prudent

15. SCANTY:

    (A) redundant   (B) mediocre   (C) calming

    (D) profuse   (E) partisan

16. PROSAIC:

    (A) poetic   (B) unique   (C) rabid

    (D) disdainful   (E) condescending

17. DIDACTIC:

    (A) dubious   (B) imbecilic   (C) punctual

    (D) rhetorical   (E) reverent

18. COLLOQUIAL:

    (A) poetic   (B) separate   (C) formal

    (D) analogical   (E) anonymous

19. COHESIVE:

    (A) adhesive   (B) opposed   (C) smooth

    (D) adverse   (E) fragmented

20. OBLIGATORY:

    (A) promising   (B) permissible   (C) heaven

    (D) optional   (E) responsible

21. OPAQUE:

    (A) permeable   (B) similar   (C) visible

    (D) opulent   (E) translucent

22. SUNDER:

    (A) unite   (B) create noise   (C) oust

    (D) rise above   (E) freeze

23. NARCISSISTIC:

    (A) flowery   (B) detrimental   (C) gentle

    (D) modest   (E) polite

24. FOSTER:

    (A) destroy   (B) relate   (C) parent

    (D) abort   (E) revere

25. LIVID:

    (A) homeless   (B) bright   (C) calm

    (D) elusive   (E) opulent

26. SUPPRESS:

    (A) justify   (B) advocate   (C) free

    (D) level   (E) immunize

27. DESTITUTE:

    (A) organized   (B) ornate   (C) moral

    (D) wealthy   (E) obsequious

28. PAINSTAKING:

    (A) healthful   (B) sordid   (C) careless

    (D) sadistic   (E) lethal

29. PAROCHIAL:

    (A) melancholy   (B) blasphemous   (C) sporting

    (D) irreligious   (E) broad-minded

30. MANDATE:

    (A) emphasis   (B) sophism   (C) pinnacle

    (D) request   (E) meander

31. LUCID:

    (A) obscure   (B) tedious   (C) calm

    (D) frightening   (E) intelligent

32. IGNOBLE:

    (A) brave   (B) honorable   (C) royal

    (D) attentive   (E) informal

33. PERTINENT:

    (A) respectful   (B) detailed   (C) dreary

    (D) blatant   (E) irrelevant

34. ABSTINENCE:

    (A) indulgence   (B) concurrence   (C) hedonism

    (D) diligence   (E) alcoholism

35. FRUGAL:

    (A) unplanned   (B) temperamental   (C) regal

    (D) ethical   (E) extravagant

36. FORTUITOUS:

    (A) lethargic   (B) unprotected   (C) weak

    (D) unlucky   (E) antagonistic

37. UNEQUIVOCAL:

    (A) versatile   (B) equal   (C) noisy

    (D) unclear   (E) truthful

38. CONTEMPT:

    (A) respect   (B) pettiness   (C) politeness

    (D) resistance   (E) compliance

39. GRAVITY:

  (A) antipathy   (B) derision   (C) buoyancy

  (D) eloquence   (E) effervescence

40. AUSTERE:

  (A) measurable   (B) resilient   (C) indulgent

  (D) indirect   (E) destitute

41. PASSIVE:

  (A) thoughtless   (B) supportive   (C) retentive

  (D) contemporary   (E) assertive

42. STAGNANT:

  (A) celibate   (B) active   (C) effluent

  (D) feminine   (E) polluted

43. ADVERSE:

  (A) friendly   (B) quiescent   (C) poetic

  (D) burly   (E) petty

44. CRAVEN:

  (A) difficult   (B) reptilian   (C) pungent

  (D) birdlike   (E) courageous

45. HEED:

  (A) adjust   (B) resist   (C) attend

  (D) encourage   (E) order

46. IMPARTIAL:

  (A) biased   (B) complete   (C) eternal

  (D) articulate   (E) raucous

47. VINDICATE:

  (A) remove   (B) absolve   (C) evoke

  (D) accuse   (E) ferret

48. DERISION:

    (A) elimination   (B)   attention   (C) praise

    (D) entrance   (E)   recession

49. REPREHENSIBLE:

    (A) released   (B)   aghast   (C) awry

    (D) incidental   (E)   commendable

50. RELEGATE:

    (A) promote   (B)   nullify   (C) include

    (D) obliterate   (E)   placate

51. VAIN:

    (A) addicted   (B)   modest   (C) unscented

    (D) proud   (E)   choleric

52. LAGGARD:

    (A) haggard   (B)   lustrous   (C) haphazard

    (D) advanced   (E)   industrious

53. LABYRINTHINE:

    (A) inconsistent   (B)   amazing   (C) direct

    (D) incredulous   (E)   mythological

54. SLANDER:

    (A) praise   (B)   comfort   (C) discipline

    (D) risk   (E)   digress

55. PITTANCE:

    (A) mound   (B)   plethora   (C) quirk

    (D) grandeur   (E)   phlegm

56. SOLACE:

    (A) lunation   (B)   turmoil   (C) distress

    (D) valance   (E)   spontaneity

57. DEFERENT:

    (A) current   (B) constructive   (C) erratic

    (D) unyielding   (E) applicant

58. FICKLE:

    (A) bland   (B) cascading   (C) caustic

    (D) dubious   (E) faithful

59. EXOTIC:

    (A) ethnic   (B) diverse   (C) realistic

    (D) mundane   (E) enigmatic

60. THWART:

    (A) imprison   (B) mystify   (C) assist

    (D) fluctuate   (E) saturate

Drill 14: Word Choice Skills

➤ **Directions:** Choose the correct option.

1.   His <u>principal</u> reasons for resigning were his <u>principles</u> of right and wrong.

    (A) principal . . . principals

    (B) principle . . . principals

    (C) principle . . . principles

    (D) No change is necessary.

2.   The book tells about Alzheimer's disease—how it <u>affects</u> the patient and what <u>effect</u> it has on the patient's family.

    (A) effects . . . affect

    (B) affects . . . affect

    (C) effects . . . effects

    (D) No change is necessary.

3. The <u>amount</u> of homeless children we can help depends on the <u>number</u> of available shelters.

    (A) number . . . number

    (B) amount . . . amount

    (C) number . . . amount

    (D) No change is necessary.

4. All students are <u>suppose to</u> pass the test before <u>achieving</u> upper-division status.

    (A) suppose to . . . acheiving

    (B) suppose to . . . being achieved

    (C) supposed to . . . achieving

    (D) No change is necessary.

5. The reason he <u>succeeded</u> is <u>because</u> he worked hard.

    (A) succeeded . . . that

    (B) seceded . . . that

    (C) succede . . . because of

    (D) No change is necessary.

➤ **Directions:** Select the sentence that clearly and effectively states the idea and has no structural errors.

6. (A) South of Richmond, the two roads converge together to form a single highway.

    (B) South of Richmond, the two roads converge together to form an interstate highway.

    (C) South of Richmond, the two roads converge to form an interstate highway.

    (D) South of Richmond, the two roads converge to form a single interstate highway.

7. (A) The student depended on his parents for financial support.

    (B) The student lacked the ways and means to pay for his room and board, so he depended on his parents for this kind of money and support.

    (C) The student lacked the ways and means or the wherewithal to support himself, so his parents provided him with the financial support he needed.

    (D) The student lacked the means to pay for his room and board, so he depended on his parents for financial support.

8. (A) Vincent van Gogh and Paul Gauguin were close personal friends and companions who enjoyed each other's company and frequently worked together on their artwork.

   (B) Vincent van Gogh and Paul Gauguin were friends who frequently painted together.

   (C) Vincent van Gogh was a close personal friend of Paul Gauguin's, and the two of them often worked together on their artwork because they enjoyed each other's company.

   (D) Vincent van Gogh, a close personal friend of Paul Gauguin's, often worked with him on their artwork.

9. (A) A college education often involves putting away childish thoughts, which are characteristic of youngsters, and concentrating on the future, which lies ahead.

   (B) A college education involves putting away childish thoughts, which are characteristic of youngsters, and concentrating on the future.

   (C) A college education involves putting away childish thoughts and concentrating on the future.

   (D) A college education involves putting away childish thoughts and concentrating on the future which lies ahead.

10. (A) I had the occasion to visit an Oriental pagoda while I was a tourist on vacation and visiting in Kyoto, Japan.

   (B) I visited a Japanese pagoda in Kyoto.

   (C) I had occasion to visit a pagoda when I was vacationing in Kyoto, Japan.

   (D) On my vacation, I visited a Japanese pagoda in Kyoto.

Drill 15: Sentence Structure Skills

➤ **Directions:** Choose the sentence that expresses the thought most clearly and that has no error in structure.

1. (A) Many gases are invisible, odorless, and they have no taste.

   (B) Many gases are invisible, odorless, and have no taste.

   (C) Many gases are invisible, odorless, and tasteless.

   (D) Many gases are invisible and odorless and tasteless.

2. (A) Everyone agreed that she had neither the voice or the skill to be a speaker.

   (B) Everyone agreed that she had neither the voice nor the skill to be a speaker.

   (C) Everyone agreed that she had either the voice nor the skill to be a speaker.

   (D) Everyone agreeed she had no voice or skill to be a speaker.

3. (A) The mayor will be remembered because he kept his campaign promises and because of his refusal to accept political favors.

    (B) The mayor will be remembered because he kept his campaign promises and because he refused to accept political favors.

    (C) The mayor will be remembered because of his refusal to accept political favors and he kept his campaign promises.

    (D) The mayor will be remembered because he refused to accept political favors and he kept compaign promises.

4. (A) While taking a shower, the doorbell rang.

    (B) While I was taking a shower, the doorbell rang.

    (C) While taking a shower, someone rang the doorbell.

    (D) While taking a shower the doorbell rang.

5. (A) He swung the bat, while the runner stole second base.

    (B) The runner stole second base while he swung the bat.

    (C) While he was swinging the bat, the runner stole second base.

    (D) He stole second base while swinging the bat.

➤ **Directions:** Choose the correct option.

6. Nothing grows as well in Mississippi as <u>cotton. Cotton</u> being the state's principal crop.

    (A) cotton, cotton

    (B) cotton; cotton

    (C) cotton cotton

    (D) No change is necessary.

7. It was a heartwrenching <u>movie; one</u> that I had never seen before.

    (A) movie and

    (B) movie, one

    (C) movie. One

    (D) No change is necessary.

8.   Traffic was stalled for three miles on the <u>bridge. Because</u> repairs were being made.

(A) bridge because

(B) bridge; because

(C) bridge, because

(D) No change is necessary.

9.   The ability to write complete sentences comes with <u>practice writing</u> run-on sentences seems to oc-cur naturally.

(A) practice, writing

(B) practice. Writing

(C) practice and

(D) No change is necessary.

10. Even though she had taken French classes, she could not understand native French <u>speakers they</u> all spoke too fast.

(A) speakers, they

(B) speakers. They

(C) speaking

(D) No change is necessary.

Drill 16: Verbs

➤ **Directions:** Choose the correct option.

1.   If you <u>had been concerned</u> about Marilyn, you <u>would have went</u> to greater lengths to ensure her safety.

(A) had been concern . . . would have gone

(B) was concerned . . . would have gone

(C) had been concerned . . . would have gone

(D) No change is necessary.

2. Susan <u>laid</u> in bed too long and missed her class.

    (A) lays   (C) lied

    (B) lay   (D) No change is necessary.

3. The Great Wall of China <u>is</u> fifteen hundred miles long; it <u>was built</u> in the third century B.C.

    (A) was . . . was built   (C) has been . . . was built

    (B) is . . . is built   (D) No change is necessary.

4. Joe stated that the class <u>began</u> at 10:30 a.m.

    (A) begins   (C) was beginning

    (B) had begun   (D) No change is necessary.

5. The ceiling of the Sistine Chapel <u>was</u> painted by Michelangelo; it <u>depicted</u> scenes from the Creation in the Old Testament.

    (A) was . . . depicts   (C) has been . . . depicting

    (B) is . . . depicts   (D) No change is necessary.

6. After Christmas <u>comes</u> the best sales.

    (A) has come   (C) is coming

    (B) come   (D) No change is necessary.

7. The bakery's specialty <u>are</u> wedding cakes.

    (A) is   (C) be

    (B) were   (D) No change is necessary.

8. Every man, woman, and child <u>were given</u> a life preserver.

    (A) have been given   (C) was given

    (B) had gave   (D) No change is necessary.

9. Hiding your mistakes <u>don't</u> make them go away.

    (A) doesn't   (C) have not

    (B) do not   (D) No change is necessary.

10. The Board of Regents <u>has recommended</u> a tuition increase.

    (A) have recommended   (C) had recommended

    (B) has recommend   (D) No change is necessary.

Drill 17: Pronouns

➤ **Directions:** Choose the correct option.

1. My friend and <u>myself</u> bought tickets for *Cats*.

    (A) I   (C) us

    (B) me   (D) No change is necessary.

2. Alcohol and tobacco are harmful to <u>whomever</u> consumes them.

    (A) whom   (C) whoever

    (B) who   (D) No change is necessary.

3. Everyone is wondering <u>whom</u> her successor will be.

    (A) who   (C) who'll

    (B) whose   (D) No change is necessary.

4. Rosa Lee's parents discovered that it was <u>her who</u> wrecked the family car.

    (A) she who   (C) her whom

    (B) she whom   (D) No change is necessary.

5. A student <u>who</u> wishes to protest <u>his or her</u> grades must file a formal grievance in the Dean's office.

    (A) that . . . their   (C) whom . . . their

    (B) which . . . his   (D) No change is necessary.

6. One of the best things about working for this company is that <u>they pay</u> big bonuses.

    (A) it pays   (C) they paid

    (B) they always pay   (D) No change is necessary.

7. Every car owner should be sure that <u>their</u> automobile insurance is adequate.

    (A) your   (C) its

    (B) his or her   (D) No change is necessary.

8.   My mother wants me to become a teacher, but I'm not interested in <u>it</u>.

(A)   this   (C)   that

(B)   teaching   (D)   No change is necessary.

9.   Since I had not paid my electric bill, <u>they</u> sent me a delinquent notice.

(A)   the power company   (C)   it

(B)   he   (D)   No change is necessary.

10.   Margaret seldom wrote to her sister when <u>she</u> was away at college.

(A)   who   (C)   her sister

(B)   her   (D)   No change is necessary.

Drill 18: Adjectives and Adverbs

➤ **Directions:** Choose the correct option.

1.   Although the band performed <u>badly</u>, I feel <u>real bad</u> about missing the concert.

(A)   badly . . . real badly   (C)   badly . . . very bad

(B)   bad . . . badly   (D)   No change is necessary.

2.   These reports are <u>relative simple</u> to prepare.

(A)   relatively simple   (C)   relatively simply

(B)   relative simply   (D)   No change is necessary.

3.   He did <u>very well</u> on the test although his writing skills are not <u>good</u>.

(A)   real well . . . good   (C)   good . . . great

(B)   very good . . . good   (D)   No change is necessary.

4.   Shake the medicine bottle <u>good</u> before you open it.

(A)   very good   (C)   well

(B)   real good   (D)   No change is necessary.

5.   Though she speaks <u>fluently</u>, she writes <u>poorly</u> because she doesn't observe <u>closely</u> or think <u>clear</u>.

    (A)   fluently . . . poorly . . . closely . . . clearly

    (B)   fluent . . . poor . . . close . . . clear

    (C)   fluently . . . poor . . . closely . . . clear

    (D)   No change is necessary.

➤ **Directions:** Select the sentence that clearly and effectively states the idea and has no structural errors.

6.   (A)   Los Angeles is larger than any city in California.

    (B)   Los Angeles is larger than all the cities in California.

    (C)   Los Angeles is larger than any other city in California.

    (D)   Los Angles is larger than most cities in California.

7.   (A)   Art history is as interesting as, if not more interesting than, music appreciation.

    (B)   Art history is as interesting, if not more interesting than, music appreciation.

    (C)   Art history is as interesting as, if not more interesting, music appreciation.

    (D)   Art history is more interesting than music appreciation.

8.   (A)   The baseball team here is as good as any other university.

    (B)   The baseball team here is as good as all the other universities.

    (C)   The baseball team here is as good as any other university's.

    (D)   The baseball team is as good as any other.

9.   (A)   I like him better than you.

    (B)   I like him better than I like you.

    (C)   I like him better.

    (D)   I like him best.

10.   (A)   You are the most stingiest person I know.

    (B)   You are the most stingier person I know.

    (C)   You are the stingiest person I know.

    (D)   You are more stingy.

Drill 19: Spelling

> **Directions:** Identify the misspelled word in each set.

1. (A) probly

    (B) accommodate

    (C) acquaintance

    (D) probability

2. (A) auxiliary

    (B) atheletic

    (C) beginning

    (D) useful

3. (A) environment

    (B) existence

    (C) Febuary

    (D) January

4. (A) ocassion

    (B) occurrence

    (C) omitted

    (D) committed

5. (A) perspiration

    (B) referring

    (C) priviledge

    (D) knowledge

➤ **Directions:** Choose the correct option.

6.   <u>Preceding</u> the <u>business</u> session, lunch will be served in a <u>separate</u> room.

    (A) preceeding . . . business . . . seperate

    (B) proceeding . . . bussiness . . . seperate

    (C) proceeding . . . business . . . seperite

    (D) No change is necessary.

7.   Monte <u>inadvertently</u> left <u>several</u> of his <u>libary</u> books in the cafeteria.

    (A) inadverdently . . . serveral . . . libery

    (B) inadvertently . . . several . . . library

    (C) inadvertentely . . . several . . . librery

    (D) No change is necessary.

8.   Sam wished he had more <u>liesure</u> time so he could <u>persue</u> his favorite hobbies.

    (A) leisure . . . pursue

    (B) Liesure . . . pursue

    (C) leisure . . . persue

    (D) No change is necessary.

9.   One of my <u>favrite charecters</u> in <u>litrature</u> is Bilbo from *The Hobbit*.

    (A) favrite . . . characters . . . literature

    (B) favorite . . . characters . . . literature

    (C) favourite . . . characters . . . literature

    (D) No change is necessary.

10.   Even <u>tho</u> Joe was badly hurt in the <u>accidant</u>, the company said they were not <u>lible</u> for damages.

    (A) though . . . accidant . . . libel

    (B) though . . . accident . . . liable

    (C) though . . . acident . . . liable

    (D) No change is necessary.

> ## Drill 20: Punctuation

> ➤ **Directions:** Choose the correct option.

1. Indianola, <u>Mississippi, where B.B. King and my father grew up,</u> has a population of less than 50,000 people.

    (A) Mississippi where, B.B. King and my father grew up,

    (B) Mississippi where B.B. King and my father grew up,

    (C) Mississippi; where B.B. King and my father grew up,

    (D) No change is necessary.

2. John Steinbeck's best known novel *The Grapes of Wrath* is the story of the <u>Joads an Oklahoma family</u> who were driven from their dustbowl farm and forced to become migrant workers in California.

    (A) Joads, an Oklahoma family

    (B) Joads, an Oklahoma family,

    (C) Joads; an Oklahoma family

    (D) No change is necessary.

3. All students who are interested in student teaching next <u>semester, must submit an application to the Teacher Education Office.</u>

    (A) semester must submit an application to the Teacher Education Office.

    (B) semester, must submit an application, to the Teacher Education Office.

    (C) semester: must submit an application to the Teacher Education Office.

    (D) No change is necessary.

4. Whenever you travel by <u>car, or plane, you</u> must wear a seatbelt.

    (A) car or plane you   (C) car or plane, you

    (B) car, or plane you   (D) No change is necessary.

5. Wearing a seatbelt is not just a good <u>idea, it's</u> the law.

    (A) idea; it's   (C) idea. It's

    (B) idea it's   (D) No change is necessary.

6.   Senators and representatives can be reelected <u>indefinitely; a</u> president can only serve two terms.

   (A) indefinitely but a   (C)   indefinitely a

   (B) indefinitely, a   (D)   No change is necessary.

7.   Students must pay a penalty for overdue library <u>books, however, there</u> is a grace period.

   (A) books; however, there   (C)   books: however, there

   (B) books however, there   (D)   No change is necessary.

8.   Among the states that seceded from the Union to join the Confederacy in 1860-1861 <u>were:</u> Mississippi, Florida, and Alabama.

   (A) were   (C)   were.

   (B) were;   (D)   No change is necessary.

9.   The art exhibit displayed works by many famous <u>artists such as</u>: Dali, Picasso, and Michelangelo.

   (A) artists such as;   (C)   artists. Such as

   (B) artists such as   (D)   No change is necessary.

10.   The National Shakespeare Company will perform <u>the following plays:</u> *Othello, Macbeth, Hamlet,* and *As You Like It.*

   (A) the following plays,   (C)   the following plays

   (B) the following plays;   (D)   No change is necessary.

Drill 21: Capitalization

➤ **Directions:** Choose the correct option.

1.   Mexico is the southernmost country in <u>North America</u>. It borders the United States on the north; it is bordered on the <u>south</u> by Belize and Guatemala.

   (A) north America . . . South

   (B) North America . . . South

   (C) North america . . . South

   (D) No change is necessary.

2.   (A)   Until 1989, Tom Landry was the only Coach the Dallas cowboys ever had.

     (B)   Until 1989, Tom Landry was the only coach the Dallas Cowboys ever had.

     (C)   Until 1989, Tom Landry was the only Coach the Dallas Cowboys ever had.

     (D)   Until 1989 Tom Landry was the only coach the Dallas cowboys ever had.

3.   The <u>Northern Hemisphere</u> is the half of the <u>earth</u> that lies north of the <u>Equator.</u>

     (A)   Northern hemisphere . . . earth . . . equator

     (B)   Northern hemisphere . . . Earth . . . Equator

     (C)   Northern Hemisphere . . . earth . . . equator

     (D)   No change is necessary.

4.   (A)   My favorite works by Ernest Hemingway are "The Snows of Kilamanjaro," *The Sun Also Rises,* and *For Whom the Bell Tolls.*

     (B)   My favorite works by Ernest Hemingway are "The Snows Of Kilamanjaro," *The Sun Also Rises,* and *For Whom The Bell Tolls.*

     (C)   My favorite works by Ernest Hemingway are "The Snows of Kilamanjaro," *The Sun also Rises,* and *For whom the Bell Tolls.*

     (D)   My favorite works by Ernest Hemingway are The Snows Of Kilamanjaro and *The Sun Also Rises* and *For Whom The Bell Tolls.*

5.   Aphrodite (<u>Venus in Roman Mythology</u>) was the <u>Greek</u> goddess of love.

     (A)   Venus in Roman mythology . . . greek

     (B)   venus in roman mythology . . . Greek

     (C)   Venus in Roman mythology . . . Greek

     (D)   No change is necessary.

6.   The <u>Koran</u> is considered by <u>Muslims</u> to be the holy word.

     (A)   koran . . . muslims   (C)   Koran . . . muslims

     (B)   koran . . . Muslims   (D)   No change is necessary.

7. (A) The freshman curriculum at the community college includes english, a foreign language, Algebra I, and history.

    (B) The freshman curriculum at the community college includes English, a foreign language, Algebra I, and history.

    (C) The Freshman curriculum at the Community College includes English, a foreign language, Algebra I, and History.

    (D) The Freshman Curriculum at the community College inlcudes English, a Foreign Language, Algebra I, and History.

8. At the <u>spring</u> graduation ceremonies, the university awarded more than 2,000 <u>bachelor's</u> degrees.

    (A) Spring . . . Bachelor's   (C)   Spring . . . bachelor's

    (B) spring . . . Bachelor's   (D)   No change is necessary.

9. The fall of the <u>Berlin wall</u> was an important symbol of the collapse of <u>Communism</u>.

    (A) berlin Wall . . . communism

    (B) Berlin Wall . . . communism

    (C) berlin wall . . . Communism

    (D) No change is necessary.

10. A photograph of <u>mars</u> was printed in <u>the *New York Times*</u>.

    (A) Mars . . . *The New York Times*

    (B) mars . . . *The New York times*

    (C) mars . . .*The New York Times*

    (D) No change is necessary.

Answer Key

Drill 1

1. (J)	4. (C)	7. (I)	10. (E)	13. (A)
2. (G)	5. (H)	8. (D)	11. (D)	14. (E)
3. (A)	6. (B)	9. (F)	12. (C)	15. (B)

Drill 2

1. (D)	4. (F)	7. (E)	10. (H)	13. (B)
2. (G)	5. (A)	8. (C)	11. (D)	14. (E)
3. (I)	6. (J)	9. (B)	12. (A)	15. (C)

Drill 3

1. (E)	4. (A)	7. (C)	10. (D)	13. (E)
2. (H)	5. (I)	8. (G)	11. (C)	14. (D)
3. (J)	6. (B)	9. (F)	12. (A)	15. (B)

Drill 4

1. (D)	4. (I)	7. (C)	10. (G)	13. (B)
2. (E)	5. (J)	8. (F)	11. (D)	14. (C)
3. (A)	6. (B)	9. (H)	12. (A)	15. (E)

Drill 5

1. (H)	4. (B)	7. (I)	10. (G)	13. (A)
2. (F)	5. (J)	8. (E)	11. (B)	14. (E)
3. (A)	6. (C)	9. (D)	12. (D)	15. (C)

Drill 6

1. (G)	4. (J)	7. (D)	10. (H)	13. (A)
2. (A)	5. (C)	8. (I)	11. (D)	14. (C)
3. (E)	6. (B)	9. (F)	12. (E)	15. (B)

Drill 7

1. (F)	4. (B)	7. (C)	10. (J)	13. (D)
2. (E)	5. (H)	8. (G)	11. (B)	14. (C)
3. (A)	6. (I)	9. (D)	12. (E)	15. (A)

Drill 8

1. (D)	4. (G)	7. (E)	10. (J)	13. (A)
2. (A)	5. (B)	8. (I)	11. (C)	14. (E)
3. (H)	6. (C)	9. (F)	12. (B)	15. (D)

Drill 9

1. (D)	4. (A)	7. (B)	10. (H)	13. (B)
2. (I)	5. (J)	8. (F)	11. (A)	14. (E)
3. (G)	6. (E)	9. (C)	12. (D)	15. (C)

Drill 10

1. (H)	4. (A)	7. (F)	10. (G)	13. (A)
2. (I)	5. (J)	8. (C)	11. (B)	14. (C)
3. (E)	6. (B)	9. (D)	12. (D)	15. (E)

Drill 11

1. (F)	4. (H)	7. (C)	10. (G)	13. (E)
2. (I)	5. (B)	8. (D)	11. (C)	14. (A)
3. (A)	6. (J)	9. (E)	12. (B)	15. (D)

Drill 12

1. (J)	4. (I)	7. (D)	10. (E)	13. (D)
2. (A)	5. (C)	8. (G)	11. (E)	14. (A)
3. (B)	6. (H)	9. (F)	12. (C)	15. (B)

Drill 13

1. (C)	13. (A)	25. (C)	37. (D)	49. (E)
2. (B)	14. (C)	26. (B)	38. (A)	50. (A)
3. (A)	15. (D)	27. (D)	39. (E)	51. (B)
4. (E)	16. (B)	28. (C)	40. (C)	52. (E)
5. (A)	17. (B)	29. (E)	41. (E)	53. (C)
6. (E)	18. (C)	30. (D)	42. (B)	54. (A)
7. (E)	19. (E)	31. (A)	43. (A)	55. (B)
8. (B)	20. (D)	32. (B)	44. (E)	56. (C)
9. (E)	21. (E)	33. (E)	45. (B)	57. (D)
10. (C)	22. (A)	34. (A)	46. (A)	58. (E)
11. (B)	23. (D)	35. (E)	47. (D)	59. (D)
12. (E)	24. (A)	36. (D)	48. (C)	60. (C)

Drill 14

1. (D)	4. (C)	7. (A)	10. (B)
2. (D)	5. (A)	8. (B)	
3. (A)	6. (C)	9. (C)	

Drill 15

1. (C)	4. (B)	7. (B)	10. (B)
2. (B)	5. (A)	8. (A)	
3. (B)	6. (A)	9. (B)	

Drill 16

1. (C)	4. (A)	7. (A)	10. (D)
2. (B)	5. (A)	8. (C)	
3. (D)	6. (B)	9. (A)	

Drill 17

1. (A)	4. (A)	7. (B)	10. (C)
2. (C)	5. (D)	8. (B)	
3. (A)	6. (A)	9. (A)	

Drill 18

1. (C)	4. (C)	7. (A)	10. (C)
2. (A)	5. (A)	8. (C)	
3. (D)	6. (C)	9. (B)	

Drill 19

1. (A)	4. (A)	7. (B)	10. (B)
2. (B)	5. (C)	8. (A)	
3. (C)	6. (D)	9. (B)	

Drill 20

1. (D)	4. (C)	7. (A)	10. (D)
2. (A)	5. (A)	8. (A)	
3. (A)	6. (D)	9. (B)	

Drill 21

1. (D)	4. (A)	7. (B)	10. (A)
2. (B)	5. (C)	8. (D)	
3. (C)	6. (D)	9. (B)	

Essay

Essay Writing Review

The FTCE-GKT contains one writing exercise. You will have 50 minutes to plan and write an essay on one of two topic choices. You must write on only one of the two choices of topic. Since you will have only 50 minutes to complete the essay, efficient use of your time is essential.

Your work will be scored holistically by two judges. The personal views you express will not be an issue; however, the skill with which you express those views, the logic of your arguments, and the degree to which you support your position will be very important in the scoring. Your essay will be scored both on substance and on the composition skills demonstrated.

Writing under pressure can be frustrating, but if you study this review, practice and polish your essay skills, and have a realistic sense of what to expect, you can turn problems into possibilities. The following review will show you how to plan and write a logical, coherent, and interesting essay.

Why Essays Exist

People write essays for purposes other than testing. Some of our best thinkers have written essays that we continue to read from generation to generation. Essays offer the reader a logical, coherent, and imaginative written composition showing the nature or consequences of a single controlling idea when considered from the writer's unique point of view. Writers use essays to communicate their opinion or position on a topic to readers who cannot be present during their live conversation. Writers use essays to help readers understand or learn about something that readers should or may want to know or do. Essays always express more or less directly the author's opinion, belief, position, or knowledge (backed by evidence) about the idea or object in question.

Pre-Writing/Planning

Before you begin to actually write, there are certain preliminary steps you need to take. A few minutes spent planning pays off—your final essay will be more focused, well-developed, and clearer. For a 50-minute essay, you should spend about five to ten minutes on the pre-writing process.

Skill 1: Determine the Purpose for Writing

For this test you will need to recognize and generate the elements of an excellent essay. In essence, you will be taking the principles covered in this review and utilizing them to create your own original essay. With that in mind, read carefully the standards and explanations below to prepare you for what to look for in your own essay response.

Read the essay question very carefully and ask yourself the following questions:

- What is the meaning of the topic statement?

- Is the question asking me to persuade the reader of the validity of a certain opinion?

- Do I agree or disagree with the statement? What will be my thesis (main idea)?

- What kinds of examples can I use to support my thesis? Explore personal experiences, historical evidence, current events, and literary subjects.

Skill 2: Formulate a Thesis or Statement of Main Idea

In academic writing, two purposes dominate essays:

1. Persuasion through argumentation using one, some, or all of the logical patterns described here.

2. Informing and educating through analysis and using one, some, or all of the logical patterns described here.

All of an essay's organizational strategies may be used to argue in writing. The author offers reasons and/or evidence so an audience will be inclined to believe the position that the author presents about the idea under discussion. Writers use seven basic strategies to organize information and ideas in essays to help prove their point (thesis). All of these strategies might be useful in arguing for an idea and persuading a reader to see the issue the writer's way. Your job is to use strategies that are appropriate to demonstrate your thesis. For example, you may wish to use comparison and contrast to demonstrate that one thing or idea is better or worse than another.

The following seven steps can be used to prove a thesis:

Seven Steps to Prove a Thesis

1. Show how a *process* or procedure does or should work, step by step, in time.

2. *Compare or contrast* two or more things or ideas to show important differences or similarities.

3. *Identify a problem* and then explain how to solve it.

4. *Analyze* into its components, or *classify* by its types or categories an idea or thing to show how it is put together, how it works, or how it is designed.

5. *Explain* why something happens to produce a particular result or set of results.

6. *Describe* the particular individual characteristics, beauty and features of a place, person(s), time, or idea.

7. *Define* what a thing is or what an idea means.

Depending upon the purpose of the essay, one pattern tends to dominate the discussion question. (For example, the writer might use *description* and *explanation* to define the varied meanings of "love.")

Skill 3: Organize Ideas and Details Effectively

Decide how many paragraphs you will write. In a 30-minute exercise, you will probably have time for no more than four or five paragraphs. In such a format, the first paragraph will be the introduction, the next two or three will develop your thesis with specific examples, and the final paragraph should be a strong conclusion.

The Introduction

The focus of your introduction should be the thesis statement. This statement allows your reader to understand the point and direction of your essay. The statement identifies the central idea of your essay and should clearly state your attitude about the subject. It will also dictate the basic content and organization of your essay. If you do not state your thesis clearly, your essay will suffer.

The thesis is the heart of the essay. Without it, readers won't know what your major message or central idea is in the essay.

The thesis must be something that can be argued or needs to be proven, not just an accepted fact. For example, "Animals are used every day in cosmetic and medical testing" is a fact—it needs no proof. But if the writer says, "Using animals for cosmetic and medical testing is cruel and should be stopped," we have a point that must be supported and defended by the writer.

The thesis can be placed in any paragraph of the essay, but in a short essay, especially one written for evaluative exam purposes, the thesis is most effective when placed in the last sentence of the opening paragraph.

Consider the following sample question:

ESSAY TOPIC:

"That government is best which governs least."

ASSIGNMENT:

Do you agree or disagree with this statement? Choose a specific example from current events, personal experience, or your reading to support your position.

After reading the topic statement, decide if you agree or disagree. If you agree with this statement, your thesis statement could be the following:

> "Government has the right to protect individuals from interference but no right
> to extend its powers and activities beyond this function."

This statement clearly states the writer's opinion in a direct manner. It also serves as a blueprint for the essay. The remainder of the introduction should give two or three brief examples that support your thesis.

Supporting Paragraphs

The next two or three paragraphs of your essay will elaborate on the supporting examples you gave in your introduction. Each paragraph should discuss only one idea. Like the introduction, each paragraph should be coherently organized, with a topic sentence and supporting details.

The topic sentence is to each paragraph what the thesis statement is to the essay as a whole. It tells the reader what you plan to discuss in that paragraph. It has a specific subject and is neither too broad nor too narrow. It also establishes the author's attitude and gives the reader a sense of the direction in which the writer is going. An effective topic sentence also arouses the reader's interest.

Although it may occur in the middle or at the end of the paragraph, the topic sentence usually appears at the beginning of the paragraph. Placing it at the beginning is advantageous because it helps you stay focused on the main idea.

The remainder of each paragraph should support the topic sentence with examples and illustrations. Each sentence should progress logically from the previous one and be centrally connected to your topic sentence. Do not include any extraneous material that does not serve to develop your thesis.

Conclusion

Your conclusion should briefly restate your thesis and explain how you have shown it to be true. Since you want to end your essay on a strong note, your conclusion should be concise and effective.

Do not introduce any new topics that you cannot support. If you were watching a movie that suddenly shifted plot and characters at the end, you would be disappointed or even angry. Similarly, conclusions must not drift away from the major focus and message of the essay. Make sure your conclusion is clearly on the topic and represents your perspective without any confusion about what you really mean and believe. The reader will respect you for staying true to your intentions.

The conclusion is your last chance to grab and impress the reader. You can even use humor, if appropriate, but a dramatic close will remind the reader you are serious, even passionate, about what you believe.

Skill 4: Provide Adequate, Relevant Supporting Material

You may employ any one of the seven steps previously listed to prove any thesis that you maintain is true. You may also call on evidence from one or all of the four following kinds of evidence to support the thesis of your essay. Identify which kind(s) of evidence you can use to prove the points of your essay. In test situations, most essayists use anecdotal evidence or analogy to explain, describe, or prove a thesis. But if you know salient facts or statistics, don't hesitate to call upon them.

1. **Hard data** (facts, statistics, scientific evidence, research)—documented evidence that has been verified to be true.

2. **Anecdotal evidence**—stories from the writer's own experience and knowledge that illustrate a particular point or idea.

3. **Expert opinions**—assertions or conclusions, usually by authorities, about the matter under discussion.

4. **Analogies**—show a resemblance between one phenomenon and another.

Skill 5: Use Effective Transitions

Transitions are like the links of a bracelet, holding the beads or major points of your essay together. They help the reader follow the smooth flow of your ideas and show a connection between major and minor ideas. Transitions are used either at the beginning of a paragraph, or to show the connections among ideas within a single paragraph. Without transitions, you will jar the reader and distract him from your true ideas.

Here are some typical transitional words and phrases:

Linking similar ideas

again	for example	likewise
also	for instance	moreover
and	further	nor
another	furthermore	of course
besides	in addition	similarly
equally important	in like manner	too

Linking dissimilar/contradictory ideas

although	however	on the other hand
and yet	in spite of	otherwise
as if	instead	provided that
but	nevertheless	still
conversely	on the contrary	yet

Indicating cause, purpose, or result

as	for	so
as a result	for this reason	then
because	hence	therefore
consequently	since	thus

Indicating time or position

above	before	meanwhile
across	beyond	next
afterwards	eventually	presently
around	finally	second
at once	first	thereafter
at the present time	here	thereupon

Indicating an example or summary

as a result	in any event	in other words
as I have said	in brief	in short
for example	in conclusion	on the whole
for instance	in fact	to sum up

Skill 6: Demonstrate Mature Command of Language

Common Writing Errors

The four writing errors most often made by beginning writers are run-ons (also known as fused sentences), fragments, lack of subject-verb agreement, and incorrect use of the object:

1. **Run-ons:** "She swept the floor it was dirty" is a run-on, because the pronoun "it" stands as a noun subject and starts a new sentence. A period or semicolon is needed after "floor."

2. **Fragments:** "Before Jimmy learned how to play baseball" is a fragment, even though it has a subject and verb (Jimmy learned). The word "before" fragmentizes the clause, and the reader needs to know what happened before Jimmy learned how to play baseball.

3. **Problems with subject-verb agreement:** "Either Maria or Robert are going to the game" is incorrect because either Maria is going or Robert is going, but not both. The sentence should say, "Either Maria or Robert is going to the game."

4. **Incorrect object:** Probably the most common offender in this area is saying "between you and I," which sounds correct, but isn't. "Between" is a preposition that takes the objective case "me." The correct usage is "between you and me."

The FTCE-GKT test graders also cite lack of thought and development, misspellings, incorrect pronouns or antecedents, and lack of development as frequently occurring problems. Finally, keep in mind that clear, coherent handwriting always works to your advantage. Readers will appreciate an essay they can read with ease.

Five Words Weak Writers Overuse

Weak and beginning writers overuse the vague pronouns "you, we, they, this, and it" often without telling exactly who or what is represented by the pronoun.

1. Beginning writers often shift to second person **"you,"** when the writer means "a person." This shift confuses readers and weakens the flow of the essay. Although "you" is commonly accepted in creative writing, journalism, and other arenas, in a short, formal essay, it is best to avoid "you" altogether.

2. **"We"** is another pronoun that should be avoided. If by "we" the writer means "Americans," "society," or some other group, then he or she should say so.

3. **"They"** is often misused in essay writing, because it is overused in conversation: "I went to the doctor, and they told me to take some medicine." Tell the reader who "they" are.

4. **"This"** is usually used incorrectly without a referent: "She told me she received a present. This sounded good to me." This what? This idea? This news? This present? Be clear—don't make your readers guess what you mean. The word "this" should be followed by a noun or referent.

5. **"It"** is a common problem among weak writers. To what does "it" refer? Your readers don't appreciate vagueness, so take the time to be clear and complete in your expression of ideas.

Use Your Own Vocabulary

Is it a good idea to use big words that sound good in the dictionary or thesaurus, but that you don't really use or understand? No. So whose vocabulary should you use? Your own. You will be most comfortable with your own level of vocabulary.

This "comfort zone" doesn't give you license to be informal in a formal setting or to violate the rules of standard written English, but if you try to write in a style that is not yours, your writing will be awkward and lack a true voice.

You should certainly improve and build your vocabulary at every opportunity, but remember: you should not attempt to change your vocabulary level at this point.

Avoid the Passive Voice

In writing, the active voice is preferable because it is emphatic and direct. A weak passive verb leaves the doer unknown or seemingly unimportant. However, the passive voice is essential when the action of the verb is more important than the doer, when the doer is unknown, or when the writer wishes to place the emphasis on the receiver of the action rather than on the doer.

Skill 7: Avoid Inappropriate Use of Slang, Jargon, and Clichés

The requirements for informal spoken English are much more relaxed than the rigid rules for "standard written English." While slang, colloquialisms, and other informal expressions are acceptable and sometimes very appropriate in casual speech, they are inappropriate in academic and business writing. More often than not, writers, especially student writers, do not make a distinction between the two: they use the same words, grammar, and sentence structure from their everyday speech in their college papers, albeit unsuccessfully.

The FTCE does not require you to know grammatical terms such as *gerund, subject complement,* or *dependent clause,* although general familiarity with such terms may be helpful to you in determining whether a sentence or part of a sentence is correct or incorrect. You should watch for errors in grammar, spelling, punctuation, capitalization, sentence structure, and word choice. Remember: this is a test of written language skills; therefore, your responses should be based on what you know to be correct for written work, not what you know to be appropriate for a casual conversation. For instance, in informal speech, you might say "Who are you going to choose?" But in formal academic writing, you would write "Whom are you going to choose?" Your choices, then, should be dictated by requirements for *written*, not *conversational* English.

Skill 8: Use a Variety of Sentence Patterns Effectively

Parallelism

Sentences should use the same kind of grammatical construction for all items in a series—those usually joined by a coordinating conjunction (*and, but, or,* and *nor*). "No smoking, eating, or drinking" is parallel; "No smoking, food, or drinking" is not, because *food* is not a verb form. Making elements parallel also requires knowledge of parallel correlative pairs, that is, the use of appropriate pairs together: *neither* and *nor, either* and *or, both* with *and, whether* with *or,* and *not only* with *but also.*

Parallel structure is used to express matching ideas. It refers to the grammatical balance of a series of any of the following:

> **Phrases.** The squirrel ran *along the fence, up the tree,* and *into his hole* with a mouthful of acorns.
>
> **Adjectives.** The job market is flooded with *very talented, highly motivated,* and *well-educated* young people.
>
> **Nouns.** You will need a *notebook, pencil,* and *dictionary* for the test.
>
> **Clauses.** The children were told to decide *which toy they would keep* and *which toy they would give away.*
>
> **Verbs.** The farmer *plowed, planted,* and *harvested* his corn in record time.
>
> **Verbals.** *Reading, writing,* and *calculating* are fundamental skills we should all possess.
>
> **Correlative Conjunctions.** *Either* you will do your homework *or* you will fail. *Note:* Correlative conjunctions must be used as pairs and not mixed with other conjunctions, such as *neither* with *or* or *not only* with *also.*
>
> **Near-parallelisms.** Sometimes a string of seemingly parallel thoughts are not in fact parallel. Consider this sentence: "I *have quit* my job, *enrolled* in school, and *am looking* for a reliable babysitter." In this sentence the writer has already *quit* and *enrolled* but is still looking for a babysitter; therefore she cannot include all three in a parallel structure. A good revision of this sentence is, "I have quit my job and enrolled in school, and I am looking for a babysitter."

Misplaced and Dangling Modifiers

Many people, probably including at least some parents of your students, consider misplaced and dangling modifiers to be a sure sign of ignorance about the English language. Although this belief on their part may be unfair, teachers need to be aware that it is firmly held. As the name suggests, a misplaced modifier is one that is in the wrong place in the sentence. Misplaced modifiers come in all forms—words, phrases, and clauses. Sentences containing misplaced modifiers are often very comical: *Mom made me eat the spinach instead of my brother.* Misplaced modifiers, like the one in this sentence, are usually too far away from the word or words they modify. This sentence should read *Mom made me, instead of my brother, eat the spinach.*

Such modifiers as *only, nearly,* and *almost* should be placed next to the word they modify and not in front of some other word, especially a verb, that they are not intended to modify. For example, *I only sang for one reason* is wrong if the writer means to say that there was *only one* reason for singing.

A modifier is misplaced if it appears to modify the wrong part of the sentence or if the reader cannot be certain what part of the sentence the writer intended it to modify. To correct a misplaced modifier, move the modifier next to the word it describes.

> UNREVISED: She served hamburgers to the men on paper plates.
>
> REVISED: She served hamburgers on paper plates to the men.

A *squinting modifier* is one that may refer to either a preceding or a following word, leaving the reader uncertain about what it is intended to modify. Correct a squinting modifier by moving it next to the word it is intended to modify.

> UNREVISED: Snipers who fired on the soldiers often escaped capture.
>
> REVISED: Snipers who often fired on the soldiers escaped capture. OR
> Snipers who fired on the soldiers escaped capture often.

A *dangling modifier* is a modifier or verb in search of a subject: the modifying phrase (usually a participle phrase—an *-ing* word group or an *-ed* or an *-en* word group—or an infinitive phrase—a *to* + *verb* word group) has nothing to modify. It is figuratively *dangling* at the beginning or the end of a sentence. The sentences often look and sound correct at first glance: *To be a student government officer, your grades must be above average.* However, the verbal modifier has nothing to describe. *You* are supposed *to be a student government officer*; *your grades* cannot become an officer.

To correct a dangling modifier, reword the sentence by either (1) changing the modifying phrase to a clause with a subject, or (2) changing the subject of the sentence to the word that should be modified. Here are some other examples of correct revision of dangling modifiers:

> UNREVISED: Shortly after leaving home, the accident occurred.
>
> REVISED: Shortly after we left home, the accident occurred.

> UNREVISED: To get up on time, a great effort was needed.
>
> REVISED: To get up on time, I made a great effort.

Sentence Fragments

A fragment is an incomplete construction that either (1) lacks a subject or a verb or (2) is preceded by a subordinating conjunction (e.g., *because, which, when, although*). A complete construction, such as a sentence or an independent clause, expresses a complete thought.

> UNREVISED: Traffic was stalled for ten miles on the freeway. Because repairs were being made on potholes. (The second "sentence" is a dependent, or subordinate, clause.)
>
> REVISED: Traffic was stalled for ten miles on the freeway because repairs were being made on potholes.

> UNREVISED: It was a funny story. One that I had never heard before. (The
> second "sentence" has no verb for its subject, "One.")

> REVISED: It was a funny story, one that I had never heard.

Run-On/Fused Sentences

A run-on, or fused, sentence is not necessarily a long sentence or a sentence that the reader considers too long; in fact, a run-on might consist of two short sentences: *Dry ice does not melt it evaporates.* A run-on results when the writer fuses, or runs together, two separate sentences without any correct mark of punctuation separating them.

> UNREVISED: Knowing how to use a dictionary is no problem each dictionary has a section in the front of the book that tells you how.

> REVISED: Knowing how to use a dictionary is no problem. Each dictionary has a section in the front of the book that tells you how.

The most common type of run-on sentence is characterized by a comma splice—the incorrect use of only a comma to separate what are really two separate sentences. There are three quick ways to fix a comma splice: (1) replace the comma with a period and start a new sentence; (2) replace the comma with a semicolon; and (3) add a coordinating conjunction, such as *and* or *but,* after the comma.

> UNREVISED: Bob bought dress shoes, a suit, and a nice shirt, he needed them for his sister's wedding.

> REVISED: Bob bought dress shoes, a suit, and a nice shirt. He needed them for his sister's wedding.

> UNREVISED: One common error in writing is incorrect spelling, the other is the occasional use of faulty diction.

> REVISED: One common error in writing is incorrect spelling; the other is the occasional use of faulty diction.

> UNREVISED: We have never won the track championship, we have won the cross-country title.

> REVISED: We have never won the track championship, but we have won the cross-country title.

If one of the complete thoughts is subordinate to the other, you may also use a subordinate conjunction to connect the two:

> UNREVISED: Neal won the award, he had the highest score.

> REVISED: Neal won the award because he had the highest score.

Subordination, Coordination, and Predication

Suppose that you wanted to combine the information in these two sentences to create one statement: *I studied a foreign language. I found English quite easy.* How you decide to combine this information should be determined by the relationship you'd like to show between the two facts. *I studied a foreign language, and I found English quite easy* adds little or nothing to the original meaning. The **coordination** of the two ideas (connecting them with the coordinating conjunction *and*) is therefore ineffective. Using **subordination** instead (connecting the sentences with a subordinating conjunction) clearly shows the relationship between the expressed ideas:

> *After I studied a foreign language, I found English quite easy.* OR
>
> *Because I studied a foreign language, I found English quite easy.*

When using any conjunction—coordinating or subordinating—be sure that the sentence parts you are joining are in agreement:

> UNREVISED: She loved him dearly but not his dog.
>
> REVISED: She loved him dearly, but she did not love his dog. OR
>   She loved him, but not his dog, dearly.

Another common mistake is to forget that each member of the pair must be followed by the same kind of construction.

> UNREVISED: She complimented her friends both for their bravery and thanked them for their kindness.
>
> REVISED: She both complimented her friends for their bravery and thanked them for their kindness.

While refers to time and should not be used as a substitute for *though, and,* or *but.*

> UNREVISED: While I'm usually interested in Fellini movies, I'd rather not go tonight.
>
> REVISED: Although I'm usually interested in Fellini movies, I'd rather not go tonight.

Where refers to a place and should not be used as a substitute for *that.*

> UNREVISED: We read in the paper where they are making strides in DNA research.
>
> REVISED: We read in the paper that they are making great strides in DNA research.

After words such as *reason* and *explanation,* use *that,* not *because.*

> UNREVISED: His explanation for his tardiness was because his alarm did
> not go off.

> REVISED: His explanation for his tardiness was that his alarm did not
> go off.

Skill 9: Maintain Consistent Point of View

Depending on the audience, essays may be written from one of three points of view:

1. *Subjective/Personal* Point of View:

    "I think . . ."

    "I believe cars are more trouble than they are worth."

    "I feel . . ."

2. *Second Person* Point of View (We . . . You; I . . . You):

    "If *you* own a car, *you* will soon find out that it is more trouble than
    it is worth."

3. *Third Person* Point of View (focuses on the idea, not what "I" think of it):

    "*Cars* are more trouble than *they* are worth."

It is very important to maintain a consistent point of view throughout your essay. If you begin writing in the first-person ("I"), do not shift to the second- or third-person in the middle of the essay. Such inconsistency is confusing to your reader and will be penalized by the graders of your essay.

Skill 10: Observe the Conventions of Standard American English

Make sure to leave yourself enough time at the end to read over your essay for errors such as misspellings, omitted words, or incorrect punctuation. You will not have enough time to make large-scale revisions, but take this chance to make any small changes that will make your essay stronger. Consider the following when proofreading your work:

- Are all your sentences really sentences? Have you written any fragments or run-on sentences?

- Are you using vocabulary correctly?

- Did you leave out any punctuation? Did you capitalize correctly?

- Are there any misspellings, especially of difficult words?

If you have time, read your essay backwards from end to beginning. By doing so, you may catch errors that you missed reading forward only.

Drill: Essay Writing Scoring

➤ **Directions:** You have 50 minutes to plan and write an essay on the topic below. You may write on one of the assigned topic choices only.

Make sure to give specific examples to support your thesis. Proofread your essay carefully and take care to express your ideas clearly and effectively.

ESSAY TOPIC:

In the last 20 years, the deterioration of the environment has become a growing concern among both scientists and ordinary citizens.

ASSIGNMENT:

Choose one pressing environmental problem, explain its negative impact and discuss possible solutions.

Drill: Essay Writing Scoring

This Answer Key provides three sample essays that represent possible responses to the essay topic. Compare your own response to those given on the next few pages. Allow the strengths and weaknesses of the sample essays help you to critique your own essay and improve your writing skills.

ESSAY I (Score: 5–6)

There are many pressing environmental problems facing both this country and the world today. Pollution, the misuse and squandering of resources, and the cavalier attitude many people express all contribute to the problem. But one of the most pressing problems this country faces is the apathetic attitude many Americans have towards recycling.

Why is recycling so imperative? There are two major reasons. First, recycling previously used materials conserves precious national resources. Many people never stop to think that reserves of metal ores are not unlimited. There is only so much gold, silver, tin, and other metals in the ground. Once it has all been mined, there will never be any more unless we recycle what has already been used.

Second, the United States daily generates more solid waste than any other country on earth. Our disposable consumer culture consumes fast food meals in paper or styrofoam containers, uses disposable diapers with plastic liners that do not biodegrade, receives pounds, if not tons, of unsolicited junk mail every year, and relies more and more on prepackaged rather than fresh food.

No matter how it is accomplished, increased recycling is essential. We have to stop covering our land with garbage, and the best ways to do this are to reduce our dependence on prepackaged goods and to minimize the amount of solid waste disposed of in landfills. The best way to reduce solid waste is to recycle it. Americans need to band together to recycle, to preserve our irreplaceable natural resources, reduce pollution, and preserve our precious environment.

Analysis

This essay presents a clearly defined thesis, and the writer elaborates on this thesis in a thoughtful and sophisticated manner. Various aspects of the problem under consideration are presented and explored, along with possible solutions. The support provided for the writer's argument is convincing and logical. There are few usage or mechanical errors to interfere with the writer's ability to communicate effectively. This writer demonstrates a comprehensive understanding of the rules of written English.

ESSAY II (Score: 3–4)

A pressing environmental problem today is the way we are cutting down too many trees and not planting any replacements for them. Trees are beneficial in many ways, and without them, many environmental problems would be much worse.

One of the ways trees are beneficial is that, like all plants, they take in carbon dioxide and produce oxygen. They can actually help clean the air this way. When too many trees are cut down in a small area, the air in that area is not as good and can be unhealthy to breath.

Another way trees are beneficial is that they provide homes for many types of birds, insects, and animals. When all the trees in an area are cut down, these animals lose their homes and sometimes they can die out and become extinct that way. Like the spotted owls in Oregon, that the loggers wanted to cut down the trees they lived in. If the loggers did cut down all the old timber stands that the spotted owls lived in, the owls would have become extinct.

But the loggers say that if they can't cut the trees down then they will be out of work, and that peoples' jobs are more important than birds. The loggers can do two things—they can either get training so they can do other jobs, or they can do what they should have done all along, and start replanting trees. For every mature tree they cut down, they should have to plant at least one tree seedling.

Cutting down the trees that we need for life, and that lots of other species depend on, is a big environmental problem that has a lot of long term consequences. Trees are too important for all of us to cut them down without thinking about the future.

Analysis

This essay has a clear thesis, which the author does support with good examples. But the writer shifts between the chosen topic, which is that indiscriminate tree-cutting is a pressing environmental problem, and a list of the ways in which trees are beneficial and a discussion about the logging profession. Also, while there are few mistakes in usage and mechanics, the writer does have some problems with sentence structure. The writing is pedestrian and the writer does not elaborate on the topic as much as he or she could have. The writer failed to provide the kind of critical analysis that the topic required.

ESSAY III (Score: 1–2)

The most pressing environmental problem today is that lots of people and companies don't care about the environment, and they do lots of things that hurt the environment.

People throw littur out car windows and don't use trash cans, even if their all over a park, soda cans and fast food wrappers are all over the place. Cigarette butts are the worst cause the filters never rot. Newspapers and junk mail get left to blow all over the neighborhood, and beer bottles too.

Companies pollute the air and the water. Sometimes the ground around a company has lots of toxins in it. Now companies can buy credits from other companies that let them pollute the air even more. They dump all kinds of chemicals into lakes and rivers that kills off the fish and causes acid rain and kills off more fish and some trees and small animals and insects and then no one can go swimming or fishing in the lake.

People need to respect the environment because we only have one planet, and if we keep polluting it pretty soon nothing will grow and then even the people will die.

Analysis

The writer of this essay does not define his or her thesis for this essay. Because of this lack of a clear thesis, the reader is left to infer the topic from the body of the essay. It is possible to perceive the writer's intended thesis; however, the support for this thesis is very superficial. The writer presents a list of common complaints about polluters, without any critical discussion of the problems and possible solutions. Many sentences are run-ons and the writer has made several spelling errors. While the author manages to communicate his or her position on the issue, he or she does so on such a superficial level and with so many errors in usage and mechanics that the writer fails to demonstrate an ability to effectively communicate.

FTCE

**Florida Teacher Certification Examination
General Knowledge Test**

Practice Test 1

Answer Sheet – Practice Test 1

Subtest I: Reading

1. Ⓐ Ⓑ Ⓒ Ⓓ
2. Ⓐ Ⓑ Ⓒ Ⓓ
3. Ⓐ Ⓑ Ⓒ Ⓓ
4. Ⓐ Ⓑ Ⓒ Ⓓ
5. Ⓐ Ⓑ Ⓒ Ⓓ
6. Ⓐ Ⓑ Ⓒ Ⓓ
7. Ⓐ Ⓑ Ⓒ Ⓓ
8. Ⓐ Ⓑ Ⓒ Ⓓ
9. Ⓐ Ⓑ Ⓒ Ⓓ
10. Ⓐ Ⓑ Ⓒ Ⓓ

11. Ⓐ Ⓑ Ⓒ Ⓓ
12. Ⓐ Ⓑ Ⓒ Ⓓ
13. Ⓐ Ⓑ Ⓒ Ⓓ
14. Ⓐ Ⓑ Ⓒ Ⓓ
15. Ⓐ Ⓑ Ⓒ Ⓓ
16. Ⓐ Ⓑ Ⓒ Ⓓ
17. Ⓐ Ⓑ Ⓒ Ⓓ
18. Ⓐ Ⓑ Ⓒ Ⓓ
19. Ⓐ Ⓑ Ⓒ Ⓓ
20. Ⓐ Ⓑ Ⓒ Ⓓ

21. Ⓐ Ⓑ Ⓒ Ⓓ
22. Ⓐ Ⓑ Ⓒ Ⓓ
23. Ⓐ Ⓑ Ⓒ Ⓓ
24. Ⓐ Ⓑ Ⓒ Ⓓ
25. Ⓐ Ⓑ Ⓒ Ⓓ
26. Ⓐ Ⓑ Ⓒ Ⓓ
27. Ⓐ Ⓑ Ⓒ Ⓓ
28. Ⓐ Ⓑ Ⓒ Ⓓ
29. Ⓐ Ⓑ Ⓒ Ⓓ
30. Ⓐ Ⓑ Ⓒ Ⓓ

31. Ⓐ Ⓑ Ⓒ Ⓓ
32. Ⓐ Ⓑ Ⓒ Ⓓ
33. Ⓐ Ⓑ Ⓒ Ⓓ
34. Ⓐ Ⓑ Ⓒ Ⓓ
35. Ⓐ Ⓑ Ⓒ Ⓓ
36. Ⓐ Ⓑ Ⓒ Ⓓ
37. Ⓐ Ⓑ Ⓒ Ⓓ
38. Ⓐ Ⓑ Ⓒ Ⓓ
39. Ⓐ Ⓑ Ⓒ Ⓓ
40. Ⓐ Ⓑ Ⓒ Ⓓ

Subtest II: Mathematics

1. Ⓐ Ⓑ Ⓒ Ⓓ
2. Ⓐ Ⓑ Ⓒ Ⓓ
3. Ⓐ Ⓑ Ⓒ Ⓓ
4. Ⓐ Ⓑ Ⓒ Ⓓ
5. Ⓐ Ⓑ Ⓒ Ⓓ
6. Ⓐ Ⓑ Ⓒ Ⓓ
7. Ⓐ Ⓑ Ⓒ Ⓓ
8. Ⓐ Ⓑ Ⓒ Ⓓ
9. Ⓐ Ⓑ Ⓒ Ⓓ
10. Ⓐ Ⓑ Ⓒ Ⓓ
11. Ⓐ Ⓑ Ⓒ Ⓓ

12. Ⓐ Ⓑ Ⓒ Ⓓ
13. Ⓐ Ⓑ Ⓒ Ⓓ
14. Ⓐ Ⓑ Ⓒ Ⓓ
15. Ⓐ Ⓑ Ⓒ Ⓓ
16. Ⓐ Ⓑ Ⓒ Ⓓ
17. Ⓐ Ⓑ Ⓒ Ⓓ
18. Ⓐ Ⓑ Ⓒ Ⓓ
19. Ⓐ Ⓑ Ⓒ Ⓓ
20. Ⓐ Ⓑ Ⓒ Ⓓ
21. Ⓐ Ⓑ Ⓒ Ⓓ
22. Ⓐ Ⓑ Ⓒ Ⓓ

23. Ⓐ Ⓑ Ⓒ Ⓓ
24. Ⓐ Ⓑ Ⓒ Ⓓ
25. Ⓐ Ⓑ Ⓒ Ⓓ
26. Ⓐ Ⓑ Ⓒ Ⓓ
27. Ⓐ Ⓑ Ⓒ Ⓓ
28. Ⓐ Ⓑ Ⓒ Ⓓ
29. Ⓐ Ⓑ Ⓒ Ⓓ
30. Ⓐ Ⓑ Ⓒ Ⓓ
31. Ⓐ Ⓑ Ⓒ Ⓓ
32. Ⓐ Ⓑ Ⓒ Ⓓ
33. Ⓐ Ⓑ Ⓒ Ⓓ

34. Ⓐ Ⓑ Ⓒ Ⓓ
35. Ⓐ Ⓑ Ⓒ Ⓓ
36. Ⓐ Ⓑ Ⓒ Ⓓ
37. Ⓐ Ⓑ Ⓒ Ⓓ
38. Ⓐ Ⓑ Ⓒ Ⓓ
39. Ⓐ Ⓑ Ⓒ Ⓓ
40. Ⓐ Ⓑ Ⓒ Ⓓ
41. Ⓐ Ⓑ Ⓒ Ⓓ
42. Ⓐ Ⓑ Ⓒ Ⓓ
43. Ⓐ Ⓑ Ⓒ Ⓓ
44. Ⓐ Ⓑ Ⓒ Ⓓ
45. Ⓐ Ⓑ Ⓒ Ⓓ

Subtest III: English Language Skills

1. Ⓐ Ⓑ Ⓒ Ⓓ
2. Ⓐ Ⓑ Ⓒ Ⓓ
3. Ⓐ Ⓑ Ⓒ Ⓓ
4. Ⓐ Ⓑ Ⓒ Ⓓ
5. Ⓐ Ⓑ Ⓒ Ⓓ
6. Ⓐ Ⓑ Ⓒ Ⓓ
7. Ⓐ Ⓑ Ⓒ Ⓓ
8. Ⓐ Ⓑ Ⓒ Ⓓ
9. Ⓐ Ⓑ Ⓒ Ⓓ
10. Ⓐ Ⓑ Ⓒ Ⓓ

11. Ⓐ Ⓑ Ⓒ Ⓓ
12. Ⓐ Ⓑ Ⓒ Ⓓ
13. Ⓐ Ⓑ Ⓒ Ⓓ
14. Ⓐ Ⓑ Ⓒ Ⓓ
15. Ⓐ Ⓑ Ⓒ Ⓓ
16. Ⓐ Ⓑ Ⓒ Ⓓ
17. Ⓐ Ⓑ Ⓒ Ⓓ
18. Ⓐ Ⓑ Ⓒ Ⓓ
19. Ⓐ Ⓑ Ⓒ Ⓓ
20. Ⓐ Ⓑ Ⓒ Ⓓ

21. Ⓐ Ⓑ Ⓒ Ⓓ
22. Ⓐ Ⓑ Ⓒ Ⓓ
23. Ⓐ Ⓑ Ⓒ Ⓓ
24. Ⓐ Ⓑ Ⓒ Ⓓ
25. Ⓐ Ⓑ Ⓒ Ⓓ
26. Ⓐ Ⓑ Ⓒ Ⓓ
27. Ⓐ Ⓑ Ⓒ Ⓓ
28. Ⓐ Ⓑ Ⓒ Ⓓ
29. Ⓐ Ⓑ Ⓒ Ⓓ
30. Ⓐ Ⓑ Ⓒ Ⓓ

31. Ⓐ Ⓑ Ⓒ Ⓓ
32. Ⓐ Ⓑ Ⓒ Ⓓ
33. Ⓐ Ⓑ Ⓒ Ⓓ
34. Ⓐ Ⓑ Ⓒ Ⓓ
35. Ⓐ Ⓑ Ⓒ Ⓓ
36. Ⓐ Ⓑ Ⓒ Ⓓ
37. Ⓐ Ⓑ Ⓒ Ⓓ
38. Ⓐ Ⓑ Ⓒ Ⓓ
39. Ⓐ Ⓑ Ⓒ Ⓓ
40. Ⓐ Ⓑ Ⓒ Ⓓ

Practice Test 1

Subtest I: Reading

TIME: 40 Minutes
40 Questions

> **DIRECTIONS:** A number of questions follow each of the passages in the reading section. Answer the questions by choosing the best answer from the four choices given.

Questions 1 and 2 refer to the following passage:

America's national bird, the mighty bald eagle, is being threatened by a new menace. Once decimated by hunters and loss of habitat, this newest danger is suspected to be from the intentional poisoning by livestock ranchers. Authorities have found animal carcasses injected with restricted pesticides. These carcasses are suspected to have been placed to attract and kill predators such as the bald eagle in an effort to preserve young grazing animals. It appears that the eagle is being threatened again by the consummate predator, humans.

1. One can conclude from this passage that

  (A) the pesticides used are detrimental to the environment.
  (B) the killing of eagles will protect the rancher's rangeland.
  (C) ranchers must obtain licenses to use the pesticides.
  (D) the poisoning could result in the extinction of the bald eagle.

2. The author's attitude is one of

  (A) detached observation.   (C) informed acceptance.
  (B) concerned interest.   (D) unbridled anger.

Questions 3 and 4 refer to the graph below.

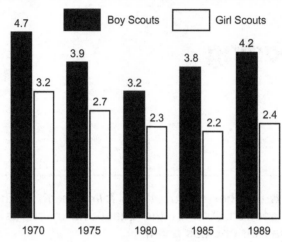

Number of Boys and Girls in Scouting in 1989 (in millions)

Source: 1991 Census Bureau's Statistical Abstract of the U.S.

3. In what year was the involvement in scouting closest to being equal between girls and boys?

    (A) 1970   (C) 1980
    (B) 1975   (D) 1985

4. How much difference between the number of boys and the number of girls involved in scouting was there (in millions) in 1970?

    (A) 1.6 million   (C) 1.5 million
    (B) .9 million   (D) 2.4 million

5. The disparaging remarks about her performance on the job made Alice uncomfortable. The word "disparaging" is closest in meaning to

    (A) complimentary.   (C) technical.
    (B) evil.   (D) insulting.

Questions 6 to 8 refer to the following passage:

INSTRUCTIONS FOR ABSENTEE VOTING

These instructions describe conditions under which voters may register for or request absentee ballots to vote in the November 2, 2004, election.

(1) If you moved on or prior to October 5, 2004, and did not register to vote at your new address, you are not eligible to vote in this election.

(2) If you move after this date, you may vote via absentee ballot or at your polling place, using your previous address as your address of registration for this election.

(3) You must register at your new address to vote in future elections.
(4) The last day to request an absentee ballot is October 28, 2004.
(5) You must be a registered voter in the county.
(6) You must sign your request in your own handwriting.
(7) You must make a separate request for each election.
(8) The absentee ballot shall be issued to the requesting voter in person or by mail.

6. A voter will be able to participate in the November 2, 2004, election as an absentee if he or she

   (A) requested an absentee ballot on November 1, 2004.
   (B) voted absentee in the last election.
   (C) moved as a registered voter on October 13, 2004.
   (D) moved on October 5, 2004.

7. On October 15, 2004, Mr. Applebee requested an absentee ballot for his daughter, a registered voting college student, to enable her to participate in the election process. Mr. Applebee will most likely need clarification on which of the following instructions?

   (A) 2   (C) 5
   (B) 4   (D) 6

8. Which of the following best describes the most important piece of information for potential voters who want to participate in the election process, either in person or by absentee ballot?

   (A) Do not change precincts.
   (B) Do register to vote in the appropriate precinct.
   (C) You may vote at your nearest polling place.
   (D) The last day to register is always October 28.

Questions 9 and 10 refer to the following statement:

   The atrophy and incapacity that occur when a broken bone is encased in plaster and immobilized clearly demonstrate what a sedentary lifestyle can do to the human body.

9. In the passage above, "atrophy and incapacity" refer to

   (A) a strengthened condition brought about by rest.
   (B) a decrease in size and strength.
   (C) a type of exercise.
   (D) rest and recuperation.

10. Which of the following statements does NOT reflect the author's view of sedentary living?

   (A) If you don't use it, you lose it.
   (B) Mobility is affected by lifestyle.
   (C) A sedentary lifestyle is a healthy lifestyle.
   (D) A body is as a body does.

Questions 11 to 15 refer to the following passage:

Frederick Douglass was born Frederick Augustus Washington Bailey in 1817 to a white father and a slave mother. Frederick was raised by his grandmother on a Maryland plantation until he was eight. It was then that he was sent to Baltimore by his owner to be a servant to the Auld family. Mrs. Auld recognized Frederick's intellectual acumen and defied the law of the state by teaching him to read and write. When Mr. Auld warned that education would make the boy unfit for slavery, Frederick sought to continue his education in the streets. When his master died, Frederick was returned to the plantation to work in the fields at age 16. Later, he was hired out to work in the shipyards in Baltimore as a ship caulker. He plotted an escape but was discovered before he could get away. It took five years before he made his way to New York City and then to New Bedford, Massachusetts, eluding slave hunters by changing his name to Douglass.

At an 1841 anti-slavery meeting in Massachusetts, Douglass was invited to give a talk about his experiences under slavery. His impromptu speech was so powerful and so eloquent that it thrust him into a career as an agent for the Massachusetts Anti-Slavery Society.

Douglass wrote his autobiography in 1845 primarily to counter those who doubted his authenticity as a former slave. This work became a classic in American literature and a primary source about slavery from the point of view of a slave. Douglass went on a two-year speaking tour abroad to avoid recapture by his former owner and to win new friends for the abolition movement. He returned with funds to purchase his freedom and to start his own anti-slavery newspaper. He became a consultant to Abraham Lincoln and throughout Reconstruction fought doggedly for full civil rights for freedmen; he also supported the women's rights movement.

11. According to the passage, Douglass's autobiography was motivated by

    (A) the desire to make money for his anti-slavery movement.
    (B) the desire to start a newspaper.
    (C) his interest in authenticating his life as a slave.
    (D) his desire to educate people about slavery.

12. The central idea of the passage is that Frederick Douglass

    (A) was influential in changing the laws regarding the education of slaves.
    (B) was one of the most eminent human rights leaders of the century.
    (C) was a personal friend and confidant to a president.
    (D) wrote a classic in American literature.

13. According to the author of this passage, Mrs. Auld taught Frederick to read because

    (A) Frederick wanted to learn like the other boys.
    (B) she recognized his natural ability.
    (C) he needed to read to work in the home.
    (D) she obeyed her husband's wishes in the matter.

14. The title that best expresses the ideas of this passage is

    (A) The History of the Anti-Slavery Movement.
    (B) The Dogged Determination of Frederick Douglass.
    (C) Frederick Douglass's Contributions to Freedom.
    (D) The Oratorical and Literary Brilliance of Frederick Douglass.

15. In the context of the passage, "impromptu" is closest in meaning to

    (A) unprepared.   (C) forceful.
    (B) in a quiet manner.   (D) elaborate.

Question 16 refers to the following passage:

Acupuncture practitioners, those who use the placement of needles at strategic locations under the skin to block pain, have been tolerated by American physicians since the 1930s. This form of Chinese treatment has been used for about 3,000 years and until recently has been viewed suspiciously by the West. New research indicates that acupuncture might provide relief for sufferers of chronic back pain, arthritis, and, recently, pain experienced by alcoholics and drug users as they kick the habit.

16. According to the passage, acupuncture has been found to help people suffering from all of the following EXCEPT

    (A) recurring back pain.   (C) liver disease.
    (B) alcoholics in withdrawal.   (D) drug addicts in withdrawal.

Question 17 refers to the following passage:

Each time a person opens his or her mouth to eat, he or she makes a nutritional decision. These selections make a definitive difference in how an individual looks, feels, and performs at work or play. When a good assortment of food in appropriate amounts is selected and eaten, the consequences are likely to be desirable levels of health and energy to allow one to be as active as needed. Conversely, when choices are less than desirable, the consequences can be poor health or limited energy or both. Studies of American diets, particularly the diets of the very young, reveal unsatisfactory dietary habits as evidenced by the numbers of overweight and out-of-shape young children.

17. The author's attitude toward Americans' dietary habits may be characterized as

    (A) concerned.   (C) angry.
    (B) informational.   (D) amused.

Question 18 refers to the following passage:

Commercial enterprises frequently provide the backdrop for the birth of a new language. When members of different language communities need to communicate or wish to bargain with each other, they may develop a new language through a process called "pidginization." A pidgin language, or pidgin, never becomes a native language; rather, its use is limited to business transactions with members of other language communities. Pidgins consist of very simple grammatical structures and small vocabularies. They have tended to develop around coastal areas where seafarers first made contact with speakers of other languages.

18. The passage suggests which of the following about pidgins?

    (A) We could expect to hear pidgins along the west coast of Africa and in the Pacific islands.
    (B) Pidgins are located in inland mountain regions.
    (C) Pidgins become the main language after several generations of use.
    (D) Pidgins are the languages of seafarers.

Question 19 refers to the following passage:

There are two ways of measuring mass. One method to determine the mass of a body is to use a beam-balance. By this method, an unknown mass is placed on one pan at the end of a beam. The known masses are added to the pan at the other end of the beam until the pans are balanced. Since the force of gravity is the same on each pan, the masses must also be the same on each pan. When the mass of a body is measured by comparison with known masses on a beam-balance, it is called the gravitational mass of the body.

The second method to determine the mass of a body is distinctly different; this method uses the property of inertia. To determine mass in this way, a mass is placed on a frictionless horizontal surface. When a known force is applied to it, the magnitude of the mass is measured by the amount of acceleration produced upon it by the known force. Mass measured in this way is said to be the inertial mass of the body in question. This method is seldom used because it involves both a frictionless surface and a difficult measurement of acceleration.

19. Which of the following statements can best be supported from the passage?

    (A) The gravitational and inertia mass methods measure different properties of the object.
    (B) The masses are equal when the weights are equal and cause the beam to be balanced.
    (C) Gravitational and inertial measurements do not give the same numerical value for mass.
    (D) The mass of a body depends on where it is located in the universe.

Question 20 refers to the following statement:

Her introductory remarks provided a segue into the body of the speech.

20. In this context the word "segue" means

    (A) delivery.   (C) direction.
    (B) a pause.   (D) credential.

Questions 21 to 23 refer to the following passage:

One of the many tragedies of the Civil War was the housing and care of prisoners. The Andersonville prison, built by the Confederates in 1864 to accommodate 10,000 Union prisoners, was not completed when prisoners started arriving. Five months later the total number of men incarcerated there had risen to 31,678.

The sounds of death and dying were not diminished by surrender of weapons to a captor. Chances of survival for prisoners in Andersonville were not much better than in the throes of combat. Next to overcrowding, inadequate shelter caused unimaginable suffering. The Confederates were not equipped with the manpower, tools, or supplies necessary to house such a population of captives; prisoners themselves gathered lumber, logs, anything they could find to construct some sort of protection from the elements. Some prisoners dug holes in the ground, risking suffocation from cave-ins, but many hundreds were left exposed to the wind, rain, cold, and heat.

Daily food rations were exhausted by the sheer numbers they had to serve, resulting in severe dietary deficiencies. The overcrowding, meager rations, and deplorable unsanitary conditions resulted in rampant disease and a high mortality rate. The consequences of a small scratch or wound could result in death in Andersonville. During the prison's 13-month existence, more than 12,000 prisoners died and were buried in the Andersonville cemetery. Most of the deaths were caused by diarrhea, dysentery, gangrene, and scurvy that could not be treated due to inadequate staff and supplies.

21. What is the central idea of the passage?

    (A) The prison was never fully completed.
    (B) Prison doctors were ill-equipped to handle emergencies.
    (C) Andersonville prison was not adequate to care for three times as many prisoners as it could hold.
    (D) Many prisoners died as a result of shelter cave-ins.

22. From this passage the author's attitude toward the Confederates is one of

    (A) impartiality.   (C) indifference.
    (B) contempt.   (D) denial.

23. The first sentence of the second paragraph of this passage can best be described as

    (A) a digression.   (C) an exposé.
    (B) a hypothesis.   (D) an irony.

Question 24 refers to the following statement:

Maria commented to Joe, "Ted's nose is out of joint because he wasn't invited to the reception."

24. Someone hearing the conversation would most likely conclude that Ted

    (A) had a swollen nose.
    (B) was upset about not being asked to the reception.
    (C) was not invited to the reception because his nose was hurt.
    (D) had a bandage on his nose at the reception.

Questions 25 to 27 refer to the following passage:

To the Shakers, perfection was found in the creation of an object that was both useful and simple. Their Society was founded in 1774 by Ann Lee, an Englishwoman from the working classes who brought eight followers to New York with her. "Mother Ann" established her religious community on the belief that worldly interests were evil.

To gain entrance into the Society, believers had to remain celibate, have no private possessions, and avoid contact with outsiders. The order came to be called "Shakers" because of the feverish dance the group performed. Another characteristic of the group was the desire to seek perfection in their work.

Shaker furniture was created to exemplify specific characteristics: simplicity of design, quality of craftsmanship, harmony of proportion, and usefulness. While Shakers did not create any innovations in furniture designs, they were known for fine craftsmanship. The major emphasis was on function, and not on excessive or elaborate decorations that contributed nothing to the product's usefulness.

25. The passage indicates that members of the religious order were called the Shakers because

 (A) they shook hands at their meetings.
 (B) they did a shaking dance at their meetings.
 (C) they took their name from the founder.
 (D) they were named after the township where they originated.

26. Which of the following is the most appropriate substitute for the use of the term "innovations" in the third paragraph?

 (A) Corrections   (C) Functions
 (B) Changes   (D) Brocades

27. The passage suggests which of the following about the Shakers?

 (A) Shakers believed in form over function in their designs.
 (B) Shaker furniture has seen a surge in popularity.
 (C) Shakers appeared to believe that form follows function.
 (D) Shaker furniture is noted for the use of brass hardware.

Questions 28 and 29 refer to the following passage:

James Dean began his career as a stage actor, but in motion pictures he symbolized the confused, restless, and idealistic youth of the 1950s. He excelled at film parts that called for brooding, impulsive characterizations, the personification of frustrated youthful passion. Dean made three such movies: *East of Eden, Rebel Without a Cause,* and *Giant,* and established himself as a cult hero. Tragically, his career was cut short in an automobile crash before the release of *Giant.*

28. One conclusion that could be drawn from this passage is that

    (A) James Dean was not well regarded because of the kind of characters he portrayed.
    (B) James Dean had to be replaced by another actor in *Giant* due to his death.
    (C) James Dean was adept at portraying sensitive, youthful characters.
    (D) James Dean was a promising stage actor.

29. The author's attitude is one of

    (A) regret.   (C) pessimism.
    (B) anger.   (D) indifference.

Questions 30 to 32 refer to the following passage:

Benjamin Franklin began writing his autobiography in 1771, but he set it aside to assist the colonies in gaining independence from England. After a hiatus of 13 years, he returned to chronicle his life, addressing his message to the younger generation. In this significant literary work of early United States, Franklin portrays himself as benign, kindhearted, practical, and hardworking. He established a list of ethical conduct and recorded his transgressions when he was unsuccessful in overcoming temptation. Franklin wrote that he was unable to arrive at perfection, "yet I was, by the endeavor, a better and happier man than I otherwise should have been if I had not attempted it."

30. Which of the following is the LEAST appropriate substitute for the use of the term "ethical" near the end of the passage?

    (A) Moral   (C) Virtuous
    (B) Depraved   (D) Qualifiable

31. The passage suggests which of the following about Franklin's autobiography?

    (A) It was representative of early American literature.
    (B) It fell short of being a major work of literary quality.
    (C) It personified Franklin as a major political figure.
    (D) It was a notable work of early American literature.

32. Which of the following slogans best describes Franklin's assessment of the usefulness of attempting to achieve perfection?

    (A) Cleanliness is next to Godliness.
    (B) Nothing ventured, nothing gained.
    (C) Ambition is its own reward.
    (D) Humility is everything.

Questions 33 to 35 refer to the graph below:

How the Average Consumer Spent Money in 2002
Total: $25,893

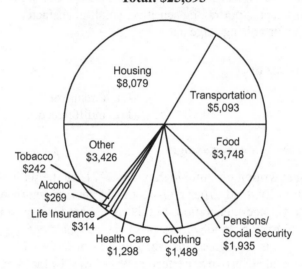

Source: Census Bureau's Statistical Abstract of the U.S.

33. According to the graph, the average consumer spent approximately 50 percent of her/his earnings on

   (A) housing and health care costs.
   (B) transportation and housing.
   (C) food.
   (D) transportation and pensions.

34. After transportation, the next greatest amount of money was spent on

   (A) clothing.   (C) food.
   (B) other.   (D) pensions/social security.

35. According to the graph, expenditure on health care was approximately equal to

   (A) clothing.   (C) food.
   (B) pensions.   (D) other.

Questions 36 to 38 refer to the following passage:

The scarlet flamingo is practically a symbol of Florida. Once the West Indian flamingo population wintered in Florida Bay and as far north as St. John's River and Tampa Bay, but the brilliantly colored birds abandoned these grounds around 1885 due to the decimation of their numbers by feather hunters. The flock at Hialeah Race Track is descended from a handful of birds imported from Cuba in the 1930s. It took seven years before the first flamingo was born in captivity, but several thousand have since been hatched.

Flamingo raisers found that the birds require a highly specialized diet of shrimps and mollusks to maintain their attractive coloring. It is speculated that hunters as well as the birds' selective breeding habits perhaps caused the disappearance of these beautiful birds from the wild in North America.

36. The central idea of the passage is that the flamingos of Florida

    (A) are a symbol of Florida.
    (B) are no longer found in the wild in North America.
    (C) came from Cuba.
    (D) eat shrimps and mollusks.

37. The word "decimation" is closest in meaning to

    (A) desecration.   (C) eradication.
    (B) restoration.   (D) appeasement.

38. According to the passage, which of the following is responsible for the flamingo's brilliant plumage?

    (A) Selective breeding
    (B) Their diet of marine organisms
    (C) Shallow water plants
    (D) Fish and water snakes

Questions 39 and 40 refer to the following passage:

Teachers should be cognizant of the responsibility they have for the development of children's competencies in basic concepts and principles of free speech. Freedom of speech is not merely the utterance of sounds into the air, rather, it is couched in a set of values and legislative processes that have developed over time. These values and processes are a part of our political conscience as Americans. Teachers must provide ample opportunities for children to express themselves effectively in an environment where their opinions are valued. Children should have ownership in the decision-making process in the classroom and should be engaged in activities where alternative resolutions to problems can be explored. Because teachers have such tremendous power to influence in the classroom, they must be careful to refrain from presenting their own values and biases that could "color" their students' belief systems. If we want children to develop their own voices in a free society, then teachers must support participatory democratic experiences in the daily workings of the classroom.

39. The title that best expresses the ideas in the passage is

    (A) The Nature of the Authoritarian Classroom.
    (B) Concepts and Principles of Free Speech.
    (C) Exploring Freedom in American Classrooms.
    (D) Developing Children's Citizenship Competencies.

40. It can be inferred from the passage that instructional strategies that assist children in the development of citizenship competencies include all of the following EXCEPT

    (A) children's participation in rule making.
    (B) fostering self-esteem.
    (C) indoctrination in principles of society.
    (D) consideration of cultural and gender differences.

Subtest II: Mathematics

TIME: 100 Minutes
45 Questions

DIRECTIONS: Each of the questions or incomplete statements below is followed by four suggested answers or completions. Select the one that is best in each case.

---

1. Simplify the following expression: $6 + 2(x - 4)$.

   (A) $4x - 16$ (C) $2x - 2$
   (B) $2x - 14$ (D) $-24x$

2. Simplify by following the order of operations: $9 - 5 \div (8 - 3) \times 3 + 6$

   (A) $7\dfrac{1}{5}$ (C) 22

   (B) 12 (D) 1

3. If six cans of beans cost $1.50, what is the price of eight cans of beans?

   (A) $.90   (C) $1.60
   (B) $1.00   (D) $2.00

4. Bonnie's average score on three tests is 71. Her first two test scores are 64 and 87. What is her score on test three?

   (A) 62   (C) 74
   (B) 71   (D) 151

5. Jeannie was trying to guess the name of the three-dimensional figure that Xavier was describing. Xavier's figure had:

   - 5 vertices

   - 1 rectangular base

   - 4 triangular lateral faces

What is the name of Xavier's figure?

(A) rectangular prism   (C) triangular prism
(B) rectangular pyramid   (D) triangular pyramid

6. Carla's garden was 15 feet long by 8 feet wide. What is the perimeter of Carla's garden in feet?

(A) 120   (C) 46
(B) 23   (D) 80

7. Which ordered pair is *not* a solution to the inequality: $y < \dfrac{1}{2}x - 5$?

(A) (4, 8)   (C) (10, –1)
(B) (32, 10)   (D) (6, –5)

8. If $2x^2 + 5x - 3 = 0$ and $x > 0$, then what is the value of x?

(A) $-\dfrac{1}{2}$ (C) 1

(B) $\dfrac{1}{2}$ (D) $\dfrac{3}{2}$

9. Which answer choice shows the best unit price?

(A) 12 apples for $6.96   (C) 5 apples for $2.80
(B) 15 apples for $8.10   (D) 13 apples for $7.41

10. According to the following chart, in what year was the total sales of Brand X televisions the greatest?

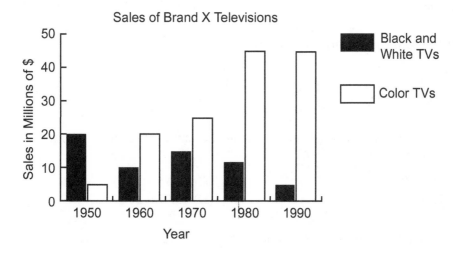

(A) 1960   (C) 1980
(B) 1970   (D) 1990

11. How many odd prime numbers are there between 1 and 20?

   (A) 7   (C) 9
   (B) 8   (D) 10

12. The map shows part of the East Village neighborhood in NYC. Which street is perpendicular to Avenue A (found right above Tompkins Square)?

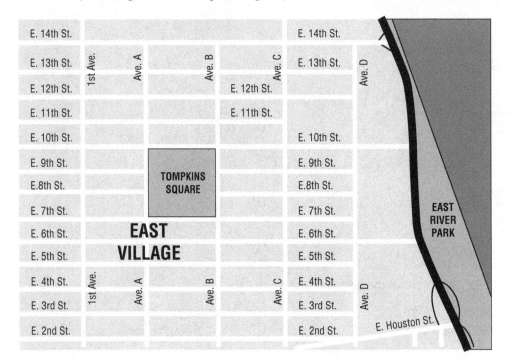

   (A) Avenue B   (C) E. 11th Street
   (B) Avenue C   (D) 1st Avenue

13. Solve the following inequality for x: $8 - 2x \leq 10$.

   (A) $x \leq 1$ (C) $x \geq -1$

   (B) $x \leq -1$ (D) $x \leq \dfrac{5}{3}$

14. Calculate the expression shown below and write the answer in scientific notation.
   0.003×1.25

   (A) 0.375×10^{-2} (C) 3.75×10^{-3}
   (B) 0.375×10^{2} (D) 3.75×10^{3}

15. Find the 7th number in the geometric sequence: $-1, 3, -9, 27 \ldots$

   (A) -729 (C) 243
   (B) 729 (D) -243

16. Find the next number in the pattern: 1, 8, 27, 64 …

    (A) 101   (C) 83
    (B) 71   (D) 125

17. One day the temperature in Buffalo, NY was 15° Celsius (C). The formula $F = \dfrac{9}{5}C + 32$ can be used to convert this temperature to degrees Fahrenheit (F). Find the temperature that is equivalent to 15°C in degrees Fahrenheit.

    (A) 47   (C) 85
    (B) 59   (D) 40

18. Find the slope of the line passing through the points W and Z in the following figure.

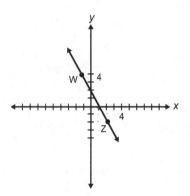

    (A) $-\dfrac{1}{2}$ (C) −2

    (B) $\dfrac{1}{4}$ (D) 2

19. Using the metric system, find the measure of the black line below to the nearest millimeter.

    (A) 3.3 mm   (C) .33 mm
    (B) 33 mm   (D) 330 mm

20. Which of the ordered pairs is a solution of the inequality $y \leq -3x - 1$?

    (A) (2, 3)   (C) (1, −2)
    (B) (−5, 15)   (D) (0, −1)

21. The formula relating the Celsius (C) and the Fahrenheit (F) scales of temperature is shown below.

$$F = \frac{9}{5}C + 32$$

Find the temperature in the Celsius scale when the temperature is 86° F.

(A) 25°

(B) 30°

(C) 105°

(D) 124.6°

22. It is 358 miles from Pensacola to Jacksonville. If the scale on a map is 1 inch = 50 miles, what would be the distance on the map from Pensacola to Jacksonville to the nearest quarter of an inch?

(A) 7 inches

(B) $7\frac{1}{4}$ inches

(C) $7\frac{1}{2}$ inches

(D) $7\frac{3}{4}$ inches

23. Mrs. Wall has $300,000. She wishes to give each of her six children an equal amount of her money. Which of the following methods will result in the amount that each child is to receive?

   (A) 6 × 300,000
   (B) 6 ÷ 300,000

   (C) 300,000 ÷ 6
   (D) 300,000 – 6

24. Referring to the figure below, what is the length of $\overline{PQ}$?

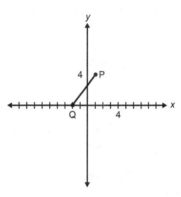

   (A) $2\sqrt{5}$
   (B) $5\sqrt{2}$

   (C) 5
   (D) 7

25. Ms. Rossi needs to catch the 7:35 a.m. train into the city. It takes her $\frac{1}{3}$ of an hour to drive to the train station, 25 minutes to shower and get dressed, 10 minutes to eat breakfast, and 15 minutes to blowdry her hair. What is the latest time that Ms. Rossi can get up in order to get to her train on time?

   (A) 6:15 a.m.
   (B) 6:25 a.m.

   (C) 6:45 a.m.
   (D) 6:50 a.m.

26. What is the probability that a six-sided die will land on a prime number?

   (A) $\frac{1}{2}$

   (B) $\frac{2}{3}$

   (C) $\frac{1}{6}$

   (D) $\frac{5}{6}$

27. Ricky drove from Town A to Town B in 3 hours. His return trip from Town B to Town A took 5 hours because he drove 15 miles per hour slower on the return trip. How fast did Ricky drive on the trip from Town A to Town B?

   (A) 25.5 mph
   (B) 32 mph

   (C) 37.5 mph
   (D) 45 mph

28. At a certain company, there are 41 employees. In the past year, 20 of the employees got fired. If the company wants their employees to feel that their jobs are safe, which statement below would encourage them?

    (A) Almost 50% of our employees lost their jobs last year.
    (B) Only 20 of our employees lost their jobs last year.
    (C) More than 50% of our employees kept their jobs last year.
    (D) Just about $\frac{1}{2}$ of our employees lost their jobs last year.

29. Carlos was applying for a position at a large store. The weekly salaries of the 16 employees are listed below:

    350, 400, 400, 400, 400, 400, 400, 400, 400, 600, 600, 600, 600, 675, 675, 675

    If Carlos asks what the average weekly salary for an employee is, which measure of central tendency will be the highest: the mean, median, or mode?

    (A) The mean and the median will be the highest.
    (B) The mean will be the highest.
    (C) The mode and mean will be the highest.
    (D) The median will be the highest.

30: Which answer below shows the correct simplification of $150 \div (6 + 3 \times 8) - 5$?

    (A) 0   (C) $\frac{150}{67}$

    (B) $-\frac{105}{36}$ (D) 5

31. Simplify the following expression.

    $$\frac{x^2 \times x^7}{x}$$

    (A) x^6 (C) x^8
    (B) x^7 (D) x^{10}

32. List the fractions shown below from least to greatest.

    $$\frac{1}{9}, \frac{2}{15}, \frac{3}{21}$$

    (A) $\frac{1}{9}, \frac{2}{15}, \frac{3}{21}$ (C) $\frac{1}{9}, \frac{3}{21}, \frac{2}{15}$

    (B) $\frac{3}{21}, \frac{1}{9}, \frac{2}{15}$ (D) $\frac{2}{15}, \frac{1}{9}, \frac{3}{21}$

33. A rectangular box with a square base is shown below. If the volume of the box is 256 cubic feet and the height of the box is one-half the length of a side of the base, find the height of the box.

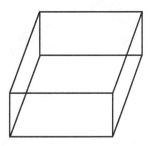

(A) 4 feet   (C) 8 feet

(B) 6 feet   (D) 10 feet

34. If $x = -3$, then find the value of $-x^2 + 2x$.

(A) −15   (C) 3

(B) −3   (D) 15

35. Dante tossed three coins. Use the tree diagram below to find the probability that two of the three coins will land on heads.

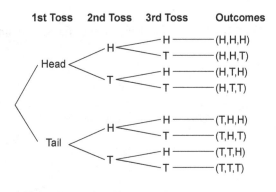

(A) $\dfrac{3}{8}$ (C) $\dfrac{1}{4}$

(B) $\dfrac{1}{2}$ (D) $\dfrac{5}{8}$

36. In a barn there were cows and people. If we counted 30 heads and 104 legs in the barn, how many cows and how many people were in the barn?

(A) 16 cows and 14 people   (C) 22 cows and 8 people

(B) 18 cows and 16 people   (D) 24 cows and 4 people

37. What geometric translation are the footprints below an example of?

    (A) translation   (C) reflection
    (B) rotation   (D) dilation

38. A box is 11 inches long, 19 inches wide, and 12 inches high. Find the volume of the box in cubic inches.

    (A) 569   (C) 2508
    (B) 1138   (D) 1800

39. What is $\dfrac{1}{2}+\dfrac{1}{3}$?

    (A) $\dfrac{1}{5}$ (C) $\dfrac{2}{6}$

    (B) $\dfrac{2}{5}$ (D) $\dfrac{5}{6}$

40. Given that $\overline{BC} \parallel \overline{DE}$ in the following figure, write down the pair of similar (~) triangles.

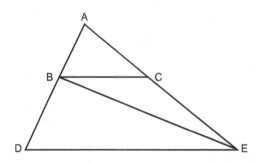

    (A) $\triangle ABC \sim \triangle ADE$ (C) $\triangle ABC \sim \triangle AED$
    (B) $\triangle ABC \sim \triangle ABE$ (D) $\triangle BCE \sim \triangle BAC$

41. The cost of gas heating a house in Riverview, Florida, is $1.83 per cubic foot. What is the monthly gas bill if the customer uses 145 cubic feet?

    (A) $265.35   (C) $183.00
    (B) $145.00   (D) $79.23

42. Twenty-two second grade students were asked what type of pet they wanted to have. Their results are shown in the bar graph. Which statement about the results is true?

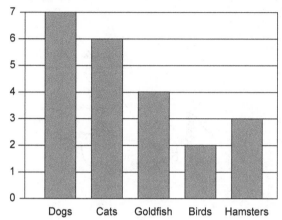

(A) Two more students want dogs than want cats.
(B) Twice as many students want goldfish as want hamsters.
(C) Fewer students want cats than want birds.
(D) Three times more students want cats than birds.

43. The wear-out mileage of a certain tire is normally distributed with a mean of 30,000 miles and a standard deviation of 2,500 miles, as shown below. What is the percentage of tires that will last at least 30,000 miles?

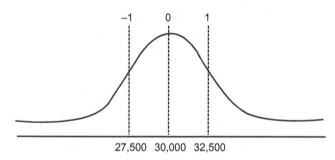

(A) 40%   (C) 50%
(B) 45%   (D) 55%

44. Heather bought 5 new books. In how many different orders can Heather read her 5 books?

(A) 25   (C) 120
(B) 60   (D) 100

45. Suppose a person 2 m tall casts a shadow 1 m long when a tree has an 8 m shadow. How high is the tree?

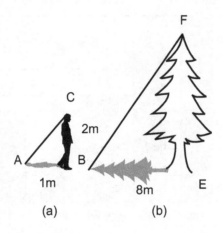

(A) 8 m   (C) 14 m

(B) 10 m   (D) 16 m

Subtest III: English Language Skills

TIME: 40 Minutes
40 Questions

Part A: Usage

> **DIRECTIONS:** Each of the following sentences may contain an error in diction, usage, idiom, or grammar. Some sentences are correct. Some sentences contain one error. No sentence contains more than one error.
>
> If there is an error, it will appear in one of the underlined portions labeled A, B, or C. If there is no error, choose the portion labeled D. If there is an error, select the letter of the portion that must be changed in order to correct the sentence.
>
> **EXAMPLE:**
>
> He drove <u>slowly</u> and <u>cautiously</u> in order to <u>hopefully</u> avoid having an
>   **A**   **B**   **C**
> accident. <u>No error</u>.
>   **D**   Ⓐ Ⓑ ● Ⓓ

1. In 1877 Chief Joseph of the Nez Perces, <u>together with</u> 250 warriors and 500 women and children,
                                         A
   <u>were praised</u> by newspaper reporters for bravery during the 115-day fight <u>for</u> freedom. <u>No error</u>.
     B   **C**   **D**

2. The ideals <u>upon which</u> American society <u>is based</u> <u>are</u> primarily those of Europe and not ones derived
            A   **B** **C**
   from the native Indian culture. <u>No error</u>.
                           D

3. <u>An astute and powerful</u> woman, Frances Nadel <u>was</u> a beauty contest winner before she became
           A   **B**
   president of the company <u>upon the death</u> of her husband. <u>No error</u>.
                      C   **D**

4. Representative Wilson pointed out, however, that the legislature <u>had not finalized</u> the state budget
   A

   and salary increases <u>had depended</u> on decisions <u>to be made</u> in a special session. <u>No error</u>.
   B   **C**   **D**

5. Now the city librarian, doing more than checking out books, must help <u>to plan</u> puppet shows and
   A

   movies for children, garage sales for <u>used</u> books, and <u>arranging for</u> guest lecturers and exhibits for
   B   **C**

   adults. <u>No error</u>.
   D

6. In order <u>to completely understand</u> the psychological <u>effects</u> of the bubonic plague, one must realize
   A   **B**

   that one-fourth to one-third of the population in an <u>affected</u> area died. <u>No error</u>.
   C   D

7. Rural roads, known in the United States as farm to market roads, have always been a vital <u>link in</u>
   A

   the economy of <u>more advanced</u> nations because transportation of goods to markets <u>is</u> essential.
   B   **C**

   <u>No error</u>.
   D

8. <u>Many a</u> graduate wishes to return to college and <u>abide in</u> the protected environment of a university,
   A   **B**

   particularly if <u>someone else</u> pays the bills. <u>No error</u>.
   C   **D**

9. <u>Confronted with</u> a choice of either cleaning up his room or <u>cleaning out</u> the garage, the teenager
   A   **B**

   became very <u>aggravated</u> with his parents. <u>No error</u>.
   C   **D**

10. My brother and <u>I</u> dressed as quickly as we could, but we missed the school bus, <u>which</u> made <u>us</u> late
    A   **B**   **C**

    for class today. <u>No error</u>.
    D

11. <u>Among</u> the activities offered at the local high school <u>through</u> the community education program <u>are</u>
    A   **B**   **C**

    singing in the couples' chorus, ballroom dancing, and Chinese cooking. <u>No error</u>.
    D

12. If you are <u>disappointed by</u> an inexpensive bicycle, then an option you might consider is to work this
A

summer and <u>save</u> your money for a <u>more expensive</u> model. <u>No error</u>.
B **C** **D**

13. Also being presented to the city council this morning <u>is</u> the mayor's city budget for next year and
A

plans to renovate the <u>existing</u> music theater, so the session <u>will focus</u> on financial matters. <u>No error</u>.
B **C** **D**

14. Even a movement <u>so delicate</u> as a <u>fly's walking</u> triggers the Venus flytrap to grow extra cells on the
A **B**

outside of <u>its</u> hinge, immediately closing the petals of the trap. <u>No error</u>.
C **D**

15. Although outwardly Thomas Hardy seemed quite <u>the picture</u> of <u>respectability</u> and contentment, his
A **B**

works, especially the prose, <u>deals with</u> the theme of man's inevitable suffering. <u>No error</u>.
C **D**

16. Though unequal in social standing, the everyday lives of ancient Egyptian kings and commoners
<u>alike</u> are visible in the pictures of <u>them</u> found <u>inside of</u> tombs and temples. <u>No error</u>.
A **B** **C** **D**

17. Sometimes considered <u>unsafe for</u> crops, land around river deltas <u>can be</u> excellent land for farming
A **B**

because periodic flooding deposits silt rich <u>in</u> nutrients. <u>No error</u>.
C **D**

18. For years, people concerned with the environment <u>have compiled</u> information that <u>show</u> many
A **B**

species are extinct and others <u>are either</u> endangered or bordering on becoming endangered. <u>No error</u>.
C **D**

19. Little is known about Shakespeare's boyhood or his early career as an actor and playwright, but he
<u>appears to have been</u> a financial success because he bought many properties, including <u>one of the finest</u>
A **B**

homes in Stratford, the town he <u>was born in</u>. <u>No error</u>.
C **D**

20. *Scared Straight*, a program designed <u>to inhibit</u> criminal behavior in juvenile offenders <u>who</u> seemed
A **B**

bound for prison as adults, had a significant <u>affect</u> on the youngsters. <u>No error</u>.
C **D**

21. The average American tourist feels <u>quite</u> at home in a Japanese stadium filled <u>at capacity</u> with sports
                           A   **B**

    fans watching Japan's <u>most</u> popular sport, baseball. <u>No error</u>.
                           C   **D**

22. My brother is engaged to a woman <u>who</u> my parents <u>have</u> not met because she has not yet
                                         A   **B**

    <u>emigrated from</u> her native country of Ecuador. <u>No error</u>.
            C   **D**

23. Colonel Jones <u>denies that</u> he illegally delivered funds to a foreign government agent or that <u>he</u> was
                  A   **B**

    involved in <u>any other</u> covert activity. <u>No error</u>.
                 C   **D**

24. In the United States, <u>testing for</u> toxicity, determining the proper dose and timing between doses, and
                         A

    evaluating the vaccine for <u>effectiveness</u> <u>is</u> the method used in researching new drugs. <u>No error</u>.
                                B   **C**   **D**

25. George wants <u>to know if</u> <u>it is her</u> driving that expensive red sports car at a rate of speed
                   A   **B**

    <u>obviously exceeding</u> the posted speed limit. <u>No error</u>.
             C   **D**

Part B: Sentence Correction

DIRECTIONS: In each of the following sentences, some portion of the sentence is underlined. Under each sentence are four choices. The first choice has the same wording as the original. The other three choices are reworded. Sometimes the first choice containing the original wording is the best; sometimes one of the other choices is the best. Choose the letter of the best choice. Your choice should produce a sentence which is not ambiguous or awkward and which is correct, clear, and precise.

This is a test of correct and effective English expression. Keep in mind the standards of English usage, punctuation, grammar, word choice, and construction.

EXAMPLE:

When you listen to opera, <u>a person may not appreciate it</u>.

    (A) a person may not appreciate it.
    (B) it may not be appreciated by a person.
    (C) you may not appreciate it.
    (D) appreciating it may be a problem for you.

26. <u>Being that you bring home more money than I do</u>, it is only fitting you should pay proportionately more rent.

    (A) Being that you bring home more money than I do
    (B) When more money is made by you than by me
    (C) Because you bring home more money than I do
    (D) If your bringing home more money than me

27. So tenacious is their grip on life, that sponge cells will regroup and form a new sponge even <u>when they are</u> squeezed through silk.

    (A) when they are
    (B) as they will be
    (C) after they have been
    (D) because they should be

28. <u>Seeing as how the plane is late</u>, wouldn't you prefer to wait for a while on the observation deck?

    (A) Seeing as how the plane is late
    (B) When the plane comes in
    (C) Since the plane is late
    (D) Being as the plane is late

29. Only with careful environmental planning can we protect the <u>world we live in</u>.

    (A) world we live in
    (B) world in which we live in
    (C) living in this world
    (D) world in which we live

30. In the last three years we have added more varieties of vegetables to our garden <u>than those you suggested in the beginning</u>.

    (A) than those you suggested in the beginning
    (B) than the ones we began with
    (C) beginning with your suggestion
    (D) which you suggested in the beginning

31. As you know, I am not easily fooled by flattery, and while <u>nice words please you</u>, they don't get the job done.

    (A) nice words please you
    (B) nice words are pleasing
    (C) nice words please a person
    (D) flattering words please people

32. Some pieces of the puzzle, in spite of Jane's search, <u>are still missing and probably will never be found</u>.

    (A) are still missing and probably will never be found
    (B) is missing still but never found probably
    (C) probably will be missing and never found
    (D) are still probably missing and to never be found

33. *Gone With the Wind* <u>is the kind of a movie</u> producers would like to release because it would bring them fame.

    (A) is the kind of a movie   (C) is the kind of movie
    (B) is the sort of movie   (D) is the category of movie

34. Eighteenth-century architecture, with its columns and balanced lines, <u>was characteristic of those of previous times in Greece and Rome</u>.

    (A) was characteristic of those of previous times in Greece and Rome
    (B) is similar to characteristics of Greece and Rome
    (C) is similar to Greek and Roman building styles
    (D) was similar to architecture of Greece and Rome

35. Plato, one of the famous Greek philosophers, won many wrestling prizes when he was a young man, thus <u>exemplifying the Greek ideal of balance between the necessity for physical activity and using one's mind</u>.

    (A) exemplifying the Greek ideal of balance between the necessity for physical activity and using one's mind
    (B) serving as an example of the Greek ideal of balance between physical and mental activities
    (C) an example of balancing Greek mental and athletic games
    (D) this as an example of the Greek's balance between mental physical pursuits

36. Allied control of the Philippine Islands during World War II proved to be <u>another obstacle as the Japanese scattered resistance</u> until the end of the war.

    (A) another obstacle as the Japanese scattered resistance
    (B) difficult because of the Japanese giving resistance
    (C) as another scattered obstacle due to Japanese resistance
    (D) difficult because the Japanese gave scattered resistance

37. Flooding abated and the river waters receded as the <u>rainfall finally let up</u>.

    (A) rainfall finally let up
    (B) rain having let up
    (C) rainfall, when it finally let up
    (D) raining finally letting up

38. Unless China slows its population growth to zero, that country <u>would still have</u> a problem feeding its people.

    (A) would still have
    (B) might have had still
    (C) will still have
    (D) would have still

39. In *The Music Man*, Robert Preston portrays a fast-talking salesman who comes to a small town in Iowa <u>inadvertently falling in love with</u> the librarian.

    (A) inadvertently falling in love with
    (B) and inadvertently falls in love with
    (C) afterwards he inadvertently falls in love with
    (D) when he inadvertently falls in love with

40. Many naturalists have a reverence for the woods and wildlife, <u>which exhibits itself through their</u> writings or paintings.

    (A) which exhibits itself through their
    (B) and this exhibits itself through their
    (C) and exhibiting itself in
    (D) when they produce

Subtest IV: Essay

TIME: 50 Minutes

> <u>DIRECTIONS:</u> **Two topics are presented below. Select one of the topics as the basis for your essay. READ THE TOPICS VERY CARE-FULLY TO MAKE SURE YOU KNOW WHAT YOU ARE BEING ASKED TO DO.**

TOPIC 1:

In the twentieth century, the concept of heroism is dead. Do you agree or disagree with the statement? Support your opinion with specific examples from history, current events, literature, or personal experience.

OR

TOPIC 2:

Television often causes the viewer to lose touch with reality and become completely passive and unaware. Like other addictions, television provides a pleasurable es-cape route from action to inaction. Do you agree or disagree with these statements? Support your opinion with specific examples from history, current events, literature, or personal experience.

Practice Test 1

ANSWER KEY

Subtest I — Reading

1.	(D)	11.	(C)	21.	(C)	31.	(D)
2.	(B)	12.	(B)	22.	(A)	32.	(B)
3.	(C)	13.	(B)	23.	(D)	33.	(B)
4.	(C)	14.	(C)	24.	(B)	34.	(C)
5.	(D)	15.	(A)	25.	(B)	35.	(A)
6.	(C)	16.	(C)	26.	(B)	36.	(B)
7.	(D)	17.	(A)	27.	(C)	37.	(C)
8.	(B)	18.	(A)	28.	(C)	38.	(B)
9.	(B)	19.	(B)	29.	(A)	39.	(D)
10.	(C)	20.	(C)	30.	(B)	40.	(C)

Subtest II — Mathematics

1.	(C)	13.	(C)	25.	(B)	37.	(B)
2.	(B)	14.	(C)	26.	(A)	38.	(C)
3.	(D)	15.	(A)	27.	(C)	39.	(D)
4.	(A)	16.	(D)	28.	(B)	40.	(A)
5.	(B)	17.	(B)	29.	(B)	41.	(A)
6.	(C)	18.	(C)	30.	(A)	42.	(D)
7.	(A)	19.	(B)	31.	(C)	43.	(C)
8.	(B)	20.	(D)	32.	(A)	44.	(C)
9.	(B)	21.	(B)	33.	(A)	45.	(D)
10.	(C)	22.	(B)	34.	(A)		
11.	(A)	23.	(C)	35.	(A)		
12.	(C)	24.	(C)	36.	(C)		

Subtest III — English Language Skills

1.	(B)	11.	(D)	21.	(B)	31.	(B)
2.	(D)	12.	(A)	22.	(A)	32.	(A)
3.	(B)	13.	(A)	23.	(B)	33.	(C)
4.	(B)	14.	(A)	24.	(D)	34.	(D)
5.	(C)	15.	(C)	25.	(B)	35.	(B)
6.	(A)	16.	(C)	26.	(C)	36.	(D)
7.	(B)	17.	(D)	27.	(C)	37.	(A)
8.	(D)	18.	(B)	28.	(C)	38.	(C)
9.	(C)	19.	(C)	29.	(D)	39.	(B)
10.	(B)	20.	(C)	30.	(A)	40.	(B)

Detailed Explanations of Answers

Subtest I: Reading

1. **(D)**

   It is implied that the poisoning of animal carcasses in the habitat of bald eagles presents a new danger of extinction for America's symbol. Choices (A) and (C) are not mentioned in the passage. Choice (B) suggests a reason for the poisoning; however, the overall focus of the passage does not support this.

2. **(B)**

   The author's use of words such as "mighty bald eagle" and "threatened by a new menace" supports concern for the topic. Therefore, choices (A) and (C) are not applicable. The author appears for the most part to be objective. Choice (D) is too strong to be correct.

3. **(C)**

   In 1980, the difference between the numbers of boys and girls in scouting was .9 million. This represents the closest margin, the largest being 1.6 in 1985.

4. **(C)**

   In 1970, the difference between the numbers of boys and girls in scouting was 1.5 million.

5. **(D)**

   If Alice is uncomfortable with remarks about her performance on the job, it could mean either that the remarks were unkind or that compliments might lead to embarrassment. However, the prefix "dis" means to take away or not. In this instance then, we can assume that the remarks were not complimentary, choice (A). Nothing in the text indicates that the remarks were evil or technical, choices (B) and (C).

6. **(C)**

   Choice (C) fulfills requirements stated in rules 2 and 4 of the instructions for absentee voting. All other choices do not.

7. **(D)**

   Mr. Applebee's daughter must sign her own request for an absentee ballot. Since the passage indicates that she is registered, the most important instruction for her is number 6, choice (D).

8. **(B)**

   Choices (A) and (D) are not stated in the passage. Choice (C) is not true unless voters have registered, choice (B).

9. **(B)**

   Atrophy and incapacity mean to experience a decrease in size and strength.

10. **(C)**

    The passage associates loss of mobility with a sedentary lifestyle.

11. **(C)**

    Douglass was interested in raising social consciousness about slavery. The passage stresses his interest in refuting those who doubted his claim to have been a slave.

12. **(B)**

    Choice (A) is not supported by the text. All other choices, while true, are irrelevant to the question.

13. **(B)**

    This choice is supported by the statement, "Mrs. Auld recognized Frederick's intellectual acumen . . ." Choice (D) contradicts information in the passage. The passage does not support choices (A) and (C).

14. **(C)**

    Choices (A) and (B) are either too broad or too general. Choice (D) is too specific and limited to cover the information in the passage.

15. **(A)**

An "impromptu" speech is one given suddenly without preparation.

16. **(C)**

All other choices are mentioned as providing relief from pain.

17. **(A)**

Use of terms "good," "consequences," and "desirable" indicate a concern for a healthy diet. Choice (B) contradicts the author's attitude. Choices (C) and (D) are not supported by the text.

18. **(A)**

Choices (B) and (C) are contradicted in the passage, and choice (D) is not relevant.

19. **(B)**

All other choices are not supported in the text.

20. **(C)**

A "segue" provides a direction or lead into the speech.

21. **(C)**

The passage states that housing of prisoners was "one of the many tragedies of the Civil War," and that "overcrowding, meager rations . . . resulted in rampant disease and a high mortality rate," implying that the prison facility was inadequate for the number of prisoners. All other choices are discussed, but the main issue was overcrowded conditions.

22. **(A)**

The author emphasizes a lack of supplies and manpower to care for the prisoners, not a lack of interest in doing so by the Confederates. Hence, choices (B), (C), and (D) are not appropriate.

23. **(D)**

An irony is a result that is the opposite of what might be expected or appropriate. The passage implies that being captured was not a guarantee of survival in Andersonville. This choice is supported by the second sentence of the second paragraph.

24. **(B)**

The figure of speech "his or her nose is out of joint" is an expression used to indicate that someone feels slighted. It has nothing to do with the condition of someone's nose.

25. **(B)**

This choice is supported by the second paragraph of the passage. All other choices are irrelevant to information in the passage.

26. **(B)**

"Innovations" means changes or new features that have been introduced.

27. **(C)**

The passage discusses the importance of usefulness as well as simplicity to the Shakers; therefore, the function of the piece of furniture would be more important than the particular form. Choices (A) and (D) are contradictory to the information given, while choice (B) is beyond information given in the text.

28. **(C)**

The passage states that Dean "symbolized the confused, restless, and idealistic youth," which implies that he was adept at portraying sensitive, youthful characters. Choices (A) and (B) are contradictory to information in the text. Choice (D) is a conclusion not supported by the text.

29. **(A)**

The author's use of the word "tragically" in reference to Dean's death indicates a feeling of regret.

30. **(B)**

Depraved means corrupted or perverted. All other choices have to do with accepted standards of conduct.

31. **(D)**

The author states that Franklin's work was a "significant literary work of early United States." Each of the other choices is not supported by the text.

32. **(B)**

The final sentence of the paragraph supports this choice. Choice (C) might apply, but choice (B) is closest to the overall mood of the passage. Choices (A) and (E) are not relevant to the question.

33. **(B)**

Transportation and housing total about half of the $25,892.

34. **(C)**

According to the graph, food is next after transportation in amount of expense paid by the consumer.

35. **(A)**

According to the graph, health care was closest to clothing in total amount spent.

36. **(B)**

The author's use of the word "decimation" as well as the last sentence in the second paragraph supports this choice. All other choices are secondary to the central idea of the passage.

37. **(C)**

"Decimation" is the eradication or destruction of a large part of something.

38. **(B)**

This choice is supported by the first sentence of the second paragraph. All other choices are irrelevant to the discussion of the flamingo's plumage.

39. **(D)**

The first and last sentences of the passage support this choice. Choice (A) contradicts information in the passage, and choices (B) and (C) are too broad in nature and go beyond the scope of the passage.

40. **(C)**

Reviewing the author's discussion of developing children's citizenship competencies, we may conclude that indoctrination is contradictory to information given in the passage.

NOTATION: $m\angle PQR$ will represent "the measure of angle PQR."

1. **(C)**
    When simplifying algebraic expressions, always work from left to right. First perform all multiplications and divisions; then, once this is done, start again from the left and do all additions and subtractions.

    SUGGESTION: It can be helpful to translate the algebraic statement to English. For example, $6 + 2(x - 4)$ is "six plus two *times* the quantity x minus 4." The word *times* indicates multiplication, so we must first perform $2(x - 4)$ by using the *distributive property* $a(b - c) = ab - ac$:

    $$6 + 2(x - 4) = 6 + 2 \times x - 2 \times 4 = 6 + 2x - 8.$$

    Then we perform the subtraction to combine the terms 6 and 8:

    $$6 + 2x - 8 = 2x + (6 - 8) = 2x - 2.$$

    Note that we did not combine the $2x$ term with the other terms. This is because they are not *like terms*. Like terms are terms that have the same variables (with the same exponents). Since the terms 6 and 8 have no variable x, they are not like terms with $2x$.

2. **(B)**
    Follow the order of operations to simplify the problem.

$9 - 5 \div (8 - 3) \times 3 + 6$	The problem
$9 - 5 \div (5) \times 3 + 6$	Simplify within parentheses.
$9 - 1 \times 3 + 6$	Do division.
$9 - 3 + 6$	Do multiplication.
$6 + 6$	Do subtraction.
12	Do addition.

3. **(D)**
    Let x be the cost of one can of beans. Then $6x$ is the cost of six cans of beans. So $6x = \$1.50$. Dividing both sides of the equation by 6, we get $x = \$.25$ and, hence, since $8x$ is the cost of eight cans of beans, we have

    $$8x = 8 \times \$.25 = \$2.00.$$

4. **(A)**

Let t_1, t_2, and t_3 represent Bonnie's scores on tests one, two, and three, respectively. Then the equation representing Bonnie's average score is

$$\frac{t_1 + t_2 + t_3}{3} = 71.$$

We know that $t_1 = 64$ and $t_2 = 87$. Substitute this information into the equation above:

$$\frac{64 + 87 + t_3}{3} = 71$$

Combining 64 and 87 and then multiplying both sides of the equation by 3 gives us

$$3 \times \frac{151 + t_3}{3} = 3 \times 71$$

or $\qquad 151 + t_3 = 213.$

Now subtract 151 from both sides of the equation so that

$$t_3 = 213 - 151 = 62.$$

5. **(B)**

A figure with 1 rectangular base and 4 triangular lateral faces will be a rectangular pyramid. The net below shows the 5 two-dimensional shapes that make up the three-dimensional shape.

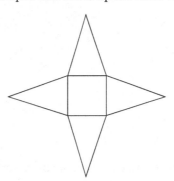

6. **(C)**

The perimeter of a shape is the distance around it. A rectangle has two equal lengths and two equal widths. Therefore, to find the perimeter, you must find the following sum: 15 + 15 + 8 + 8. This sum is 46.

7. **(A)**

When you substitute the ordered pair (4, 8) into the inequality $y < \frac{1}{2}x - 5$, you get a false statement. Therefore, you know that (4, 8) is *not* a solution to the inequality.

$$y < \frac{1}{2}x - 5$$

$$8 < \frac{1}{2}(4) - 5$$

$$8 < 2 - 5$$

$8 < -3$, which is false.

8. **(B)**

To solve the equation

$$2x^2 + 5x - 3 = 0,$$

we can factor the left side of the equation to get

$$(2x - 1)(x + 3) = 0.$$

Then use the following rule (this rule is sometimes called the Zero Product Property): If $a \times b = 0$, then either $a = 0$ or $b = 0$. Applying this to our problem gives us

$$2x - 1 = 0 \text{ or } x + 3 = 0.$$

Solve these two equations:

$$2x - 1 = 0 \rightarrow 2x = 1 \rightarrow x = \frac{1}{2} \text{ or } x + 3 = 0 \rightarrow x = -3.$$

But $x > 0$, so $x = \frac{1}{2}$.

9. **(B)**

Divide each price by the number of apples to find the price for one apple. The lowest price per apple is the best unit price. $8.10 \div 15 = 0.54$. This is the lowest unit price and therefore, the best price.

10. **(C)**

First find the total sales for each year by reading the graph for the sales of (i) black and white televisions and (ii) color televisions. Then combine these numbers:

1950	$20,000,000 + $5,000,000 = $25,000,000
1960	$10,000,000 + $20,000,000 = $30,000,000

1970	$15,000,000 + $25,000,000 = $40,000,000
1980	$10,000,000 + $45,000,000 = $55,000,000
1990	$5,000,000 + $45,000,000 = $50,000,000

The greatest total sales occurred in 1980.

11. (A)

A prime number is an integer which is greater than one and which has no integer divisors other than 1 and itself. So, the prime numbers between 1 and 20 (not including 1 and 20) are: 2, 3, 5, 7, 11, 13, 17, 19. But 2 is not an odd number, so the odd primes between 1 and 20 are: 3, 5, 7, 11, 13, 17, 19. Hence, there are seven odd primes between 1 and 20.

12. (C)

Two lines are perpendicular if they meet at right angles. In the diagram Avenue B, Avenue C, and 1st Avenue are all parallel to Avenue A. E. 11th Street is perpendicular to Avenue A.

13. (C)

To solve this inequality, we shall use the following rules:

(i)   If $a \leq b$ and c is any number, then $a + c \leq b + c$.

(ii) If $a \leq b$ and $c < 0$, then $ca \geq cb$.

The goal in solving inequalities, as in solving equalities, is to change the inequality so that the variable is isolated (i.e., by itself on one side). So, in the equation $8 - 2x \leq 10$, we want the term $-2x$ by itself. To achieve this, use rule (i) above and add -8 to both sides obtaining

$$8 - 2x + (-8) \leq 10 + (-8)$$

or $-2x \leq 2$.

Now we use rule (ii) and multiply both sides of the inequality by $-\frac{1}{2}$ as follows:

$$-\frac{1}{2} \times -2x \geq -\frac{1}{2} \times 2$$

or $x \geq -1$.

14. (C)

Since 0.003 has three numbers to the right of the decimal point and 1.25 has two numbers to the right of the decimal point, our answer will have (three plus two) or five numbers to the right of the decimal point. Multiplying 0.003 and 1.25, we get 0.00375, since 3 times 125 is 375. Numbers of the form

$A \times 10^n$, where A is a number between 0 and 1 inclusive, and n is an integer, are in scientific notation. Thus, 0.00375 in scientific notation is 3.75×10^{-3}. Notice that when the exponent $n < 0$, the original number is smaller than A.

15. (A)

A geometric sequence is a series of numbers where each number is found by multiplying the one before it by the same number. Find the number that you multiply each term by to get the next term in the sequence in order to continue the pattern.

$$-1 \times -3 = 3$$
$$3 \times -3 = -9$$
$$-9 \times -3 = 27$$

Therefore, you can continue the pattern by multiplying each term by -3. You are asked to find the 7th number in the sequence. ($-1, 3, -9, 27, -81, 243, -729$). The 7th number in the sequence is -729.

16. (D)

This pattern is neither geometric nor arithmetic. If you examine the number closely, you can see that they are all cube numbers. A cube number is found by raising a number to the third power. To find the next number in the pattern, cube 5. The answer is 125 as shown below in the table.

n	n^3
1	$1 \times 1 \times 1 = 1$
2	$2 \times 2 \times 2 = 8$
3	$3 \times 3 \times 3 = 27$
4	$4 \times 4 \times 4 = 64$
5	$5 \times 5 \times 5 = 125$

17. (B)

Use the formula given and substitute 15 for the Celsius temperature. This will get you the equivalent Fahrenheit temperature.

$$F = \frac{9}{5}C + 32$$

$$F = \frac{9}{5}(15) + 32$$

$$F = 27 + 32$$

$$F = 59$$

18. **(C)**

Note that the line passing through W and Z slants downward as we look at it from left to right. This means our slope should be a negative number! To find the slope of the line passing through the points (x_1, y_1), and (x_2, y_2) we use the following formula:

$$\text{slope} = \frac{y_2 - y_1}{x_2 - x_1}.$$

Our points are $W = (-1, 4)$ and $Z = (2, -2)$ and so our slope is

$$\frac{(-2) - 4}{2 - (-1)} = \frac{-6}{3} = -2.$$

19. **(B)**

The numbers on the ruler indicate centimeters. The small lines between each number are millimeters. The red line is 3 centimeters and 3 millimeters long. Every centimeter is equal to 10 millimeters, so the line is $30 + 3$ millimeters long; it is 33 millimeters long.

20. **(D)**

To find the ordered pair that is a solution to the inequality $y \le -3x - 1$, substitute in each (x, y) pair to find one that makes a true statement. The statement below is true. Therefore, $(0, -1)$ is a solution to the inequality.

$$y \le -3x - 1$$
$$-1 \le -3(0) - 1$$
$$-1 \le -1$$

21. **(B)**

Substituting $F = 86$ into the formula

$$F = \frac{9}{5}C + 32$$

we get

$$86 = \frac{9}{5}C + 32.$$

To solve for C, first subtract 32 from both sides:

$$86 - 32 = \frac{9}{5}C + 32 - 32$$

or

$$54 = \frac{9}{5}C.$$

Now multiply both sides of this equation by the reciprocal of $\frac{9}{5}$ which is $\frac{5}{9}$:

$$\left(\frac{5}{9}\right)54 = \left(\frac{5}{9}\right)\frac{9}{5}C \text{ or } \frac{270}{9} = C \text{ or } C=30$$

22. **(B)**

Set up and solve a proportion to find how long 358 miles would be on the map.

$$\frac{1}{50} = \frac{x}{358}$$

$$50x = 358$$

$$x = 358 \div 50$$

$$x = 7.16$$

The length on the map should be 7.16 inches. However, the directions say to round to the nearest quarter of an inch. Ask yourself is 7.16 closer to 7 or closer to $7\frac{1}{4}$? It is closer to $7\frac{1}{4}$ because $7\frac{1}{4}$ is equivalent to 7.25. 7.16 is .09 from 7.25 and .16 from 7. The answer is $7\frac{1}{4}$.

23. **(C)**

Another way to phrase the second sentence is: She wants to divide her money equally among her six children. Therefore, each child is to receive $300,000 \div 6$.

24. **(C)**

To find the distance between two points (x_1, y_1) and (x_2, y_2), we may use the following formula:

$$d = \sqrt{(x_2 - x_1)^2 + (y_2 - y_1)^2}$$

For our two points, $P = (1, 4)$ and $Q = (-2, 0)$, the above formula gives us the length of segment PQ:

$$d = \sqrt{(-2 - 1)^2 + (0 - 4)^2} = \sqrt{(-3)^2 + (4)^2} = \sqrt{9 + 16} = \sqrt{25} = 5.$$

25. (B)

Find the amount of time Ms. Rossi needs before her train. Then subtract that amount of time from 7:35 to find the time Ms. Rossi needs to get up. Add the following: $\frac{1}{3}$ of an hour + 25 minutes + 10 minutes + 15 minutes. How many minutes are in $\frac{1}{3}$ of an hour? An hour has 60 minutes, and one-third of 60 is 20. So add: $20 + 25 + 10 + 15$. This equals 70 minutes. Now subtract 70 minutes from 7:35. One hour (or 60 minutes) before 7:35 is 6:35. Then subtract another 10 minutes to get you to 6:25.

26. (A)

The prime numbers between 1 and 6 are 2, 3, and 5. Therefore, the probability that a six-sided die will land on a prime number is $\frac{3}{6}$, which can be simplified to $\frac{1}{2}$.

27. (C)

Let s_1 and s_2 be Ricky's speed (rate) on the trip from A to B and the return trip from B to A, respectively. Then, since he drove 15 miles per hour slower on the return trip, $s_2 = s_1 - 15$. Recall that rate times time equals distance. So the distance from A to B is $(s_1)3 = 3s_1$ and the distance from B to A is

$$(s_2)5 = 5s_2 = 5(s_1 - 15) = 5s_1 - 75.$$

But the distance from Town A to Town B is the same as the distance from Town B to Town A, so we have the following equation:

$$3s_1 = 5s_1 - 75.$$

To solve this equation, first add 75 to both sides of the equation:

$$3s_1 + 75 = 5s_1 - 75 + 75 \text{ or } 3s_1 + 75 = 5s_1.$$

Now to isolate the variable, subtract $3s_1$ from both sides:

$$3s_1 + 75 - 3s_1 = 5s_1 - 3s_1 \text{ or } 75 = 2s_1.$$

To finish the problem, divide both sides of the equation by 2:

$$s_1 = \frac{75}{2} = 37.5.$$

Thus, Ricky drove 37.5 miles per hour on his trip from Town A to Town B.

28. (B)

Even though each answer choice represents the same statistics, they are not interpreted in the same way. Saying "Only 20 of our employees lost their jobs last year" does not sound as bad as "Almost 50% of our employees lost their jobs last year." Therefore, answer choice (B) would be more encouraging to employees.

29. (B)

The weekly salary which occurs the most is $400, so that is the mode. There are 16 salaries listed, and the middle two are both $400, so the median is $400. As you can see, these values are the same. It is not necessary to find the mean to recognize that the four values of 600 and the three values of 675 will pull the mean up above $400. You can deduce that the mean will be higher than the mode or the median.

30. (A)

Simplify the following by using the order of operations.

$150 \div (6 + 3 \times 8) - 5$	The problem
$150 \div (6 + 24) - 5$	Simplify inside parentheses (multiplication first)
$150 \div (30) - 5$	Simplify inside parentheses (addition next)
$5 - 5$	Do division.
0	Do subtraction.

31. (C)

Recall the following Laws of Exponents:

$$x^p \times x^q = x^{p+q} \text{ and } \frac{x^p}{x^q} = x^{p-q}.$$

So, $x^2 \times x^7 = x^{2+7} = x^9$. Hence,

$$\frac{x^2 \times x^7}{x} = \frac{x^9}{x^1} = x^{9-1} = x^8.$$

32. (A)

We need to write the three fractions with the same denominator. So, find the least common multiple (LCM) of 9, 15, and 21.

$$9 = 3^2, 15 = 3 \times 5, \text{ and } 21 = 3 \times 7$$

Therefore, the LCM is

$$3^2 \times 5 \times 7 = 315.$$

Then

$$\frac{1}{9} = \frac{5 \times 7}{5 \times 7} \times \frac{1}{9} = \frac{35}{315},$$

$$\frac{2}{15} = \frac{3 \times 7}{3 \times 7} \times \frac{2}{15} = \frac{42}{315},$$

and
$$\frac{3}{21} = \frac{3 \times 5}{3 \times 5} \times \frac{3}{21} = \frac{45}{315}.$$

Clearly,
$$\frac{35}{315} < \frac{42}{315} < \frac{45}{315}$$

and hence, in order, from least to greatest, we have:
$$\frac{1}{9}, \frac{2}{15}, \frac{3}{21}.$$

33. **(A)**

The volume of a rectangular box is the area of the base times the height. So if we let s be the length of each side of the base (it is a square), the area of the base is s^2. The height of the box is one-half the length of a side of the base. Thus, the height is $\frac{1}{2} s$. The volume is then

$$V = s^2 \times \frac{1}{2} s = \frac{1}{2} s^3.$$

But the volume is given as 256. Substituting this into the equation

$$V = \frac{1}{2} s^3$$

gives us:

$$256 = \frac{1}{2} s^3.$$

Now multiply both sides of the equation by 2 to get

$$512 = s^3$$

But, $512 = 8^3$ so that we have $8^3 = s^3$ or $s = 8$. The height of the box is

$$\frac{1}{2} s = \frac{1}{2} \times 8 = 4 \text{ feet}.$$

34. **(A)**

If $x = -3$ then

$$-x^2 + 2x = -(-3)^2 + 2(-3) = -(9) + (-6) = -15.$$

35. (A)

The third column shows which of the outcomes have two heads (and one tail). Count them to see that three of the eight outcomes have two heads (and one tail). Therefore, the probability is $\dfrac{3}{8}$.

36. (C)

Let x be the number of people in the barn. Then, since each person and cow has only one head, the number of cows must be $30 - x$. Since people have two legs, the number of human legs totals $2x$. Similarly, since the number of legs each cow has is 4, the total number of cow legs in the barn is $4(30 - x)$. Thus, we have this equation:

$$2x + 4(30 - x) = 104.$$

To solve this equation, use the distributive property:

$$a(b - c) = ab - ac.$$

We get

$$4(30 - x) = (4 \times 30) - (4 \times x) = 120 - 4x.$$

Our equation reduces to:

$$2x + 120 - 4x = 104 \text{ or } 120 - 2x = 104.$$

Now subtract 120 from both sides of the equation to get

$$-2x = 104 - 120 = -16.$$

Dividing both sides of the equation by -2: $x = 8$. Therefore, there were 8 people and $30 - 8 = 22$ cows in the barn.

37. (B)

The footsteps show a rotation because one of the feet is turned, and the only transformation that could turn a shape is a rotation.

38. (C)

To find the volume of a rectangular prism, a box, multiply the length by the width by the height. $11 \times 19 \times 12 = 2508$

39. (D)

First of all, the least common multiple (LCM) of 2 and 3 is $2 \times 3 = 6$, so let's rewrite the expression so that both fractions have 6 as a common denominator:

$$\frac{1}{2} + \frac{1}{3} = \frac{3}{3} \times \frac{1}{2} + \frac{2}{2} \times \frac{1}{3} = \frac{3}{6} + \frac{2}{6} = \frac{5}{6}.$$

40. **(A)**

Two triangles are similar if we can find two pairs of angles, one in each triangle, that are congruent. Given that $\overline{BC} \parallel \overline{DE}$ we know that $(\angle ABC, \angle BDE)$ and $(\angle ACB, \angle CED)$ are two pairs of corresponding and hence congruent angles. Thus, taking care in the order that we write the triangles so that we match the correct angles, $\triangle ABC \sim \triangle ADE$.

41. **(A)**

Multiply $1.83 by 145 and the answer is $265.35.

42. **(D)**

The number of students who want cats is 6, and the number of students who want birds is 2. Because 6 is three times 2, this is the correct answer.

43. **(C)**

In a normal distribution, half the data are always above the mean. Since 30,000 miles is the mean, half or 50 percent of the tires will last at least 30,000 miles.

44. **(C)**

This is a permutation problem that can be solved by simplifying 5! 5! is the same as $5 \times 4 \times 3 \times 2 \times 1$, which equals 120.

45. **(D)**

This can be solved using ratio and proportion. Thus, 2 is to 1 as x is to 8.

$$\frac{2}{1} = \frac{x}{8}$$

so $x = 16$ m.

Correlation with FTCE Competency/Skill

Competency/Skill	Problem Number
	Total of 8 in section 1
1.1	14, 31, 32
1.2	23, 39
1.3	11
1.4	2, 30
	Total of 10 in section 2
2.1	6, 38
2.2	9, 27, 41
2.3	22
2.4	17, 21
2.5	25
2.6	19
	Total of 9 in section 3
3.1	5
3.2	3, 24, 40, 45
3.3	18, 33
3.4	12, 37

Competency/Skill	Problem Number
	Total of 9 in section 4
4.1	15, 16
4.2	1, 34
4.3	8, 13, 36
4.4	7, 20
	Total of 9 in section 5
5.1	10, 42
5.2	28
5.3	4, 43
5.4	29
5.5	26
5.6	35, 44

Key: 1.3 means Competency 1 Skill 3

Competency/Skill		Approximate # of Questions
	MATHEMATICS The test center will provide a 4-function calculator. The test center will provide a reference sheet.	
1	**Knowledge of number sense, concepts, and operations**	**8**
	1 Compare the relative value of real numbers (e.g., integers, fractions, decimals, percents, irrational numbers, and numbers expressed in exponential or scientific notation.)	
	2 Solve real-world problems involving addition, subtraction, multiplication, and division of rational numbers (e.g., whole numbers, integers, decimals, percents, and fractions including mixed numbers).	
	3 Apply basic number theory concepts including the use of primes, composites, factors, and multiples in solving problems.	
	4 Apply the order of operations with or without grouping symbols.	
2	**Knowledge of measurement (using customary or metric units)**	**10**
	1 Solve real-world problems involving length, weight, mass, perimeter, area, capacity, and volume.	
	2 Solve real-world problems involving rated measures (e.g., miles per hour, meters per second, cost per item, and cost per unit).	
	3 Solve real-world problems involving scaled drawings (e.g., maps, blueprints, and models).	
	4 Solve real-world problems involving the change of units of measures of length, weight, mass, capacity, and time.	
	5 Solve real-world problems involving estimates of measures including length, weight, mass, temperature, time, money, perimeter, area, and volume.	
	6 Choose the correct reading, to a specified degree of accuracy, using instruments (e.g., scales, rulers, thermometers, measuring cups, protractors, and gauges).	

Competency/Skill		Approximate # of Questions
3	**Knowledge of geometry and spatial sense**	9
	1 Identify and/or classify simple two- and three-dimensional figures according to their properties.	
	2 Solve real-world and mathematical problems involving ratio, proportion, similarity, congruence, and the Pythagorean relationship.	
	3 Identify the location of ordered pairs of integers in all four quadrants of a coordinate system (graph) and use the coordinate system to apply the concepts of slope and distance to solve problems.	
	4 Identify real-world examples that represent geometric concepts including perpendicularity, parallelism, tangency, symmetry, and transformations (e.g., flips, slides, and turns).	
4	**Knowledge of algebraic thinking**	9
	1 Analyze and generalize patterns including arithmetic and geometric sequences.	
	2 Interpret algebraic expressions using words, symbols, variables, tables, and graphs.	
	3 Solve equations and inequalities graphically or algebraically.	
	4 Determine whether a number or ordered pair is among the solutions of given equations or inequalities.	
5	**Knowledge of data analysis and probability**	9
	1 Analyze data and solve problems using data presented in histograms, bar graphs, ,circle graphs, pictographs, tables, and charts.	
	2 Identify how the presentation of data can lead to different or inappropriate interpretations.	
	3 Calculate range, mean, median, and mode(s) from sets of data and interpret the meaning of the measures of central tendency (i.e., mean, median, and mode) and dispersion (i.e., range and standard deviation).	
	4 Identify how the measures of central tendency (i.e., mean, median, or mode) can lead to different interpretations.	
	5 Calculate the probability of a specified outcome.	
	6 Solve and interpret real-world problems involving probability using counting procedures, tables, tree diagrams, and the concepts of permutations and combinations.	

Subtest III: English Language Skills

1. **(B)**

"Were praised" is a plural verb; since the subject is Chief Joseph, a singular proper noun, the verb should be "was praised." The intervening phrase of choice (A), "*together with* 250 warriors and 500 women and children," does not change the singular subject. Choice (C), "for," is idiomatically correct in that phrase.

2. **(D)**

Choice (A), "upon which," is a correct prepositional phrase. Choice (B), "is based," agrees with its subject, "society." In choice (C), "are" agrees with its subject, "ideals."

3. **(B)**

Two past actions are mentioned. The earlier of two past actions should be indicated by past perfect tense, so the answer is "had been." Choice (A) contains two adjectives as part of an appositive phrase modifying the subject, and choice (C), "upon the death," is idiomatically correct.

4. **(B)**

Choice (B) should be "depend," not "had depended," because that use of past perfect would indicate prior past action. There is a series of events in this sentence: first, the legislature "had not finalized" the budget (A); then, Representative Wilson "pointed out" this failure. Choice (B) needs to be present tense as this situation still exists, and choice (C) is future action.

5. **(C)**

In order to complete the parallelism, choice (C) should be "arrangements." "To plan" (A) is an infinitive phrase followed by noun objects: "puppet shows and movies" and "garage sales." Choice (B), "used," is a participate modifying books.

6. **(A)**

An infinitive, "to understand," should never be split by any adverbial modifier, "completely." Choice (B), "effects," is the noun form, and choice (C), "affected," is the adjective form.

7. **(B)**

    "More" is used to compare two things. Since the number of nations is not specified, "more" cannot be used in this sentence. Choice (A) is idiomatically correct; choice (C), "is," agrees in number with its subject, "transportation."

8. **(D)**

    Choice (B) is idiomatically correct. In "someone else," (C), "else" is needed to indicate a person other than the student would pay the bills.

9. **(C)**

    Choice (C) should read, "became very irritated." "To aggravate" means "to make worse"; "to irritate" means "to excite to impatience or anger." A situation is "aggravated" and becomes worse, but one does not become "aggravated" with people. Choices (A), and (B) are correctly used idioms.

10. **(B)**

    The reference in choice (B) is vague because it sounds as if the bus made the two students late. Choice (A) is a correct subject pronoun; choice (C) is a correct object pronoun.

11. **(D)**

    Choice (A), "among," indicates choice involving more than two things. The preposition in (B) is correct. "Are," (C), is a plural verb, agreeing in number with the compound subject "singing . . . dancing . . . cooking."

12. **(A)**

    One is "disappointed by" a person or action but "disappointed in" what is not satisfactory. Parallel with "to work," choice (B), "save," had the word "to" omitted. Choice (C) compares the two models, one "inexpensive" and one "more expensive."

13. **(A)**

    The verb should be plural, "are," in order to agree with the compound subject, "budget . . . plans." Choice (C) is part of an infinitive phrase which includes a participle, "existing," (B). Choice (C) is idiomatically correct.

14. **(A)**

The expression should be phrased "as delicate as." Choice (B) uses a possessive before a gerund; and choice (C) is a possessive pronoun of neuter gender which is appropriate to use in referring to a plant.

15. **(C)**

The verb "deal" must agree with the subject, "works," and not a word in the intervening phrase. Choices (A) and (B), "the picture of respectability," describe the subject; (C) is idiomatically correct.

16. **(C)**

The word "of" in "inside of" is redundant and should not be used. Choice (A), "alike," is appropriate when comparing two classes of people. Choice (B), "them," is correct pronoun usage.

17. **(D)**

Choice (A), "unsafe for," is idiomatically correct. Choice (B), "can be," is grammatically correct. The preposition "in," choice (C), is correct.

18. **(B)**

The verb in this subordinate clause is incorrect; the clause begins with "that," and this word refers to "information." Therefore, the clause, in order to agree with the antecedent, must read "that shows." The verb "shows" should not be made to agree with "species" and "others." Choice (A), "have compiled," agrees in number with people. "Either" in choice (C) is correctly placed after the verb to show a choice of "endangered" or "becoming endangered."

19. **(C)**

Do not end a sentence with a preposition; the phrase should read, "in which he was born." The verb shows proper time sequence in choice (A); choice (B) is correct pronoun usage and correct superlative degree of adjective.

20. **(C)**

The noun form "effect" is the correct one to use. Choice (A), "to inhibit," is an infinitive; in choice (B), the nominative case "who" is the correct subject of "seemed."

21. **(B)**

The idiom should be "filled to capacity." The adverb in choice (A), "quite," is correct. Choice (C), "most," is appropriate for the superlative degree.

22. **(A)**

The subordinate clause, "who my parents have not met," has as its subject "parents," which agrees with choice (B), "have . . . met." Therefore, the pronoun is a direct object of the verb and should be in the objective case, "whom." Choice (C) is idiomatically correct.

23. **(B)**

The pronoun reference is unclear. The meaning of the sentence indicated that Colonel Jones denies involvement in any other covert activity. The agent from a foreign country may or may not have been involved in other covert activities, but that is not the issue here. The verb tense of choice (A) is correct. The word "other" in choice (C) is necessary to the meaning of the sentence.

24. **(D)**

Choice (A), "testing," is parallel to "determining" and "evaluating." In choice (B), "effectiveness" is correct. In choice (C), "is" must be singular because all three steps mentioned comprise the one process.

25. **(B)**

Choice (A) is correct. Choice (B) should read "it is she"; nominative case pronoun is required following a linking verb. The correct form of the modifiers appears in choice (C).

26. **(C)**

"Because" is the correct word to use in the cause-and-effect relationship in this sentence. Choice (A), "being that," and choice (D), "than me," are not grammatically correct. Choice (B), "is made by you," is in the passive voice and not as direct as choice (C).

27. **(C)**

"After they have been" completes the proper time sequence. Choice (A), "when," and choice (B), "will be," are the wrong time sequences. Choice (D), "should be," is an idea not contained in the original sentence.

28. **(C)**

"Since the plane is late" shows correct time sequence and good reasoning. Choice (A), "seeing as how," and choice (D), "being as," are poor wording. Choice (B), "when," is the wrong time, logically, to be on the observation deck.

29. **(D)**

Since a sentence should not end with a preposition, choices (A) and (B) are eliminated. Choice (C), "living in this world," introduces a new concept.

30. **(A)**

The construction, "than those," clarifies the fact that more vegetables have been added. Choice (C), "your suggestion," and choice (D), "which," do not contain the idea of adding more varieties of vegetables. Choice (B) ends with a redundant preposition.

31. **(B)**

The voice must be consistent with "I," so (B) is the only possible correct answer. All other choices have a noun or pronoun that is not consistent with "I": choice (A), "you," choice (C), "a person," and choice (D), "people."

32. **(A)**

The correct answer has two concepts—pieces are missing and pieces will probably never be found. Choice (B) has a singular verb, "is." Choice (C) indicates the pieces "probably will be" missing, which is not the problem. Choice (D) indicates the pieces are "probably" missing, which is illogical because the pieces either are or are not missing.

33. **(C)**

Choice (A), "the kind of a," is incorrect grammatical structure. Choice (D) introduces the new concept of "category." Choice (B), "sort of," is poor wording.

34. **(D)**

Choice (D) is clear and concise and shows the correct comparison of architecture. The antecedent of "those" in choice (A) is not clear. Choice (B) is comparing "characteristics," not just architecture. Choice (C) is awkward.

35. **(B)**

Choice (B) is clear and direct. Choice (A) is too wordy. Choice (C) has the wrong concept, "balancing games." Choice (D), "this as an example," is poorly worded.

36. **(D)**

An opposing force "gives" scattered resistance; therefore, choice (A) is incorrect. Choices (B) and (C) are poorly worded and do not have the correct meaning.

37. **(A)**

Choice (A) produces a complete sentence: "rainfall" is the subject and "let up" is the verb. None of the other choices produces a complete sentence.

38. **(C)**

This choice uses the correct tense, "will have," showing action in the future. All the other verbs listed do not show correct future verb construction.

39. **(B)**

The correct choice has a compound verb: "comes" and "falls in love." The salesman comes to town first, then meets and falls in love with the librarian. Choice (A), with its misplaced participial phrase, sounds as if either the town or Iowa is in love with the librarian. Choice (C) would produce a run-on sentence. Choice (D) has an unclear tense.

40. **(A)**

Choice (A) has clear reference. Choice (B) will produce a run-on sentence. Choice (C) does not indicate whose writings or paintings. Choice (D) sounds as if the only time naturalists feel reverence is when they write or paint.

Essay Scoring Guide

The FTCE-GKT essay sections are scored by two writing experts on the basis of the criteria outlined below. In addition to comparing your essay to those included in our practice tests, you may use these guidelines to estimate your score on this section. Remember that your score is the sum of the scores of two writing experts, so provided you respond to the assigned topic, your score will fall somewhere between two and twelve. Scores will be assigned based on the following guidelines:

SCORE of 6:   The paper has a clearly established main idea that the writer fully develops with specific details and examples. Organization is notably logical and coherent. Point of view is consistently maintained. Vocabulary and sentence structure are varied and effective. Errors in sentence structure, usage, and mechanics are few and insignificant.

SCORE of 5:   The paper has a clearly established main idea that is adequately developed and recognizable through specific details and/or examples. Organization follows a logical and coherent pattern. Point of view is mostly maintained. Vocabulary and sentence structure are mostly varied and effective. Occasional errors in sentence structure, usage, and mechanics do not interfere with the writer's ability to communicate.

SCORE of 4:   The paper has an adequately sated main idea that is developed with some specific details and examples. Supporting ideas are presented in a mostly logical and coherent manner. Point of view is somewhat maintained. Vocabulary and sentence structure are somewhat varied and effective. Occasional errors in sentence structure, usage, and mechanics may interfere with writer's ability to communicate.

SCORE of 3:   The paper states a main idea that is developed with generalizations or lists. The paper may contain occasional lapses in logic and coherence, and organization is mechanical. Point of view is ambiguous. Vocabulary and sentence structure are repetitious and often ineffective. A variety of errors in sentence structure, usage, and mechanics sometimes interferes with the writer's ability to communicate.

SCORE of 2:   The paper presents an incomplete or ambiguous main idea. Support is developed with generalizations and lists. Organization is mechanical. The paper contains occasional lapses in logic and coherence. Point of view is confusing and distracting. Word choice is simplistic, and sentence structure is disjointed. Errors in sentence structure, usage, and mechanics frequently interfere with the writer's ability to communicate.

SCORE of 1: The paper has no evident main idea. Development is inadequate and/or irrelevant. Organization is illogical and/or incoherent. Point of view has not been established. Vocabulary and sentence structure are garbled and confusing. Significant and numerous errors in sentence structure, usage, and mechanics interfere with the writer's ability to communicate.

Subtest IV: Sample Essays with Commentary

Topic 1

Strong Response

A poll was recently conducted to determine American heroes. Sadly, most of the heroes listed in the top ten are cartoon characters or actors who portray heroic roles. What does this say about American ideals? Perhaps we do not know enough, or perhaps we know too much in order to have heroes. Having access to instant information about a variety of military, political, and religious figures, citizens of modern society have outgrown the innocence of previous centuries.

The ancient hero possessed many idealized virtues, such as physical strength, honesty, courage, and intelligence. Oedipus saved his people from pestilence by solving the riddle of the Sphinx. As leader, he was sworn to find the murderer of the previous king; Oedipus' brave pursuit of justice was conducted with honesty and integrity. Beowulf, another famous ancient hero, existed at a time when life was wild, dangerous, unpredictable.

Modern society is missing several of the ingredients necessary to produce a hero of this calibre. For one thing, there are no mythical monsters such as the Sphinx or Grendel. War is left as the stuff of heroic confrontation, but modern wars only add to our confusion. Men have been decorated for killing their brothers and friends in the Civil War; America fought the Germans in World War I and the Germans and Japanese in World War II, but our former enemies are our current allies. As for honesty, modern role models too often let us down. The media exposes politicians who are involved in scandal, sports figures who do drugs, and religious leaders who make multi-million dollar incomes.

No wonder Americans name Superman and actors John Wayne and Clint Eastwood to the list of modern heroes. These heroes are larger than life on the theatre screen, and their vices are at least predictable and reasonably innocuous. Wisely, we have chosen those who will not surprise us with ugly or mundane reality.

Analysis

This essay has a score range of 5-6. It is the strongest of the four essays. Although it is not perfect, it shows a good command of the English language and depth of thought. The writer employs a traditional essay structure: the first paragraph is the introduction and ends with the thesis statement; the second and third paragraphs discuss traditional and contemporary heroes, as stated in the last sentence of the thesis paragraph; the fourth paragraph concludes. Each of the two body paragraphs has a clear topic sentence. The writer gives several distinct examples to support his ideas. Vocabulary is effective, and sentence structure is varied.

Topic 2

Strong Response

In the past thirty years, television has become a very popular passtime for almost everyone. From the time the mother places the baby in his jumpseat in front of the television so that she can relax and have a second cup of coffee until the time the senior citizen in the retirement home watches Vanna White turn the letters on "Wheel of Fortune," Americans spend endless hours in front of the "boob tube." I believe that television can become an addiction that provides an escape from the problems of the world and from facing responsibility for your own life.

When my mother was a little girl, what did children do to entertain themselves? They played. Their games usually involved social interaction with other children as well as imaginatively creating entertainment for themselves. They also developed hobbies like woodworking and sewing. Today few children really know how to play with each other or entertain themselves. Instead, they sit in front of the television, glued to cartoons that are senseless and often violent. Even if they watch educational programs like "Sesame Street," they don't really have to do anything but watch and listen to what the answer to the question is.

Teenagers, also, use television as a way of avoiding doing things that will help them mature. How many kids do much homework anymore? Why not? Because they come home from school tired and relax in front of the television. Even if they watch a controversial program about some problem in the world like AIDS or the war in the Middle East, they don't usually do anything about it.

In addition, young mothers use television to escape their own problems. The terrible woes of the people on the soap operas make their problems seem less important. This means that they don't need to solve their own problems.

Although it may seem as if television is really great for older people, I think even my grandma would have more fun if she had more interests rather than just watching quiz shows. I know she has blotted out the "real world" when she expects us to act like perfect kids when she comes to visit.

In conclusion, I believe that television really can become an addiction that allows people of all ages to avoid facing their own problems and lose themselves in the problems of other people.

Analysis

This essay has a score range of 5-6. It has a traditional structure; the first paragraph introduces the topic, even suggesting the chronological organization of the essay. Each of the next four paragraphs has a clear topic sentence and details that develop it. The concluding paragraph, although only one sentence in length, restates the main idea. The essay is, therefore, clearly unified around the writer's opinion, which the writer tries to prove in a logical fashion. The writer effectively employs transitional words to relate the main ideas, varied sentence structure, and controlled vocabulary. Although the writer misspells *pastime*, uses the colloquial word *kids*, and has some problem with parallelism, repetition, and pronoun usage, the essay is well written considering the time limit.

FTCE

**Florida Teacher Certification Examination
General Knowledge Test**

Practice Test 2

Answer Sheet – Practice Test 2

Subtest I: Reading

1. Ⓐ Ⓑ Ⓒ Ⓓ	11. Ⓐ Ⓑ Ⓒ Ⓓ	21. Ⓐ Ⓑ Ⓒ Ⓓ	31. Ⓐ Ⓑ Ⓒ Ⓓ
2. Ⓐ Ⓑ Ⓒ Ⓓ	12. Ⓐ Ⓑ Ⓒ Ⓓ	22. Ⓐ Ⓑ Ⓒ Ⓓ	32. Ⓐ Ⓑ Ⓒ Ⓓ
3. Ⓐ Ⓑ Ⓒ Ⓓ	13. Ⓐ Ⓑ Ⓒ Ⓓ	23. Ⓐ Ⓑ Ⓒ Ⓓ	33. Ⓐ Ⓑ Ⓒ Ⓓ
4. Ⓐ Ⓑ Ⓒ Ⓓ	14. Ⓐ Ⓑ Ⓒ Ⓓ	24. Ⓐ Ⓑ Ⓒ Ⓓ	34. Ⓐ Ⓑ Ⓒ Ⓓ
5. Ⓐ Ⓑ Ⓒ Ⓓ	15. Ⓐ Ⓑ Ⓒ Ⓓ	25. Ⓐ Ⓑ Ⓒ Ⓓ	35. Ⓐ Ⓑ Ⓒ Ⓓ
6. Ⓐ Ⓑ Ⓒ Ⓓ	16. Ⓐ Ⓑ Ⓒ Ⓓ	26. Ⓐ Ⓑ Ⓒ Ⓓ	36. Ⓐ Ⓑ Ⓒ Ⓓ
7. Ⓐ Ⓑ Ⓒ Ⓓ	17. Ⓐ Ⓑ Ⓒ Ⓓ	27. Ⓐ Ⓑ Ⓒ Ⓓ	37. Ⓐ Ⓑ Ⓒ Ⓓ
8. Ⓐ Ⓑ Ⓒ Ⓓ	18. Ⓐ Ⓑ Ⓒ Ⓓ	28. Ⓐ Ⓑ Ⓒ Ⓓ	38. Ⓐ Ⓑ Ⓒ Ⓓ
9. Ⓐ Ⓑ Ⓒ Ⓓ	19. Ⓐ Ⓑ Ⓒ Ⓓ	29. Ⓐ Ⓑ Ⓒ Ⓓ	39. Ⓐ Ⓑ Ⓒ Ⓓ
10. Ⓐ Ⓑ Ⓒ Ⓓ	20. Ⓐ Ⓑ Ⓒ Ⓓ	30. Ⓐ Ⓑ Ⓒ Ⓓ	40. Ⓐ Ⓑ Ⓒ Ⓓ

Subtest II: Mathematics

1. Ⓐ Ⓑ Ⓒ Ⓓ	12. Ⓐ Ⓑ Ⓒ Ⓓ	23. Ⓐ Ⓑ Ⓒ Ⓓ	34. Ⓐ Ⓑ Ⓒ Ⓓ
2. Ⓐ Ⓑ Ⓒ Ⓓ	13. Ⓐ Ⓑ Ⓒ Ⓓ	24. Ⓐ Ⓑ Ⓒ Ⓓ	35. Ⓐ Ⓑ Ⓒ Ⓓ
3. Ⓐ Ⓑ Ⓒ Ⓓ	14. Ⓐ Ⓑ Ⓒ Ⓓ	25. Ⓐ Ⓑ Ⓒ Ⓓ	36. Ⓐ Ⓑ Ⓒ Ⓓ
4. Ⓐ Ⓑ Ⓒ Ⓓ	15. Ⓐ Ⓑ Ⓒ Ⓓ	26. Ⓐ Ⓑ Ⓒ Ⓓ	37. Ⓐ Ⓑ Ⓒ Ⓓ
5. Ⓐ Ⓑ Ⓒ Ⓓ	16. Ⓐ Ⓑ Ⓒ Ⓓ	27. Ⓐ Ⓑ Ⓒ Ⓓ	38. Ⓐ Ⓑ Ⓒ Ⓓ
6. Ⓐ Ⓑ Ⓒ Ⓓ	17. Ⓐ Ⓑ Ⓒ Ⓓ	28. Ⓐ Ⓑ Ⓒ Ⓓ	39. Ⓐ Ⓑ Ⓒ Ⓓ
7. Ⓐ Ⓑ Ⓒ Ⓓ	18. Ⓐ Ⓑ Ⓒ Ⓓ	29. Ⓐ Ⓑ Ⓒ Ⓓ	40. Ⓐ Ⓑ Ⓒ Ⓓ
8. Ⓐ Ⓑ Ⓒ Ⓓ	19. Ⓐ Ⓑ Ⓒ Ⓓ	30. Ⓐ Ⓑ Ⓒ Ⓓ	41. Ⓐ Ⓑ Ⓒ Ⓓ
9. Ⓐ Ⓑ Ⓒ Ⓓ	20. Ⓐ Ⓑ Ⓒ Ⓓ	31. Ⓐ Ⓑ Ⓒ Ⓓ	42. Ⓐ Ⓑ Ⓒ Ⓓ
10. Ⓐ Ⓑ Ⓒ Ⓓ	21. Ⓐ Ⓑ Ⓒ Ⓓ	32. Ⓐ Ⓑ Ⓒ Ⓓ	43. Ⓐ Ⓑ Ⓒ Ⓓ
11. Ⓐ Ⓑ Ⓒ Ⓓ	22. Ⓐ Ⓑ Ⓒ Ⓓ	33. Ⓐ Ⓑ Ⓒ Ⓓ	44. Ⓐ Ⓑ Ⓒ Ⓓ
			45. Ⓐ Ⓑ Ⓒ Ⓓ

Subtest III: English Language Skills

1. Ⓐ Ⓑ Ⓒ Ⓓ	11. Ⓐ Ⓑ Ⓒ Ⓓ	21. Ⓐ Ⓑ Ⓒ Ⓓ	31. Ⓐ Ⓑ Ⓒ Ⓓ
2. Ⓐ Ⓑ Ⓒ Ⓓ	12. Ⓐ Ⓑ Ⓒ Ⓓ	22. Ⓐ Ⓑ Ⓒ Ⓓ	32. Ⓐ Ⓑ Ⓒ Ⓓ
3. Ⓐ Ⓑ Ⓒ Ⓓ	13. Ⓐ Ⓑ Ⓒ Ⓓ	23. Ⓐ Ⓑ Ⓒ Ⓓ	33. Ⓐ Ⓑ Ⓒ Ⓓ
4. Ⓐ Ⓑ Ⓒ Ⓓ	14. Ⓐ Ⓑ Ⓒ Ⓓ	24. Ⓐ Ⓑ Ⓒ Ⓓ	34. Ⓐ Ⓑ Ⓒ Ⓓ
5. Ⓐ Ⓑ Ⓒ Ⓓ	15. Ⓐ Ⓑ Ⓒ Ⓓ	25. Ⓐ Ⓑ Ⓒ Ⓓ	35. Ⓐ Ⓑ Ⓒ Ⓓ
6. Ⓐ Ⓑ Ⓒ Ⓓ	16. Ⓐ Ⓑ Ⓒ Ⓓ	26. Ⓐ Ⓑ Ⓒ Ⓓ	36. Ⓐ Ⓑ Ⓒ Ⓓ
7. Ⓐ Ⓑ Ⓒ Ⓓ	17. Ⓐ Ⓑ Ⓒ Ⓓ	27. Ⓐ Ⓑ Ⓒ Ⓓ	37. Ⓐ Ⓑ Ⓒ Ⓓ
8. Ⓐ Ⓑ Ⓒ Ⓓ	18. Ⓐ Ⓑ Ⓒ Ⓓ	28. Ⓐ Ⓑ Ⓒ Ⓓ	38. Ⓐ Ⓑ Ⓒ Ⓓ
9. Ⓐ Ⓑ Ⓒ Ⓓ	19. Ⓐ Ⓑ Ⓒ Ⓓ	29. Ⓐ Ⓑ Ⓒ Ⓓ	39. Ⓐ Ⓑ Ⓒ Ⓓ
10. Ⓐ Ⓑ Ⓒ Ⓓ	20. Ⓐ Ⓑ Ⓒ Ⓓ	30. Ⓐ Ⓑ Ⓒ Ⓓ	40. Ⓐ Ⓑ Ⓒ Ⓓ

Practice Test 2

Subtest I: Reading

TIME: 40 Minutes
         40 Questions

> **DIRECTIONS:** A number of questions follow each of the passages in the reading section. Answer the questions by choosing the best answer from the four choices given.

Questions 1 to 5 refer to the following passage:

Spa water quality is maintained through a filter to ensure cleanliness and clarity. Wastes such as perspiration, hairspray, and lotions, which cannot be removed by the spa filter, can be controlled by shock treatment or super chlorination every other week. Although the filter traps most of the solid material to control bacteria and algae and to oxidize any organic material, the addition of disinfectants such as bromine or chlorine is necessary.

As all water solutions have a pH that controls corrosion, proper pH balance is also necessary. A pH measurement determines if the water is acid or alkaline. Based on a 14-point scale, a pH reading of 7.0 is considered neutral while a lower reading is considered acidic, and a higher reading indicates alkalinity or basic. High pH (above 7.6) reduces sanitizer efficiency, clouds water, promotes scale formation on surfaces and equipment, and interferes with filter operation. When pH is high, add a pH decrease such as sodium bisulphate (e.g., Spa Down). Because the spa water is hot, scale is deposited more rapidly. A weekly dose of a stain and scale fighter also will help to control this problem. Low pH (below 7.2) is equally damaging, causing equipment corrosion, water that is irritating, and rapid sanitizer dissipation. To increase pH, add sodium bicarbonate (e.g., Spa Up).

The recommended operating temperature of a spa (98°–104°) is a fertile environment for the growth of bacteria and viruses. This growth is prevented when appropriate sanitizer levels are continuously monitored. Bacteria can also be controlled by maintaining a proper bromine level of 3.0 to 5.0 parts per million (ppm) or a chlorine level of 1.0–2.0 ppm. As bromine tablets should not be added directly to the water, a bromine floater will properly dispense the tablets. Should chlorine be the chosen sanitizer, a granular form is recommended, as liquid chlorine or tablets are too harsh for the spa.

1. Although proper chemical and temperature maintenance of spa water is necessary, the most important condition to monitor is

    (A) preventing growth of bacteria and viruses.
    (B) preventing equipment corrosion.
    (C) preventing scale formation.
    (D) preventing cloudy water.

2. Of the chemical and temperature conditions in a spa, the condition most dangerous to one's health is

    (A) spa water temperature above 104°.
    (B) bromine level between 3.0 and 5.0.
    (C) pH level below 7.2.
    (D) spa water temperature between 90° and 104°.

3. The primary purpose of the passage is to

    (A) relate that maintenance of a spa can negate the full enjoyment of the spa experience.
    (B) convey that the maintenance of a spa is expensive and time consuming.
    (C) explain the importance of proper spa maintenance.
    (D) detail proper spa maintenance.

4. The spa filter can be relied upon to

    (A) control algae and bacteria.
    (B) trap most solid material.
    (C) assure an adequate level of sanitation.
    (D) maintain clear spa water.

5. Which chemical should one avoid when maintaining a spa?

    (A) Liquid chlorine   (C) Sodium bisulfate
    (B) Bromine   (D) Baking soda

Questions 6 to 10 refer to the following passage:

The relationship of story elements found in children's generated stories to reading achievement was analyzed. Correlations ranged from .61101 ($p = .64$) at the beginning of first grade to .83546 ($p = .24$) at the end of first grade, to .85126 ($p = .21$) at the end of second grade, and to .82588 ($p = .26$) for fifth/sixth grades. Overall, the correlation of the story elements to reading achievement appeared to indicate a high positive correlation trend even though it was not statistically significant.

Multiple regression equation analyses dealt with the relative contribution of the story elements to reading achievement. The contribution of certain story elements was substantial. At the beginning of first grade, story conventions added 40 percent to the total variance while the other increments were not significant. At the end of first grade, story plot contributed 44 percent to the total variance, story conventions contributed 20 percent, and story sources contributed 17 percent. At the end of second grade, the story elements contributed more equal percentages to the total partial correlation of .8513. Although none of the percentages were substantial, story plot (.2200), clausal connectors (.1858), and T-units (.1590) contributed the most to the total partial correlation. By the fifth and sixth grades three other story elements—T-units (.2241), story characters (.3214), and clausal connectors (.1212)—contributed most to the total partial correlation. None of these percentages was substantial.

6. Which of the following is the most complete and accurate definition of the term "statistically significant" as used in the passage?

   (A) Consists of important numerical data
   (B) Is educationally significant
   (C) Permits prediction of reading achievement by knowing the story elements
   (D) Indicates two measures (reading achievement and story elements) give the same information

7. The passage suggests which of the following conclusions about the correlation of story elements to reading achievement?

   (A) That there are other more important story elements that should also be included in the analyses
   (B) That children's inclusion of story elements in their stories causes them to achieve higher levels in reading
   (C) That these story elements are important variables to consider in reading achievement
   (D) That correlations of more than 1.0 are needed for this study to be statistically significant

8. The relative contribution of story conventions and story plot in first grade suggests that

   (A) children may have spontaneously picked up these story elements as a result of their exposure to stories.
   (B) children have been explicitly taught these story elements.
   (C) these story elements were not important because in fifth/sixth grades other story elements contributed more to the total partial correlation.
   (D) children's use of story conventions and plots were not taken from story models.

9. The content of the passage suggests that the passage would most likely appear in which of the following?

   (A) *Psychology Today*   (C) *Language Arts*
   (B) *The Creative Writer*   (D) *Reading Research Quarterly*

10. "None of these percentages were substantial" is the last statement in the passage. It refers to

    (A) the story elements for fifth/sixth grades.
    (B) the story elements for second grade.
    (C) the story elements at the end of first grade.
    (D) the story elements for all of the grades, i.e., first grade, second grade, and fifth/sixth grade.

Questions 11 to 13 refer to the following passage:

There is an importance of learning communication and meaning in language. Yet the use of notions such as communication and meaning as the basic criteria for instruction, experiences, and materials in classrooms may misguide a child in several respects. Communication in the classroom is vital. The teacher should use communication to help students develop the capacity to make their private responses become public responses. Otherwise, one's use of language would be in danger of being what the younger generation refers to as mere words, mere thoughts, and mere feelings.

Learning theorists emphasize specific components of learning: behaviorists stress behavior in learning; humanists stress the affective in learning; and cognitivists stress cognition in learning. All three of these components occur simultaneously and cannot be separated from each other in the learning process. In 1957, Festinger referred to dissonance as the lack of harmony between what one does (behavior) and what one believes (attitude). Attempts to separate the components of learning either knowingly or unknowingly create dissonances wherein language, thought, feeling, and behavior become diminished of authenticity. As a result, ideas and concepts lose their content and vitality, and the manipulation and politics of communication assume prominence.

11. Which of the following best describes the author's attitude toward the subject discussed?

(A) A flippant disregard   (C) A passive resignation
(B) A mild frustration   (D) An informed concern

12. The primary purpose of the passage is to

(A) discuss the relationships between learning and communication.
(B) assure teachers that communication and meaning are the basic criteria for learning in classrooms.
(C) stress the importance of providing authentic communication in classroom learning.
(D) address the role of communication and meaning in classrooms.

13. Which of the following is the most complete and accurate definition of the term "mere" as used in the passage?

(A) Small   (C) Little
(B) Minor   (D) Insignificant

Questions 14 to 16 refer to the following passage:

In 1975, Sinclair observed that it had often been supposed that the main factor in learning to talk is being able to imitate. Schlesinger (1975) noted that at certain stages of learning to speak, a child tends to imitate everything an adult says to him or her, and it therefore seems reasonable to accord to such imitation an important role in the acquisition of language.

Moreover, various investigators have attempted to explain the role of imitation in language. In his discussion of the development of imitation and cognition of adult speech sounds, Nakazema (1975) stated that although the parent's talking stimulates and accelerates the infant's articulatory activity, the parent's phoneme system does not influence the child's articulatory mechanisms. Slobin and Welsh (1973) suggested that imitation is the reconstruction of the adult's utterance and that the child does so by employing the grammatical rules that he has developed at a specific time. Schlesinger proposed that by imitating the adult the child practices new grammatical constructions. Brown and Bellugi (1964) noted that a child's imitations resemble spontaneous speech in that they drop inflections, most function words, and sometimes other words. However, the word order of imitated sentences usually was preserved. Brown and Bellugi assumed that imitation is a function of what the child attended to or remembered. Shipley et al. (1969) suggested that repeating an adult's utterance assists the child's comprehension. Ervin (1964) and Braine (1971) found that a child's imitations do not contain more advanced structures than his or her spontaneous utterances; thus, imitation can no longer be regarded as the simple behavioristic act that earlier scholars assumed it to be.

14. The author of the passage would tend to agree with which of the following statements?

(A) Apparently, children require practice with more advanced structures before they are able to imitate.
(B) Apparently, children only imitate what they already do, using whatever is in their repertoire.
(C) Apparently, the main factor in learning to talk remains being able to imitate.
(D) Apparently, children cannot respond meaningfully to a speech situation until they have reached a stage where they can make symbol-orientation responses.

15. The primary purpose of the passage is to

(A) explain the role of imitation in language acquisition.
(B) assure parents of their role in assisting imitation in language acquisition.
(C) relate the history of imitation in language acquisition.
(D) discuss relationships between psychological and physiological processes in language acquisition.

16. An inference that parents may make from the passage is that they should

(A) be concerned when a child imitates their language.
(B) focus on developing imitation in their child's language.
(C) realize that their child's imitations may reflect several aspects of language acquisition.
(D) realize that their talking may over-stimulate their child's articulatory activity.

Questions 17 and 18 refer to the following passage:

A major problem with reading/language arts instruction is that practice assignments from workbooks often provide short, segmented activities that do not really resemble the true act of reading. Perhaps more than any computer application, word processing is capable of addressing these issues.

17. The author would tend to agree that a major benefit of computers in reading/language arts instruction is

(A) that the reading act may be more closely resembled.
(B) that short segmented assignments will be eliminated.
(C) that computer application will be limited to word processing.
(D) that reading practice will be eliminated.

18. The appropriate use of a word processor to assist in making practice resemble a reading act is

   (A) detailed.   (C) unstated.
   (B) desirable.   (D) alluded.

Questions 19 to 21 refer to the following passage:

In view of the current emphasis on literature-based reading instruction, a greater understanding by teachers of variance in cultural, language, and story components should assist in narrowing the gap between reader and text and improve reading comprehension. Classroom teachers should begin with students' meaning and intentions about stories before moving students to the commonalities of story meaning based on common background and culture. With teacher guidance, students should develop a fuller understanding of how complex narratives are when they are generating stories as well as when they are reading stories.

19. Which of the following is the intended audience for the passage?

   (A) Teachers using literature-based curriculum
   (B) Professors teaching a literature course
   (C) Parents concerned about their child's comprehension of books
   (D) Teacher educators teaching reading methods courses

20. Which of the following is the most complete and accurate definition of the term "variance" as used in the passage?

   (A) Change   (C) Diversity
   (B) Fluctuations   (D) Deviation

21. The passage supports a concept of meaning primarily residing in

   (A) culture, language, and story components.
   (B) comprehension.
   (C) students' stories only.
   (D) students and narratives.

Questions 22 to 25 refer to the following passage:

As noted by Favat in 1977, the study of children's stories has been an ongoing concern of linguists, anthropologists, and psychologists. The past decade has witnessed a surge of interest in children's stories from researchers in these and other disciplines. The use of narratives for reading and reading instruction has been commonly accepted by the educational community. The notion that narrative is highly structured and that children's sense of narrative structure is more highly developed than expository structure has been proposed by some researchers.

Early studies of children's stories followed two approaches for story analysis: the analysis of story content or the analysis of story structure. Story content analysis has centered primarily on examining motivational and psychodynamic aspects of story characters as noted in the works of Erikson and Pitcher and Prelinger in 1963 and Ames in 1966. These studies have noted that themes or topics predominate and that themes change with age.

Early research on story structure focused on formal models of structure, such as story grammar and story schemata. These models specified basic story elements and formed sets of rules similar to sentence grammar for ordering the elements.

The importance or centrality of narrative in a child's development of communicative ability has been proposed by Halliday (1976) and Hymes (1975). Thus, the importance of narrative for language communicative ability and for reading and reading instruction has been well documented. However, the question still remains about how these literacy abilities interact and lead to conventional reading.

22. This passage is most probably directed at which of the following audience?

(A) Reading educators
(B) Linguists
(C) Psychologists
(D) Reading researchers

23. According to the passage, future research should address

(A) how story structure and story schema interact with comprehension.
(B) how children's use and understanding of narrative interacts and leads to conventional reading.
(C) how story content interacts with story comprehension.
(D) how narrative text structure differs from expository text structure.

24. The major distinction between story content and story structure is that

(A) story content focuses on motivational aspects whereas story structure focuses on rules similar to sentence grammar.
(B) story content focuses on psychodynamic aspects whereas story structure focuses on formal structural models.
(C) story content and story structure essentially refer to the same concepts.
(D) story content focuses primarily on characters whereas story structure focuses on story grammar and schemata.

25. Which of the following is the most complete and accurate definition of the term "surge" as used in the following sentence? The past decade has witnessed a surge of interest in children's stories from researchers in these and other disciplines.

(A) A heavy swell
(B) A sudden rise
(C) A sudden increase
(D) A sudden rush

Questions 26 to 29 refer to the following passage:

Seldom has the American school system not been the target of demands for change to meet the social priorities of the times. This theme has been traced through the following significant occurrences in education: Benjamin Franklin's advocacy in 1749 for a more useful type of education; Horace Mann's zealous proposals in the 1830s espousing the tax-supported public school; John Dewey's early twentieth century attack on traditional schools for not developing the child effectively for his or her role in society; the post-Sputnik pressure for academic rigor; the prolific criticism and accountability pressures of the 1970s;

and the ensuing disillusionment and continued criticism of schools until this last decade of the twentieth century. Indeed, the waves of criticism about American education have reflected currents of social dissatisfaction for any given period of this country's history.

As dynamics for change in the social order result in demands for change in the American educational system, so in turn insistence has developed for revision of teacher education (witness the more recent Holmes report (1986)). Historically, the education of American teachers has reflected evolving attitudes about public education. With slight modifications, the teacher education pattern established following the demise of the normal school during the early 1900s has persisted in most teacher preparation programs. The pattern has been one requiring certain academic and professional (educational) courses often resulting in teachers prone to teach as they had been taught.

26. The author of this passage would probably agree with which of the following statements?

    (A) Social dissatisfaction should drive change in the American school systems.
    (B) Teacher education programs have changed greatly since normal schools were eliminated.
    (C) Critics of American education reflect vested interests.
    (D) Teachers' teaching methods tend to reflect what they have learned in their academic and professional courses.

27. The evolving attitudes about public education are

    (A) stated.   (C) alluded.
    (B) unstated.   (D) unwarranted.

28. One possible sequence of significant occurrences in education noted in the passage is

    (A) Mann's tax-supported public schools, post-Sputnik pressures for academic rigor, and the Holmes' report.
    (B) Franklin's more useful type of education, Dewey's educating children for their role in society, and Mann's tax-supported public schools.
    (C) Franklin's more useful type of education, the Holmes' report, and accountability pressures of the 1970s.
    (D) Mann's tax-supported public schools, accountability pressures of the 1970s, and the post-Sputnik pressures for academic rigor.

29. Which of the following statements most obviously implies dissatisfaction with preparation of teachers in the United States?

    (A) Demands for change in the American education system lead to insistence for revision of teacher education programs.
    (B) The pattern of teacher education requires certain academic and professional education courses.
    (C) The education of U.S. teachers has reflected evolving attitudes about public education.
    (D) Teacher education has changed very little since the decline of the normal school.

Questions 30 to 33 refer to the following passage:

HAWK ON A FRESHLY PLOWED FIELD

My Lord of the Field, proudly perched on the sod,
You eye with disdain
And mutter with wings
As steadily each furrow I tractor-plod.
"Intruder!" you glare, firmly standing your ground,
Proclaim this fief yours
By Nature so willed—
Yet bound to the air on my very next round.
You hover and soar, skimming close by the earth,
Distract me from work
To brood there with you
Of changes that Man wrought your land—for his worth.
In medieval days, lords were god over all:
Their word was the law.
Yet here is this hawk
A ruler displaced—Man and Season forestall.
My Lord of the Field, from sight you have flown.
For purpose untold,
When brave, you return
And perch once again, still liege-lord—but Alone.

Jacqueline K. Hultquist (1952)

30. Which of the following is the most complete and accurate definition of the term "liege-lord" as used in the passage?

(A) Monarch
(B) King
(C) Sovereign
(D) Master

31. Which of the following best describes the author's attitude toward the hawk?

(A) Romantic
(B) Pensive
(C) Intimidating
(D) Fearful

32. Which of the following groups of words about the hawk carry human qualities?

(A) Mutter, brood, and ruler
(B) Brave, disdain, and perch
(C) Brave, brood, and distract
(D) Mutter, disdain, and skimming

33. Which of the following is the most complete and accurate definition of the term "medieval" as used in the passage?

(A) Antiquated
(B) Feudal

(C) Old
(D) Antediluvian

Questions 34 to 37 refer to the following passage:

Reduced to its simplest form, a political system is really no more than a device enabling groups of people to live together in a more or less orderly society. As they have developed, political systems generally have fallen into the broad categories of those which do not offer direct subject participation in the decision-making process, and those which allow citizen participation—in form, if not in actual effectiveness.

Let us consider, however, the type of political system that is classified as the modern democracy in a complex society. Such a democracy is defined by Lipset (1963) as "a political system which supplies regular constitutional opportunities for changing the governing officials, and a social mechanism which permits the largest possible part of the population to influence major decisions by choosing among alternative contenders for political office."

Proceeding from another concept (that of Easton and Dennis), a political system is one of inputs, conversion, and outputs by which the wants of a society are transformed into binding decisions. Easton and Dennis (1967) observed: "To sustain a conversion process of this sort, a society must provide a relatively stable context for political interaction, set of general rules for participating in all parts of the political process." As a rule, this interaction evolves around the settling of differences (satisfying wants or demands) involving the elements of a "political regime," which consists of minimal general goal constraints, norms governing behavior, and structures of authority for the input-output function.

In order to persist, a political system would seem to need a minimal support for the political regime. To insure the maintenance of such a support is the function of political socialization, a process varying according to political systems but toward the end of indoctrinating the members to the respective political system. "To the extent that the maturing members absorb and become attached to the overarching goals of the system and its basic norms and come to approve its structure of authority as legitimate, we can say that they are learning to contribute support to the regime." The desired political norm (an expectation about the way people will behave) is that referred to as political efficacy—a feeling that one's action can have an impact on government.

Adapted from Easton, B. and J. Dennis, "The Child's Acquisition of Regime Norms: Political Efficacy" *American Political Science Review,* March 1967.

34. Political efficacy according to the passage is

(A) most likely to be found where citizen participation is encouraged.
(B) in an expanding concept of political efficiency.
(C) in a diminishing concept of political efficiency.
(D) in a figurehead political system.

35. Political socialization is a process which

    (A) occurs only in democracies.
    (B) occurs in any type of political system.
    (C) occurs less frequently in recent years.
    (D) occurs when members reject the goals of the system.

36. As used in the passage, which of the following is the most complete and accurate definition of the term "conversion"?

    (A) Transformation   (C) Resolution
    (B) Changeover   (D) Passing

37. The major distinction between the concepts of Easton and Dennis as opposed to the concepts of Lipset is

    (A) that the concepts of Easton and Dennis are based on the wants of a society, whereas Lipset's concepts are based on change of governing officials.
    (B) that Easton and Dennis' concepts are based on arbitrary decisions, whereas Lipset's concepts are based on influencing major decisions.
    (C) that Easton and Dennis' concepts must have a set of general rules, whereas Lipset's concepts provide for irregular constitutional opportunities.
    (D) that Easton and Dennis' concepts evolve around the settling of differences, whereas Lipset's concepts permit the largest conflict possible.

Questions 38 to 40 refer to the following passage:

Assignment: Research for a White Paper Proposing U.S. Foreign Policy

Imagine you are in charge (or assigned to) a foreign policy desk in the U.S. Department of State. Select one of the following regions (descriptors are merely suggestions):

Western Europe—A Changing Alliance

Eastern Europe—Out from Behind the Iron Curtain

The U.S.S.R.—Still an Enigma

The Middle East—History and Emotions

Africa—Rising Expectations in the Postwar Continent

South and Southeast Asia—Unrest in Far Away Places

The Far East—Alienation and Alliance

The Western Hemisphere—Neighbors; Pro and Con

Through research, prepare a White Paper for that area which will indicate:

1. a General Policy Statement toward the nations of that region;

2. a statement as to how World War II set the stage for that policy;

3. a summary of the major events since 1945 in that region which have affected U.S. foreign policy;

4. a list of suggested problems and/or possibilities for near-future interactions of that region and the U.S.

38. In order to complete this assignment, research into which of the following disciplines (areas of study) would be most appropriate?

    (A) History, Economics, Political Science, and Language
    (B) History, Political Science, Education, and Economics
    (C) Political Science, Economics, Geography, and Religion
    (D) History, Political Science, Economics, and Culture

39. Which of the following is the most complete and accurate definition of the term "Enigma" as used in the passage?

    (A) Riddle   (C) Secret
    (B) Puzzle   (D) Mystery

40. Which of the following is the most appropriate secondary school audience for the assignment?

    (A) Students in a World Geography class
    (B) Students in a World History class
    (C) Students in an Economics class
    (D) Students in an American Government class

Subtest II: Mathematics

TIME: 100 Minutes
45 Questions

> **DIRECTIONS:** Each of the questions or incomplete statements below is followed by four suggested answers or completions. Select the one that is best in each case.

1. Which of the statements below is true?

   (A) $4^3 = 3^4$

   (B) $5^0 \times 8^2 > 2^5$

   (C) $7^4 + 7^3 = 7^7$

   (D) $5^2 + 5^8 = 5^{10}$

2. The mean IQ score for 1,500 students is 100, with a standard deviation of 15. Assuming normal curve distribution, how many students have an IQ between 85 and 115? Refer to the figure shown below.

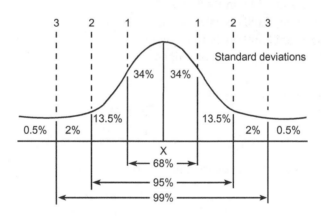

   (A) 750

   (B) 1,020

   (C) 1,275

   (D) 1,425

3. Complete the following and express the answer in scientific notation.

$$\frac{4.8 \times 10^5}{2.4 \times 10^3}$$

   (A) 2.0×10^8

   (B) 2.0×10^2

   (C) 7.2×10^2

   (D) 7.2×10^8

4. The number 80 written in prime factorization is:

   (A) $2^4 \times 5$ (C) $2^5 \times 3$
   (B) $4^2 \times 5$ (D) 10×2^3

5. Two college roommates spent $2,000 for their total monthly expenses. A pie graph below indicates a record of their expenses.

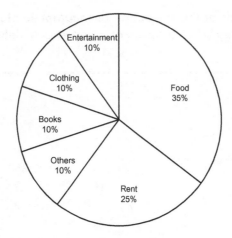

   Based on the above information, which of the following statements is accurate?

   (A) The roommates spent $700 on food alone.
   (B) The roommates spent $300 on entertainment alone.
   (C) The roommates spent $300 on clothing alone.
   (D) The roommates spent $300 on books alone.

6. Find the next number in the pattern: 39, 33, 27...

   (A) 24   (C) 22
   (B) 21   (D) 20

7. Which one of the points below lies on the line $y = 3x - 5$?

   (A) $(-2, -11)$ (C) $(0, 5)$
   (B) $(3, 5)$ (D) $(-3, -4)$

8. Simplify the following: $|8 - 6| + 3 \div 3 \times 4^2 - 2$

   (A) 22   (C) $\dfrac{74}{3}$

   (B) 16   (D) $\dfrac{34}{3}$

9. An elephant in a zoo weighs 8.25 tons. How many pounds does the elephant weigh?

    (A) 1,650 pounds
    (B) 8,250 pounds

    (C) 16,500 pounds
    (D) 82,500 pounds

10. Terence wants to find the average height of a student in his high school. Which would be the best sample?

    (A) The 17 students in his math class
    (B) All of the 10th grade girls
    (C) 15 students from each of the grades 9 through 12
    (D) The 30 players on the varsity and junior varsity basketball teams

11. Alejandra's bedroom is twice as long as it is wide. If the area of her room is 288 square feet, what is the length of her bedroom?

    (A) 12 feet
    (B) 24 feet

    (C) 20 feet
    (D) 18 feet

12. A cardboard shipping box is 14 inches long, 16 inches wide, and 20 inches high. Find the volume of the box in cubic feet to the nearest hundredth.

    (A) 373.3
    (B) 2.59

    (C) 31.1
    (D) 137.3

13. A collection of data has a very large outlier. Which measure of central tendency will the outlier affect, and in what way?

    (A) The median will be much higher.
    (B) The mode will be much higher.

    (C) The range will be much higher.
    (D) The mean will be much higher.

14. A bag contains 12 blue tiles, 6 red tiles, and 2 green tiles. What is the probability that you will select a green tile if you pick a tile from the bag at random?

    (A) $\dfrac{2}{18}$

    (B) $\dfrac{2}{20}$

    (C) $\dfrac{1}{20}$

    (D) $\dfrac{1}{18}$

15. Danny is traveling to his sister's house, which is 300 miles from his apartment. Danny drove 3.5 hours at a constant rate of 55 miles per hour before stopping for lunch. How many more miles does Danny have to drive to get to his sister's?

    (A) 192.5
    (B) 107.5

    (C) 214
    (D) 158

16. Comparing unit prices is helpful when trying to find the best price at the supermarket. Which of the following would be the best deal?

    8 bagels for $2.80

    10 bagels for $3.35

    15 bagels for $4.35

    (A) 15 bagels for $4.35
    (B) 10 bagels for $3.35
    (C) 8 bagels for $2.80
    (D) 10 bagels for $3.35 or 8 bagels for $2.80

17. The scale drawing of a volleyball court is 3 inches by 6 inches. The scale is 1 inch is equal to 3 meters. What is the area of the volleyball court in square meters?

    (A) 18   (C) 102
    (B) 54   (D) 162

18. Find the next number in the sequence: 1, 5, 25, 125…

    (A) 625   (C) 525
    (B) 225   (D) 425

19. Suppose that a pair of pants and a shirt cost $65 and the pants cost $25 more than the shirt. What did they each cost?

    (A) The pants cost $40 and the shirt costs $25.
    (B) The pants cost $43 and the shirt costs $22.
    (C) The pants cost $45 and the shirt costs $20.
    (D) The pants cost $50 and the shirt costs $15.

20. There are five members on a basketball team. Supposing each member shakes hands with every other member of the team before the game starts, how many handshakes will there be in all?

    (A) 8   (C) 10
    (B) 9   (D) 12

21. The Four Seasons hotel in Miami, Florida is 794 feet tall. How many yards high is the building?

    (A) $264\frac{2}{3}$ (C) $66\frac{1}{3}$

    (B) 2382   (D) 350

22. Ms. Koch baked a chicken for 145 minutes. How many hours is 145 minutes?

(A) $2\frac{1}{4}$ (C) $2\frac{5}{12}$

(B) $2\frac{1}{2}$ (D) $2\frac{7}{8}$

23. The length of a picture frame is 2 inches more than twice its width. If the perimeter of the picture frame is 88 inches, what is the length of the frame in inches?

(A) 14   (C) 60
(B) 22   (D) 30

24. Below is a rectangular pyramid ABCDE.

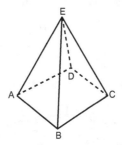

How many vertices does it have?

(A) 4   (C) 6
(B) 5   (D) 7

25. Tom bought a piece of land selling for $20,000. If he had to pay 20 percent of the price as a down payment, how much was the down payment?

(A) $2,500   (C) $4,500
(B) $4,000   (D) $5,000

26. A personal computer sells for $3,200 to the general public. If you purchase one in the university, the price is reduced by 20 percent. What is the sale price of the computer?

(A) $640   (C) $2,560
(B) $2,410   (D) $3,180

27. In order for Sue to receive a final grade of C, she must have an average greater than or equal to 70% but less than 80% on five tests. Suppose her grades on the first four tests were 65%, 85%, 60%, and 90%. What range of grades on the fifth test would give her a C in the course?

    (A) 40 up to but excluding 95
    (B) 45 up to but excluding 95
    (C) 49 up to but excluding 98
    (D) 50 up to but excluding 100

28. A certain company produces two types of lawnmowers. Type A is self-propelled while type B is not. The company can produce a maximum of 18 mowers per week. It can make a profit of $15 on mower A and a profit of $20 on mower B. The company wants to make at least 2 mowers of type A but not more than 5. They also plan to make at least 2 mowers of type B. Let x be the number of type A produced, and let y be the number of type B produced.

    From the above, which of the following is NOT one of the listed constraints?

    (A) $x \leq 5$ (C) $y < 5$
    (B) $x + y \leq 18$ (D) $y \geq 2$

29. Find the measure of the angle shown below to the nearest degree.

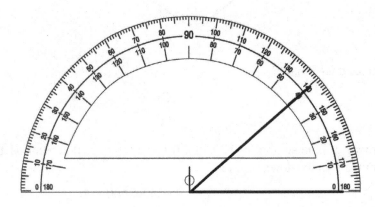

    (A) 41 degrees   (C) 139 degrees
    (B) 39 degrees   (D) 141 degrees

30. What is the best name for the polygon described below?

    • Four sides

    • Opposite sides are equal in length

    (A) Square   (C) Parallelogram
    (B) Quadrilateral   (D) Rectangle

31. George has four ways to get from his house to the park. He has seven ways to get from the park to the school. How many ways can George get from his house to school by way of the park?

    (A) 4
    (B) 7
    (C) 28
    (D) 11

32. In which quadrant would you find the point (–3, –8)?

    (A) I
    (B) II
    (C) III
    (D) IV

33. The map below shows the center of Florida City and the streets surrounding it. Which street is parallel to NW 3rd Street (above and to the left of Florida City)?

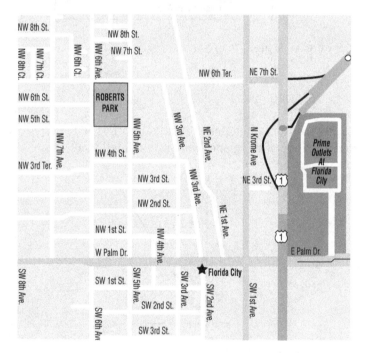

    (A) NE 2nd Avenue
    (B) N. Krome Avenue
    (C) NW 6th Street
    (D) NW 6th Avenue

34. The property tax rate of the town of Grandview is $32 per $1,000 of assessed value. What is the tax if the property is assessed at $50,000?

    (A) $32
    (B) $1,000
    (C) $1,562
    (D) $1,600

35. A portion of land is in the shape of a right triangle. The legs are 35 feet and 75 feet. What is the length of the hypotenuse of the land (to the nearest foot)?

    (A) 10
    (B) 83
    (C) 110
    (D) 6850

36. Mary had been selling printed shirts in her neighborhood. She made this pictograph to show how much money she made each week.

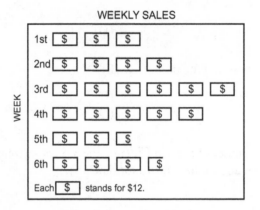

How many weeks were sales more than $55?

(A) 1 week
(B) 2 weeks

(C) 3 weeks
(D) 4 weeks

37. Laura gets an hourly rate for helping out at her dad's office. The graph below shows Laura's earnings. If you found the slope of the graph, what would it tell you?

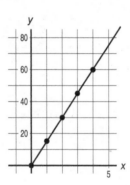

(A) The number of hours Laura worked
(B) The total amount of money Laura earned
(C) The number of hours Laura works for 0 dollars
(D) Laura's hourly rate

38. What type of transformation is illustrated in the diagram below?

   (A) Translation   (C) Reflection
   (B) Rotation   (D) Dilation

39. Which word phrase below is the correct translation of the algebraic expression in the box?

$$5(x - 3)$$

   (A) Five times x decreased by three
   (B) The quotient of five and the difference of x and three
   (C) Three less than five multiplied by x
   (D) Five times the quantity x minus three

40. The diagram below shows the location of Kaylie, who is in the water, and the lifeguard. If Kaylie should need the lifeguard's help, how many feet would he have to travel to get to her? Note: Each unit on the graph is equal to 10 feet.

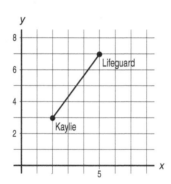

   (A) 5 feet   (C) 50 feet
   (B) 7 feet   (D) 70 feet

41. How many 12 oz. cans of orange juice would it take to give 75 people each an 8 oz. cup of orange juice?

   (A) 112 cans   (C) 600 cans
   (B) 75 cans   (D) 50 cans

42. A car rental agency charges $139 per week plus $0.08 per mile for an average size car. How far can you travel to the nearest mile on a maximum budget of $350?

    (A) 2,637 mi.   (C) 2,110 mi.
    (B) 2,640 mi.   (D) 1,737 mi.

43. Pencils come in packages of 12 and notebooks come in packages of 5. What are the fewest packages of pencils and notebooks you would have to buy to have the same number of items of each?

    (A) 3 packages of pencils and 6 packages of notebooks
    (B) 12 packages of pencils and 5 packages of notebooks
    (C) 5 packages of pencils and 12 packages of notebooks
    (D) 6 packages of pencils and 3 packages of notebooks

44. Peter took a 1,500-mile trip in 5 days. Each day, he drove 30 miles more than the day before. How many miles did he cover on the first day?

    (A) 375 mi.   (C) 230 mi.
    (B) 294 mi.   (D) 240 mi.

45. The ordered pair (7, –20) is a solution of which equation?

    (A) $y = -3x + 1$ (C) $y = -4x + 2$
    (B) $y = -x + 7$ (D) $y = -2x + 3$

Subtest III: English Language Skills

TIME: 40 Minutes
40 Questions

Part A: Usage

> **DIRECTIONS:** Each of the following sentences may contain an error in diction, usage, idiom, or grammar. Some sentences are correct. Some sentences contain one error. No sentence contains more than one error.
>
> If there is an error, it will appear in one of the underlined portions labeled A, B, or C. If there is no error, choose the portion labeled D. If there is an error, select the letter of the portion that must be changed in order to correct the sentence.
>
> **EXAMPLE:**
>
> He drove <u>slowly</u> and <u>cautiously</u> in order to <u>hopefully</u> avoid having an accident.
>   **A**   **B**   **C**
>
> <u>No error</u>.
>   **D**
>
>   Ⓐ Ⓑ ● Ⓓ

1. *Huckleberry Finn*, by <u>general consensus agreement</u> Mark Twain's greatest work, is <u>supremely</u> the
                              A   **B**
   American <u>Classic</u>; it is also one of the great books of the world. <u>No error</u>.
             C   **D**

2. The U.S. Constitution <u>supposes</u> what the history of all governments <u>demonstrate</u>, that the executive
                                   A   **B**
   is the branch <u>most</u> interested in war and most prone to it. <u>No error</u>.
                     C   **D**

3. Mama, the <u>narrator</u> of Alice Walker's short story "Everyday Use," speaks fondly of her daughter
               A
   upon her return home after a long absence <u>like</u> Mama is <u>proud</u> of her. <u>No error</u>.
                                            B   **C**   **D**

4. <u>Nearly</u> one hundred years after the impoverished Vincent Van Gogh died, his paintings <u>had sold</u> for
   A   **B**
   more than a <u>million dollars</u>. <u>No error</u>.
                C   **D**

5. Many athletes recruited for football by college coaches <u>expect</u> that they will, <u>in fact</u>, receive an
                                          A   **B**

    education when they <u>accept</u> a scholarship. <u>No error</u>.
                         C   **D**

6. <u>Hopefully</u>, by the end of the <u>Twentieth Century</u>, computer scientists will invent machines with enough
   A   **B**

    intelligence to work without breaking down <u>continually</u>. <u>No error</u>.
                                     C   **D**

7. Studies <u>showing</u> that the earth includes a <u>vast series</u> of sedimentary rocks, some with embedded fossils
          A   **B**

    <u>that</u> prove the existence of ancient organisms. <u>No error</u>.
    C   **D**

8. When Martin Luther King, Jr., wrote his famous letter from the Birmingham jail, he advocated neither

    evading <u>or</u> defying the law; <u>but</u> he accepted the idea that a penalty <u>results from</u> breaking a law, even an
            A   **B**   **C**

    unjust one. <u>No error</u>.
              D

9. <u>The Eighteenth Century</u> philosopher Adam Smith asserted that a nation <u>achieves</u> the best economic
          A   **B**

    results when individuals work both for their own interests and <u>to gain more goods</u>. <u>No error</u>.
                                             C   **D**

10. According to Niccolo Machiavelli, wise rulers <u>cannot</u> and <u>should not</u> keep their word when such
                                      A   **B**

    integrity would be to their disadvantage and when the reasons for the promise no longer <u>exist</u>. <u>No error</u>.
                                                   C   **D**

11. The Milky Way galaxy, which <u>comprises</u> millions of stars, has both thin and congested spots, but
                               A

    shines <u>their</u> <u>brightest</u> in the constellation Sagittarius. <u>No error</u>.
           B   **C**   **D**

12. <u>To learn</u> an ancient language <u>like</u> Latin or Greek is one way to discover the roots of Western Culture;
    A   **B**

    studying Judeo-Christian religious beliefs <u>is</u> another. <u>No error</u>.
                            C   **D**

13. Many political conservatives <u>contribute</u> the problems of modern American society to the twin evils of
    A
    the New Deal and <u>secular humanism</u>, both <u>of which</u> are presumed to stem from Marxism. <u>No error</u>.
    B   **C**   **D**

14. <u>Having minimal exposure</u> to poetry when they attended school, most Americans <u>chose</u> to watch
    A   **B**
    television or <u>to read</u> popular magazines for entertainment. <u>No error</u>.
    C   **D**

15. What makes <u>we</u> humans <u>different from</u> other animals <u>can be defined</u> at least partly by our powerful
    A   **B**   **C**
    and efficient intelligence. <u>No error</u>.
    D

16. When one contrasts the ideas of the Romantic William Wordsworth <u>with</u> those of Neoclassicist John
    A
    Dryden, <u>one finds</u> that neither of the poets <u>differ</u> as much as one would expect. <u>No error</u>.
    B   **C**   **D**

17. Carl Jung's hypothesis of the collective unconscious suggests that we inherit <u>cultural-experimental</u>
    A
    memory in the form of mythological archetype, <u>which arise</u> from repeated <u>patterns</u> of human behavior.
    B   **C**
    <u>No error</u>.
    D

18. Bertrand Russell believed that a free person's liberation is <u>effected</u> by a contemplation of <u>Fate</u>; one
    A   **B**
    achieves emancipation through passionate pursuit of eternal things, <u>not through</u> the pursuit of private
    C
    happiness. <u>No error</u>.
    D

19. <u>Latin American</u> literature includes the works of Gabriel Garcia Marquez, Pablo Neruda, and Jorge
    A
    Luis Borges; each of these <u>acclaimed</u> artists has won <u>their</u> share of prizes. <u>No error</u>.
    B   **C**   **D**

20. The reason <u>a large percentage</u> of American college students <u>located</u> Moscow in California is <u>because</u>
    A   **B**   **C**
    they were not required to learn the facts of geography. <u>No error</u>.
    D

21. Astronomers and physicists <u>tell</u> us that the universe is <u>constant</u> expanding and that it <u>comprises</u>
                    A   **B**   **C**
    numerous galaxies like ours. <u>No error</u>.
                        D

22. <u>Less</u> students chose liberal arts and <u>sciences</u> majors in the 1980s than in the 1960s <u>because of</u> the
    A   **B**   **C**
    contemporary view that a college education is a ticket to enter the job market. <u>No error</u>.
                                                  D

23. Span of control is the term <u>that</u> refers to the <u>limits</u> of a leader's <u>ability for managing</u> those employees
                        A   **B**   **C**
    under his/her supervision. <u>No error</u>.
                      D

24. <u>Because some</u> people believe <u>strongly</u> that channelling, the <u>process by which</u> an individual goes into
    A   **B**   **C**
    a trance-like state and communicates the thoughts of an ancient warrior or guru to an audience, helps
    them cope with modern problems, but others condemn the whole idea as mere superstition. <u>No error</u>.
                                                                   D

25. The reed on a woodwind instrument is <u>essential</u> <u>being that</u> it controls the quality of <u>tone and sound</u>.
                                    A   **B**   **C**
    <u>No error</u>.
    D

Part B: Sentence Correction

DIRECTIONS: In each of the following sentences some portion of the sentence is underlined. Under each sentence are four choices. The first choice has the same wording as the original. The other three choices are reworded. Sometimes the first choice containing the original wording is the best; sometimes one of the other choices is the best. Choose the letter of the best choice. Your choice should produce a sentence that is not ambiguous or awkward and that is correct, clear, and precise.

This is a test of correct and effective English expression. Keep in mind the standards of English usage, punctuation, grammar, word choice, and construction.

EXAMPLE:

When you listen to opera, <u>a person may not appreciate it</u>.

(A) a person may not appreciate it.
(B) it may not be appreciated by a person.
(C) you may not appreciate it.
(D) appreciating it may be a problem for you.

26. Two-thirds of American 17-year-olds do not know that the Civil War <u>takes place</u> between 1850–1900.

(A) takes place
(B) took place
(C) had taken place
(D) have taken place

27. Both professional and amateur ornithologists, <u>people that study birds</u>, recognize the Latin or scientific names of bird species.

(A) people that study birds
(B) people which study birds
(C) the study of birds
(D) people who study birds

28. Many of the oil-producing states spent their huge surplus tax revenues during the oil boom of the 1970s and early 1980s <u>in spite of the fact that</u> oil production from new wells began to flood the world market as early as 1985.

(A) in spite of the fact that
(B) even in view of the fact that
(C) even though
(D) when it was clear that

29. The president of the community college reported <u>as to the expectability of the tuition increase as well as the actual amount</u>.

    (A) as to the expectability of the tuition increase as well as the actual amount
    (B) that the tuition will likely increase by a specific amount
    (C) as to the expectability that tuition will increase by a specific amount
    (D) about the expected tuition increase of five percent

30. Although Carmen developed an interest in classical music, <u>she did not read notes and had never played an instrument</u>.

    (A) she did not read notes and had never played an instrument
    (B) she does not read notes and has never played an instrument
    (C) it is without being able to read notes or having played an instrument
    (D) it is without reading notes nor having played an instrument

31. Political candidates must campaign on issues and ideas that strike a chord within their constituency but <u>with their goal to sway</u> undecided voters to support their candidacy.

    (A) with their goal to sway
    (B) need also to sway
    (C) aiming at the same time to sway
    (D) also trying to sway

32. The major reasons students give for failing courses in college <u>is that they have demanding professors and work at</u> full- or part-time jobs.

    (A) is that they have demanding professors and work at
    (B) are demanding professors and they work at
    (C) are demanding professors, in addition to working at
    (D) are that they have demanding professors and that they have

33. <u>Having command of color, symbolism, as well as technique</u>, Georgia O'Keeffe is considered to be a great American painter.

    (A) Having command of color, symbolism, as well as technique
    (B) Having command of color, symbolism, and her technical ability
    (C) Because of her command of color, symbolism, and technique
    (D) With her command of color and symbolism and being technical

34. <u>Whether the ancient ancestors of American Indians actually migrated or did not</u> across a land bridge now covered by the Bering Strait remains uncertain, but that they could have has not been refuted by other theories.

    (A) Whether the ancient ancestors of American Indians actually migrated or did not
    (B) That the ancient ancestors of American Indians actually did migrate
    (C) Whether in actuality the ancient ancestors of American Indians migrated or not
    (D) That the ancient ancestors of American Indians may actually have migrated

35. Caution in scientific experimentation can <u>sometimes be related more to integrity than to lack of knowledge</u>.

    (A) sometimes be related more to integrity than to lack of knowledge
    (B) sometimes be related more to integrity as well as lack of knowledge
    (C) often be related to integrity as to lack of knowledge
    (D) be related more to integrity rather than lack of knowledge

36. Separated by their successful rebellion against England from any existing form of government, the citizens of the United States <u>have developed a unique constitutional political system</u>.

    (A) have developed a unique constitutional political system
    (B) had developed their constitutional political system uniquely
    (C) have developed their political system into a very unique constitutional one
    (D) have a unique political system, based on a constitution

37. <u>Returning to the ancestral home after 12 years, the house itself seemed much smaller to Joe</u> than it had been when he visited it as a child.

    (A) Returning to the ancestral home after 12 years, the house itself seemed much smaller to Joe
    (B) When Joe returned to the ancestral home after 12 years, he thought the house itself much smaller
    (C) Joe returned to the ancestral home after 12 years, and then he thought the house itself much smaller
    (D) After Joe returned to the ancestral home in 12 years, the house itself seemed much smaller

38. Historians say that the New River of North Carolina, Virginia, and West Virginia, <u>which is 2,700 feet above sea level and 2,000 feet above</u> the surrounding foothills, is the oldest river in the United States.

    (A) which is 2,700 feet above sea level and 2,000 feet above
    (B) with a height of 2,700 feet above sea level as well as 2,000 feet above that of
    (C) 2,700 feet higher than sea level and ascending 2,000 feet above
    (D) located 2,700 feet high above sea level while measuring 2,000 feet above

39. <u>The age of 36 having been reached</u>, the Ukrainian-born Polish sailor Teodor Josef Konrad Korzeniowski changed his name to Joseph Conrad and began a new and successful career as a British novelist and short story writer.

    (A) The age of 36 having been reached
    (B) When having reached the age of 36
    (C) When he reached the age of 36
    (D) At 36, when he reached that age

40. During the strike, Black South African miners threw a cordon around the <u>gold mine, and they thereby blocked it to all white workers</u>.

    (A) gold mine, and they thereby blocked it to all white workers
    (B) gold mine, by which all white workers were therefore blocked
    (C) gold mine and therefore blocking it to all white workers
    (D) gold mine, thereby blocking it to all white workers

Subtest IV: Essay

TIME: 50 Minutes

DIRECTIONS: Two topics are presented below. Select one of the topics as the basis for your essay. **READ THE TOPICS VERY CAREFULLY TO MAKE SURE YOU KNOW WHAT YOU ARE BEING ASKED TO DO.**

TOPIC 1:

Many leaders have suggested over the last few years that instead of a military draft we should require all young people to serve the public in some way for a period of time. The service could be military or any other reasonable form of public service. Do you agree or disagree with the statement? Support your opinion with specific examples from history, current events, literature, or personal experience.

OR

TOPIC 2:

The old saying "Experience is the best teacher" suggests to some people that they would benefit more from learning on the job or in the world than from continuing their formal education in the school or college classroom.

ASSIGNMENT:

Write an essay in which you discuss the relative values of experiential and academic learning. Support your view with specific examples from literature, history, current events, or personal experience.

Practice Test 2

ANSWER KEY

Subtest I — Reading

1.	(A)	11.	(D)	21.	(D)	31.	(B)
2.	(A)	12.	(C)	22.	(D)	32.	(A)
3.	(C)	13.	(D)	23.	(B)	33.	(B)
4.	(B)	14.	(B)	24.	(B)	34.	(A)
5.	(A)	15.	(A)	25.	(C)	35.	(B)
6.	(C)	16.	(C)	26.	(D)	36.	(A)
7.	(C)	17.	(A)	27.	(B)	37.	(A)
8.	(A)	18.	(C)	28.	(A)	38.	(D)
9.	(D)	19.	(A)	29.	(D)	39.	(B)
10.	(A)	20.	(C)	30.	(D)	40.	(D)

Subtest II — Mathematics

1.	(B)	13.	(D)	25.	(B)	37.	(D)
2.	(B)	14.	(B)	26.	(C)	38.	(A)
3.	(B)	15.	(B)	27.	(D)	39.	(D)
4.	(A)	16.	(A)	28.	(C)	40.	(C)
5.	(A)	17.	(D)	29.	(B)	41.	(D)
6.	(B)	18.	(A)	30.	(C)	42.	(A)
7.	(A)	19.	(C)	31.	(C)	43.	(C)
8.	(B)	20.	(C)	32.	(C)	44.	(D)
9.	(C)	21.	(A)	33.	(C)	45.	(A)
10.	(C)	22.	(C)	34.	(D)		
11.	(B)	23.	(D)	35.	(B)		
12.	(B)	24.	(B)	36.	(B)		

Subtest III — English Language Skills

1.	(A)	11.	(B)	21.	(B)	31.	(B)
2.	(B)	12.	(A)	22.	(A)	32.	(D)
3.	(B)	13.	(A)	23.	(C)	33.	(C)
4.	(B)	14.	(B)	24.	(A)	34.	(B)
5.	(A)	15.	(A)	25.	(B)	35.	(A)
6.	(A)	16.	(C)	26.	(B)	36.	(A)
7.	(A)	17.	(D)	27.	(D)	37.	(B)
8.	(A)	18.	(D)	28.	(C)	38.	(A)
9.	(C)	19.	(C)	29.	(B)	39.	(C)
10.	(D)	20.	(C)	30.	(A)	40.	(D)

Detailed Explanations
of Answers

Subtest I: Reading

1. **(A)**

   Choices (B) and (D) present minor problems in spa maintenance. As bacteria and viruses are controlled by both temperature and chemicals, it becomes a possible source of health problems if ignored.

2. **(A)**

   Choices (B), (C), and (D) are correct levels or degrees.

3. **(C)**

   Choices (A) and (B) represent an inference that goes beyond the scope of the passage and would indicate biases of the reader. Although the passage explains spa maintenance, choice (D), the information is not adequate to serve as a detailed guide.

4. **(B)**

   The other choices, (A) and (C), refer to chemical or temperature maintenance. Although choice (D) helps to ensure clarity, choice (B) is explicitly stated in the passage.

5. **(A)**

   Choices (B), (C), and (D) are appropriate chemicals. Although chlorine is an alternative to bromine, this passage indicates it should be granular as indicated in choice (A).

6. **(C)**

   Choices (A) and (B) appear to be acceptable, whereas choice (D) indicates a perfect correlation. Choice (C) is correct as the passage is about correlational statistical significance, which permits prediction.

7. **(C)**

   Choice (A) goes beyond the information provided in the passage. Choice (B) is incorrect as correlation cannot indicate causality. Choice (D) is not statistically possible. The high positive correlation trend indicates that these variables are important to consider for future research. Thus, choice (C) is correct.

8.   **(A)**

Choices (B), (C), and (D) represent inferences that are based on inadequate information, which go beyond the scope of the passage. As these story elements are not taught explicitly in the first grade or prior to entering school, children apparently have picked up these elements from their exposures to stories as indicated by choice (A).

9.   **(D)**

Although the content might be appropriate for each of the journals, choices (A), (B), and (C), the style of writing suggests that it would be most appropriate for choice (D), *Reading Research Quarterly*, as this passage reports research results.

10.   **(A)**

The passage provides information for the grade level and mentions if it was significant or substantial. As this statement follows information provided for fifth/sixth grades, it refers to that level, thus choice (A).

11.   **(D)**

Choices (A), (B), and (C) all connote extreme or inappropriate attitudes not expressed in the passage. The author presents an informed concern—choice (D).

12.   **(C)**

For the other choices, (A), (B), and (D), the criteria, the role, the discussion, and the assurance for communication or learning are not provided in the passage. The passage stresses the importance of authenticity in communication—choice (C).

13.   **(D)**

Each of the choices is a possible definition, but the passage overall suggests that communication needs to be developed so that students' responses may become more significant and authentic—choice (D).

14.   **(B)**

Choices (A) and (D) are not supported by the passage. Choice (C) represents an incorrect conclusion. Choice (B) is supported by the various investigators' explanations.

15. **(A)**

As stated explicitly in the passage, the various investigators have attempted to explain the role of imitation in language—choice (A). The other choices go beyond the scope of the passage.

16. **(C)**

As the investigators studied different aspects of language while attempting to explain the role of imitation in language, choice (C) is correct. The other choices go beyond the scope of the passage.

17. **(A)**

The passage explicitly states that computers are capable of addressing the issues of practice and the true act of reading, choice (A). The other choices represent inferences that are not supported by the passage.

18. **(C)**

Although the reader might make inferences to select choices (A), (B), and (D), ways to use a word processor to make practice resemble the true reading act are not stated in the passage. Thus, choice (C) is the correct answer.

19. **(A)**

Although audiences in choices (B), (C), and (D) may benefit from the information provided in the passage, the passage explicitly states that a greater understanding of the information in the passage should assist teachers—choice (A).

20. **(C)**

Each of the choices is a definition of variance. However, for this passage, choice (C) is the most appropriate.

21. **(D)**

Although meaning is found in the components of each choice, the passage states that we should begin with students' meaning before moving to the commonalities of story meaning—choice (D).

22. **(D)**

As the passage presents information by various researchers on children's stories, the passage ends with an unanswered question that still needs to be addressed by reading researchers as provided in choice (D).

23. **(B)**

Although more information may be needed about story content and story structure as indicated in choices (A), (C), and (D), the main question that remains to be answered is choice (B).

24. **(B)**

Each choice provides partially correct information about story content and story structure; choice (B) provides the most complete response.

25. **(C)**

Each choice is a possible definition. However, choice (C) is most appropriate as there was an increased interest by researchers in these and other areas even though it has been an ongoing concern of some researchers.

26. **(D)**

Choice (B) is not supported by the passage. Choices (A) and (C) go beyond the passage. The last sentence states "The pattern . . . resulting in teachers prone to teach as they had been taught"—thus choice (D).

27. **(B)**

The other choices, (A), (C), and (D), are not supported by the passage. Although the passage mentions that teacher education has reflected evolving attitudes about education, the attitudes are not spelled out—choice (B).

28. **(A)**

Only choice (A) has the correct sequence; the other sequences are incorrect.

29. **(D)**

Choices (A), (B), and (C) are statements about education, teacher education, and teachers. Choice (D)'s statement that teacher education has changed very little implies that this lack of change could be a source of dissatisfaction.

30. **(D)**

Choices (A), (B), and (C) suggest rights either by heredity or supreme authority. The hyphenated term "liege-lord" connotes both entitled rights and power to command respect. Thus choice (D), "master" (one who assumes authority and property rights through ability and power to control), best represents the hawk.

31. **(B)**

Choices (C) and (D) are not supported by the passage. Choice (A) represents a possible conclusion, but choice (B) suggests real thought about the hawk.

32. **(A)**

Each of the other choices contains a term that does not refer to human qualities. The other qualities may refer to the hawk, e.g., perch, or to the author of the passage, e.g., disdain.

33. **(B)**

Choice (D) is incorrect because of definition. Choices (A) and (C) are possible definitions, but *feudal* most clearly denotes an association to the Middle Ages.

34. **(A)**

The passage explicitly states that political efficacy is a feeling that one's actions can have an impact on government—choice (A). Choices (B), (C), and (D) are not supported by the passage.

35. **(B)**

Choices (A), (C), and (D) are not supported by the passage. The passage states ". . . political social-ization, a process varying according to political systems but toward the end of indoctrinating the members to the respective political system"—choice (B).

36. **(A)**

Although the other choices (B), (C), and (D) are possible definitions, the passage explicitly states that "a political system is one of inputs, conversions, and outputs by which the wants of a society are transformed into binding decisions"—thus choice (A).

37. **(A)**

Choices (B), (C), and (D) contain an incorrect concept of either Easton and Dennis or Lipset. Only choice (A) has the correct concepts for both Easton and Dennis and Lipset.

38. **(D)**

Choices (A), (B), and (C) each contain an area that is considered a component of culture, such as religion, education, and language. Thus, choice (D) is the most appropriate response.

39. **(B)**

Although each definition appears appropriate, choices (A), (C), and (D) assume that a solution is known, or has been known at one time, and could be solved. Choice (B) suggests a situation that is intricate enough to perplex the mind. Choice (B) is most appropriate for this passage as a definition of enigma is an inexplicable situation.

40. **(D)**

Although choices (A), (B), and (C) may touch on such a topic, the roles and functions of governmental offices and departments are generally addressed in an American Government class. Thus, choice (D) is correct.

Subtest II: Mathematics

1. **(B)**

    Simplify the expressions to find the true statement. Remember, anything (except 0) to the 0 power is 1. 8^2 means 8×8, and 2^5 means $2 \times 2 \times 2 \times 2 \times 2$.

    $$5^0 \times 8^2 > 2^5$$

    $$1 \times 64 > 32$$

    $$64 > 32$$

2. **(B)**

    The mean IQ score of 100 is given. One standard deviation above the mean is 34% of the cases, with an IQ score up to 115. One standard deviation below the mean is another 34% of the cases, with an IQ score down to 85. So, a total of 68% of the students have an IQ between 85 and 115. Therefore, $1{,}500 \times .68 = 1{,}020$.

3. **(B)**

    Divide 4.8 by 2.4 to get 2.0. Then, to divide 10^5 by 10^3, keep the base the same and subtract the exponents to get 10^2. The correct answer is 2.0×10^2.

4. **(A)**

    $2^4 \times 5$ is the only set of prime factors that multiply together to get 80.
    $$2 \times 2 \times 2 \times 2 \times 5 = 80$$

5. **(A)**

    $$\$2{,}000 \times .35 = \$700.$$

    The rest have wrong computations.

6. **(B)**

    This is an arithmetic sequence, which means that there is a common difference between each number and the following one. The common difference is -6. Therefore, subtract 6 from 27 to find the next number in the pattern. $27 - 6 = 21$.

7.   (A)

Substitute in each (x, y) pair to find the one that makes a true statement.

$$y = 3x - 5$$
$$-11 = 3(-2) - 5$$
$$-11 = -6 - 5$$
$$-11 = -11$$

8.   (B)

Follow the order of operations to simplify the expression.

$|8 - 6| + 3 \div 3 \times 4^2 - 2$	The problem.
$2 + 3 \div 3 \times 4^2 - 2$	Simplify inside grouping symbols (absolute value bars are grouping symbols)
$2 + 3 \div 3 \times 16 - 2$	Simplify exponents.
$2 + 1 \times 16 - 2$	Do division.
$2 + 16 - 2$	Do multiplication.
$18 - 2$	Do addition.
16	Do subtraction.

9.   (C)

There are 2,000 pounds in a ton. Multiply 8.25 by 2,000 to get 16,500 pounds.

10.   (C)

The best sample would be the one which contains the least bias. A sampling of students from each grade would be the best sample.

11.   (B)

This problem can be solved by guess and check or by algebra. To determine the length and width of Alejandra's room by guess and check, look for two numbers that multiply to get 288. One number must be twice the other number. Using algebra, you can write the following key:

$$w = \text{width}$$

$$2w = \text{length}$$

The equation that represents the area is:

$$w(2w) = 288$$

$$2w^2 = 288 \qquad \text{Divide both sides by 2}$$

$$w^2 = 144 \qquad \text{Take the square root of both sides.}$$

$$w = 12 \qquad \text{The width of Alejandra's room is 12 feet.}$$

$$2w = 24 \qquad \text{The length of her room is 24 feet}$$

12. (B)

The first step is to find the volume of the box in cubic inches (because the measurements are given in inches). The volume of a box is found by using the formula $V = lwh$. The volume is $14 \times 16 \times 20$, which equals 4480 cubic inches. To find the number of cubic feet in 4480 inches, you need to know how many cubic inches there are in a cubic foot. A cubic foot is 12 inches by 12 inches by 12 inches, which equals 1728 cubic inches. Divide 4480 by 1728 to find the number of cubic feet in 1728. Then round the answer to the nearest hundredth, as instructed. There are approximately 2.59 cubic feet in 4480 cubic inches.

13. (D)

A large outlier will pull the mean up, so (D) is the correct answer. The range, too, will be higher, but the range is not a measure of central tendency.

14. (B)

There are 2 green tiles and a total of $12 + 6 + 2 = 20$ tiles. The probability of selecting a green tile is $\dfrac{2}{20}$.

15. (B)

Using the formula $D = RT$ (distance equals rate times time), you can find that Danny drove $3.5 \times 55 = 192.5$ miles before stopping for lunch. To find how many more miles he has to drive, subtract 192.5 from 300, the total number of miles Danny must drive.

$$300 - 192.5 = 107.5.$$

16. (A)

Divide the total price by the number of bagels to find the unit price for one bagel. The best deal (at 29 cents per bagel) is 15 bagels for $4.35.

17. (D)

To solve this problem, first set up and solve proportions to find the length and width of the volleyball court in real life.

$$\frac{1}{3} = \frac{3}{x}$$

$x = 9$ The width of the volleyball court in real life is 9 meters.

$$\frac{1}{3} = \frac{6}{x}$$

$x = 18$ The length of the volleyball court in real life is 18 meters.

Now, find the area of the court by multiplying length by width. $9 \times 18 = 162$. The area of the volleyball court is 162 square meters.

18. (A)

This sequence shows a geometric sequence. Each number is found by multiplying the previous number by 5. To find the next number, multiply 125 by 5, which is 625.

19. (C)

Let the variable S stand for the cost of the shirt. Then the cost of the pair of pants is $S + 25$ and

$$S + (S + 25) = 65$$

$$2S = 65 - 25$$

$$2S = 40$$

$$S = 20$$

$20 (cost of shirt)

$20 + $25 = $45 (cost of pants)

20. (C)

The possible handshakes are illustrated by listing all the possible pairs of letters. Thus,

AB   AC   AD   AE

BC   BD   BE

CD   CE

DE

(a total of 10 handshakes)

21. (A)

There are 3 feet in every yard, so divide 794 by 3 to find the number of yards in 794 feet. The answer is $264\frac{2}{3}$ yards.

22. (C)

There are 60 minutes in an hour, so divide 145 by 60 to find the number of hours in 145 minutes. There are two hours and 25 minutes in 145 minutes. 25 minutes is $\frac{25}{60}$ of an hour, which can be simplified to $\frac{5}{12}$. Therefore, 145 minutes is the same as $2\frac{5}{12}$ hours.

23. (D)

You can solve this problem using algebra. Write a key for the length and width of the picture frame.

w = width

$2w + 2$ = length

To find the perimeter of a rectangle, add all four sides together. That is two widths and two lengths. Write an equation and solve it.

$w + w + 2w + 2 + 2w + 2 = 88$

$6w + 4 = 88$ Collect like terms.

$6w = 84$ Subtract 4 from both sides.

$w = 14$ The width is 14 inches.

Substitute in 14 for w in $2w + 2$ to find the length. $2(14) + 2 = 30$. The length is 30 inches.

24. (B)

Points ABCDE are the vertices. Thus, 5 is correct.

25. (B)

Let

D = down payment

$D = \$20,000 \times .20$

$D = \$4,000$

26. **(C)**

      20% of $3,200 = $640 (amount price reduced)

      $3,200 − $640 = $2,560 (sale price)

27. **(D)**

Let x = 5th grade

$$\text{Average} = \frac{65+85+60+90+x}{5}$$

For Sue to obtain a C, her average must be greater than or equal to 70 but less than 80.

$$70 \leq \frac{65+85+60+90+x}{5}$$

$$70 \leq \frac{300+x}{5} < 80$$

$$5(70) \leq 5(300 + x) \div 5 < 5(80)$$

$$350 \leq 300 + x < 400$$

$$350 - 300 \leq x < 400 - 300$$

$$50 \leq x < 100$$

Thus, a grade of 50 up to but not including a grade of 100 will result in a C.

28. **(C)**

All but (C) are constraints. The constraint for y is to at least make two mowers.

29. **(B)**

When an angle is opening to the right, use the inside scale. The angle is 39 degrees.

30. **(C)**

Although all four answer choices have four sides, the best answer is a parallelogram. You cannot choose square or rectangle because you do not know if the angles are right angles.

31. **(C)**

Simple multiplication: $7 \times 4 = 28$.

32. **(C)**

Ordered pairs with negative *x*- and *y*-coordinates are in Quadrant III. Point (−3, −8) is shown graphed below.

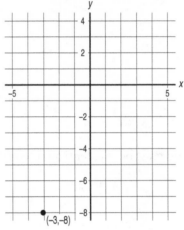

33. **(C)**

The only street which is parallel to NW 3rd Street is NW 6th Street. The two streets are parallel because they will never intersect.

34. **(D)**

First find out how many shares of $1,000 there are in $50,000.

$50,000 ÷ 1,000 = 50

Then, multiply the shares by the cost (50 × $32) and the answer is $1,600.

35. **(B)**

Substitute the values of 35 and 75 as legs in the Pythagorean theorem to find the hypotenuse.

$$a^2 + b^2 = c^2$$
$$35^2 + 75^2 = c^2$$
$$1225 + 5625 = c^2$$
$$6850 = c^2$$
$$83 \approx c$$

36. **(B)**

    If each ⬚ $ stands for $12, weeks 3 and 4 had a sale of $72 and $60, respectively. The rest are below $55.

37. **(D)**

    The slope of a line is the rate. Every hour that Laura works she earns $15.

38. **(A)**

    A translation is a shifting up, down, left, or right. This diagram illustrates a translation. Since you do not know which is the original footprint and which is the image, you don't know if the translation is to the left or to the right; however, you do not need to know this to answer the question correctly.

39. **(D)**

    In order to indicate that the amount in parentheses $(x - 3)$ is being multiplied by 5, you must say, "the quantity x minus three".

40. **(C)**

    There are two steps to solve this problem. First you have to find the distance between the two points on the graph, and then you have to find the distance it represents using 1 unit = 10 feet. The coordinates for the lifeguard are (5, 7), and the coordinates for Kaylie are (2, 3). Use the distance formula to find the distance.

    $$\text{Distance} = \sqrt{(x_2 - x_1)^2 + (y_2 - y_1)^2}$$
    $$\text{Distance} = \sqrt{(5-2)^2 + (7-3)^2}$$
    $$\text{Distance} = \sqrt{(3)^2 + (4)^2}$$
    $$\text{Distance} = \sqrt{9+16}$$
    $$\text{Distance} = \sqrt{25}$$
    $$\text{Distance} = 5$$

    Now that you know the distance between the points on the graph is 5 units, use the scale given (1 unit = 10 feet) to find the distance. 5 × 10 = 50. The distance between Kaylie and the lifeguard is 50 feet.

41. **(D)**

    First, find out how many ounces of orange juice are needed. So, multiply 75 × 8 oz. = 600 oz. needed. Then, divide 600 by 12 oz. = 50 12 oz. cans needed to serve 75 people with 8 oz. of juice each.

42. **(A)**

m = number of miles you can travel

$\$0.08m$ = amount spent for m miles travelled at 8 cents per mile,

(rental fee + mileage charge = total amount spent)

$\$139 + \$0.08m = \$350$

$139 - 139 + 0.08m = 350 - 139$

$$\frac{0.08m}{0.08} = \frac{211}{0.08}$$

$m = 2{,}637.5$

$m = 2{,}637$

Therefore, you can travel 2,637 miles (if you go 2,638 miles you have travelled too far).

43. **(C)**

To answer this question, first you must find the least common multiple of 5 and 12. This is 60. The next step is to find how many packages 60 notebooks is and how many packages 60 pencils is. Pencils come 12 in a package, so divide 60 by 12 to get 5; there will be 5 packages of pencils. Notebooks come in packages of 5, do divide 60 by 5 to get 12; there will be 12 packages of notebooks.

44. **(D)**

Let m = number of miles covered the 1st day.

$m + 30$ = number of miles covered the 2nd day,

$m + 30 + 30$ = number of miles covered the 3rd day,

$m + 30 + 30 + 30$ = number of miles covered the 4th day,

$m + 30 + 30 + 30 + 30$ = number of miles covered the 5th day.

$m + m + 30$ and so on . . . = 1,500

$5m + 30\,(10) = 1{,}500$

$5m + 300 = 1{,}500$

$5m = 1{,}500 - 300$

$5m = 1{,}200$

$$m = \frac{1{,}200}{5}$$

$m = 240$ mi.

45. (A)

Substitute (7, –20) into each of the equations until you find one that is true.

$$y = -3x + 1$$
$$-20 = -3(7) + 1$$
$$-20 = -21 + 1$$
$$-20 = -20$$ This is a true statement. (7, –20) is a solution to the equation.

Correlation with FTCE Competency/Skill

Competency/ Skill	Problem Number
	Total of 8 in section 1
1.1	14, 31, 32
1.2	23, 39
1.3	11
1.4	2, 30
	Total of 10 in section 2
2.1	6, 38
2.2	9, 27, 41
2.3	22
2.4	17, 21
2.5	25
2.6	19
	Total of 9 in section 3
3.1	5
3.2	3, 24, 40, 45
3.3	18, 33
3.4	12, 37

Competency/ Skill	Problem Number
	Total of 9 in section 4
4.1	15, 16
4.2	1, 34
4.3	8, 13, 36
4.4	7, 20
	Total of 9 in section 5
5.1	10, 42
5.2	28
5.3	4, 43
5.4	29
5.5	26
5.6	35, 44

Key: 1.3 means Competency 1 Skill 3

Competency/Skill	Approximate # of Questions
MATHEMATICS The test center will provide a 4-function calculator. The test center will provide a reference sheet.	
1 Knowledge of number sense, concepts, and operations	**8**
1 Compare the relative value of real numbers (e.g., integers, fractions, decimals, percents, irrational numbers, and numbers expressed in exponential or scientific notation.) 2 Solve real-world problems involving addition, subtraction, multiplication, and division of rational numbers (e.g., whole numbers, integers, decimals, percents, and fractions including mixed numbers). 3 Apply basic number theory concepts including the use of primes, composites, factors, and multiples in solving problems. 4 Apply the order of operations with or without grouping symbols.	
2 Knowledge of measurement (using customary or metric units)	**10**
1 Solve real-world problems involving length, weight, mass, perimeter, area, capacity, and volume. 2 Solve real-world problems involving rated measures (e.g., miles per hour, meters per second, cost per item, and cost per unit). 3 Solve real-world problems involving scaled drawings (e.g., maps, blueprints, and models). 4 Solve real-world problems involving the change of units of measures of length, weight, mass, capacity, and time. 5 Solve real-world problems involving estimates of measures including length, weight, mass, temperature, time, money, perimeter, area, and volume. 6 Choose the correct reading, to a specified degree of accuracy, using instruments (e.g., scales, rulers, thermometers, measuring cups, protractors, and gauges).	

Competency/Skill		Approximate # of Questions
3	**Knowledge of geometry and spatial sense**	**9**
	1 Identify and/or classify simple two- and three-dimensional figures according to their properties.	
	2 Solve real-world and mathematical problems involving ratio, proportion, similarity, congruence, and the Pythagorean relationship.	
	3 Identify the location of ordered pairs of integers in all four quadrants of a coordinate system (graph) and use the coordinate system to apply the concepts of slope and distance to solve problems.	
	4 Identify real-world examples that represent geometric concepts including perpendicularity, parallelism, tangency, symmetry, and transformations (e.g., flips, slides, and turns).	
4	**Knowledge of algebraic thinking**	**9**
	1 Analyze and generalize patterns including arithmetic and geometric sequences.	
	2 Interpret algebraic expressions using words, symbols, variables, tables, and graphs.	
	3 Solve equations and inequalities graphically or algebraically.	
	4 Determine whether a number or ordered pair is among the solutions of given equations or inequalities.	
5	**Knowledge of data analysis and probability**	**9**
	1 Analyze data and solve problems using data presented in histograms, bar graphs, ,circle graphs, pictographs, tables, and charts.	
	2 Identify how the presentation of data can lead to different or inappropriate interpretations.	
	3 Calculate range, mean, median, and mode(s) from sets of data and interpret the meaning of the measures of central tendency (i.e., mean, median, and mode) and dispersion (i.e., range and standard deviation).	
	4 Identify how the measures of central tendency (i.e., mean, median, or mode) can lead to different interpretations.	
	5 Calculate the probability of a specified outcome.	
	6 Solve and interpret real-world problems involving probability using counting procedures, tables, tree diagrams, and the concepts of permutations and combinations.	

Subtest III: English Language Skills

1. **(A)**

    Choice (A) is obviously wordy, "consensus" meaning the same as "general agreement," so it is the best choice. None of the others has a usage error. Choice (B) underscores the claim made in the whole sentence by establishing the book as the "best" American work. Finally, choice (C) is acceptable because of commas in other parts of the sentence. Choice (D) clearly does not apply.

2. **(B)**

    This question has several potential errors. Choice (A) calls to question the attribution of human rationality to an inanimate object, but since the Constitution actually does have logical premises, we can correctly say that the document can posit the premise stated. Choice (C) is acceptable because the superlative is referenced within the sentence; one should know that the U.S. government has three branches. That leaves choices (B) and (D). Choice (B) is the verb in the clause beginning with the word "what"; it is plural, and therefore, incorrect because it does not agree with its subject "history," a singular noun. Do not be fooled by the intervening plural word "governments." Since choice (B) is the error, choice (D) would no longer be considered.

3. **(B)**

    Even though people use "like" as a conjunction in conversation and public speaking, it is a preposition, and formal written English requires "as," "as if," or "as though" when what follows is a clause. No other choice is even suspect.

4. **(B)**

    One could question the use of "nearly" (A), but it is correct. One might argue also that "million dollars" (C) should be written "$1 million," but choice (B) is so clearly an incorrect use of the past perfect tense that the other possibilities, remote at best, pale by comparison. The simple past tense ("sold"), the present progressive tense ("are selling"), or the present perfect progressive tense ("have been selling") could each be used correctly depending on the meaning intended.

5. **(A)**

    This choice is not as obvious, but authorities agree that the use of "expect" to mean "suppose" or "believe" (the usage here) is either informal or colloquial, but again not formal written English. The next most likely choice, (D), would suggest that informal or colloquial usage is appropriate. The third most likely choice, (C), brings to mind the distinction between "accept" and "except," a word pair often confused. However, "accept" is correct here.

6. **(A)**

Regardless of its popular usage "hopefully" is an adverb trying to be a clause ("it is hoped" or "I hope"). However, instances still exist that require a distinction between the two uses. To be clear, use, "hopefully" when you mean "in a hopeful manner." ["He wished hopefully that she would accept his proposal of marriage."] Choice (C) appears suspicious. "Continually" means recurrence at intervals over a period of time, so it is correctly used to imply that machines do break down often. (B) Capitalizing "Twentieth Century" is also appropriate as it is here used as the specific historical period (like the "Middle Ages"). We would not capitalize the phrase if it were used simply to count, as in "The twentieth century from now will surely find enormous changes in the world." It is incorrect to hyphenate a number-noun phrase like this one when it stands alone as a noun phrase.

7. **(A)**

The two most suspicious choices are (A) and (C) because the item is a sentence fragment. No reasonable substitute for (C) would solve both the logic problem (incomplete thought) and the punctuation problem (comma splice if you omit "that"). Changing "showing" to "show" would, however, make the clause into a complete sentence with correct punctuation. Choice (B) does not provoke suspicion.

8. **(A)**

Again, the two most questionable choices, (A) and (B), compete for our attention. The use of "but" makes sense because it shows contrast to the previous idea. ("Don't evade or defy the law, *but* if caught breaking a law, accept the penalty.") The use of "or," however, is clearly not parallel to the immediately preceding use of "neither." The proper phrase is "neither . . . nor" for negative alternate choices. Choice (C) does not demand a second look.

9. **(C)**

This choice involves parallel construction, or the lack of it. The word "both" introduces a pair of phrases, one a prepositional phrase ("for their own interests"), the other an infinitive phrase ("to gain more goods"). Aside from being inelegant, "to gain more goods" is also not the same structure and should be changed to "their own gain" to make the two phrases perfectly parallel. Choice (C) is not problematic. Choice (A) is another candidate because of the capitalization and the lack of a hyphen between "Eighteenth" and "Century." The capitalization is correct and no hyphen is needed when the phrase becomes an adjective that has meaning as a single phrase, which the capitalization suggests, or if the first word forms a familiar pair with the following word and if there is no danger of confusion. [The sentence clearly does not mean that Smith is the eighteenth (small "e") philosopher, but *the* Eighteenth Century philosopher.]

10. **(D)**

The other choices all fail to exhibit inappropriate usage. Choice (A), "cannot," is spelled as one word; choice (B), "should not," is parallel to "cannot" and adds meaning necessary to the thought. Finally, choice (C) is a third-person plural verb agreeing with its subject, "reasons."

11. **(B)**

"Milky Way galaxy" is the singular antecedent, for which the pronoun referent should be "its" (inanimate object). Do not be confused by the intervening words ("stars" and "spots"); it is the galaxy which shines in this sentence, not the stars or the spots. Choice (A) is the correct usage of "comprises." Choice (C) is appropriate because the sentence has an internally supplied superlative sense; it does not need a "brightest of" phrase.

12. **(A)**

Again, non-parallel structure is the key of this and many other test items. Because of the overwhelming importance of understanding balance in sentence structure, tests like this one emphasize parallel sentence structures. "To learn" clashes with "studying" in the parallel clause. You cannot choose "studying." "Learning" substituted for "To learn" would make the clauses parallel. Choice (B) is a correct use of "like" as a preposition (objects: "Latin," "Greek"). Choice (C) is correctly singular as the verb of the noun phrase "studying . . . beliefs."

13. **(A)**

This is a colloquial, nonstandard substitution for the correct word, "attribute." Choice (B) is correctly lowercase, not capitalized. Choice (C) is a correct, if a bit stiff, phrase.

14. **(B)**

This is an incorrect simple past verb tense. You have to spot the context clue "most Americans" "attended" school in the past, which suggests they no longer do so now. They must then "choose" their entertainment. Choice (A) is questionable, but the present participial phrase suggests coincidence with the time "most Americans" "attended school." It is, therefore, correct. Choice (C) is correctly an infinitive that is parallel to "to watch."

15. **(A)**

The two most questionable choices are (A) and (B). Choice (A) is incorrectly a subjective case pronoun when it should be objective (object of verb "makes," subject "What"). If you know the difference between "different from" (correctly used in this sentence) and "difference than" (correctly used only to introduce a clause), then choice (B) is no longer viable. Besides being a passive construction, choice (C) has no objectionable qualities; it is grammatically correct.

16. **(C)**

This is a case of subject-verb disagreement related to the definition of the word "neither" (subject) as singular. Its verb must also be singular, and "differ" is plural. Choice (A) correctly uses English idiom ("compare to"—"contrast with"). Choice (B) is a singular verb agreeing with its subject, "one."

17. **(D)**

Everything in the sentence is acceptable or correct usage, even though some of it may be a bit stuffy and pedantic, i.e., choice (A). Choice (B) correctly agrees with its subject "which" (plural, antecedent "archetypes"). Choice (C) might be considered redundant ("repeated" and "patterns"), but that is not apparent from the context.

18. **(D)**

You are likely to have chosen either (A) or (B) here. The affect/effect word pair often confuses students, and this instance is one in which "effected" is correctly used as a verb meaning "brought about" or "caused to happen." The question in choice (B) is whether or not to capitalize the word "Fate." When it refers to the collective term for the Greek concept of destiny (actually gods, the Fates), as it does here, it is appropriately capitalized. Choice (C) does not seem questionable.

19. **(C)**

Again, the problem here is pronoun-antecedent agreement. "Their" does not refer to the three writers collectively; its antecedent is "each," which is always singular, not plural ("each one"). There is nothing wrong with choices (A) and (B).

20. **(C)**

The error here is known as faulty predication ("reason . . . is because"). The usage rule is that "because" is redundant for "reason." Choice (A) is appropriate, if a bit general (not 30 or 70 percent, for example). The verb in choice (B) is correct and in the past tense.

21. **(B)**

Choice (A) is a verb correctly in agreement with its compound subject. Choice (C) correctly uses the word "comprises" and makes it agree with its subject. Only (B) seems incorrect. The structure requires the adverb form "constantly," since it describes an adjective, "expanding."

22. **(A)**

This is the classic confusion of "less" for the correct "fewer." "Few(er)" refers to countable things or persons; "little (less)" refers to things that can be measured or estimated but not itemized.

23. **(C)**

Choice (A) is a correct use of the relative pronoun. Nothing is unusual about (B). (C) is the culprit here: it should be the infinitive form to adhere to the idiom, "ability to (verb)."

24. **(A)**

The sentence as it stands is illogical. Removing "Because" will make it sensible. (B) is an appropriate adverb modifying "believe"; (C) is a clear and effective subordination of an explanation of a term.

25. **(B)**

"Being that" is colloquial for "because," which is better for at least the reason that it is shorter, but also that it is more formal. No other choices seem out of bounds.

26. **(B)**

This question of appropriate verb tense requires the simple past tense verb "took" because the Civil War happened in a finite time period in the past. The other choices all fail that test. The original is present tense, and does not logically fit the facts. Choice (D) is the present perfect tense, which suggests a continuous action from the past to the present. Choice (C) is the past perfect tense, which suggests a continuing action from one time in the past to another in the more recent past.

27. **(D)**

We can eliminate fairly quickly choice (C) as either an inappropriate or awkward appositive to "ornithology," instead of "ornithologists." Neither is (A) the best choice even though some may consider it acceptable. Likewise, choice (B) tends to be limited to nonrestrictive clauses, unlike this one. Choice (D) then correctly uses a "personal" relative pronoun.

28. **(C)**

Choices (A), (C), and (D) are the best candidates because they are more concise than the other two choices. Each does express the same idea, but (D) does not as strongly indicate the contrast between the two clauses in the sentence as do choices (A) and (C). Choice (C) clearly makes its point in fewer words and is the better choice.

29. **(B)**

The phrase "as to" often is overblown and unclear, so it is best to eliminate it when there are other choices. Likewise, "expectability" does not exactly roll off your tongue. That leaves choices (B) and (D). Choice (D) adds a definite figure, unwarranted by the original sentence. It also is duller than (B), which does change the wording for the better and also indicates that the "actual amount" is to be announced, rather than that it is already known.

30. **(A)**

Choices (C) and (D) introduce unnecessary absolute phrases beginning with "it," which makes the sentences wordy. They can be eliminated immediately. Between (A) and (B) the difference boils down to the present tense vs. the past tense. Choice (A) uses past tenses, which seem better in sequence to follow the past tense verb "developed."

31. **(B)**

Choices (A), (C), and (D) can be disqualified quickly because they are not parallel to the structure of the main clause. Choice (B) reads well and has the virtue of brevity.

32. **(D)**

The choices are easy to discern in this sentence. The original verb does not agree with its subject, nor is the structure parallel. Choice (B) does not have parallel structure (phrase and clause). Choice (C) does not logically agree with the subject ("reasons") since it names one ("demanding professors") but relegates the other reason to an afterthought. Choice (D) has both parallel structure and subject-verb agreement; it also names two reasons.

33. **(C)**

The original suffers from inadequate causal relationship and non-parallel structure. Choice (D) is unnecessarily wordy; (D) is still not parallel. Choice (B) switches its structure at the end. Although it is technically parallel, it is still awkward because of the addition of the possessive pronoun "her." Choice (C) solves both problems by clearly showing cause and by being parallel (three nouns in series).

34. **(B)**

This sentence presents an incomplete comparison and a redundancy ("Whether"/"or did not"/ "remains uncertain"). Choice (B) eliminates both problems clearly. Choice (C) is worse in both respects. Choice (D) clears up the syntax but leaves some redundancy ("may actually have"/"remains uncertain"). Choice (B) eliminates both problems clearly.

35. **(A)**

The sentence as is reads well; it is perfectly balanced. Choice (B) introduces an incomplete comparison ("more" but no "than"). Choice (C) awkwardly uses "as to." Choice (D) makes a scrambled mess by introducing an illogical structure.

36. **(A)**

"Unique" means just that; it should not have qualifiers like "very" or "nearly." That eliminates choice (C). Choice (B) changes the meaning by making the development unique, instead of the system. Choice (D) uses an inappropriate verb tense because the first of the sentence suggests the Revolutionary War period, definitely in the past.

37. **(B)**

The original sentence, (A), has a dangling modifier (participial phrase). The house cannot return to itself, nor can "it" (pronoun for house). Choice (D) seems to leave something out: "returned to . . . home in 12 years." Choice (C) solves the original problem but is unnecessarily wordy. Choice (B) properly solves the dangling modifier problem by subordinating the return in an adverbial clause.

38. **(A)**

Choice (A) is the only response that makes sense. Each of the others introduces illogical comparisons or structures (non-parallel); (B) and (D) are also verbose. Choice (C) is concise but not parallel.

39. **(C)**

This sentence suggests causal relationships between the parts of the sentence that do not belong there. Choice (B) echoes the original (A) in that regard. Choice (D) has garbled syntax. (C) shows clearly that the cause-effect relationship is, rather, a time relationship.

40. **(D)**

This is essentially a problem of wordiness. (D) is the shortest and most clear of all the choices. The syntax of (B) complicates the idea unnecessarily. (C) does not use the appropriate conjunctive adverb; "thereby" is more precise than "therefore" when referring to an event.

Essay Scoring Guide

The FTCE-GKT essay sections are scored by two writing experts on the basis of the criteria outlined below. In addition to comparing your essay to those included in our practice tests, you may use these guidelines to estimate your score on this section. Remember that your score is the sum of the scores of two writing experts, so provided you respond to the assigned topic, your score will fall somewhere between two and twelve. Scores will be assigned based on the following guidelines:

SCORE of 6: The paper has a clearly established main idea that the writer fully develops with specific details and examples. Organization is notably logical and coherent. Point of view is consistently maintained. Vocabulary and sentence structure are varied and effective. Errors in sentence structure, usage, and mechanics are few and insignificant.

SCORE of 5: The paper has a clearly established main idea that is adequately developed and recognizable through specific details and/or examples. Organization follows a logical and coherent pattern. Point of view is mostly maintained. Vocabulary and sentence structure are mostly varied and effective. Occasional errors in sentence structure, usage, and mechanics do not interfere with the writer's ability to communicate.

SCORE of 4: The paper has an adequately stated main idea that is developed with some specific details and examples. Supporting ideas are presented in a mostly logical and coherent manner. Point of view is somewhat maintained. Vocabulary and sentence structure are somewhat varied and effective. Occasional errors in sentence structure, usage, and mechanics may interfere with writer's ability to communicate.

SCORE of 3: The paper states a main idea that is developed with generalizations or lists. The paper may contain occasional lapses in logic and coherence, and organization is mechanical. Point of view is ambiguous. Vocabulary and sentence structure are repetitious and often ineffective. A variety of errors in sentence structure, usage, and mechanics sometimes interferes with the writer's ability to communicate.

SCORE of 2: The paper presents an incomplete or ambiguous main idea. Support is developed with generalizations and lists. Organization is mechanical. The paper contains occasional lapses in logic and coherence. Point of view is confusing and distracting. Word choice is simplistic, and sentence structure is disjointed. Errors in sentence structure, usage, and mechanics frequently interfere with the writer's ability to communicate.

SCORE of 1: The paper has no evident main idea. Development is inadequate and/or irrelevant. Organization is illogical and/or incoherent. Point of view has not been established. Vocabulary and sentence structure are garbled and confusing. Significant and numerous errors in sentence structure, usage, and mechanics interfere with the writer's ability to communicate.

Subtest IV: Sample Essays with Commentary

Topic 1

Strong Response

The cynic in me wants to react to the idea of universal public service for the young with a reminder about previous complaints aimed at the military draft. These complaints suggest that wars might never be fought if the first people drafted were the adult leaders and lawmakers. Still the idea of universal public service sounds good to this concerned citizen who sees everywhere—not just in youth—the effects of a selfish and self-indulgent culture.

One reads and hears constantly about young people who do not care about the problems of our society. These youngsters seem interested in money and the luxuries money can buy. They do not want to work from the minimum wage up, but want instead to land a high paying job without "paying their dues." An informal television news survey of high school students a few years ago suggested that students had the well entrenched fantasy that with no skills or higher education they would not accept a job paying less than $20 an hour. Perhaps universal service helping out in an urban soup kitchen for six months would instill a sense of selflessness rather than selfishness.

The shiny gleam of a new expensive sports sedan bought on credit by a recent accounting student reflects self indulgence that might be toned down by universal service. That self indulgence may reflect merely a lack of discipline, but it also may reflect a lack of purpose in life. Philosophers, theologians and leaders of all types suggest throughout the ages that money and objects do not ultimately satisfy. Helping others—service to our fellow human beings—often does. Universal public service for that accounting student might require a year helping low income or senior citizens prepare income tax forms. This type of service would dim that self indulgence, give the person some experience in the real world, and also give satisfaction that one's life is not lived only to acquire things.

Universal service might also help young people restore faith in their nation and what it means to them. Yes, this is the land of opportunity, but it is also a land of forgotten people, and it is a land that faces outside threats. Part of the requisite public service should remind young people of their past and of their responsibility to the future.

Analysis

This essay has a score range of 5–6. It uses a traditional structure: the first paragraph states the topic, the second and third present development with specific examples from personal observation. The fourth ends the essay, but it is not as strong a conclusion as it could be. The writer probably ran out of time. The essay as a whole is unified and uses pertinent examples to support the opinion stated. The sentence structure varies, and the vocabulary is effective. Generally, it is well done within the time limit.

Topic 2

Strong Response

Years ago, before formal education was available, everybody learned what they needed to know by experience. The prehistoric hunter-gatherers had assigned roles in the tribe or community, and each person learned their role by following an expert around and by practicing skills like hurling a spear or keeping a fire going. In a way, they were "learning on the job." Today, however, learning on the job no longer works for many of the technologically oriented jobs in the marketplace. People need some academic learning before or at the same time as experiential learning.

In the distant past of low technology, people learned how to do their work by practicing it under the direction of a parent or another experienced adult. Even the so-called primitive people had to learn how to hunt and what plants are edible in the process of becoming hunters and gatherers. There was no manual and no school of hunting or gathering. They learned skills at the knee of their elders. As technology advanced, more knowledge became necessary. And when agricultural life began to dominate, skills such as knowing when and what to plant were learned by experience, often harsh experience at that. As technology advances farther into the use of complex machinery, more people will need more formal training. An IBM television commercial a few years ago showed how farmers can be more productive when they use an IBM personal computer to help manage their business. You don't have to go to college to learn how to use a computer, but you probably need some specialized formal training.

Today, job recruiters constantly say that they need workers who can learn by experience, who are prepared by academic training to learn work skills. If you want to work in accounting, for instance, you need to learn the rules and practices of accounting before you can start working. Then you learn even more in the practice of auditing other people's books. Some jobs also require a lot of formal education before you can work in that job. Real estate sales, for example, requires a state license that can only be acquired after a certain number of hours of formal training. Even relatively skilled jobs that do not require college degrees may require some prior academic training. If you have little or no knowledge of applied mathematics, you will have a hard time doing carpentry or machinery work.

On the other hand, classroom training is often out of touch with the "real world." Part of that is by design. Most people will not use directly a subject like algebra in their work. They won't write essays or interpret poetry. These academic skills often are used to do other academic work, but they can contribute to the ability to learn by experience. Algebra and poetry interpretation both train us in abstract thinking and creative problem solving, which should make us more valuable to an employer. Essay writing skills can be adapted fairly easily to business writing requirements. In other words, a large part of our academic learning prepares us to learn academically at a higher level or to apply the skills we learn in schools and college to real jobs.

Even college graduates are often assigned to a person on the job who is supposed to help the new employee learn by experience. Sometimes, though, there is no such help and the school of experience becomes the school of "hard knocks." Each time the new employee makes an error, they can either learn from that error and adapt or, ultimately, lose their job. By the same token, the new employee can learn through success as well. If they find out how to enter data into a microcomputer software program like a spreadsheet in accounting, they can build on that success and try to use or write a macro (a sort of mini-program) to help them become even more productive.

So, it seems that both academic learning and learning by experience are valuable in a technologically advanced culture. The best and most satisfying jobs aren't learned overnight or just in school or college. They require a mixture of academic or formal training and experience that helps them build on the academic learning.

Analysis

This essay has a score range of 5–6. The introduction is well thought-out and presents a strong thesis. The body paragraphs are detailed and support the thesis clearly and completely. Their sound structure steps through the author's argument clearly and there are few grammatical or punctuation errors. The conclusion could be stronger, but based on the length and considering the time constraints, it is adequate. The author uses language well except for a persistent pronoun-antecedent agreement problem and a few grammatical errors.

FTCE

Florida Teacher Certification Examinations General Knowledge Test

Practice Test 3

Answer Sheet – Practice Test 3

Subtest I: Reading

1. Ⓐ Ⓑ Ⓒ Ⓓ
2. Ⓐ Ⓑ Ⓒ Ⓓ
3. Ⓐ Ⓑ Ⓒ Ⓓ
4. Ⓐ Ⓑ Ⓒ Ⓓ
5. Ⓐ Ⓑ Ⓒ Ⓓ
6. Ⓐ Ⓑ Ⓒ Ⓓ
7. Ⓐ Ⓑ Ⓒ Ⓓ
8. Ⓐ Ⓑ Ⓒ Ⓓ
9. Ⓐ Ⓑ Ⓒ Ⓓ
10. Ⓐ Ⓑ Ⓒ Ⓓ

11. Ⓐ Ⓑ Ⓒ Ⓓ
12. Ⓐ Ⓑ Ⓒ Ⓓ
13. Ⓐ Ⓑ Ⓒ Ⓓ
14. Ⓐ Ⓑ Ⓒ Ⓓ
15. Ⓐ Ⓑ Ⓒ Ⓓ
16. Ⓐ Ⓑ Ⓒ Ⓓ
17. Ⓐ Ⓑ Ⓒ Ⓓ
18. Ⓐ Ⓑ Ⓒ Ⓓ
19. Ⓐ Ⓑ Ⓒ Ⓓ
20. Ⓐ Ⓑ Ⓒ Ⓓ

21. Ⓐ Ⓑ Ⓒ Ⓓ
22. Ⓐ Ⓑ Ⓒ Ⓓ
23. Ⓐ Ⓑ Ⓒ Ⓓ
24. Ⓐ Ⓑ Ⓒ Ⓓ
25. Ⓐ Ⓑ Ⓒ Ⓓ
26. Ⓐ Ⓑ Ⓒ Ⓓ
27. Ⓐ Ⓑ Ⓒ Ⓓ
28. Ⓐ Ⓑ Ⓒ Ⓓ
29. Ⓐ Ⓑ Ⓒ Ⓓ
30. Ⓐ Ⓑ Ⓒ Ⓓ

31. Ⓐ Ⓑ Ⓒ Ⓓ
32. Ⓐ Ⓑ Ⓒ Ⓓ
33. Ⓐ Ⓑ Ⓒ Ⓓ
34. Ⓐ Ⓑ Ⓒ Ⓓ
35. Ⓐ Ⓑ Ⓒ Ⓓ
36. Ⓐ Ⓑ Ⓒ Ⓓ
37. Ⓐ Ⓑ Ⓒ Ⓓ
38. Ⓐ Ⓑ Ⓒ Ⓓ
39. Ⓐ Ⓑ Ⓒ Ⓓ
40. Ⓐ Ⓑ Ⓒ Ⓓ

Subtest II: Mathematics

1. Ⓐ Ⓑ Ⓒ Ⓓ
2. Ⓐ Ⓑ Ⓒ Ⓓ
3. Ⓐ Ⓑ Ⓒ Ⓓ
4. Ⓐ Ⓑ Ⓒ Ⓓ
5. Ⓐ Ⓑ Ⓒ Ⓓ
6. Ⓐ Ⓑ Ⓒ Ⓓ
7. Ⓐ Ⓑ Ⓒ Ⓓ
8. Ⓐ Ⓑ Ⓒ Ⓓ
9. Ⓐ Ⓑ Ⓒ Ⓓ
10. Ⓐ Ⓑ Ⓒ Ⓓ
11. Ⓐ Ⓑ Ⓒ Ⓓ

12. Ⓐ Ⓑ Ⓒ Ⓓ
13. Ⓐ Ⓑ Ⓒ Ⓓ
14. Ⓐ Ⓑ Ⓒ Ⓓ
15. Ⓐ Ⓑ Ⓒ Ⓓ
16. Ⓐ Ⓑ Ⓒ Ⓓ
17. Ⓐ Ⓑ Ⓒ Ⓓ
18. Ⓐ Ⓑ Ⓒ Ⓓ
19. Ⓐ Ⓑ Ⓒ Ⓓ
20. Ⓐ Ⓑ Ⓒ Ⓓ
21. Ⓐ Ⓑ Ⓒ Ⓓ
22. Ⓐ Ⓑ Ⓒ Ⓓ

23. Ⓐ Ⓑ Ⓒ Ⓓ
24. Ⓐ Ⓑ Ⓒ Ⓓ
25. Ⓐ Ⓑ Ⓒ Ⓓ
26. Ⓐ Ⓑ Ⓒ Ⓓ
27. Ⓐ Ⓑ Ⓒ Ⓓ
28. Ⓐ Ⓑ Ⓒ Ⓓ
29. Ⓐ Ⓑ Ⓒ Ⓓ
30. Ⓐ Ⓑ Ⓒ Ⓓ
31. Ⓐ Ⓑ Ⓒ Ⓓ
32. Ⓐ Ⓑ Ⓒ Ⓓ
33. Ⓐ Ⓑ Ⓒ Ⓓ

34. Ⓐ Ⓑ Ⓒ Ⓓ
35. Ⓐ Ⓑ Ⓒ Ⓓ
36. Ⓐ Ⓑ Ⓒ Ⓓ
37. Ⓐ Ⓑ Ⓒ Ⓓ
38. Ⓐ Ⓑ Ⓒ Ⓓ
39. Ⓐ Ⓑ Ⓒ Ⓓ
40. Ⓐ Ⓑ Ⓒ Ⓓ
41. Ⓐ Ⓑ Ⓒ Ⓓ
42. Ⓐ Ⓑ Ⓒ Ⓓ
43. Ⓐ Ⓑ Ⓒ Ⓓ
44. Ⓐ Ⓑ Ⓒ Ⓓ
45. Ⓐ Ⓑ Ⓒ Ⓓ

Subtest III: English Language Skills

1. Ⓐ Ⓑ Ⓒ Ⓓ
2. Ⓐ Ⓑ Ⓒ Ⓓ
3. Ⓐ Ⓑ Ⓒ Ⓓ
4. Ⓐ Ⓑ Ⓒ Ⓓ
5. Ⓐ Ⓑ Ⓒ Ⓓ
6. Ⓐ Ⓑ Ⓒ Ⓓ
7. Ⓐ Ⓑ Ⓒ Ⓓ
8. Ⓐ Ⓑ Ⓒ Ⓓ
9. Ⓐ Ⓑ Ⓒ Ⓓ
10. Ⓐ Ⓑ Ⓒ Ⓓ

11. Ⓐ Ⓑ Ⓒ Ⓓ
12. Ⓐ Ⓑ Ⓒ Ⓓ
13. Ⓐ Ⓑ Ⓒ Ⓓ
14. Ⓐ Ⓑ Ⓒ Ⓓ
15. Ⓐ Ⓑ Ⓒ Ⓓ
16. Ⓐ Ⓑ Ⓒ Ⓓ
17. Ⓐ Ⓑ Ⓒ Ⓓ
18. Ⓐ Ⓑ Ⓒ Ⓓ
19. Ⓐ Ⓑ Ⓒ Ⓓ
20. Ⓐ Ⓑ Ⓒ Ⓓ

21. Ⓐ Ⓑ Ⓒ Ⓓ
22. Ⓐ Ⓑ Ⓒ Ⓓ
23. Ⓐ Ⓑ Ⓒ Ⓓ
24. Ⓐ Ⓑ Ⓒ Ⓓ
25. Ⓐ Ⓑ Ⓒ Ⓓ
26. Ⓐ Ⓑ Ⓒ Ⓓ
27. Ⓐ Ⓑ Ⓒ Ⓓ
28. Ⓐ Ⓑ Ⓒ Ⓓ
29. Ⓐ Ⓑ Ⓒ Ⓓ
30. Ⓐ Ⓑ Ⓒ Ⓓ

31. Ⓐ Ⓑ Ⓒ Ⓓ
32. Ⓐ Ⓑ Ⓒ Ⓓ
33. Ⓐ Ⓑ Ⓒ Ⓓ
34. Ⓐ Ⓑ Ⓒ Ⓓ
35. Ⓐ Ⓑ Ⓒ Ⓓ
36. Ⓐ Ⓑ Ⓒ Ⓓ
37. Ⓐ Ⓑ Ⓒ Ⓓ
38. Ⓐ Ⓑ Ⓒ Ⓓ
39. Ⓐ Ⓑ Ⓒ Ⓓ
40. Ⓐ Ⓑ Ⓒ Ⓓ

Practice Test 3

Subtest I: Reading

TIME: 40 Minutes
40 Questions

> <u>DIRECTIONS:</u> A number of questions follow each of the passages in the reading section. Answer the questions by choosing the best answer from the four choices given.

Questions 1 to 3 refer to the following passage:

Representatives of the world's seven richest and most industrialized nations held a three-day economic summit in London on July 14–16, 1991. On the second day of the summit, Mikhail Gorbachev, who appealed for help, was offered support by the seven leaders for his economic reforms and his "new' thinking" regarding political reforms. However, because the allies were split on giving a big aid package to Gorbachev, the seven leaders decided to provide help in the form of technical assistance in fields such as banking and energy, rather than in hard cash.

1. Which of the following statements best synthesizes what the passage is about?

    (A) A seven-nation economic summit was held in London in July 1991.
    (B) Mikhail Gorbachev appealed for help and the seven leaders agreed to support his economic reforms.
    (C) At a three-day economic summit held in London in July 1991, leaders of the world's seven richest and most industrialized nations agreed to provide technical assistance to Gorbachev.
    (D) Representatives of the world's seven most industrialized nations, at a summit conference in London, were split on giving Gorbachev assistance in the form of hard cash.

2. The passage implies that

    (A) under the leadership of Gorbachev, the Soviet Union is faced with a financial crisis.
    (B) Gorbachev's "new thinking" on democratic reforms needs support from the seven nations meeting in London.
    (C) the seven leaders meeting in London were split on giving Gorbachev economic and political support.
    (D) with the support of political and economic reforms along with provisions for technical assistance from the seven nations that met in London, the Soviet Union, under the leadership of Gorbachev, can achieve political and economic stability.

3. The passage suggests that technical assistance will be provided to the Soviet Union
   (A) only in the fields of banking and energy.
   (B) in the fields of banking and energy and possibly other fields also.
   (C) by the U.S. in the fields of banking and energy.
   (D) by all seven nations—U.S., Great Britain, France, Germany, Italy, Canada, and Japan.

Questions 4 to 6 refer to the following passage:

A follow-up survey of the 1990 census showed an estimated undercount of 5.2 million people nationwide. This "undercount" was greatest in California where approximately 1.1 million people were not recorded. This estimated undercount was based on a post-census survey of 171,390 households nationwide. Failure to achieve an accurate count would affect federal funding and political representation. If the higher numbers were used, California would gain eight congressional seats instead of seven and about $1 billion in federal funds. Last July 14, 1991, however, Commerce Secretary Robert Mosbacher decided to stick to the original figures of the 1990 census.

4. Which of the following statements gives the main idea of the passage you just read?

   (A) California will gain an additional congressional seat and more federal money if the 1.1 million people undercounted in the census are included.
   (B) An undercount in the census, if not considered, will be a disadvantage to any state.
   (C) A post-census survey is necessary in getting to a more accurate population figure for the states.
   (D) California will suffer the most because of the 1.1 million undercount in the 1990 census.

5. If the 1.1 million undercount was considered for California

   (A) it would settle any political dispute arising from the undercount.
   (B) it would give California eight congressional seats and $1 billion in federal funds.
   (C) it would discourage the practice of a post-census survey.
   (D) it would reverse the decision made by Commerce Secretary Mosbacher.

6. What would it mean for California if the original figures of the 1990 census were to remain the same?

   (A) No additional federal funding will be given.
   (B) There will be no additional political representation.
   (C) The amount of federal funding and number of congressional seats will remain the same.
   (D) The results of the follow-up survey of the 1990 census will be meaningless.

Questions 7 to 10 refer to the following passage:

A big toxic spill took place on the upper Sacramento River in California on July 13, 1991, about 10 p.m., when a slow moving Southern Pacific train derailed north of the town of Dansmuir. A tank car containing 19,500 gallons of pesticide broke open and spilled into the river. This pesticide is used to kill soil pests. Since the spill, thousands of trout and other fish were poisoned along a 45-mile stretch of river. In addition, 190 people were treated at a local hospital for respiratory and related illnesses. Residents along the river have been warned to stay away from the tainted water. Once this water reaches Lake Shasta, a source of water for millions of Californians, samples will be taken to assess the quality of the water.

7. Which of the following statements conveys the message in the passage?

   (A) Pesticides intended to kill soil pests can be dangerous to all living things.
   (B) Water uncontaminated by pesticides is safe to drink.
   (C) Take every precaution not to come in contact with the pesticide-infected water.
   (D) Pesticides that killed thousands of trout and other fish will not necessarily kill human beings.

8. The Southern Pacific train that derailed was

   (A) a passenger train.
   (B) a cargo train.
   (C) a cargo and passenger train.
   (D) a special train.

9. The most serious problem that can come about as a result of the toxic spill is

   (A) possible movement of residents in Dansmuir to another place of residence.
   (B) the negative effects on those whose livelihood depends on the fishing industry.
   (C) when the tainted water reaches Lake Shasta, which is a source of water supply for millions of Californians.
   (D) the uncertain length of time it will take to make the tainted water safe and healthy again.

10. This unfortunate incident of toxic spill resulting from train derailment implies

   (A) the need for more environmental protection.
   (B) other means for transporting pesticides need to be considered.
   (C) that there should be an investigation as to the cause of the train derailment and effective measures to prevent its occurrence again should be applied.
   (D) that there should be research on how to expedite making infected water safe and healthy again.

Questions 11 to 13 refer to the following passage:

Labor Day, a national holiday observed in the United States, is really a day we should remember to give thanks to the labor unions. In the days before the unions became effective, a holiday meant a day off, but the loss of a day's pay to working people. It was not until World War II that unions succeeded, through negotiations with the federal government, in making paid holidays a common practice.

11. The main idea in the passage you just read is

   (A) the role labor unions played in employer-employee relations.
   (B) Labor Day as a national holiday in the U.S.
   (C) the role labor unions played in effecting paid holidays.
   (D) the dispute between paid and unpaid holidays.

12. The passage implies that before World War II

   (A) a holiday gave working people a chance to rest from work.
   (B) Labor Day meant losing a day's pay.
   (C) a holiday was a day to make up for upon returning to work.
   (D) labor unions were ineffective.

13. As a national holiday, Labor Day should really be a day to remember and be thankful for

(A) working people.

(C) labor unions.

(B) paid holidays.

(D) a free day.

Question 14 refers to the following passage:

President Bush's proposed educational "program of choice" will give parents more say in choosing schools for their children. This will encourage states and local districts to change their laws so that parents can apply their tax dollars toward the public or private school to which they choose to send their children, rather than be forced to send their child to the public school in their district or pay for private school tuition.

14. President Bush's proposed educational program implies

(A) the freedom to choose.

(B) competition among schools.

(C) school standards need to be raised.

(D) curricula should be improved.

Question 15 refers to the following passage:

Ash from Mt. Pinatubo in the Philippines has been found to contain gold and other precious metals. However, officials warned against any hopes of a new "gold rush." They found gold content of only 20 parts per billion, which is far below commercial levels. Other metals found were chromium, copper, and lithium.

15. The passage indicates

(A) the possibility of existing gold mines beneath Mt. Pinatubo.

(B) the need for further exploration of what else lies beneath the volcano.

(C) other active volcanoes might be worth exploring as possible gold resources.

(D) that the gold content of the ash from Mt. Pinatubo does not warrant a commercial level.

16. Which of the following makes a good title for the passage you just read?

(A) A New Gold Rush

(B) Ash Content from Mt. Pinatubo

(C) A Philippine Discovery

(D) Precious Metals

17. What might be a possible research project resulting from the ash content finding of Mt. Pinatubo?

(A) Research on the ash content from the eruption of Mt. Fujiyama in Japan

(B) Potential market value of the gold and other metals content in the volcanic ash from Mt. Pinatubo

(C) Further excavation into possible gold underneath Mt. Pinatubo

(D) Research on what lies underneath active volcanoes

Questions 18 to 20 refer to the following passage:

Gary Harris, a farmer from Conrad, Montana, has invented and patented a motorcycle helmet. It provides a brake light, which can signal traffic intentions to other drivers behind. In the U.S., all cars sold are now required to carry a third, high-mounted brake light. Harris' helmet will meet this requirement for motorcyclists.

18. The passage tells about

(A) a new invention for motorcyclists.
(B) a brake light for motorcyclists.
(C) Harris' helmet.
(D) Gary Harris, inventor.

19. An implication regarding the new invention is

(A) the new brake light requirement for cars should likewise apply to motorcycles.
(B) the new brake light requirement for cars cannot apply to motorcycles.
(C) if you buy a car from outside of the U.S., you are exempted from the brake light requirement.
(D) as an inventor, Gary Harris can make more money if he leaves farming.

20. Because of the new brake light requirement for cars

(A) drivers can readily see the traffic signals of car drivers ahead of them.
(B) less accidents can happen on the road.
(C) car prices will go up and will be less affordable to buy.
(D) more lights on the road can be hazardous.

Questions 21 to 24 refer to the following passage:

Lead poisoning is considered by health authorities to be the most common and devastating environmental disease of young children. According to studies made, it affects 15% to 20% of urban children and from 50% to 75% of inner-city, poor children. As a result of a legal settlement, all of California's medical-eligible children, ages one through five, will now be routinely screened annually for lead poisoning. Experts estimate that more than 50,000 cases will be detected in California because of the newly mandated tests. This will halt at an early stage a disease that leads to learning disabilities and life-threatening disorders.

21. Lead poisoning among young children, if not detected early, can lead to

(A) physical disabilities.
(B) mental disabilities.
(C) learning disabilities.
(D) death.

22. The new mandate to screen all young children for lead poisoning is required of

(A) all young children in California.
(B) all children with learning disabilities.
(C) all medical-eligible children, ages one through five, in California.
(D) all school-age children in California.

23. According to findings, more cases of lead poisoning are found among

    (A) urban children.   (C) immigrant children.
    (B) inner-city, poor children.   (D) children in rural areas.

24. The implication of this new mandate in California regarding lead poisoning is

    (A) non-eligible children will not be screened.
    (B) children older than five years will not be screened.
    (C) middle-class children will not be screened.
    (D) thousands of young children in California will remain at risk for lead poisoning.

Question 25 refers to the following passage:

As millions of children returned to school in the year 1991–1992, teachers in California had to face the reality of what many consider as the worst fiscal crisis to hit the schools in more than a decade. This crisis caused reductions in teaching positions, increases in class sizes, cuts in teacher paychecks in some school districts, reductions in special programs, reductions in school supplies, etc.

25. Those who will be most affected by the effects of the financial crisis in California schools are

    (A) the teachers.   (C) the paraprofessionals.
    (B) the school administrators.   (D) the students.

Questions 26 to 28 refer to the following passage:

The U.S. Postal Service issued a 50-cent stamp in Anchorage, Alaska, on October 12, 1991, to commemorate the 500th anniversary of the arrival of the Italian explorer Christopher Columbus in the New World. The stamp depicts how Americans may have appeared to Asians crossing the Bering Strait. The stamp series showed the pre-Columbian voyages of discovery.

26. Which of the following makes an appropriate title for the passage?

    (A) The Discovery of the Americas
    (B) 500th Anniversary of the Discovery of America
    (C) The Significance of the Bering Strait
    (D) A Commemorative New U.S. Postal Stamp

27. The passage implies that

    (A) historical facts need to be verified.
    (B) Christopher Columbus was not the first to arrive in the New World.
    (C) Native Americans came from Asia.
    (D) history books need to be rewritten.

28. Which of the following would you consider as the most historically significant?

    (A) Asians crossed over the Bering Strait to the New World before Columbus came.
    (B) It has been 500 years since Christopher Columbus arrived in the New World.
    (C) A tribute to Christopher Columbus was held on October 12, 1991.
    (D) There were other voyages undertaken before Christopher Columbus'.

Questions 29 and 30 refer to the following passage:

A 150 million-year-old allosaurus skeleton, which appears to be intact, was found on September 9, 1991, by a Swiss team in north-central Wyoming. This Zurich-based company sells fossils to museums. They were digging on private property, but the fossil actually showed up on federal land.

Immediately, the federal government sealed off the site along the foot of Big Horn Mountains in Wyoming and deployed rangers from the Bureau of Land Management to prevent vandalism. Paleontologists believe that this discovery could lead them to a vast dinosaur graveyard.

29. The passage you just read can best be utilized by a classroom teacher in

    (A) reading.   (C) zoology.
    (B) biology.   (D) history.

30. A teaching strategy that the classroom teacher can use appropriately with the students regarding the allosaurus fossil discovery is

    (A) the problem-solving approach.
    (B) the survey approach.
    (C) the deductive approach.
    (D) the historical approach.

Questions 31 to 33 refer to the following passage:

Popular U.S. attractions such as Disneyland, the Golden Gate Bridge, Las Vegas, and the Statue of Liberty have attracted millions of foreign tourists whose spending helped the U.S. post a $31.7 billion service trade surplus in 1990 compared with a $101 billion merchandise trade deficit in the same year. The heavy-spending Japanese tourists accounted for the biggest portion of the tourism trade surplus, spending $5.5 billion more touring the U.S. than U.S. tourists spent visiting Japan. Canadians also outspent American tourists to Canada by $2.2 billion.

31. The main idea in the passage is

    (A) foreign tourists in the U.S. spend more than American tourists spend abroad.
    (B) Japanese tourists are the biggest spenders among tourists to the U.S.
    (C) Canadians rank second to Japan in tourism spending in the U.S.
    (D) tourism is very important to the economy of the U.S.

32. A significant implication of the passage is

 (A) that the U.S. should increase its tourist spending in Japan.
 (B) that tourist spending in the U.S. reduces its trade deficit.
 (C) that Canada needs to improve its tourism attractions.
 (D) that Japan has more money on which to spend on tourism than any other country.

33. Based on the passage, which of the following would be an appropriate topic of discussion with students?

 (A) International relations
 (B) Global relations
 (C) Balance in global tourism industry
 (D) Interdependency of nations

Questions 34 and 35 refer to the following passage:

San Francisco was named the world's favorite travel destination in the prestigious 1991 *Conde Nast Traveler* magazine poll. It was considered the best city in the world that year, beating out Florence, Italy (No. 2), and London and Vienna, which tied for No. 3. A red-carpet gala in the City Hall rotunda is planned in which Mayor Agnos will laud the city's 60,000 tourism industry workers including hotel maids, taxi drivers, bellhops, and others in the local hospitality industry.

34. An appropriate title for the passage is

 (A) San Francisco: World's Favorite Travel Destination.
 (B) A Gala for San Francisco's Tourism Workers.
 (C) San Francisco: Top in Ranking.
 (D) Top City in 1991.

35. The prestigious citation for the city of San Francisco could mean in practical terms

 (A) more openings for tourism industry workers.
 (B) higher pay demands from hotel maids, bellhops, and other workers.
 (C) more tourists will come to the city.
 (D) more money coming to the city from its tourism industry.

Questions 36 to 38 refer to the following passage:

Results of a study released by the College Board and the Western Interstate Commission for Higher Education projected that in 1994, the majority of California's high school graduates would be non-white and that by 1995, one-third of all the nation's students would be from minority groups. It is also predicted that, nationally, the total non-white and Hispanic student population for all grade levels would increase from 10.4 million in 1985–1986 to 13.7 million in 1994–1995. The figures suggest that, in the 1990s, equal educational opportunity for all students had taken hold as our nation's number one priority.

36. The passage suggests that, in the 1990s,

    (A) this nation was, educationally, at risk.
    (B) something needed to be done to reduce the growing numbers of minority students in the school system.
    (C) urgent educational reforms were needed to provide equal opportunity for all students.
    (D) immigration laws should have been strictly enforced to balance the numbers of white and non-white student populations.

37. Because of changes in demographics, what preparation would have been needed in California in the area of teacher preparation?

    (A) Recruit more minority teachers
    (B) Enforce school desegregation
    (C) Encourage non-Hispanic, white students to enroll in private schools
    (D) Revise teacher preparation programs to reflect appropriate preparation for multicultural classrooms

38. What problem could have resulted from the increasing minority population in the nation?

    (A) Strong resentment from mainstream whites towards the school system
    (B) Increase in enrollment in private and parochial schools
    (C) "White flight" to the suburbs, where minorities had not yet become the majority
    (D) Inappropriate and inadequate school curriculum and teacher preparation to meet the needs in multicultural classrooms

Questions 39 and 40 refer to the following passage:

The United States' final offer on a lease agreement for the Subic Bay Naval Base in the Philippines was rejected by the Philippine Senate. Hence, for the first time in nearly a century, U.S. military strategy for the Asia-Pacific region will no longer be centered on the Philippines, and the nation's economic survival and development will no longer rely on U.S. dependency. Somehow, this dependency on the U.S. has served as an impediment to the Philippines' ability to join East Asia's economic boom.

39. Which of the following best summarizes what the passage is about?

    (A) The Philippines' economic dependency on the U.S. ended with its Senate's rejection of the U.S. lease offer.
    (B) The U.S. lease offer for the Subic Bay Naval Base was rejected by the Philippine Senate. Hence, the U.S. will no longer have its military base in the Asia-Pacific region.
    (C) The Philippines is now on its own in its economic survival and development.
    (D) The U.S. military strategy for the Asia-Pacific region will no longer be on the Philippines following the Philippine Senate's rejection of the U.S. lease offer.

40. The U.S. military's pullout from Subic Bay would mean

    (A) less Americans in the Philippines.
    (B) a chance for the Philippines to survive on its own.
    (C) weakening of U.S.-Philippine relations.
    (D) less protection for the Philippines.

Subtest II: Mathematics

TIME: 100 Minutes
45 Questions

> <u>DIRECTIONS:</u> Each of the questions or incomplete statements below is followed by four suggested answers or completions. Select the one that is best in each case.

1.   Which of the statements below is false?

   (A) $3^2 + 3^2 = 3^4$

   (B) $4^3 \cdot 4^1 = 4^4$

   (C) $\dfrac{10^6}{10^2} = 10^4$

   (D) $30 + 5^0 = 31$

2.   Which is the correct prime factorization of 200?

   (A) $(10)(10)(2)$

   (B) $(2^3)(5^2)$

   (C) $(3^2)(5^2)$

   (D) $(2^4)(5)$

3.   Pens come in packages of 8 and pencils come in packages of 12. If your order contained more than 45 and less than 60 of each item, how many packages of pens and pencils did you order?

   (A)   4 packages of pens and 6 packages of pencils
   (B)   3 packages of pens and 2 packages of pencils
   (C)   6 packages of pens and 4 packages of pencils
   (D)   5 packages of pens and 5 packages of pencils

4.   How much water is needed to add to a half-pint of syrup with 60 percent sugar to obtain a drink with 5 percent sugar?

   (A)   3 pints

   (B)   4 pints

   (C)   5.5 pints

   (D)   7 pints

5.   Which of the following must be true about triangle *ABC*?

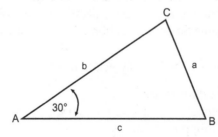

(A) Angle a is the smallest angle.
(B) Side a is not the longest side.
(C) Angle b or c must be a right angle.
(D) Side b must be greater than side a in measurement.

6. Simplify the following: $25 - (6 - 4)^3 \div 2 + |-3|$

(A) 24   (C) 21
(B) 11.5   (D) 18.5

7. A solid cube of wood has a volume of 8. What would be the volume of a cube whose sides are twice the length of this cube?

(A) 28   (C) 36
(B) 32   (D) 64

8. Tommy is driving 500 miles to his favorite vacation spot. Tommy drove 6.5 hours at a constant rate of 60 miles per hour before stopping to refuel. How many more miles does Tommy have to drive after getting gas?

(A) 390   (C) 250
(B) 110   (D) 430

9. Bob has 50 coins, all nickels and dimes, worth a total of $4.85. How many nickels does he possess?

(A) 15   (C) 37
(B) 7   (D) 3

10. The scale drawing of a football field is 18.3 centimeters by 9.8 centimeters. The scale is 1 cm equals 5 meters. What is the area of the football field in square meters?

(A) 179.34   (C) 4483.5
(B) 896.7   (D) 2112.45

11. If ten babies drink a total of ten gallons of milk in ten days, how many gallons of milk will 20 babies drink in 20 days?

(A) 20   (C) 30
(B) 25   (D) 40

12. Jane has three kinds of coins, quarters, dimes, and nickels, totalling 24 in number and worth $3.00. How many coins of each kind does she have?

(A) Jane has 12 nickels, 4 dimes, and 8 quarters.
(B) Jane has 9 nickels, 8 dimes, and 7 quarters.
(C) Jane has 6 nickels, 12 dimes, and 6 quarters.
(D) There is no unique answer; further information is needed.

13. A piece of artwork is in the shape of a parallelogram. All of its sides measure 4, and both of its diagonals measure $4\sqrt{2}$. What is its area in square units?

   (A) 16
   (B) $4\sqrt{3}$
   (C) It cannot be determined from the information given.
   (D) $8\sqrt{3}$

14. Jack gave one-third of his money to his daughter and one-quarter of his money to his son. He then had $150,000 left. How much money did he have before he gave away some?

   (A) $225,000   (C) $360,000
   (B) $300,000   (D) $400,000

15. An average adult giraffe weighs 1.3 tons. How many pounds is that?

   (A) 260   (C) 2600
   (B) 130   (D) 1300

16. In which quadrant would you find the point (2, –18)?

   (A) I   (C) III
   (B) II   (D) IV

17. What is the slope of segment *AB* shown in $\triangle ABC$ on the coordinate grid?

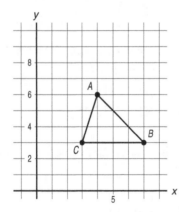

   (A) –3   (C) 1
   (B) –1   (D) 3

18. Norman lives six blocks north and six blocks east of Bob. The town is made up of all square blocks. How many ways can Bob walk to Norman's house walking only 12 blocks?

   (A) 2 ways   (C) 36 ways
   (B) 924 ways   (D) Infinitely many ways

19. The map shows New York City's Midtown area. Which street is perpendicular to Ninth Avenue?

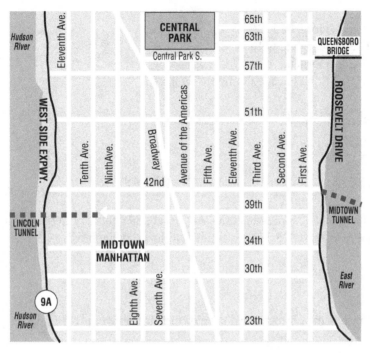

(A) Tenth Avenue   (C) Park Avenue

(B) Broadway   (D) 34th Street

20. Donald gave Louie a number of marbles to share with Dewey and Huey. Making sure that he got his share, Louie took one-third of the marbles and hid them. Dewey, after hearing from Donald that he is entitled to one-third of the marbles as well, went and hid one-third of the remaining marbles. Not knowing what was going on, Daisy took two marbles from the pile. When Huey came, there were only 10 marbles left. How many marbles did Donald give to Louie in the beginning?

(A) 18

(B) 24

(C) 27

(D) That number cannot be found for lack of information.

21. An artist is making a sketch of some items. He is using the scale 1 cm (sketch) = 5.5 cm (actual size). How long will the artist's sketch of an item 75 cm long be? Round your answer to the nearest centimeter.

(A) 14   (C) 85

(B) 413   (D) 306

22. Joan is eight years older than Georgette. Joan was twice as old as Georgette eight years ago. How old are they now?

    (A) Joan is 28 and Georgette is 20.
    (B) Joan is 26 and Georgette is 18.
    (C) Joan is 24 and Georgette is 16.
    (D) Further information is needed to figure their ages.

23. What is the next number in the sequence that follows?
    23, 29, 35, 41...

    (A) 46   (C) 48
    (B) 47   (D) 49

24. Sarah bought 10 pounds of apples and nuts. Apples are 89 cents a pound, and nuts are $1.29 a pound. She spent a total of $10.10. How many pounds of nuts did she buy?

    (A) 2   (C) 4
    (B) 3   (D) 5

25. Which word phrase is the correct translation of the algebraic expression in the box?

$$\frac{y}{2} - 3$$

    (A) Half of y, minus three   (C) The product of y and two, decreased by three
    (B) Three less than the quotient of two and y (D) Subtract three from double y

26. Which expression is equivalent to the one below?

$$-3\left(\frac{x}{3} - 1\right)$$

    (A) $-3x + 3$ (C) $x - 1$
    (B) $-x + 3$ (D) $x + 1$

27. What is the 8th number in the sequence: $-2, 4, -8, 16$ ...?

    (A) 256   (C) 128
    (B) -256 (D) -128

28. Which ordered pair is *not* a solution to the following inequality?
    $$y < 4x + 4$$

    (A) $(2, -2)$ (C) $(1, 5)$
    (B) $(0, 0)$ (D) $(-1, 2)$

29. Which ordered pair below is *not* on the line $y = -x + 8$?

    (A) (3, 5)   (C) (−4, 12)
    (B) (−2, 6)   (D) (0, 8)

30. The pictograph shows the number of taxi drivers in five cities in Massachusetts. Which statement about the data in the pictograph is *false*?

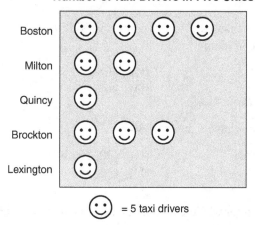

Number of Taxi Drivers in Five Cities

= 5 taxi drivers

    (A) Each whole face represents 5 taxi drivers.
    (B) There are 3 taxi drivers in Brockton.
    (C) There are more taxi drivers in Boston than in Milton and Lexington combined.
    (D) There are 5 more taxi drivers in Milton than in Quincy.

31. The bar graph below shows the average annual salary of an employee at Company C. This bar graph is misleading because . . .

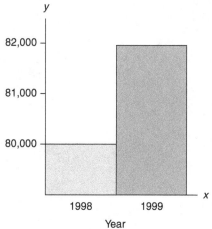

    (A) the number of employees in Company C is not known
    (B) 1998 and 1999 are only one year apart
    (C) the scale on the *y*-axis does not start at 0 and it looks like salaries tripled
    (D) $80,000 is a very large number

32. What is the measurement of an angle of a regular pentagon?

    (A) 72°   (C) 84°
    (B) 108°   (D) 104°

33. Which data set has a mean of 10?

    (A) (4, 5, 10, 13, 17)   (C) (2, 10, 10, 10, 11)
    (B) (3, 5, 5, 8, 13)   (D) (7, 8, 8, 12, 15)

34. The longest side of a triangle measures 2 and the shortest side measures 1. What cannot be the measurement of the angle between them?

    (A) 30°   (C) 70°
    (B) 60°   (D) 90°

35. Which group of numbers does *not* have a mean of 30?

    (A) (20, 30, 30, 40)   (C) (30, 30, 30)
    (B) (22, 24, 15, 19, 40, 60)   (D) (15, 49)

36. Which is a reasonable explanation for why the median of a set of data may not be one of the data items?

    (A) if the mean and the mode are the same
    (B) if the data items are not put into order correctly
    (C) if there is an outlier
    (D) if there is an even number of data items

37. Grace bought 24 muffins. She got 6 corn, 6 blueberry, and 12 chocolate chip. What is the probability that if Grace chooses a muffin at random she will choose a blueberry one?

    (A) $\dfrac{6}{12}$ (C) $\dfrac{6}{24}$

    (B) $\dfrac{12}{24}$ (D) $\dfrac{6}{18}$

38. Simplify the following:

    $$6 \times (8 + 2) \div 5 - 3^2$$

    (A) 3   (C) 81
    (B) 1   (D) 53

39. Using the metric system, find the measure of the black line to the nearest centimeter.

(A) 3   (C) 3.4
(B) 4   (D) 34

40. There are 10 students in the chess club. If the teacher wants to choose 3 students to represent the chess club during the next school assembly, how many different groups of 3 students can he choose?

(A) 30   (C) 60
(B) 120   (D) 300

41. The area of a circular mirror is 144π square feet. If the radius of the mirror is increased by 2 feet, what would be the area of the larger mirror in square feet?

(A) 196π (C) 121π
(B) 576π (D) 288π

42. Which picture below does not show symmetry?

(A)    (C)

(B)    (D)

43. A right triangular shaped garden has one leg that is 6 meters long and the other leg is 8 meters long. Its hypotenuse is 10 meters long. What is the area of the garden?

(A) 24   (C) 121
(B) 48   (D) 240

44. According to the graph below, during how many months was supply greater than demand?

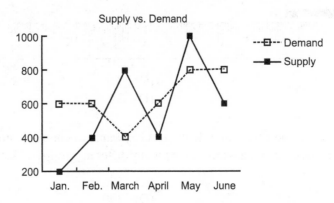

(A) 0

(B) 1

(C) 2

(D) 3

45. At what point does the equation $y = -2x + 4$ intersect the x-axis?

(A) (0, 4)

(B) (2, 0)

(C) (0, 2)

(D) (4, 0)

Subtest III: English Language Skills

TIME: 40 Minutes
40 Questions

Part A: Usage

DIRECTIONS: Each of the following sentences may contain an error in diction, usage, idiom, or grammar. Some sentences are correct. Some sentences contain one error. No sentence contains more than one error.

If there is an error, it will appear in one of the underlined portions labeled A, B, or C. If there is no error, choose the portion labeled D. If there is an error, select the letter of the portion that must be changed in order to correct the sentence.

EXAMPLE: He drove <u>slowly</u> and <u>cautiously</u> in order to <u>hopefully</u> avoid having an
                A   **B**   **C**

accident. <u>No error.</u>
     D   Ⓐ Ⓑ ● Ⓓ

---

1. Which suspension bridge <u>is</u> the <u>longest,</u> the Verrazano-Narrows Bridge in New York City <u>or</u> the
                      A   **B**   **C**
Golden Gate Bridge in San Francisco? <u>No error.</u>
                           D

2. A main function of proteins, whether <u>they come</u> from <u>plant or animal sources,</u> <u>is</u> the building of
                                   A   **B**   **C**
body tissue. <u>No error.</u>
          D

3. <u>Recognizing</u> that we <u>had worked</u> very hard to complete our project, the teacher told Janice and <u>I</u>
     A   **B**   **C**
that we could give it to her tomorrow. <u>No error.</u>
                                   D

4. <u>According to</u> the United States Constitution, the legislative branch of the government has powers
     A
<u>different than</u> <u>those</u> of the executive branch. <u>No error.</u>
       B   **C**   **D**

5. After <u>being studied</u> for the <u>preceding ten years</u> by the National Heart, Lung, and Blood Institute,
          A   **B**

    the relationship of high levels of cholesterol in the blood to the possibility of <u>having</u> heart attacks
                                                                                C

    was reported in 1984. <u>No error</u>.
                 D

6. The book *Cheaper By the Dozen* demonstrates that each of the children of Frank and Lillian Gilbreth
    <u>was expected</u> <u>to use</u> <u>his or her</u> time efficiently. <u>No error</u>.
        A   **B**   **C**   **D**

7. His aversion <u>with</u> snakes made camping an unpleasant activity <u>for him</u> and <u>one</u> that he tried dili-
               A   **B**   **C**

    gently to avoid. <u>No error</u>.
                  D

8. The story of the American pioneers, <u>those</u> who willingly left the safety of <u>their</u> homes to move into
                                     A   **B**

    unsettled territory, <u>show</u> us great courage in the face of danger. <u>No error</u>.
                      C   **D**

9. <u>Because of</u> the long, cold winters and short summers, farming in high latitudes is <u>more difficult</u>
    A   **B**

    <u>than low latitudes</u>. <u>No error</u>.
           C   **D**

10. When my sister and <u>I</u> were in Los Angeles, <u>we</u> hoped that both of us could be <u>a contestant</u> on a quiz
                     A   **B**   **C**

    show. <u>No error</u>.
           D

11. After he <u>had broke</u> the vase that his mother <u>had purchased</u> in Europe, he tried to buy a new one for
              A   **B**

    his father and <u>her</u>. <u>No error</u>.
               C   **D**

12. Some of the people <u>with whom</u> the witness <u>worked</u> were engaged in covert activities <u>on behalf of</u> the
                     A   **B**   **C**

    United States government. <u>No error</u>.
                         D

13. Because of their cold personalities and hot tempers, <u>neither</u> John Adams <u>nor</u> his son John Quincy
 A **B**

 Adams <u>were</u> especially successful in politics. <u>No error</u>.
 C **D**

14. <u>Among</u> the reasons <u>for United States participation</u> in World War II <u>were</u> the Japanese attack on the
 A **B** **C**

 naval base at Pearl Harbor on December 7, 1941. <u>No error</u>.
 D

15. Some parents make a <u>greater</u> attempt to frighten <u>their</u> children about the dangers of driving than
 A **B**

 <u>teaching</u> them safe driving habits. <u>No error</u>.
 C **D**

16. The high standard of living in Sweden <u>is shown</u> by <u>their</u> statistics <u>of life expectancy</u> and per capita
 A **B** **C**

 income. <u>No error</u>.
 D

17. The snow leopard <u>is</u> a wild mammal in Central Asia <u>that has</u> large eyes, a four-foot body, and
 A **B**

 <u>white and bluish gray in color</u>. <u>No error</u>.
 C **D**

18. Selecting a lifetime vocation, a young person may have to choose either a vocation that he enjoys
 <u>and</u> a vocation that will make <u>him</u> rich; that choice is perhaps the <u>most important</u> one he will ever
 A **B** **C**

 make. <u>No error</u>.
 D

19. Failing a test because the student is nervous <u>is</u> understandable; <u>to fail</u> because <u>he or she</u> did not study
 A **B** **C**

 is quite another matter. <u>No error</u>.
 D

20. Although she <u>had grown up</u> in the North and <u>had been</u> neither a slave <u>or</u> a slave owner, Harriet
 A **B** **C**
 Beecher Stowe vividly portrayed life on a slave-holding plantation in her famous book. <u>No error</u>.
 D

21. The reason Jason failed <u>his</u> speech was <u>because</u> he suffered <u>such stage fright</u> that he refused to give
                      A   **B**   **C**

    his final speech. <u>No error</u>.
                    D

22. After completing the typing course, he made <u>less</u> errors and typed <u>more rapidly</u> than <u>anyone else</u> in
                                        A   **B**   **C**

    his office. <u>No error</u>.
          D

23. Learning the basic components of good nutrition is <u>important for</u> the young adult <u>who want</u> <u>to gain</u>
                                      A   **B**   **C**

    <u>independence</u> by living in his or her own apartment. <u>No error</u>.
                                            D

24. Because condominiums offer the advantages of property ownership <u>along with</u> those of apartment
                                                    A

    rental, <u>this</u> <u>has made</u> condominiums popular since the 1970s. <u>No error</u>.
          B   **C**   **D**

25. Students <u>who</u> eat every day in the college cafeteria generally tire of the <u>frequent</u> repetitious menu
            A   **B**

    <u>that is provided</u>. <u>No error</u>.
          C   **D**

Part B: Sentence Correction

DIRECTIONS: in each of the following sentences some portion of the sentence is underlined. Under each sentence are four choices. The first choice has the same wording as the original. The other three choices are reworded. Sometimes the first choice containing the original wording is the best; sometimes one of the other choices is the best. Choose the letter of the best choice. Your choice should produce a sentence which is not ambiguous or awkward and which is correct, clear, and precise.

This is a test of correct and effective English expression. Keep in mind the standards of English usage, punctuation, grammar, word choice, and construction.

EXAMPLE:

When you listen to opera, <u>a person may not appreciate it</u>.

(A) a person may not appreciate it.

(B) it may not be appreciated by a person.

(C) which may not be appreciated by one.

(D) you may not appreciate it.

26. Wealthy citizens often protest <u>about the building of</u> low-cost housing in the affluent communities where they reside.

(A) about the building of
(B) whether they should build
(C) the building of
(D) whether or not they should build

27. Siblings growing up in a family do not necessarily have equal opportunities to achieve, <u>the difference being their placement in the family, their innate abilities, and their personalities</u>.

(A) the difference being their placement in the family, their innate abilities, and their personalities.
(B) because of their placement in the family, their innate abilities, and their personalities.
(C) and the difference is their placement in the family, their innate abilities, and their personalities.
(D) they have different placements in the family, different innate abilities, and different personalities.

28. Two major provisions of the United States Bill of Rights <u>is freedom of speech and that citizens are guaranteed a trial by jury</u>.

    (A) is freedom of speech and that citizens are guaranteed a trial by jury.
    (B) is that citizens have freedom of speech and a guaranteed trial by jury.
    (C) are freedom of speech and that citizens are guaranteed a trial by jury.
    (D) are freedom of speech and the guarantee of a trial by jury.

29. Poets of the nineteenth century tried <u>to entertain their readers but also with the attempt of teaching them</u> lessons about life.

    (A) to entertain their readers but also with the attempt of teaching them
    (B) to entertain their readers but also to attempt to teach them
    (C) to both entertain their readers and to teach them
    (D) both to entertain and to teach their readers

30. The city council decided to remove parking meters <u>so as to encourage</u> people to shop in Centerville.

    (A) so as to encourage
    (B) to encourage
    (C) with the desire
    (D) thereby encouraging

31. Visiting New York City for the first time, <u>the sites most interesting to Megan were</u> the Statue of Liberty, the Empire State Building, and the Brooklyn Bridge.

    (A) the sites most interesting to Megan were
    (B) Megan found that the sites most interesting to her were
    (C) Megan was most interested in
    (D) Megan was most interested in the sites of

32. Although most college professors have expertise in their areas of specialty, <u>some are more interested in continuing their research than in teaching undergraduate students</u>.

    (A) some are more interested in continuing their research than in teaching undergraduate students.
    (B) some are most interested in continuing their research rather than in teaching undergraduate students.
    (C) some prefer continuing their research rather than to teach undergraduate students.
    (D) continuing their research, not teaching undergraduate students, is more interesting to some.

33. <u>Whether adult adoptees should be allowed to see their original birth certificates or not</u> is controversial, but many adoptive parents feel strongly that records should remain closed.

    (A) Whether adult adoptees should be allowed to see their original birth certificates or not
    (B) Whether or not adult adoptees should be allowed to see their original birth certificates or not
    (C) Allowing the seeing of their original birth certificates by adult adoptees
    (D) That adult adoptees should be allowed to see their original birth certificates

34. <u>Having studied theology, music, along with medicine</u>, Albert Schweitzer became a medical missionary in Africa.

    (A) Having studied theology, music, along with medicine
    (B) Having studied theology, music, as well as medicine
    (C) Having studied theology and music, and, also, medicine
    (D) After he had studied theology, music, and medicine

35. When the Mississippi River threatens to flood, sandbags are piled along its banks, <u>and they do this to keep its waters from overflowing</u>.

    (A) and they do this to keep its waters from overflowing.
    (B) to keep its waters from overflowing.
    (C) and then its waters won't overflow.
    (D) and they keep its waters from overflowing.

36. <u>Because of the popularity of his light verse</u>, Edward Lear is seldom recognized today for his travel books and detailed illustrations of birds.

    (A) Because of the popularity of his light verse
    (B) Owing to the fact that his light verse was popular
    (C) Having written light verse that was popular
    (D) Being the author of popular light verse

37. Lincoln's Gettysburg Address, <u>despite its having been very short and delivered after a two-hour oration by Edward Everett</u>, is one of the greatest speeches ever delivered.

    (A) despite its having been very short and delivered after a two-hour oration by Edward Everett
    (B) which was very short and delivered after a two-hour oration by Edward Everett
    (C) although it was very short and delivered after a two-hour oration by Edward Everett
    (D) despite the fact that it was very short and delivered after a two-hour oration by Edward Everett

38. China, <u>which ranks third in area and first in population among the world's countries</u>, also has one of the longest histories.

    (A) which ranks third in area and first in population among the world's countries
    (B) which is the third largest in area and ranks first in population among the world's countries
    (C) in area ranking third and in population ranking first among the world's countries
    (D) third in area and first in the number of people among the world's countries

39. <u>Leonardo Da Vinci was a man who</u> was a scientist, an architect, an engineer, and a sculptor.

    (A) Leonardo Da Vinci was a man who
    (B) The man Leonardo Da Vinci
    (C) Leonardo da Vinci
    (D) Leonardo Da Vinci, a man who

40. <u>The age of 35 having been reached</u>, a natural-born United States citizen is eligible to be elected President of the United States.

    (A) The age of 35 having been reached
    (B) The age of 35 being reached
    (C) When having reached the age of 35
    (D) When he or she is 35 years old

Subtest IV: Essay

TIME: 50 Minutes

<u>DIRECTIONS:</u> Two topics are presented below. Select one of the topics as the basis for your essay. READ TOPICS VERY CAREFULLY TO MAKE SURE YOU KNOW WHAT YOU ARE BEING ASKED TO DO.

TOPIC 1:

"There is a wonderful, mystical law of nature that the three things we crave most in life—happiness, freedom, and peace of mind—are always attained by giving them to someone else." Do you agree or disagree with the statement? Support your opinion with specific examples from history, current events, literature, or personal experience.

OR

TOPIC 2:

The rising cost of health care has been a hotly debated political topic in recent years. What are your opinions on this subject?

Practice Test 3

ANSWER KEY

Subtest I — Reading

1. (C)	11. (C)	21. (D)	31. (A)
2. (D)	12. (B)	22. (C)	32. (B)
3. (B)	13. (C)	23. (B)	33. (C)
4. (A)	14. (B)	24. (D)	34. (A)
5. (B)	15. (D)	25. (D)	35. (D)
6. (C)	16. (B)	26. (D)	36. (C)
7. (C)	17. (B)	27. (B)	37. (D)
8. (B)	18. (A)	28. (A)	38. (D)
9. (C)	19. (A)	29. (C)	39. (D)
10. (C)	20. (A)	30. (D)	40. (B)

Subtest II — Mathematics

1. (A)	13. (A)	25. (A)	37. (C)
2. (B)	14. (C)	26. (B)	38. (A)
3. (C)	15. (C)	27. (A)	39. (A)
4. (C)	16. (D)	28. (D)	40. (B)
5. (B)	17. (B)	29. (B)	41. (A)
6. (A)	18. (B)	30. (B)	42. (B)
7. (D)	19. (D)	31. (C)	43. (A)
8. (B)	20. (C)	32. (B)	44. (C)
9. (D)	21. (A)	33. (D)	45. (B)
10. (C)	22. (C)	34. (D)	
11. (D)	23. (B)	35. (D)	
12. (D)	24. (B)	36. (D)	

Subtest III — English Language Skills

1. (B)	11. (A)	21. (B)	31. (C)
2. (D)	12. (D)	22. (A)	32. (A)
3. (C)	13. (C)	23. (B)	33. (D)
4. (B)	14. (C)	24. (B)	34. (D)
5. (A)	15. (C)	25. (B)	35. (B)
6. (D)	16. (B)	26. (C)	36. (A)
7. (A)	17. (C)	27. (B)	37. (C)
8. (C)	18. (A)	28. (D)	38. (A)
9. (C)	19. (B)	29. (D)	39. (C)
10. (C)	20. (C)	30. (B)	40. (D)

Detailed Explanations
of Answers

Subtest I: Reading

1. **(C)**

    The question asks for the best synthesis of the passage and (C) is the best and most complete answer. Choices (A), (B), and (D) are not as complete. For example, (A) left out the duration of the conference, (B) left out both the duration of the conference and the number of the nations represented at the summit, and (D) left out the number of nations represented and support for Gorbachev's "new thinking."

2. **(D)**

    Of the choices provided, (D) gives the most logical and sound implication of the passage. (A) falls short of the capabilities of Gorbachev's leadership; in (B) the "new thinking" referred to already has the support of the seven leaders at the summit; (C) is a rather sweeping, unfair statement.

3. **(B)**

    The mention of banking and energy did not rule out technical assistance in other fields, hence, (B) is the correct answer. Choice (A) limited the assistance to only the fields of banking and energy; in (C) the statement is only partly true—the U.S. is not alone in providing support; and in (D) technical assistance can likewise come from other nations outside of the seven.

4. **(A)**

    The question asks for the main idea in the passage and (A) gives the best and complete main idea. Choices (B) and (C) are generalizations derived from the passage and (D), while it is true and specific to the passage, is stated in the negative.

5. **(B)**

    (B) gives the most specific consequence for California. The other choices, while all plausible or possible answers, do not get to the "root" of the issue specific to California.

6. **(C)**

    Based on the passage read, the answer to this question is (C)—two things are mentioned that could affect California and these are federal funding and the number of congressional seats. While (A) and (B) are correct, they are incomplete. Choice (D) is a consequential generalization which is correct but lacks the preciseness of (C).

7. **(C)**

The question asks for the "message" conveyed in the passage. Choice (C) is the correct answer, as it gives a warning. In choice (A), pesticides cannot necessarily be dangerous to all living things—some are good for the protection of plants, for example; in (B), water can be contaminated by something other than pesticides; the statement in choice (D) may be true, but it is certainly not the best answer.

8. **(B)**

The train is definitely a cargo train, hence, (B) is the correct answer. In (A), if it were a passenger train, hundreds would have been killed; in (C), according to the clues, the choices here don't apply; and in (D) the answer used "special train" but could have appropriately used "cargo train" instead.

9. **(C)**

The question here asks for the most "serious problem" that can come about; so, of all the choices, (C) provides the most serious problem resulting from the pesticide spill for Californians. Choices (A), (B), and (D) are not life-threatening as is (C)

10. **(C)**

(C) is the most logical and straightforward answer. (C) prioritizes which action should be first taken, and is therefore the correct answer. While the choices in (A), (B), and (D) are sound answers, they don't list the most urgent thing to do.

11. **(C)**

The correct answer here is (C) because this choice synthesizes the key or main idea in the passage. The other choices, while partly true, don't give the main idea.

12. **(B)**

Before World War II, which were the depression years, one can easily presume that people were more practical or money minded, hence, Labor Day as celebrated then could mean the loss of a day's pay for working people. Hence, (B) is the correct answer. While choices (A), (C), and (D) are also possible answers they don't get to the "root" of the issue.

13. **(C)**

Explicitly given in the passage is (C), the correct answer. Choices (A), (B), and (D), while they may all be true and correct, are not what is precisely given in the passage.

14. **(B)**

The question asks for implication. The most straightforward implication of the choices provided has got to be (B). Choice (A) is too general and is actually given in the passage. Choice (C) is an eventual consequence of the proposed program and the same can be said of (D).

15. **(D)**

The gold content found in the volcanic ash from Mt. Pinatubo could easily stir or trigger a "gold rush." However, people are warned that the gold content found is not at a "commercial level." Hence, (D) is the correct answer. The other choices provided are all mere speculations.

16. **(B)**

Choice (B) is the most appropriate answer—it also synthesizes the content of the reading passage; hence, it is the correct answer. Choice (A) is incorrect. Choices (C) and (D) are somewhat applicable as titles but do not really synthesize the main idea of the passage as choice (B).

17. **(B)**

If priorities will have to be established to determine the most immediate research needed on the ash content from Mt. Pinatubo, choice (B) will have to be the most logical choice because there is already some data with which to work. Other research possibilities such as those in choices (A), (C), and (D) will have to come later.

18. **(A)**

The best and correct answer here is (A)—it's the main idea of the passage. Choice (B) is partially correct—if it has to be specific, it should refer to the brake lights on the helmet. Choice (C) is incomplete as a key or main idea of the passage and the same could be said of choice (D).

19. **(A)**

It would follow that the rationale behind the new brake light requirement for cars in. California is the same for all other vehicles on the road. Hence, choice (A) is the correct answer. (B) is illogical; in (C) any car driven in California, wherever its been bought, cannot be exempted from the requirement; in (D) Harris can go on inventing while remaining a farmer—he'll make more money doing both.

20. **(A)**

Choice (A) is the most logical and appropriate answer. Hence, it is the correct answer. Choice (B) can be, but is not necessarily true; (C) is a logical possibility but will not drastically raise car prices beyond affordability; (D) may be true, but not as road hazards.

21. **(D)**

All the choices in this question are possible answers; however, since the question asks what lead poisoning, if not detected early, "can lead to," it calls for the ultimate consequence. Hence, (D) is the correct answer inasmuch as the passage states "life-threatening disorders" as among the possible consequences.

22. **(C)**

The correct answer to this question is choice (C)—it gives the complete and precise category. Other choices are incomplete—(A) left out the age group and the medical eligibility; (B) is narrowed down and all inclusive of "children with learning disabilities" and choice (D) is incorrect.

23. **(B)**

As indicated by figures in the passage, the correct answer is (B). Other choices (A), (C), and (D) are obviously incorrect. This is an example of a question in which the incorrect choices are not possible answers. The correct answer is derived from the figures provided in the passage.

24. **(D)**

The implications provided in choices (A) through (D) are correct. However, each of the implications for (A) through (C) is narrowed down to only one specific category of children—not any one is inclusive of all that needs to be addressed. Hence, (D) is the best and appropriate answer because it addresses the thousands who will not be screened, which include those in choices (A) through (C).

25. **(D)**

If schools exist to serve the best interest of students, then the correct answer for this question is (D). Choices (A) through (C) are also correct; however, the group that will be most affected by the financial crisis in California would have to be the "students." The fact remains that schools exist to serve the best interest of students.

26. **(D)**

A title is supposed to synthesize the main idea and (D) does. Choice (A) left out the main idea of a commemorative stamp; choice (B) is incorrect because it implies Columbus discovered the Americas; choice (C) is not the main idea of the passage.

27. **(B)**

The underlying fact behind the passage is explicitly implied; therefore, (B) is the correct answer. Choice (A), while true, is a generalized implication, not addressing the specific issue; choice (C) is debatable; choice (D), like (A), is also a generalized implication.

28. **(A)**

Of the choices given, (A) is the most historically significant, and, therefore, the correct answer. Choice (B) is significant but left out the fact that Columbus was not the first to arrive in the New World, the main point in the passage; choice (C) is a mere commemoration day; and choice (D) is not specific enough as an historically significant fact.

29. **(C)**

Since zoology is the study of animals (C) is the correct and appropriate answer. The other choices, which are other subject areas, as in (A), (B), and (D), are not quite the most appropriate subject areas.

30. **(D)**

A study of a 150 million-year-old fossil will require digging up into history; hence, (D) is the correct answer. Choice (A) could be used if there is a problem focus in the passage; choices (B) and (C) are poor and incorrect choices. Survey applies to a descriptive study; deductive is an approach that proceeds from a generalization or theory.

31. **(A)**

(A) clearly synthesizes the main idea in the passage; hence, it is the correct answer. Choice (D) is merely stating a fact, which does not speak of the main idea; the same can be said of choice (C); and choice (D), while it may be true, is not really the passage's main idea.

32. **(B)**

The most sound and significant implication of the passage is stated in (B); hence, this is the correct answer. Choice (B) is not sound, and reflects rather immature reasoning; choice (C) merely states some degree of competitiveness, which is not the issue's focus; and (D) is a "so what" kind of statement and not a sound implication.

33. **(C)**

The passage is really on global tourism providing comparisons and implying some inter-nation balance in tourism trade; hence, (C) is the appropriate and correct answer. Choices (A), (B), and (D) are stated in general terms, missing out on the specific focus or topic of the passage. Hence, they are not the logical and immediate topics to discuss.

34. **(A)**

The most appropriate and complete title is expressed in (A); hence, this is the correct answer. Choice (B) merely states a planned activity and does not address the main idea; choice (C) is incomplete—it does not specify basis for ranking; the same can be said for choice (D), likewise, an incomplete title.

35. **(D)**

The best answer in considering "practical terms" will have to be (D), which is the correct answer. Choice (B) is a possible consequence but an undesirable one; and choice (C) is a true implication but the "practicality" is merely implied. (D) says this explicitly.

36. **(C)**

The suggestion in (C) is the most sound and logical if equal opportunity for all students is to be our nation's priority; hence, this is the correct answer. Choice (A) is a mere statement of concern and does not provide a plan for action; choice (B) is illogical—you cannot cut down the number of minority students who are already in the system; and (D) is only secondary to the major issue.

37. **(D)**

Since the passage points out the growing number of minority students in the classroom, priority should be in providing the appropriate teacher preparation; hence, the correct answer is (D). Choice (A) is a need but secondary to those who are already in the system; choice (B) is something that has triggered legislations since the 1950s—the natural composition of the classroom today is already desegregated. While the other choices are a need, the one that needs immediate action is (D).

38. **(D)**

The answer to this question has to tie in with the foregoing answer; hence, the correct choice should be (D). Choices (A), (B), and (C), while also problems that arose from the changes in demographics, are secondary to (D).

39. **(D)**

The most complete summary of the passage is stated in (D); hence, this is the correct answer. Choice (A) is rather put in general terms—the U.S. pullout is not the only issue related to the Philippine economy. The interdependence of nations will remain no matter what, i.e., trade relations will continue; choice (B) is incorrect. The U.S. military strategy will have to be relocated elsewhere in the Asia-Pacific region. The same can be said for choice (C)—the Philippines will not be completely on its own as it continues to maintain its trade relations with the U.S. and other trading partners.

40. **(B)**

The passage is quite explicit in stating that the U.S. presence on the Philippines has been an impediment to the nation's capability in joining East Asia's "economic boom"; hence, the correct answer is (B). Choices (A), (C), and (D) are all possible consequences but are all quite debatable.

Subtest II: Mathematics

1. **(A)**

    When multiplying terms whose bases are the same, you can add the exponents. However, when adding terms whose bases are the same, you cannot add exponents. You must simplify each term separately and then combine. $3^2 + 3^2$ is not the same as 3^4.

2. **(B)**

    The only way to find the product of 200 with prime factors is using $(2^3)(5^2)$, which is

    $$2 \times 2 \times 2 \times 5 \times 5 = 200.$$

3. **(C)**

    You are looking for a common multiple of 8 and 12 that is between 45 and 60. The only multiple of both numbers that lies between 45 and 60 is 48. The next step is to find how many packages of pencils and pens that would be. There are 8 pens in each package, so divide 48 by 8 to get 6; there will be 6 packages of pens. There are 12 pencils in each package, so divide 48 by 12 to get 4; there will be 4 packages of pencils.

4. **(C)**

    Since the sugar content is 60 percent of $\frac{1}{2}$ pint and will not be changed after the water is added, we obtain an equation by equating the sugar content before and after adding in x pints of water. The equation is then

    $$\left(\frac{1}{2}\right) \times 60\% = \left(\frac{1}{2} + x\right) \times 5\%$$

    or

    $$30 = \frac{5}{2} + 5x$$

    $$60 = 5 + 10x$$

    $$55 = 10x$$

    $$5.5 = x$$

5. **(B)**

    Since the only information we have concerning the triangle is that angle A measures $30°$, we know that in a triangle, the largest angle faces the longest side, the sum of the three angles of a triangle is $180°$, and a $30°$ angle is not the largest angle. Therefore, a is not the longest side.

6. **(A)**

Follow the order of operations to simplify this expression.

$25 - (6 - 4)^3 \div 2 + \lvert -3 \rvert$	The given expression.
$25 - (2)^3 \div 2 + 3$	Simplify inside grouping symbols.
$25 - 8 \div 2 + 3$	Simplify exponents.
$25 - 4 + 3$	Do division.
$21 + 3$	Do subtraction.
24	Do addition.

7. **(D)**

The first step is to find the side length of the cube with a volume of 8. To find the volume of a cube, raise the side length to the third power. Therefore, you must find the cube root of 8. Ask yourself, what number raised to the third power is 8? The answer is 2. The next step is to double this side length to find the length of the side of a cube whose sides are twice the length of the given cube: $2 \times 2 = 4$. Now, find the volume of a cube with a side length of 4 by using the formula $V = s^3$. $V = 4^3$. $V = 64$.

8. **(B)**

The first step is to find how many miles Tommy has driven before stopping to refuel. Use the formula $D = RT$ (distance = rate times time) to find this answer. $6.5 \times 60 = 390$. Tommy drove 390 miles before stopping. Next find the number of miles he still has to drive by subtracting 390 from 500. $500 - 390 = 110$. Tommy needs to drive 110 more miles to reach his vacation spot.

9. **(D)**

We set up two equations. Let n be the number of nickels, and let d be the number of dimes. We have

$$n + d = 50.$$

Since each nickel is worth 5 cents and each dime is worth 10 cents, we have

$$5n + 10d = 485.$$

Multiplying the first equation by 10, we obtain

$$10n + 10d = 500.$$

Subtracting the second equation from it, we obtain $5n = 15$, or $n = 3$.

10. **(C)**

First you must find the length and width of the football field in real life. Multiply 18.3 by 5 and then multiply 9.8 by 5 (you are given that 1 cm = 5 meters). In real life, the football field is 91.5 meters by 49 meters. The next step is to multiply these two measurements together to find the area (because length × width = area of a rectangle). The area of the football field in square meters is 4483.5.

11. **(D)**

Since 10 babies drink 10 gallons of milk in 10 days. 10 babies drink 1 gallon of milk per day. So, each baby drinks $\frac{1}{10}$ gallon of milk per day. Each baby drinks $20 \times \frac{1}{10} = 2$ gallons of milk in 20 days, so 20 babies will drink $2 \times 20 = 40$ gallons of milk in 20 days.

12. **(D)**

Let x be the number of nickels, y be the number of dimes, and z be the number of quarters. We have two equations:

$$x + y + z = 24$$

and
$$5x + 10y + 25z = 300$$

and three unknowns. Therefore, no unique answer can be found without one more equation.

13. **(A)**

If both of the diagonals of a parallelogram are equivalent, then you know that the shape must be a rectangle (or a square). Since you are given that the shape is a square, you can find its area by multiplying one of the sides by itself. $4 \times 4 = 16$, which is the area of the square.

14. **(C)**

Let the amount of money he had before be x. We have

$$x - \left(\frac{1}{3}\right)x - \left(\frac{1}{4}\right)x = 150,000. \text{ Then, } \frac{12}{12}x - \frac{4}{12}x - \frac{3}{12}x = 150,000.$$

Or,
$$\left(\frac{5}{12}\right)x = 150,000.$$

Therefore, $x = \dfrac{150,000}{1} \times \dfrac{12}{5} = 360,000.$

15. **(C)**

There are 2,000 pounds in a ton, so multiply 1.3 by 2000 to get 2,600. Therefore, there are 2,600 pounds in 1.3 tons.

16. **(D)**

A point with a positive *x*-coordinate and a negative *y*-coordinate will lie in Quadrant IV. The point (2, –18) is shown graphed below.

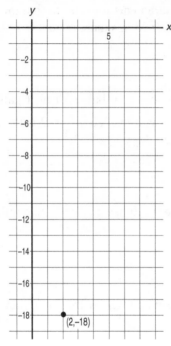

17. **(B)**

To find the slope between two points, use the slope formula. First find the coordinates of points A and B. The coordinates for point A are (4, 6), and the coordinates for point B are (7, 3).

$$\text{Slope} = \frac{y_2 - y_1}{x_2 - x_1}$$

$$\text{Slope} = \frac{6 - 3}{4 - 7}$$

$$\text{Slope} = \frac{3}{-3} = -1$$

18. **(B)**

Each way for Bob to walk to Norman's consists of six blocks northward and six blocks eastward in different orders. A specific set of intervals in which the 6 blocks northward are chosen automatically determines the intervals of the 6 blocks eastward. For example, suppose that Norman selects the 2nd, 3rd, 5th, 7th, 8th, and 11th intervals to walk northward. Then his journey of 12 blocks would appear as ENNENENNEENE. Note that the intervals for walking eastward are 1st, 4th, 6th, 9th, 10th, and 12th. The total number of ways of walking is then the same as the number of ways to choose 6 out of 12 things, and the number is

$$12 \times 11 \times 10 \times 9 \times 8 \times 7 \text{ divided by } 6 \times 5 \times 4 \times 3 \times 2, \text{ or } 924.$$

19. **(D)**

Perpendicular lines meet at right angles. The only street of the ones listed that is perpendicular to Ninth Avenue is 34th Street.

20. **(C)**

Let the number of marbles in the beginning be x. We have

$$x - \left(\frac{1}{3}\right)x - \left(\frac{1}{3}\right)\left(\frac{2}{3}\right)x - 2 = 10.$$

Then $x - \dfrac{1}{3}x - \dfrac{2}{9}x = 12$

$$\frac{9}{9}x - \frac{3}{9}x - \frac{2}{9} = 12$$

$$\frac{4}{9}x = 12$$

Thus, $x = \dfrac{12}{1} \times -\dfrac{9}{4} = 27$.

21. **(A)**

Set up and solve a proportion to answer the question.

$$\frac{1}{5.5} = \frac{x}{75}$$

$$5.5x = 75$$

$$x = 75 \div 5.5$$

$$x \approx 14$$

22. **(C)**

If we let Joan's age be x, then Georgette's age is $(x - 8)$. Solving the equation

$$(x - 8) = 2[(x - 8) - 8] = 2x - 32, \ 2x - x = 32 - 8. \text{ Thus,}$$

we obtain $x = 24$ and $x - 8 = 16$.

23. **(B)**

This is an arithmetic sequence. The common difference between numbers is 6. Add 6 to 41 to find the next number. $41 + 6 = 47$.

24. **(B)**

Suppose Sarah bought x pounds of apples and y pounds of nuts. We have the following equations to solve:

$$x + y = 10$$

$$89x + 129y = 1,010$$

Multiply the first equation by 129 to get $129x + 129y = 1,290$. Then subtract the second equation to get $40x = 280$. Solving this equation gives $x = 7$. By substitution, $7 + y = 10$, so $y = 3$.

25. **(A)**

When you divide a value by 2, it is the same as finding half of it. Therefore, half of y, minus 3 is the correct translation of the algebraic expression.

26. **(B)**

Simplify the expression by doing the Distributive Property. Multiply -3 by $\dfrac{x}{3}$ and by -1 to get $-x + 3$.

27. **(A)**

This is a geometric sequence. The value that each term is being multiplied by is -2. Continue the pattern to find the 8th number in the sequence.

$$-2, 4, -8, 16, -32, 64, -128, 256.$$

28. **(D)**

Substitute each ordered pair into the inequality to find the false statement.

$y < 4x + 4$

$2 < 4(-1) + 4$

$2 < -4 + 4$

$2 < 0$　　　　This is a false statement. $(-1, 2)$ is not a solution to the inequality.

29. **(B)**

Substitute each ordered pair into the equation to find the false statement.

$$y = -x + 8$$
$$6 = -(-2) + 8$$
$$6 = 2 + 8$$
$$6 = 10$$ This is a false statement. $(-2, 6)$ is not on the line $y = -x + 8$.

30. **(B)**

To answer the question correctly, notice that each face represents 5 taxi drivers (not one!). Read through each statement until you find the false statement. The statement "There are 3 taxi drivers in Brockton is false." There are 15 taxi drivers in Brockton.

31. **(C)**

Because the scale on the y-axis starts at $79,000, it looks like employees' salaries tripled after one year when, in fact, they only increased $2,000.

32. **(B)**

We do not need to memorize any formula. If we inscribe the regular pentagon in a circle, the angle with the vertex at the center facing each side is

$$\frac{360°}{5} = 72°,$$

and each of the other angles of that triangle must be

$$\frac{(180° - 72°)}{2} = 54°.$$

Thus, each of the angles is 108°.

33. **(D)**

Each of the data sets has five items in it. To have a mean of 10, the sum of all five items must be 50 (because $5 \times 10 = 50$). Identify the data set that has a sum of 50 to find the correct answer. Answer choice D is correct because $7 + 8 + 8 + 12 + 15 = 50$.

34. **(D)**

Since a 90° angle must be the largest in a triangle, it must face the longest side, and the angle between the longest side and the shortest side is not facing the longest side.

35. **(D)**

To find the correct set of numbers with a mean of 30, add up the numbers in each set and divide by the number of numbers in the set. Look for the set that does not have a mean of 30. In answer D, $15 + 49 = 64$. $64 \div 2 = 32$.

36. **(D)**

When there is an even number of data items, you must find the average of the two middle numbers to find the median. When this happens, you may get a number that is not in the data. For example, given the set: (3, 4, 6, 9), the two middle numbers are 4 and 6. The average of 4 and 6 is 5. Therefore, 5 would be the median. Notice that is it not one of the data items in the set.

37. **(C)**

To find the probability that Grace will select a blueberry muffin, find the ratio of the number of blueberry muffins to the total number of muffins. $\frac{6}{24}$ is the probability of selecting a blueberry muffin at random from the 24 muffins.

38. **(A)**

Simplify the expression following the order of operations.

$6 \times (8 + 2) \div 5 - 3^2$	The given expression.
$6 \times 10 \div 5 - 3^2$	Simplify within parentheses.
$6 \times 10 \div 5 - 9$	Simplify exponents.
$60 \div 5 - 9$	Do multiplication
$12 - 9$	Do division.
3	Do subtraction.

39. **(A)**

The red line is between 3 and 4 centimeters long. It is closer to 3 centimeters, and since you are to find the measure to the nearest centimeter, the answer is 3 centimeters.

40. **(B)**

You must recognize that this is a combination problem. Use the combination formula to find the answer.

$$_nC_r = \frac{n!}{r!(n-r)!} =$$

$$_{10}C_3 = \frac{10!}{3!(10-3)!} =$$

$$_{10}C_3 = 120$$

There are 120 ways of choosing groups of 3 students from 10 students.

41. **(A)**

The first step is to find the radius of the given mirror. You are told that the area is 144π square feet. You can use the area formula for a circle to find the radius. $A = \pi r^2$, so substitute the area given: $A = 144\pi$ to find that the radius is 12 feet. The next step is to find the area of a circular mirror that has a radius 2 feet greater than 12 feet. The increased radius would be 14 feet. Substitute 14 feet into the area formula of a circle to find the area.

$$A = \pi r^2$$

$$A = \pi (14)^2$$

$$A = 196\pi$$

42. **(B)**

The only picture which cannot be divided into two equal halves by a line is answer choice B.

43. **(A)**

Making a sketch will help solve this problem.

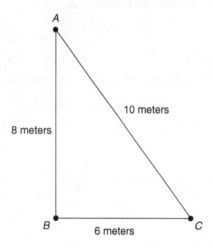

Notice that the legs of the right triangle represent the base and height of the triangle because the legs intersect at right angles. Use the formula for finding the area of a triangle.

$$A = \frac{1}{2}bh$$

$$A = \frac{1}{2}(6)(8)$$

$$A = 24$$

The area of the triangle is 24 square meters.

44. **(C)**

According to the graph, the supply was greater than the demand in March and May only.

45. **(B)**

To answer this question, you must know that every point on the *x*-axis has a *y*-coordinate of 0. Therefore, substitute *y* = 0 and solve for *x*.

$y = -2x + 4$	The linear equation given.
$0 = -2x + 4$	Substitute $y = 0$.
$-4 = -2x$	Subtract 4 from both sides.
$2 = x$	Divide both sides by –2.

Therefore, the point where the line intersects the *x*-axis is (2, 0).

Correlation with FTCE Competency/Skill

Competency/ Skill	Problem Number
	Total of 8 in section 1
1.1	14, 31, 32
1.2	23, 39
1.3	11
1.4	2, 30
	Total of 10 in section 2
2.1	6, 38
2.2	9, 27, 41
2.3	22
2.4	17, 21
2.5	25
2.6	19
	Total of 9 in section 3
3.1	5
3.2	3, 24, 40, 45
3.3	18, 33
3.4	12, 37

Competency/ Skill	Problem Number
	Total of 9 in section 4
4.1	15, 16
4.2	1, 34
4.3	8, 13, 36
4.4	7, 20
	Total of 9 in section 5
5.1	10, 42
5.2	28
5.3	4, 43
5.4	29
5.5	26
5.6	35, 44

Key: 1.3 means Competency 1 Skill 3

Competency/Skill		Approximate # of Questions
	MATHEMATICS The test center will provide a 4-function calculator. The test center will provide a reference sheet.	
1	**Knowledge of number sense, concepts, and operations**	**8**
	1 Compare the relative value of real numbers (e.g., integers, fractions, decimals, percents, irrational numbers, and numbers expressed in exponential or scientific notation.) 2 Solve real-world problems involving addition, subtraction, multiplication, and division of rational numbers (e.g., whole numbers, integers, decimals, percents, and fractions including mixed numbers). 3 Apply basic number theory concepts including the use of primes, composites, factors, and multiples in solving problems. 4 Apply the order of operations with or without grouping symbols.	
2	**Knowledge of measurement (using customary or metric units)**	**10**
	1 Solve real-world problems involving length, weight, mass, perimeter, area, capacity, and volume. 2 Solve real-world problems involving rated measures (e.g., miles per hour, meters per second, cost per item, and cost per unit). 3 Solve real-world problems involving scaled drawings (e.g., maps, blueprints, and models). 4 Solve real-world problems involving the change of units of measures of length, weight, mass, capacity, and time. 5 Solve real-world problems involving estimates of measures including length, weight, mass, temperature, time, money, perimeter, area, and volume. 6 Choose the correct reading, to a specified degree of accuracy, using instruments (e.g., scales, rulers, thermometers, measuring cups, protractors, and gauges).	

Competency/Skill		Approximate # of Questions
3	**Knowledge of geometry and spatial sense**	**9**
	1　Identify and/or classify simple two- and three-dimensional figures according to their properties.	
	2　Solve real-world and mathematical problems involving ratio, proportion, similarity, congruence, and the Pythagorean relationship.	
	3　Identify the location of ordered pairs of integers in all four quadrants of a coordinate system (graph) and use the coordinate system to apply the concepts of slope and distance to solve problems.	
	4　Identify real-world examples that represent geometric concepts including perpendicularity, parallelism, tangency, symmetry, and transformations (e.g., flips, slides, and turns).	
4	**Knowledge of algebraic thinking**	**9**
	1　Analyze and generalize patterns including arithmetic and geometric sequences.	
	2　Interpret algebraic expressions using words, symbols, variables, tables, and graphs.	
	3　Solve equations and inequalities graphically or algebraically.	
	4　Determine whether a number or ordered pair is among the solutions of given equations or inequalities.	
5	**Knowledge of data analysis and probability**	**9**
	1　Analyze data and solve problems using data presented in histograms, bar graphs, ,circle graphs, pictographs, tables, and charts.	
	2　Identify how the presentation of data can lead to different or inappropriate interpretations.	
	3　Calculate range, mean, median, and mode(s) from sets of data and interpret the meaning of the measures of central tendency (i.e., mean, median, and mode) and dispersion (i.e., range and standard deviation).	
	4　Identify how the measures of central tendency (i.e., mean, median, or mode) can lead to different interpretations.	
	5　Calculate the probability of a specified outcome.	
	6　Solve and interpret real-world problems involving probability using counting procedures, tables, tree diagrams, and the concepts of permutations and combinations.	

Subtest III: English Language Skills

1. **(B)**

    As you read the sentence, you should recognize that choice (B) presents an error in comparison. The comparison of two bridges requires the comparative form "longer." All of the other choices are acceptable in standard written English. Choice (A), "is," agrees with its singular subject "bridge"; and choice (C), "or," is a coordinating conjunction joining the names of the two bridges.

2. **(D)**

    The correct response to this question is choice (D). All labeled elements are choices acceptable in standard written English. In choice (A), the pronoun "they" is plural to agree with its antecedent, "proteins," and the verb "come" is also plural to agree with its subject, "they"; choice (B), "plant or animal sources," is idiomatic; and choice (C), "is," is singular to agree with its singular subject, "function."

3. **(C)**

    The error is choice (C), "I," which is in the nominative case. Because the words "Janice" and "I" serve as indirect objects in the sentence, the correct pronoun is the first person objective form, "me." Choice (A), "Recognizing," is a participle introducing an introductory participial phrase modifying "teacher;" choice (B), "had worked," is a verb in the past perfect tense because the action in the phrase was completed before the action in the main clause occurred.

4. **(B)**

    The error occurs at choice (C), where the preposition "from" is idiomatic after the word "different." Although some experts insist upon the use of "from" after the adjective "different," others accept the use of "different than" in order to save words. An example would be "different than you thought;" the use of "from" would require the addition of the word "what." Choice (A), "According to," is a preposition correctly introducing a prepositional phrase; and choice (C), "those," is a plural pronoun to agree with its antecedent "powers."

5. **(A)**

    Choice (A) should be a gerund in the present perfect form (having "been studied") to indicate that the action expressed by the gerund occurred before the relationship was reported. Choice (B), "preceding ten years," is idiomatic. Choice (C), "having," is a gerund introducing the phrase "having heart attacks," which is the object of the preposition "of."

6. **(D)**

    Your answer should be choice (D), indicating that this sentence contains no error in standard written English. Choice (A), "was expected," uses the third person singular form of "to be" to agree with its subject "each;" choice (B), the infinitive "to use," is idiomatic after the passive verb "was expected;" and choice (C), "his or her," is singular to agree with its antecedent, the indefinite pronoun "each," and provides gender neutrality.

7. **(A)**

    You should recognize in choice (A) that the idiomatically acceptable preposition to follow "aversion" is "to." The other choices in the sentence are acceptable in standard written English. Choice (B), "for him," is a prepositional phrase modifying "activity;" choice (C), "one," is a pronoun appropriate to refer to its antecedent "activity."

8. **(C)**

    Choice (C) contains the error because the subject of the verb "show" is "story," a singular noun that calls for the third person singular verb, "shows." The rest of the sentence represents correct usage. Choices (A) and (B), "those" and "their," are plural pronouns that agree with the antecedent "pioneers."

9. **(C)**

    Choice (C) presents an error in comparison, appearing to compare "farming" with "low latitudes" when what is intended is a comparison of "farming in high latitudes" with "farming in low latitudes." The corrected sentence reads: "Because of the long, cold winters and short summers, farming in high latitudes is more difficult than farming in low latitudes." The other choices all represent appropriate usage in standard written English. Choice (A), "Because of," is idiomatically correct as a preposition. Choice (B), "more difficult," is the comparative form appropriate to compare two items.

10. **(C)**

    The error is in choice (C). The word "contestant" is a predicate nominative in the subordinate noun clause, and it must agree in number with the plural subject of the clause, the pronoun "both," to which it refers. The noun clause should, therefore, read: "that both of us could be contestants on a quiz show." Choice (A), "I," is part of the compound subject of the introductory adverb clause and is, correctly, in the nominative case. "We" is plural to agree with its compound antecedent, "sister and I," and is in the nominative case because it is the subject of the verb "hoped."

11. **(A)**

    The error is in choice (A). The auxiliary verb "had" calls for the past participle form of the verb "break," which is "broken." All of the other choices are acceptable in standard written English. Choice (B), "had purchased," is the past perfect form of the verb to indicate action completed in the past before the action of the verb in the main clause; and choice (C), "her," is the object of the preposition "for."

12. **(D)**

This sentence contains no error in standard written English. Choice (A), the prepositional phrase "with whom," introduces an adjective clause modifying the word "people." The relative pronoun "whom" is in the objective case because it serves as the object of the preposition "with." The simple past tense "worked" is appropriate for choice (B); choice (C) is an idiomatic expression replacing the preposition "for."

13. **(C)**

Your reading of the sentence should indicate that choice (C), "were," presents an error in subject-verb agreement. A compound subject joined by "or" or "neither . . . nor" calls for a verb that agrees in number with the second part of the compound subject, which is, in this case, singular. The correct choice is the verb "was." The other choices represent correct usage. Choices (A) and (B) are correlative conjunctions.

14. **(C)**

Again the error is one of agreement of the subject and verb. Choice (C), "were," is plural; because its subject is "attack," not "reasons," which is the object of the preposition "among" and therefore cannot be the subject of the sentence, the verb should be the singular "was." Choice (A), "Among," introduces a prepositional phrase; choice (B) is an idiomatically acceptable prepositional phrase to modify the noun "reasons."

15. **(C)**

Your analysis of this sentence should disclose an error in parallelism in choice (C). "Teaching" should be replaced by "to teach," an infinitive parallel with "to frighten." Both infinitives modify the noun "attempt." The other choices all represent standard usage in written English. Choice (A), "greater," is the comparative form of the adjective, correctly used to compare two items; choice (B), "their," is a plural possessive pronoun agreeing in number with its plural antecedent, "parents."

16. **(B)**

You should recognize that the possessive pronoun in choice (B), "their," is not the appropriate pronoun to use in referring to a country. Choice (C), "of life expectancy," are both idiomatically acceptable prepositional phrases; choice (B), "is shown," is passive and agrees in number with its singular subject, "standard."

17. **(C)**

Choice (C), "white and bluish gray in color," is the third in a series of objects of the verb "has." The error lies in its lack of parallelism with the other two objects, "eyes" and "body." Corrected, the sentence reads: "The snow leopard is a wild mammal in Central Asia that has large eyes, a four-foot body, and a white and bluish gray color." The other choices are all acceptable in standard written English. Choice (A), "is," is singular to agree with its subject "leopard." Choice (B), "that has," is composed of the relative pronoun "that" referring to the noun "mammal," and the verb "has," that agrees with its subject in number.

18. **(A)**

You should recognize that choice (A), "and," is not the correct correlative conjunction to follow "either." The correct word is "or." The other choices all represent acceptable choices in standard written English. Choice (B), "him," is singular to agree with its antecedent "person" and objective because it is the object of the verb "make." Choice (C), "most important," is in the superlative form because the comparison involves more than two choices.

19. **(B)**

Choice (B), "to fail," is incorrect in standard written English. The sentence contains two parallel ideas that should be expressed with the same grammatical form. Because "Failing" is a gerund, the "infinitive" to "fail" should be replaced with "failing" to make the construction parallel. Choice (A), "is," agrees in number with its subject, "Failing"; and choice (C) is singular to agree with its antecedent, "student," and indicates no sexual preference.

20. **(C)**

You should recognize that choice (C), "or," is in error because the correlative conjunction that should follow "neither" is "nor." All other choices are correct. Choice (A), "had grown up," is idiomatically acceptable and it and choice (B), "had been," are in the past perfect tense to indicate that the actions occurred before the action mentioned in the main clause.

21. **(B)**

As you read the sentence, you should recognize that choice (B) is incorrect because "that" is the relative pronoun that should introduce a noun clause following "reason;" another option would be to revise the sentence by omitting the words "The reason," but that is not an option provided on this test. Choice (A), "his," is the correct possessive pronoun to refer to "Jason." Choice (C), "such stage fright," is idiomatic.

22. **(A)**

Your recognition that the word "less" is used with a singular noun and the word "fewer" is appropriate before a plural noun will lead you to locate the error in choice (A). Choice (B) is the comparative adverb, the correct choice to compare two people ("anyone else" is singular), and choice (C) is idiomatic as a singular indefinite pronoun.

23. **(B)**

You should recognize that the verb "want" in choice (B) does not agree with its subject "who," a pronoun that is singular to agree with its antecedent, "adult." The word ordering used in choices (A) and (C) are both idiomatic in standard written English.

24. **(B)**

As you read the sentence, you should recognize that the pronoun "this" in choice (B) does not have a clear antecedent in the sentence. The other choices are all correct in standard written English. Choice (A), "along with," is idiomatic and serves as one preposition. Choice (C), "has made," is in the present perfect tense because the action began in the past and continues into the present.

25. **(B)**

You should find the error at choice (B), where the adverb "frequently" is needed to modify the adjective "repetitious;" "frequent" is an adjective and does not correctly modify another adjective. Choice (A), the pronoun "who," correctly refers to its antecedent "Students;" and choice (C) is a relative pronoun "that" and its verb, "is provided," which comprise the adjective clause modifying "menu."

26. **(C)**

Because the verb "protest" can be transitive and have a direct object, choice (C) avoids awkward wordiness and use of the unnecessary preposition "about." Choices (B) and (D) include unnecessary words and use the pronoun "they" that has no clear antecedent.

27. **(B)**

Choice (B) best shows the causal relationship between sibling opportunities and their placement in the family, their abilities, and their personalities, and retains the subordination of the original sentence. Choice (A) provides a dangling phrase. Choice (C), with its use of the coordinating conjunction "and," treats the lack of opportunity and its cause as if they are equal ideas and does not show the causal relationship between them; choice (D) results in a run-on sentence.

28. **(D)**

Only choice (D) corrects the two major problems in the sentence, the lack of subject-verb agreement and the lack of parallelism. In choices (A) and (B), the verb "is" does not agree with its plural subject, "provisions." Choices (A) and (C) have unlike constructions serving as predicate nominatives, the noun "freedom" and the clause "that citizens are guaranteed a trial by jury." Choice (D) correctly uses the plural verb "are" to agree with the plural subject, and the predicate nominative is composed of two parallel nouns, "freedom" and "guarantee."

29. **(D)**

The errors found in the original sentence, choice (A), involve parallelism and redundancy. Choice (D) uses the parallel infinitives "to entertain" and "to teach" as direct objects and eliminates the repetition created in the use of both "tried" and "attempt" in the original sentence. Choices (B) and (C) provide parallel construction, but choice (B) retains the redundancy and choice (C) incorrectly splits the infinitive "to entertain."

30. **(B)**

Choice (B) adequately conveys the reason for removal of the parking meters with the least wordiness. Choices (A) and (C) contain unnecessary words; choice (D) has a dangling participial phrase.

31. **(C)**

Choice (C), in which "Megan" correctly follows the phrase, conveys the meaning with the least wordiness. The problem with choice (A) is the introductory participial phrase; it must be eliminated or followed immediately by the word modified. Choice (B) and (D) add words unnecessary to the meaning of the sentence.

32. **(A)**

The given sentence is acceptable in standard written English. Each of the alternate choices introduces a problem. Choice (B) uses the superlative form of the adjective, "most interested," when the comparative form "more interested" is correct for the comparison of two options; choice (C) introduces a lack of parallelism; and choice (D) is not idiomatic.

33. **(D)**

The noun clause in choice (D) is idiomatically acceptable. The use of "Whether" in choices (A) and (B) leads the writer to add "or not," words that contribute nothing to the meaning and result in awkwardness of construction. Choice (C) with its awkward gerund phrase is also not idiomatic.

34. **(D)**

This sentence presents two problems, namely use of a preposition instead of a coordinating conjunction to join the objects of the participle "having studied" and failure to show a time relationship. Choice (D) corrects both problems. Choice (B) simply replaces the preposition "along with" by "as well as"; choice (C) unnecessarily repeats the conjunction "and" rather than using the quite appropriate series construction. None of the choices (A), (B), or (C) correctly shows the time relationship.

35. **(B)**

This sentence contains the ambiguous pronoun "they," for which there is no antecedent and fails to show the relationship of the ideas expressed. Choice (B) eliminates the clause with the ambiguous pronoun and correctly expresses the reason for the sandbag placement. Choice (C) suggests that the two clauses joined by "and" are equal and does not show the subordinate relationship of the second to the first. Choice (D) retains both errors from the original sentence.

36. **(A)**

This sentence is correct in standard written English. Choice (B) introduces unnecessary words that add nothing to the meaning and make the sentence awkward and wordy; choices (C) and (D) do not correctly show relationship.

37. **(C)**

Choice (C) shows the relationship accurately and eliminates the awkward gerund construction as the object of the preposition "despite." The adjective clause in choice (B) fails to show the relationship of the original sentence; choice (D) introduces the superfluous words "the fact that."

38. **(A)**

This sentence is correct in standard written English. Choice (B) loses the strength of the parallelism in choice (A). Choice (C), although containing parallel construction, is idiomatically awkward with its participial phrases. Choices (B) and (D) all exhibit wordiness.

39. **(C)**

The original sentence, choice (A), contains the obvious and redundant words "was a man who." Choices (B) and (D) are also unnecessarily verbose. Choice (C) makes the statement in the most direct way possible and represents correct standard usage.

40. **(D)**

Choice (D) eliminates the awkward participial phrase with its passive verb, and, in direct fashion, clearly shows the desired relationship. Choices (A), (B), and (C) retain the awkward construction.

Essay Scoring Guide

The FTCE-GKT essay sections are scored by two writing experts on the basis of the criteria outlined below. In addition to comparing your essay to those included in our practice tests, you may use these guidelines to estimate your score on this section. Remember that your score is the sum of the scores of two writing experts, so provided you respond to the assigned topic, your score will fall somewhere between two and twelve. Scores will be assigned based on the following guidelines:

SCORE of 6: The paper has a clearly established main idea that the writer fully develops with specific details and examples. Organization is notably logical and coherent. Point of view is consistently maintained. Vocabulary and sentence structure are varied and effective. Errors in sentence structure, usage, and mechanics are few and insignificant.

SCORE of 5: The paper has a clearly established main idea that is adequately developed and recognizable through specific details and/or examples. Organization follows a logical and coherent pattern. Point of view is mostly maintained. Vocabulary and sentence structure are mostly varied and effective. Occasional errors in sentence structure, usage and mechanics do not interfere with the writer's ability to communicate.

SCORE of 4: The paper has an adequately stated main idea that is developed with some specific details and examples. Supporting ideas are presented in a mostly logical and coherent manner. Point of view is somewhat maintained. Vocabulary and sentence structure are somewhat varied and effective. Occasional errors in sentence structure, usage, and mechanics may interfere with writer's ability to communicate.

SCORE of 3: The paper states a main idea that is developed with generalizations or lists. The paper may contain occasional lapses in logic and coherence, and organization is mechanical. Point of view is ambiguous. Vocabulary and sentence structure are repetitious and often ineffective. A variety of errors in sentence structure, usage, and mechanics sometimes interferes with the writer's ability to communicate.

SCORE of 2: The paper presents an incomplete or ambiguous main idea. Support is developed with generalizations and lists. Organization is mechanical. The paper contains occasional lapses in logic and coherence. Point of view is confusing and distracting. Word choice is simplistic, and sentence structure is disjointed. Errors in sentence structure, usage, and mechanics frequently interfere with the writer's ability to communicate.

SCORE of 1: The paper has no evident main idea. Development is inadequate and/or irrelevant. Organization is illogical and/or incoherent. Point of view has not been established. Vocabulary and sentence structure are garbled and confusing. Significant and numerous errors in sentence structure, usage, and mechanics interfere with the writer's ability to communicate.

Subtest IV: Sample Essays with Commentary

Topic 1

Strong Response

Happiness, freedom, and peace of mind are goals that everyone wants in life. Yet they are very abstract and difficult to measure. Happiness is a frame of mind that means we enjoy what we do. Freedom is the ability to do what we want, although it is limited to not doing anything that takes away freedom from other people. Peace of mind is a feeling that we are all right and that the world is a good place. How does one achieve these important goals? They can best be acquired when we try to give them to other people rather than when we try to get them ourselves.

The people who feel happiest, experience freedom, and enjoy peace of mind are most often people who are concentrating on helping others. Mother Theresa of Calcutta is an example. Because she takes care of homeless people and is so busy, she probably doesn't have time to worry about whether she is happy, free, and peaceful. She always looks cheerful in her pictures.

There are other people in history who seem to have attained the goals we all want by helping others. Jane Addams established Hull House in the slums of Chicago to help other people, and her life must have brought her great joy and peace of mind. She gave to the mothers in the neighborhood freedom to work and know that their children were being taken care of; and Jane Addams apparently had the freedom to do what she wanted to help them.

On the other hand, there are people in literature who directly tried to find happiness, freedom, and peace of mind; and they were often miserable. The two people who come to mind are Scrooge and Silas Marner. Scrooge had been selfish in the past, and he wouldn't give anything for the poor. He wasn't a bit happy even at Christmas. Later, when he began helping others, he became happy. Silas Marner was very selfish, hoarding his money and thinking it would make him happy. Only when he tried to make little Eppie happy was he able to be happy, too, even without his stolen money.

If we want to achieve happiness, freedom, and peace of mind, we should get involved in helping others so much that we forget ourselves and find joy from the people we are helping. When we try to give away the qualities we want, we find them ourselves.

Analysis

This essay has a score range of 5–6. It is well organized, with the opening paragraph serving as the introduction and stating the thesis of the paper in its last sentence. Defining the terms serves as an effective way to introduce the paper. The last paragraph concludes the essay, restating the thesis. The three middle paragraphs support the thesis with specific examples that are adequately explained and have a single focus. Transitions effectively relate the ideas. The sentence structure varies, and the vocabulary is effective. There are no major errors in sentence construction, usage, or mechanics. Although the essay would benefit from some minor revisions, it is well done considering the time limit imposed upon the writer.

Topic 2

Strong Response

The rising cost of health care in the United States has become more than a national concern; it is now a national crisis. The situation has become so grave that the President made health care costs a major issue in his campaign and has appointed a task force to investigate ways of providing equitable health care for all Americans. One of the most pressing problems the task force is addressing is health insurance.

The cost of health insurance in this country has skyrocketed in the last two decades. Many middle class Americans cannot afford to insure themselves and their families, despite earning relatively large incomes, and for the working class, health insurance is completely out of reach. The result is that these people literally cannot afford to get sick. An illness means lost work wages, as well as exorbitant medical bills. Those who can afford to buy health insurance often find that their policy is inadequate for anything beyond rudimentary care. An unexpected surgery can involve thousands of dollars in out-of-pocket expenses, and a chronic disease like cancer or diabetes can eat up a policy's maximum allowable benefits in a matter of weeks or months.

The cost of providing group insurance has become so high that many employers, especially smaller companies, are trying to either cut benefits or find some cheaper way of providing coverage, while many prospective employees accept or reject job opportunities on the basis of benefits rather than salary.

Health-maintenance organizations (HMOs) and preferred-provider organizations (PPOs) are two common means that many employers have turned to in their attempts to regulate costs. HMOs and PPOs provide coverage for routine and preventive health care while keeping costs down by limiting benefits on certain types of care or by not covering certain expenses at all. However, these programs have serious limitations. Yearly out-of-pocket deductibles are generally high, and annual maximum benefits can be quite low. This means that for people who are in good overall health, these plans are beneficial, but if a family has an unexpected health emergency, whether it be a serious injury or a debilitating illness, these plans provide little assistance. It is also possible for a person with a rare illness not to be diagnosed because of the limitations on testing imposed by these plans.

One solution is to set national limits on how much certain procedures and tests can cost. By standardizing costs and then standardizing how much of the cost is covered by the government health care plan, costs can be managed. Many insurance companies already try to control costs by standardizing how much they will pay for various tests and procedures, but there are no regulations that restrict physicians or medical facilities from charging more than this standard rate. A national health care plan that did regulate fees would prevent some doctors and hospitals from overcharging for services. This type of fee schedule, combined with a sliding scale based on income for the amount of the fee that is covered by the government, could go far to easing this country's health care crisis. Other options are to base national health care on the plans already instituted in other countries. Canada and England are among the other countries that have instituted national health care and managed to control health care costs. A recent study showed that drug costs in Canada (for the same medications produced by the same companies) were less than half what they are in this country.

The health care problem in this country has reached crisis proportions. Many people who hold good jobs cannot afford to insure themselves or their families, and the working class and the poor cannot afford to get sick at all. Even those people who can afford health insurance find that the policies they buy do not cover catastrophic illnesses or injuries. Many employers have tried to provide health care coverage for their employees, but escalating costs have made it harder to provide comprehensive coverage. The only thing that can be said for certain is that health care reform is desperately needed, but the president's task force does not have an easy job ahead of it.

Analysis

This essay has a score rays of 5–6. If provides a clear thesis and develops that thesis in a clear and logical manner. The body of the essay expands on various aspects of the thesis, and provides concise and reasonable support. The few usage, structural, and mechanical errors do not interfere with the writer's ability to communicate effectively, and the writer demonstrates a solid understanding of the rules of written English. The essay is well-thought-out and the conclusion relates the various points raised in the essay to the general argument made throughout.

Notes

Notes

Notes

Notes

Notes

REA's Test Preps

The Best in Test Preparation

- REA Test Preps are **far more** comprehensive than any other test preparation series
- Each book contains full-length practice tests based on the most recent exams
- **Every** type of question likely to be given on the exams is included
- Answers are accompanied by **full** and **detailed** explanations

REA publishes hundreds of test prep books. Some of our titles include:

Advanced Placement Exams (APs)
Art History
Biology
Calculus AB & BC
Chemistry
Economics
English Language & Composition
English Literature & Composition
European History
French Language
Government & Politics
Latin Vergil
Physics B & C
Psychology
Spanish Language
Statistics
United States History
World History

College-Level Examination Program (CLEP)
American Government
College Algebra
General Examinations
History of the United States I
History of the United States II
Introduction to Educational Psychology
Human Growth and Development
Introductory Psychology
Introductory Sociology
Principles of Management
Principles of Marketing
Spanish
Western Civilization I
Western Civilization II

SAT Subject Tests
Biology E/M
Chemistry
French
German
Literature
Mathematics Level 1, 2
Physics
Spanish
United States History

Graduate Record Exams (GREs)
Biology
Chemistry
General
Literature in English
Mathematics
Physics
Psychology

ACT - ACT Assessment

ASVAB - Armed Services Vocational Aptitude Battery

CBEST - California Basic Educational Skills Test

CDL - Commercial Driver License Exam

COOP, HSPT & TACHS - Catholic High School Admission Tests

FE (EIT) - AM Exam

FTCE - Florida Teacher Certification Examinations

GED

GMAT - Graduate Management Admission Test

LSAT - Law School Admission Test

MAT - Miller Analogies Test

MCAT - Medical College Admission Test

MTEL - Massachusetts Tests for Educator Licensure

NJ HSPA - New Jersey High School Proficiency Assessment

NYSTCE - New York State Teacher Certification Examinations

PRAXIS PLT - Principles of Learning & Teaching Tests

PRAXIS PPST - Pre-Professional Skills Tests

PSAT/NMSQT

SAT

TExES - Texas Examinations of Educator Standards

THEA - Texas Higher Education Assessment

TOEFL - Test of English as a Foreign Language

USMLE Steps 1,2 - U.S. Medical Licensing Exams

For our complete title list,
visit www.rea.com

Research & Education Association